# CORNELL STUDIES IN CLASSICAL PHILOLOGY

EDITED BY

HARRY CAPLAN * JAMES HUTTON

G. M. KIRKWOOD * FRIEDRICH SOLMSEN

VOLUME XXXII

# Alcuin and Charlemagne:

STUDIES IN CAROLINGIAN

HISTORY AND LITERATURE

By LUITPOLD WALLACH

This work has been brought to publication with the assistance of a grant from the *Charles Edwin Bennett Fund for Research in the Classical Languages*, a fund created at Cornell University by Lawrence Bennett in memory of his father.

# Alcuin and Charlemagne:

## STUDIES IN CAROLINGIAN
## HISTORY AND LITERATURE

By *Luitpold Wallach*

University of Illinois
at Urbana

Amended by the Author

## Cornell University Press

ITHACA, NEW YORK

Reprinted with the permission of Cornell University Press

JOHNSON REPRINT CORPORATION
111 Fifth Avenue, New York, N.Y. 10003

JOHNSON REPRINT COMPANY LTD.
Berkeley Square House, London, W. 1

*To* HARRY CAPLAN

Goldwin Smith Professor of the Classical Languages
and Literature in Cornell University

# Preface

THIS book was written at Cornell University between the autumn of 1950 and the summer of 1954, though it had been begun in 1932. Of those first Carolingian studies only a short note, entitled "Amicus Amicis, Inimicus Inimicis," had appeared (in the *Zeitschrift für Kirchengeschichte*, 1933) when the political developments in Germany forced me to abandon them in favor of other historical studies that were at the time nearing completion. In 1950, reminded of Augustine's words, "nec istis temporibus desperandum est," I returned to Alcuin. The purpose of the present book is explained in the Introduction.

Alcuin's work required a critical study and rigorous analysis before its historical meaning became apparent. It is hoped that philology, with its sureness of method, may here have proved to be what the Belgian historian François L. Ganshof once called it, the "mère nourricière de l'histoire" (*Revue Belge*, 1952, p. 1275). In any case, this approach resulted in studies dealing variously with political thought and theory, with the diplomatics of letters and charters, with epigraphy, and with the procedures of Frankish law of the eighth century.

The chapters of Parts III and IV appeared in *Speculum* (1951 and 1955), in the *American Journal of Philology* (1951), in *Traditio* (1953), and in the *Harvard Theological Review* (1955).

For permission to include in the present volume these revised materials, grateful acknowledgment is made to the editors of the above-named journals, Dr. Charles R. D. Miller, Professor Henry T. Rowell, Professor Stephan Kuttner, and Professor Arthur D. Nock, and to the Johns Hopkins Press, the Fordham University Press, and the Harvard University Press. The Society for Promoting Christian Knowledge (London, England), through Mr. J. E. Padfield, kindly granted permission to reprint (with some changes) the translation of a letter by Alcuin in G. F. Browne's *Alcuin of York* (London, 1908).

I am indebted to the Faculty Research Committees of Cornell University and the University of Oklahoma for grants awarded in 1955 and 1956; to the staff of the Cornell University Library, and especially to Mr. Arthur C. Kulp and his Circulation Department, who most generously for years supplied me with the necessary books; and to the editors of the *Cornell Studies in Classical Philology* for reading the manuscript and criticizing it to my great advantage.

I should like also to express appreciation of the kind interest in my studies shown—*per multa terrarum spatia*—by Professors Bernhard Bischoff (Munich, Germany), Heinrich von Fichtenau (Vienna, Austria), François L. Ganshof (Brussels, Belgium), and Wolfram von den Steinen (Basel, Switzerland), and of the constant encouragement I have received from my friends Professors Lane Cooper and James Hutton of Cornell University.

The book is dedicated to Professor Harry Caplan, with the words of Demosthenes in mind: ἐγὼ νομίζω τὸν εὖ παθόντα δεῖν μεμνῆσθαι πάντα τὸν χρόνον.

Luitpold Wallach

*State University of New York,*
*Harpur College, Endicott, New York*
*February 6, 1958*

## PREFACE TO THE SECOND PRINTING

The second edition is a revised and amended reprint of the volume first published in 1959. Changes and corrections of the text occur on pages 40 n. 9, 88, 93, 101, 106, 192, 204, 206, and 284. Additions are appended to footnotes, and in small print to introductions and chapters, on pages 4, 28, 33, 82, 101, 177, 197, 226, 254, and at the end of the *Select Bibliography* on page 284.

University of Illinois at Urbana          L. W.
September, 1967

# Contents

# Introduction

EINHARD paid tribute to the scholarly reputation of Alcuin of York, associated with Charlemagne as teacher and friend from about 782 to 804, by calling him "a man who in any place would have been thought most learned." [1] Alcuin was indeed a "vir doctissimus undecumque," an epithet first bestowed on the Roman polyhistor Marcus Varro by Terentianus Maurus in what Augustine calls a most elegant line. Since the Venerable Bede used the same words of praise for King Aldfrid of Northumbria and for Aldhelm of Malmesbury, Einhard was placing the Saxon deacon from Northumbria where he belonged—in the tradition of Anglo-Saxon humanism.

In the service of Charlemagne, Alcuin was not only the king's

[1] *Vita Caroli*, c.25: Alcoinum...Saxonici generis hominem, virum undecumque doctissimum, praeceptorem habuit (*scil.* Charlemagne); cf. Terentianus Maurus, *De metris* 2846; Augustinus, *De civitate dei* VI.2 and XVIII.2; Bede, *Historia ecclesiastica* V.12 and V.18; *Gesta abbatum Fontanellensium* c.XVII, *MGH, Scriptores* II (1829), 293.40:...sub Heinrado abbate, viro undecumque doctissimo. Erich Auerbach, "Sermo humilis II," *Romanische Forschungen* 66 (1954), 6, questions the meaning of Einhard's designation of Alcuin; the answer is: Einhard used a topos of praise that has not been recognized as such. See also Auerbach, *Literatursprache und Publikum in der lateinischen Spätantike und im Mittelalter* (Bern, 1958), 88.

teacher in rhetoric, dialectics, and astronomy, as Einhard reported, but much more. Recent biographies by the late Arthur Kleinclausz and by Miss E. S. Duckett present vivid pictures of his work for religion and law, for king and emperor, for Church and State; [2] and his share in the reform of the liturgy in the Frankish empire has been reassessed by Father Gerald Ellard.[3] We can only agree with Etienne Gilson, admirer of the *praeceptor Galliae*, that Alcuin achieved greatness,[4] though this quality becomes more apparent from his correspondence and apologetic treatises than from the simple textbooks he compiled for elementary training in some of the liberal arts. While it is true that Alcuin's religious scholarship permits him to be placed among medieval men of approved sanctity, it is incorrect to think of him as a meek, helpless *magister*. He not infrequently presented himself as such in his letters, but it was in a vein of rhetorical understatement indicative of the conventional modesty expected of a cleric. For Alcuin, as we shall see, had an independent mind.[5] He was anything but helpless; on the contrary, he was a man of strong vitality and a large capacity for work, a man who for more than two decades was involved with Charlemagne in many undertakings of an official, and therefore also of a political, nature. Charlemagne's role in the making of his empire should not be minimized, but it is only fair to take into account the decisive significance of the success of the learned men he drew to his court in order to help him Christianize and civilize his realm. The unusual versatility of Alcuin made him

[2] Arthur Kleinclausz, *Alcuin* (Annales de l'Université de Lyon III.15; Paris, 1948); see my review in *Speculum* 24 (1949), 587–590; Eleanor Shipley Duckett, *Alcuin, Friend of Charlemagne* (New York, 1951), reviewed in *Speculum* 27 (1952), 102–106.

[3] Gerald Ellard, *Master Alcuin, Liturgist* (Chicago, 1956).

[4] Etienne Gilson, *La philosophie au moyen âge* (2nd ed.; Paris, 1944), 191–194. This book is dedicated to "Beatae memoriae Alcuini Eboracensis Galliae Praeceptoris."

[5] Cf. also Louis Halphen, *Charlemagne et l'empire carolingien* (Paris, 1949), 223.

the foremost figure in Charlemagne's brilliant entourage. His accomplishments as educator, statesman, administrator, poet, writer, and scholar were not paralleled by any of his gifted friends of the palace school fellowship, though the Goth Theodulph of Orléans may have been a better poet, the Lombard Paul the Deacon a better historian, and the Patriarch Paulinus of Aquileia a more original theologian.

Great importance must be ascribed to Alcuin's work as a statesman, that is, to his political interest in and labor for the growth of the Frankish empire. The idea that the foreigner from the British Isles played a central part in the recognition of the Frankish king as the imperial authority in the West was suggested in 1902 by Arthur Kleinclausz, is at present shared by F. L. Ganshof,[6] and has been accepted by many other historians. But there are other aspects of Alcuin's political activities that have not as yet been investigated. Some of his writings not only are literary products but, having been composed either upon the request of Charlemagne or at least with his approval, possess the character of official Frankish documents. The apologetic treatises he wrote against adoptionism [7] were not merely the work of a theologian; they represented also the official Frankish rejection of the heresy by Charlemagne, the head of his own national church.

The present investigations deal especially with the fund of Alcuin's political thought and with the extent of his political work in the service of Charlemagne. His so-called *Rhetoric* is here seen as Charlemagne's *via regia*, and not merely as a rhe-

[6] François L. Ganshof, *Le moyen âge* (Histoire des relations internationale I, ed. Pierre Renauvin; Paris, 1953), 25; also *Speculum* 24 (1949), 524, and repeatedly in his numerous Carolingian studies.—I share Ganshof's thesis; see "The genuine and the forged oath of Pope Leo III," *Traditio* XI (1955), 37–63; "The Roman Synod of December 800 and the alleged trial of Leo III," *Harvard Theological Review* 49 (1956), 123–142.

[7] See Chapter IX, p. 149 n. 7.

torical textbook. New evidence reveals that Alcuin was the editor of Charlemagne's *Libri Carolini*, the official Frankish protest against the Byzantine worship of images decreed by the Seventh Ecumenical Council of II Nicaea in 787. The proof here offered of Alcuin's anonymous authorship of some of Charlemagne's political documents confirms the great influence which the deacon from Northumbria exercised on Frankish political life.

The influence of Alcuin and his circle of friends on the events leading to the coronation of December 25, 800, has been ably reconstructed by Peter Munz, *The Origin of the Carolingian Empire* (Leicester, England 1960). A well-written account dealing with the much discussed event is presented by Robert Folz, *Le couronnement impérial de Charlemagne: 25 Decembre 800* (Paris, 1964). On the place occupied by Alcuin see E. E. Stengel, "*Imperator* und *Imperium* bei den Angelsachsen," *Deutsches Archiv für die Erforschung des Mittelalters* XVI (1960), 45 n. 46, and F. L. Ganshof, "Le programme de gouvernement impérial de Charlemagne," *Renovatio Imperii: Atti della giornata internazionale di studio per il millenario* (Ravenna, 4-5 novembre 1961: Faenza, 1963), 64f. See also below, p. 33, and the remarks made by Heinz Hürten, "Alkuin und der Episkopat im Reiche Karls des Grossen," *Historisches Jahrbuch der Görresgesellschaft* LXXXII (1963), 22 n. 2.

# CHAPTER I

# The Political Theories of Alcuin

THE political activities of Alcuin presupposed adherence to certain political theories, beliefs, or notions, which were—as we shall see—of the same traditional origin as were most of his didactic writings. Not a philosopher, Alcuin never presented his ideas on society and government in a coherent form, except to a limited degree in his *Rhetoric*.[1] But fragments of the political notions he held were interspersed throughout his numerous hortatory epistles in the form of more or less reasoned reflections on specific issues in society.[2] These notions are derived from traditional theories on politics and related subjects held by some Church fathers or propagated through a political treatise of Irish provenance that had great vogue during the ninth century. Since it has been denied that Alcuin actually adhered to "a soundly developed theory concerning temporal and divine powers,"[3] it will be necessary to connect our defense of the idea with the critical investigation of political notions actually held by Alcuin.

*On a prehistoric period.* An account of such a period, drawn according to Alcuin from ancient sources (it came, in fact, from

---

[1] See Part I, Chapters IV and V.  [2] See Chapter IV.

[3] Albert Hauck, *Kirchengeschichte Deutschlands* II (3rd and 4th ed.; Leipzig, 1912), 121.

Cicero's rhetorical treatise *On Invention*), appears in the *Rhetoric*.[4] According to this account, prehistoric men wandered aimlessly over the plains like wild beasts, relying on physical strength and not on the reasoning of the human mind. But then a great man appeared who recognized the capacities of human nature. He collected into one place the men from the plains and forests and over their protests forced them into useful and honest occupations. These savage people listened eagerly to the great man because of his reasoning power and eloquence, and then became gentle and domesticated. The great man who accomplished this civilizing feat was identified by Alcuin in a rather incongruous fashion with Charlemagne, who, as Alcuin obviously implies by this identification,[5] civilized and united barbaric Germanic tribes under his rule.

*On a primitive period in Biblical history.* "Why do we not read [in Gen. 47:3]," Alcuin asked, "that the first patriarchs were the kings of nations (reges gentium) and not the herders of sheep (pastores ovium)?"[6] Comparing the earliest rule of man over irrational animals with the rule of man over man, Alcuin

---

[4] Alcuin, *De rhetorica et de virtutibus*, ed. C. Halm, *Rhetores Latini Minores* (Leipzig, 1863), 525 f. A. J. Carlyle, *A History of Mediaeval Political Theory in the West* I (4th impression; Edinburgh-London, 1950), 211 f., apparently does not realize that Alcuin's ch. 2 is taken, almost word for word, from Cicero, *De inventione* I.2.2–3.

[5] See Chapter V, below.

[6] Alcuin, *Interrogationes et responsiones in Genesin*, no. 273, Migne, *Patrologia Latina* 100, 557A–B; Carlyle, *op. cit.*, 203, discusses this passage without realizing that it renders the opinion of Augustine quoted by Carlyle on p. 117 f. Augustine, *De civitate dei* XV.27, ed. Emanuel Hoffmann, vol. II (*CSEL* 40; Wien, 1900), p. 120.21–121.15, is literally quoted by Alcuin in the same treatise in the answer to Interrogatio 115, *PL* 100, 529B–D; no. 131, *PL* 100, 531C contains a reference to Augustine's *reges hominum* quoted in no. 273; no. 145, *PL* 100, 532D–533A, is literally taken from *De civitate dei* XVI.4, ed. Hoffmann II, p. 134.16–18, 20–25; no. 149, *PL* 100, 533C corresponds with XVI.4, ed. Hoffmann II, p. 133.11–24; no. 273, *PL* 100, 557A–B with XIX.15, ed. Hoffmann II, p. 400 f., *passim*. This influence of Augustine has remained unknown to Alcuin's recent biographers.

traced slavery to man's original iniquity and adversity. The legal position of the slave was derived by him etymologically from the Latin word for slave, *servus*, as that of one who by right of war could have been killed (iure belli possint occidi) but instead was kept and guarded (servatus est). Alcuin's entire argument, including the definition, is identical with Augustine's in *De civitate dei* XIX.15, where the rule of man over man, though contradicting man's natural condition, is said to be the remedial, divinely determined punishment for sin.

*The influence of the political theories of Isidore of Seville.* Isidore's often-quoted definition of a king (*Etymologiae* IX.3.4) was adopted by Alcuin, who wrote to King Ethelred of Northumbria: A king is so called from ruling (a regendo vero rex dicitur), and that king who rules his subjects well receives a good return from God, namely, the Kingdom of Heaven.[7] Alcuin furthermore held with the bishop of Seville (IX.3.5) that justice and piety are the principal royal virtues; he told Ethelred that princes and judges ought to rule their people with justice and piety.

But it was Isidore's *Sententiae*, one of the main sources of Alcuin's treatise *On Virtues and Vices*, that chiefly impressed upon Alcuin Isidore's ideas of the functions of rulers. God has granted leadership in government to princes (illis eos *praeesse* voluit) that they may guide the people. The princes should be helpful to the people, not harmful (*prodesse* ergo debet populis).[8] So says Isidore, and Alcuin correspondingly states that the imperial dignity of Charlemagne, ordained by God, is but for the government and the welfare of the people, *populo praeesse et prodesse.*[9] Moreover, he adopted Isidore's patristic

---

[7] Alcuin, *Epistolae*, ed. Ernst Dümmler, *MGH Epistolae* IV (*Aevi Karolini* II, Berlin, 1895), *Epist.* 18, p. 51.31.36; see also Isidore of Seville, *Sententiae* III.48.7, *PL* 83, 719A–B.

[8] *Sententiae* III.49.3, *PL* 83, 721A.

[9] *Epist.* 257, ed. Dümmler, 414.20, 802, addressed to Charlemagne. See this play on words in Augustine, *De civ. dei* XIX.19; Gregory, *Reg. Pastoralis* 2.6; *Moralia in Job* 21.15, 24.25, etc.; *Reg. S. Benedicti* 64.

theory that the rule of the king is for the correction of fallen and, therefore, sinful man, whose evil disposition should be restrained by *terror*.[10] If the word of the priest has proved powerless, this *terror* must be used by the princes of the world. Such disciplinary *terror* was ascribed by Alcuin to Charlemagne's government: it was to render nations everywhere subject to Frankish rule.[11] Furthermore, the same terror was put into foreign nations, according to Einhard, after Charlemagne had become emperor. The function of the king as an auxiliary to the priest in preventing injustice through this terror was, finally, confirmed at the Paris Synod of 829.[12]

*The influence of Pseudo-Cyprian.* The nature of royal authority, that is, the ruler's duty to his subjects, to the Church, and to himself, was often discussed by Alcuin in letters addressed to persons in ruling positions.[13] Although all these statements have an obvious practical application, they are at the same time elements of political theory that follow the Chapter (IX) on the *Unjust King* (*rex iniquus*) in Pseudo-Cyprian's *De duodecim abusivis saeculi*, an Irish treatise of the seventh century.[14] Alcuin's letter in 793 to King Ethelred of Northumbria, for example, which has the characteristics of a *speculum principis*, betrays prominently the influence of the anonymous treatise in

---

[10] *Sententiae* III.47.1, *PL* 83, 717B: Inde et in gentibus principes regesque electi sunt, ut *terrore* suo populos a malo coercerent; III.51.4, *PL* 83, 723B:...per disciplinae *terrorem*.

[11] *Epist*. 178, ed. Dümmler, 294.14: triumpho terroris vestrae; 257 D.414.25: terrorem potentiae vestrae; 17 D.47.2: humanae dignitatis terror; Einhard, *Vita Caroli* c.30:...et exteris nationibus non minimum terroris incussit.

[12] Walter Ullmann, *The Growth of Papal Government in the Middle Ages* (New York, 1956), 130 and 29.

[13] See Chapter III.

[14] Edited by Siegmund Hellmann, *Pseudo-Cyprianus de XII abusivis saeculi* (Texte und Untersuchungen, ed. A. Harnack and C. Schmidt, vol. 34.1; Leipzig, 1909). Alcuin found the chapter on the unjust king also in the *Collectio Hibernensis* (see Ch. VIII, n. 7).

its description of the king's duty to suppress all iniquities, to have wise advisers, and to protect widows and orphans.[15] And in 796 King Eardwulf of Northumbria received from Alcuin a hortatory epistle that is replete with key terms associated with the king's government according to Pseudo-Cyprian: the king is the *corrector patriae* and the corrector of his subjects; and he is responsible for the prosperity of the fatherland. Moreover, the *correctio* of his subjects will secure the *regnum* for the king himself and for his *nepotes* after him.[16]

The basic terminology of Pseudo-Cyprian's theory on the unjust king appears alike in letters addressed to rulers on the Continent and to those in the British Isles.[17] With one exception, identical topics are employed by Alcuin when chastizing his correspondents in the Frankish empire and those across the Channel. In letters sent to rulers in England, the grim picture painted by Gildas of the earlier decadent history of British princes was held up by Alcuin as a *topos* of warning.[18]

---

[15] *Epist.* 18 D.51.19: Regis est omnes iniquitates pietatis suae *potentia obprimere*—Hellmann p. 51.9: Iustitia vero regis est neminem iniuste *per potentiam opprimere;* Alcuin D.51.22: *consiliarios habere prudentes*—Hellmann p. 51.17: *sapientes...consiliarios habere;* Alcuin: D.51.29 f.: Legimus quoque..., a reference (not identified by Dümmler) to Hellmann p. 53.7–10; Alcuin D.51.30: *aeris temperies*—Hellmann p. 53.8: *aeris temperies;* Alcuin D.51.37: *viduis, pupillis,* et miseris sint quasi patres (*scil.* principes et iudices)—Hellmann p. 51.12: advenis et *pupillis et viduis* defensorem esse; etc. Alcuin's familiarity with Pseudo-Cyprian is not mentioned by Hellmann and Dümmler.

[16] *Epist.* 108 Dümmler 155.31: ad *correctionem* custoditus patriae—Hellmann p. 51.4: *correctorem* esse oportuit, and 51.7: sed qualiter alios *corrigere poterit...;* Alcuin D.155.31: *prosperitatem patriae*—Hellmann p. 52.13: *prosperitatem regni;* Alcuin D.155.33: quatenus ex *correctione* subiectorum dicioni tuae *tibi tuisque nepotibus praesens* feliciter firmetur *regnum* et *futuri regni* gloria aeternaliter concedatur—Hellmann p. 52.19–53.2: super omnia vero regis iustitia non solum *praesentis imperii* faciem fuscat, sed etiam filios suos et *nepotes* ne *post se regni hereditatem teneant,* obscurat.

[17] See Chapter IV, below.

[18] See the references to Gildas, *De excidio et conquestu Britanniae,* ed.

But the tradition of Pseudo-Cyprian left its traces also in Alcuin's correspondence with Charlemagne. Pseudo-Cyprian's list of royal duties, such as

> to correct others (alios corrigere),
> to oppress nobody (neminem opprimere),
> to defend churches (ecclesias defendere),
> to judge impartially (sine acceptione personarum iudi-
>     care),

was imitated by Alcuin, for instance, when he wrote that Charlemagne, then in Saxony, ought to be delivered of that heinous people, so that he might return home to accomplish the following program, worthy of a king:

> regna gubernare,
> iustitias facere,
> ecclesias renovare,
> populum corrigere,
> singulis personis...iusta decernere,
> oppressos defendere,
> leges statuere,
> peregrinos consolari,
> et omnibus ubique aequitatis et caelestis vitae viam
>     ostendere.[19]

*The theory of the two powers.* The relation of *regnum* and *sacerdotium*, of Church and State, was understood by Alcuin in accordance with Gelasius I's theory of the two powers gov-

---

T. Mommsen, *MGH, Auctores Antiquissimi* XIII (Berlin, 1898), in the following letters of Alcuin: *Epist.* 17 Dümmler 47.17:...patriam perdiderunt; *Epist.* 129 D.192.18: perdiderunt regnum et patriam; 108 D.155.19: vitam perdidissent et regnum; 18 D.52.5: perierunt antecessores vestri; cf. *Epist.* 232 D.377.31: quomodo perierunt reges. See now Paul Grosjean, "Le *De Excidio* chez Bede et chez Alcuin," *Analecta Bollandiana* 75 (1957), 222–226; on the Philo quotation *ibid.*, 193 f.; cf. Wallach, "Berthold of Zwiefalten's Chronicle," *Traditio* 13 (1957), 216 n. 3.

[19] *Epist.* 177 Dümmler 293.11–14: *iusta decernere;* also in *Epist.* 257 D.414.31: nisi etiam omni *dignitati iusta decernere;* cf. Prov. 8:15–16.

erning the world, as formulated in the pope's letter to the Byzantine emperor Anastasius I:

There are indeed, August Emperor, two [principles] by which this world is mainly ruled, the sacred authority of the popes (auctoritas sacrata pontificum) and the royal power (regalis potestas). Of these two, the weight of the priests (pondus sacerdotum) is much more important (tanto gravius), because it has to render account for the kings of man themselves at the divine tribunal. For you know, our most clement son, that although in dignity you occupy the leading place among mankind, yet you must bend the neck to the leaders who have charge of divine things and look to them for the means of your salvation.[20]

While Gelasius ascribed to the popes *auctoritas*, and to the emperor only *potestas* in the sense of *imperium*, or the active discharge of government, Alcuin spoke of two *potestates*, the secular power (potestas saecularis) and the spiritual power (potestas spiritalis).[21] Elsewhere he called these two powers sacerdotal and kingly (sacerdotalis atque regalis potentia).[22] The former carried, through the preaching of the word of God, the key to celestial rule; the latter carried the "sword of death" or the "sword for the punishment of criminals." When comparing these powers with each other, Alcuin used a comparative construction (multo praestantior...quam) and gave preference to the sacerdotal power, a procedure that is reminiscent of the

---

[20] See text in Carl Mirbt, *Quellen zur Geschichte des Papsttums* (4th ed.; Tübingen, 1924), no. 187, JK 632; Erich Caspar, *Geschichte des Papsttums* II (Tübingen, 1933), 64 ff.; Ernest Stein, *Histoire du Bas-Empire* II (ed. Jean-Remy Palanque; Paris, 1949), 113 f.; Lotte Knabe, *Die gelasianische Zweigestaltentheorie* (Ebering's *Historische Studien* 292; Berlin, 1936); A. K. Ziegler, "Pope Gelasius I and his teaching on the relation of Church and State," *Catholic Historical Review* 27 (1942), 412–437; Wilhelm Ensslin, "Auctoritas und Potestas," *Historisches Jahrbuch der Görresgesellschaft* 74 (1955), 661–668.

[21] Cf. Caspar, *op. cit.*, II (Tübingen, 1933), 755 ff.

[22] *Epist.* 255 Dümmler 413.12.

similarly expressed, corresponding passage in Gelasius' letter (tanto gravius est pondus sacerdotum quanto...). The priests (sacerdotes) are to put their trust in preaching the word of God (fiduciam praedicandi), while the others, that is, the seculars (ceteri...saeculares), ought to listen in humility and do what the priests ask them to do (obedientiam faciendi quae iubetis)! The seculars are the defenders of the priests, who in turn are the mediators (intercessores) for the former before God.[23] This division of power will result in a united flock under one pastor (grex...sub...pastore), so that this *patria*, Alcuin said, may be preserved by God for us and our descendants.[24]

It is quite evident from this analysis that Alcuin followed Gelasius' preference for the priests as representing the higher power, since they were concerned with the souls of all men, including the representatives of the secular power. He succinctly summarized his theory of the two powers, assigning to each its proper function, in a letter to King Ethelred of Northumbria: "It is the duty of the priests not to keep silent about the word of God; it is your duty, O princes, to obey them in humility, and diligently to perform their words." [25] The relationship between priests and rulers is, according to Alcuin, identical with that between priests and the people: the people are told by the priests what to do, and it is up to the people to listen in humility (Plebis est audire).[26]

*The royal authority of Charlemagne.* In following definite traditions concerning Church and State, Alcuin was indeed quite clear in his mind about the functions of Charlemagne as king and emperor. The terminology used to designate these functions is uniform throughout Alcuin's letters addressed to his friend Charlemagne and to other correspondents.[27]

[23] *Epist.* 16 D.44.25: illi antecessores pro vobis, vos defensores pro illis.
[24] *Epist.* 17 D.48.9 f.: et fiat haec patria ab illo *nobis nostrisque nepotibus* conservatur, a formulation influenced by Pseudo-Cyprian, see n. 16, above.
[25] *Epist.* 18 Dümmler 51.17.          [26] Alcuin, PL 101, 617C.
[27] See the general survey by Albert Hauck, *op. cit.*, 119 f.

Charlemagne was, first of all, the divinely appointed defender and protector (defensor et rector) of the Church. He was the *rector morum*, who prudently supervised the moral life of his subjects. By virtue of his being a *bonus laicus* who occupied a higher worldly position than others, and because of the sanctity of his own life, the guidance he accorded to his subjects was like the preaching (praedicatio) of eternal salvation.²⁸ The Church must thank God, Alcuin said, for giving to the Christian people in these dangerous times the most generous gift of such a pious, prudent, and just *rector* and *defensor*, who eagerly strives (in the tradition of Pseudo-Cyprian),

> to correct the evil (prava corrigere),
> to strengthen the good (recta corroborare),
> to heighten the Holy (sancta sublimare),

who rejoices in propagating the name of the most High Lord through many lands (nomen domini...*dilatare* gaudeat), who ventures to kindle the light of the catholic faith in the farthest parts of the world.²⁹ Alcuin once summarized the exalted position of Charlemagne by describing him as well-nigh infallible and calling him a *pontifex:* it was, he maintained, impossible to corrupt him.³⁰ To be sure, it was not a rhetorical overstatement when Alcuin conceded to the king competency to reform a *consuetudo* of the Church that did not appear to him sufficiently praiseworthy.³¹ Charlemagne in fact did this.³² But Alcuin reminded the emperor that his imperial power was given to him not solely for the sake of worldly government but chiefly for the sake of protecting the Church.³³

²⁸ *Epist.* 136 D.209.2–5.
²⁹ *Epist.* 121 D.176.14–19, addressed to Charlemagne in 796–797.
³⁰ Alcuin, *Adv. Elip.* I c.16, PL 101, 251D: impossibile est enim ut corrumpatur, quia....
³¹ *Epist.* 136 D.209.13.
³² See my remarks in *Harvard Theological Review* 49 (1956), 139 f.
³³ *Epist.* 308 Dümmler 471.16, 801–804: non tantum imperatoriam vestrae prudentiae potestatem a Deo solum mundi regimen, sed maxime ad ecclesiae praesidium.

The main functions of Charlemagne's royal authority were the protection and defense of the Church and the preaching and spreading (dilatatio) of the catholic faith. From these functions considered as a fact to the designation of Charlemagne's empire as an *imperium christianum*,[34] was hardly a great step, and the latter designation probably received some encouragement from the occurrence of the term in the Church's prayers for the emperor in the Good Friday liturgy of contemporary sacramentaries.[35] Geographically this *imperium* of Charlemagne comprised (see Ch. IX.iii) Germania, Gallia, Aquitania, and, as Alcuin knew from the intitulation of the *Libri Carolini*, also Italia and the provinces bordering these countries, all of them former provinces of the West Roman empire. Ideologically the *imperium christianum* was to Alcuin—as also to Charlemagne—the con-

[34] Often quoted in Alcuin's *Epistles:* 121 D.176.18: *nomen* domini dei... *dilatare* gaudeat; 110 D.157.7: christianitatis regnum atque agnitionem veri Dei *dilatavit;* 185 D.310.30: terminos custodierunt etiam et *dilataverunt christiani imperii;* 202 D.336.2: ac veluti armis *imperium christianum* fortiter *dilatare;* Alcuin, *Vita Willibrordi* ed. W. Levison, *MGH, Scriptores Rerum Merovingicarum* VII (1920), 134.3, Charlemagne: terminos *nostri dilatavit imperii; Epist.* 18 D.52.20 to King Ethelred of Northumbria: regnum dilatetur vestrum; see n. 66 below. Similiar phrases with *dilatare* occur in the *Codex Carolinus*, ed. W. Gundlach, *MGH, Epistolae* III.

[35] See Heinrich Fichtenau, "Il concetto imperiale di Carlo Magno," *Settimane di studio del Centro italiano di studi sull'alto medioevo* I (Spoleto, 1954), 22 ff. (of the reprint); Heinz Löwe in Wattenbach-Levison, *Deutschlands Geschichtsquellen im Mittelalter* (Weimar, 1953), 234; Carl Erdmann, *Forschungen zur politischen Ideenwelt des Frühmittelalters*, ed. Friedrich Baethgen (Berlin, 1951), 19; Gerald Ellard, *Master Alcuin, Liturgist* (Chicago, 1956), 194 f. Alcuin's idea of the *imperium christianum* is not at all influenced by any Anglo-Saxon conception of an *imperium* (as E. E. Stengel and others have surmised); such an idea never existed, as was shown by R. Drögereit, "Kaiseridee und Kaisertitel bei den Angelsachsen," *Zeitschrift der Savigny-Stiftung für Rechtsgeschichte* 69 (Germ. Abt., 1952), 24–73. I hope to prove (see below) that Alcuin's *imperium christianum* is the *imperium* of Charlemagne as Alcuin's ideal Christian emperor in the sense of Augustine's *felix imperator* of the *Civitas dei*.

tinuation of the Roman empire of the Christian emperors Constantine the Great, Theodosius II, Valentinian III, and Honorius, whom Alcuin considered as predecessors of Charlemagne (see Ch. VIII). This fact may further be deduced from Alcuin's identification of Charlemagne with the *imperator invictus*, the unknown Roman emperor "Octavianus Augustus," to whom Vegetius dedicated his treatise on warfare (see Ch. III, n. 5). To Alcuin the emperor at Byzantium was not the successor to the old Roman empire but only the ruler of a territory formerly belonging to the *imperium romanum* that—by the time of Alcuin—had vanished long before.[36]

*The formulary of Charlemagne's royal and imperial authority.* How well ingrained the theory of Charlemagne's authority as a ruler was in Alcuin's mind can be seen in the existence of a formulary used in his letters to Charlemagne. The formulary contains, with one exception, essentially the same elements as the theory of royal authority found in Alcuin's *Epistles* to the king in 794-795 (*Epist.* 41) and 799 (*Epist.* 178) and to the emperor in 802 (*Epist.* 257). Analysis of the identical formulaic elements in these three letters reveals the basic functions assigned by Alcuin to the ruler.

*Epist.* 41 (Dümmler 84), 794-795, Alcuin to Charlemagne:

That people is deemed blessed that has such a *rector* and *praedicator* as is Charlemagne who both ( et *utrumque*) uses the sword of triumphal power (gladius triumphalis potentiae) and the trumpet of catholic preaching (catholicae praedicationis tuba), who also, like his Biblical prototype David, everywhere subdues the nations with his victorious sword (victrici gladio *undique gentes subiciens*) and who appears before the people as a *praedicator* of God's law. Under Charlemagne's shadow the Christian people possesses security (*quiete*

[36] See the comments by Heinz Löwe, "Von Theoderich dem Grossen zu Karl dem Grossen," *Deutsches Archiv für Erforschung des Mittelalters* 9 (1952), 384 f.

populus requiescit christianus), and everywhere appears formidable to the pagan nations (et *terribilis undique gentibus extat paganis*).

*Epist.* 178 (Dümmler 294), 799, Alcuin to Charlemagne:

May God help Charlemagne everywhere to subdue through the triumph of his *terror* the hostile nations (ut triumpho *terroris* vestri *inimicos undique subiciat gentes*) and to subdue (subiciat) the wildest spirits to the Christian faith. The authority of Charlemagne's *potestas* proves him to be *rex*, and his persevering diligence in spreading the word of God makes him a *praedicator*. It is on these grounds that divine grace (*divina gratia*) has enriched Charlemagne in an extraordinary manner through these two gifts (*his duobus muneribus*), namely, the *imperium* of earthly felicity (*terrenae felicitatis imperio*) and the fullness of spiritual wisdom (*spiritalis sapientiae latitudine*). May he advance in both gifts (ut in *utroque* proficias) until he reaches the happiness of eternal beatitude (donec ad *aeternae beatitudinis* pervenias *felicitatem*).

*Epist.* 257 (Dümmler 414), 802, Alcuin to Charlemagne:

Charlemagne's imperial dignity (*dignitas imperialis*), ordained by God, is destined for nothing else but to guide and to help the people (*populo praeesse et prodesse*). Power and wisdom (*potestas et sapientia*) are given to those elected by God; *potestas*, so that the ruler may suppress the proud (*ut superbos opprimat*) and defend the lowly against the unjust (*et defendat ab inprobis humiles*); *sapientia*, so that the ruler with pious care may rule and teach his subjects (*ut regat et doceat...subjectos*). Divine grace (*divina gratia*) has exalted and honored the emperor's incomparable sublimity through those two gifts (*his duobus muneribus*) by sending the *terror* of his power over all the peoples everywhere (*terrorem* potentiae vestrae *super omnes undique gentes inmittens*) so that those people may come to Charlemagne in voluntary surrender whom war in earlier times could not subject to his rule (ut *voluntaria* subjectione ad eos veniant quos prioribus bellicus labor temporibus sibi subdere non potuit) and so the people will live in peace (*quiete populus*).

The parts of Alcuin's basic formulary of Charlemagne's royal and imperial authority are as follows:

A. Charlemagne in relation to his people is:

the *rector* and *praedicator* (*Epist.* 41);

the *rex* and *praedicator* (*Epist.* 178);

as emperor he guides and is useful, *populo praeesse et prodesse* (*Epist.* 257).

B. Charlemagne's authority is based on:

*potentia* and *praedicatio* (41);

*potestas* and the *instantia seminandi verbi dei* (178);

as emperor on *potestas* and *sapientia* (257).

C. Charlemagne's aim as ruler is the subjugation of nations everywhere:

*undique gentes subiciens* (41);

*inimicos undique subiciat gentes* (178);

as emperor to subdue through the coercive *terror* of his power, *omnes undique gentes* (257).

D. Charlemagne subjugates the nations:

*victrici gladio* (41);

*triumpho terroris* (178);

as emperor[37] through those two gifts (his *duobus muneribus*), that is, *potestas* and *sapientia* (257).

E. The result of Charlemagne's rule is:

the peace and security of the Christian people (*superna quiete populus requiescit christianus*), while he himself *terribilis*[38] *undique gentibus* extat *paganis* (41);

the *imperium* of earthly happiness, *terrenae felicitatis imperio* (178);

---

[37] This element of the formulary see, for instance, in *Epist.* 245 Dümmler 398.1: qui eum [*scil.* Charlemagne] super omnes alios reges et imperatores *sapientiae* decore honoravit et *potentia* exaltavit.

[38] This part of the formulary see, for instance, in *Epist.* 17 D.47.2: Sic tandem concordia vestra *terribilis* apparet omni; see n. 39.

as emperor the peace of the entire people, *totus pacifica
quiete populus*, and the voluntary submission under his
rule of unconquerable nations (257).

The panegyric *synkrisis* of the formulary with regard to the
imperial authority of Charlemagne is quite obvious; the *terror*
imposed on foreign nations by the sheer might of the emperor
leads to their voluntary surrender, to the cessation of war, and
subsequently to the peace of the Christian people within the
*imperium christianum* of Charlemagne.

That Alcuin's concept of *terror* as a coercive means of royal
authority originates in the political theory of Isidore of Seville
has been pointed out previously. The unresisting surrender of
foreign nations to the Roman emperor is a *topos* of Roman
historiography that was known to Alcuin in all likelihood from
his familiarity with Eutropius' *Breviary of Roman History*.[39]
There it is said of Augustus that many kings left their dominions
in order to submit to him, because they were impressed by his
might. And Eutropius reports of Antoninus Pius that this emperor was no less venerated than feared (venerabilis non minus
quam *terribilis*), so that many nations among the barbarians,
*depositis armis*, referred their controversies to him and submitted to his decisions.

The formulary of Charlemagne's functions as a ruler was by
no means a product of Alcuin's rhetorical fancy. It actually represented the official policies of Charlemagne as they were described in his letter of 796 addressed to Pope Leo III:

It is *our* part with the help of Divine Holiness to defend by armed
strength the holy Church of Christ everywhere (*undique*) from the
outward onslaught of the pagans and the ravages of the infidels (ab
incursu paganorum et ab infidelium devastatione armis defendere
foris), and to strengthen within (intus) it the knowledge of the
catholic faith.

[39] See the reference to Eutropius VII.21 below in n. 80; for Augustus
see Eutropius VII.10; for Antoninus Pius see VIII.8.

It is *your* part, most holy Father, to help our armies with your hands lifted up to God like Moses, so that by your intercession and by the leadership and gift of God the Christian people may everywhere and always have the victory over the enemies of his Holy name.[40]

The duties Charlemagne assigned to himself [41] in this letter are identical with those ascribed to him in Alcuin's formulary. This fact alone might confirm the assumption of Halphen that Alcuin was the author of this letter,[42] which indeed contains other elements characteristic of Alcuin's style. The occurrence of *undique*, referring to the king's task to defend the Church *everywhere* against the pagans, is suggestive of Alcuin's possible authorship, since this *undique* is an established part of Alcuin's formulary. There Charlemagne was hailed as defender of the Church who as *king* may defeat *undique gentes* (*Epist.* 41 and 178), the nations everywhere, and as *emperor* even *omnes undique gentes*, all the nations everywhere (*Epist.* 257).

What Alcuin expected of Charlemagne—that he defend the Church and subdue all the nations—was on the other hand a traditional wish, often repeated in the papal correspondence [43] with the Carolingians since the days of Pope Stephen II. Charlemagne's official edition (791) of a collection of papal letters, the so-called *Codex Carolinus*, contains numerous letters that express the wish that the Frankish king be victorious over *all* barbarian nations, *super omnes barbaras nationes*. Although these

[40] *Epist.* 93 Dümmler 137 f.

[41] And later to his sons; see *Divisio regnorum* of 806, *MGH, Capitularia Regum Francorum* I, no. 45, p. 129, c.15 (ed. Boretius, Hannover, 1881).

[42] Louis Halphen, *Charlemagne et l'empire carolingien* (Paris, 1949), 121; compare the *nostrum est* and *vestrum est* in Charlemagne's letter (above, n. 40) with Alcuin's *Epistles* 18 Dümmler 51.17: illorum est—vestrum est; 120 D.175.15: meum fuit—tuum est; 171 D.282.26: meum est—vestrum est; *PL* 101, 617C: sacerdotis est—populi est, etc.

[43] See *Codex Carolinus*, 498 n. 1, for a list of the numerous occurrences of the wish; for the quotation from Hadrian's letter addressed to Charlemagne see no. 62, p. 589.

wishes of the popes originally referred to the Lombards, they were retained in their correspondence with Charlemagne (after he had defeated the Lombards and become the *rex Longo-bardorum*), however, with the additional wish that God might now subject also to Charlemagne the remaining (*ceterae*) barbarian nations.[44] Charlemagne adopted this papal request by extending it to the pagan nations; and, therefore, it became his duty—in accordance with Alcuin's formulary—*undique* to protect the *ecclesia Christi*, not only in Rome, but also elsewhere. We may see in this generalization of Charlemagne's self-imposed task the hand of Alcuin, who by preference stressed the responsibility of Charlemagne's dominion for the universal church.[45]

In this vein Alcuin once wrote to Charlemagne as follows:

Spare your Christian people and defend the Church of Christ that the blessing of the King above may make you strong against the heathen. We read that one of the old poets, when praising in song the Roman emperors and describing the character that they should have, said, if I recall correctly,

*parcere subiectis et debellare superbos,*

a verse that the blessed Augustine explained with much praise in his book *On the City of God*.[46] Yet we must strive much more to follow the dictates of the Gospel than Virgil's verses.[47]

[44] *Ibid.*, no. 53, p. 575:...quia...tuis regalibus vestigiis ceteras barbaras nationes omnipotens dominus substernet. Cf. Albert Brackmann, "Die Anfänge der Slavenmission und die Renovatio Imperii des Jahres 800," *SB. Berlin Akademie* (1931), especially pp. 74–76.

[45] See Walter Ullmann, *The Growth of Papal Government in the Middle Ages* (New York, 1956), 107 n. 3: Alcuin: Universalis ecclesia quae sub...dominationis vestrae imperio conversatur.

[46] *De civitate dei* V.12, and hardly I.6, as suggested by Dümmler; see further Augustine's interpretations of *Aeneid* VI.853 in I, *Praefatio*.

[47] *Epist.* 178 Dümmler 294.25 ff., 799: *Parce populo tuo Christiano*, et ecclesias Christi defende, ut benedictio superni regis te fortem efficiat super paganos... The first words refer to Joel 2:17 *Parce, domine, parce populo tuo...*, a passage also quoted by Alcuin in *Epist.* 17, D.48.15. Cf.

The high mission of the Roman celebrated by Virgil toward the end of the sixth book of the *Aeneid* (v.853), "To be generous to the conquered and war down the proud," was criticized by Alcuin,[48] yet it was adopted by him for the imperial formulary. For the ruler possesses power, as he said, that he may suppress the proud nations *ut superbos opprimat*, and wisdom, that he may rule and teach his newly conquered subjects (ut regat et doceat subiectos).[49] The mission of the Roman as conceived by Virgil (*Aeneid* 6.851-853),

> tu regere imperio populos, Romane, memento
> (hae tibi erunt artes), pacisque imponere morem,
> parcere subiectis et debellare superbos,

was in accord with Alcuin's imperial formulary ascribed to Charlemagne in a letter poem:

> *Erige subiectos et iam depone superbos,*
> ut pax et pietas regnet ubique sacra.
> "Lift up the conquered [people] and put down the
> proud
> [nations] that peace and divine worship may rule every-
> where." [50]

Alcuin admired Charlemagne's conquest and conversion of pagan nations. He was greatly impressed to see how Charlemagne "poured the light of truth" (infudit) into those "blind minds" of the pagans: "How great will be your glory, O most blessed king, on the day of eternal retribution, when [you see] all those who through your good care were converted from the

---

E. M. Sanford, "Alcuin and the classics," *Classical Journal* 20 (1925), 526–533.

[48] Cf. Omera Floyd Long, "The attitude of Alcuin toward Virgil," *Studies in Honor of Basil L. Gildersleeve* (Baltimore, 1902), 377 ff.

[49] *Epist.* 257 Dümmler 414.22 f.

[50] No. XLV 67 f., ed. Ernst Dümmler, *MGH, Poetae Latini Aevi Carolini* I (Berlin, 1881), 259.

worship of idols to the recognition of the true God." [51] Prayers
for the success of the Roman emperor's crusade against the
pagan nations were contained in the oldest sacramentaries of
the Church. Alcuin, who edited a supplemented version of the
Gregorian Sacramentary,[52] naturally was acquainted with this
prayer: "Oremus et pro christianissimo imperatore nostro, ut
deus et dominus noster *subditas* illi *faciat omnes barbaras* nationes ad nostram perpetuam pacem." [53]

*Alcuin and the papacy.* In the relationship between Church
and State, Alcuin apportioned to Charlemagne an independent
position, which, in fact, corresponded to the king's supreme
position as head of the Frankish national church.[54] Charlemagne's autocratic dealings with the Roman See are reflections
of Alcuin's ideas on the papacy. At the outset one might assume
that Alcuin's adoption of the Gelasian theory of the two powers
provided the answer to his attitude toward the papacy. Charlemagne's letter—presumably written by Alcuin—to Leo III on
the functions of the pope apportioned a well-restricted sphere
of interest to Leo, that of prayers for the success of the Frankish
armies marching against the pagan nations, and of divine intercession for the Frankish people. It now seems that Alcuin's

[51] *Epist.* 110 D.157.8–11.        [52] See Ellard, *op. cit.*, 126 ff.

[53] See the fine study and collection of relevant prayer texts by Gerd
Tellenbach, "Römischer und christlicher Reichsgedanke in der Liturgie
des frühen Mittelalters," *SB. Heidelberg Akademie* (1934), 52; Hans
Hirsch, "Der mittelalterliche Kaisergedanke in den liturgischen Gebeten,"
*Mitteilungen des Instituts für Oesterreichische Geschichtsforschung* 44
(1930), 1–20.

[54] Cf. Etienne Delaruelle, "Charlemagne et l'église," *Revue d'histoire
de l'église de France* 39 (1953), 165–99, who suggests (p. 193) that
Cassiodorus' *Historia Tripartita* especially made the Carolingian age
familiar with the idea of the Christian empire. Alcuin, *Liber adversus
haeresin Felicis*, c.25 (*PL* 101, 97B–C), seems to have known the *Hist.
Trip.*, for the indicated passage is from H. Tr. I.14.29: Porro creaturae
eius—I.14.31: in quo bene placui, ed. Walter Jacob and Rudolph Hanslick
(*CSEL* 71; Wien, 1952), 60.201–215. That the *imperium christianum* is of
Augustinian origin will be shown subsequently; cf. also above, n. 35.

famous statement from the year 799 on the supremacy of the Frankish kingship over the papacy, and on the imperial dignity of Byzantium,[55] though called forth by exigencies which he judged correctly, also expresses his basic idea on the position of the papacy within the constellation of existing powers. Alcuin was greatly concerned about the attacks on Leo III, and he counseled Charlemagne in the matter, relying upon the king's good judgment to do what was in keeping with the pope's high office, *quid cui conveniat personae*, as he said.[56] Insisting on the traditional judicial immunity of the pontiff's person and office, Alcuin's followers successfully represented his point of view before the Roman Synod of December 800, and a public trial of Leo III never took place.[57] Recognizing the Church's need of protection, Alcuin probably agreed with Isidore of Seville:

The princes of the world now and then occupy the greatest power within the Church for the purpose of protecting through this power the ecclesiastical discipline. For the rest, these powers would not be necessary within the Church, if the princes did not command through the terror of the discipline what the priest cannot achieve through preaching [alone]. The Kingdom of Heaven often profits from the earthly kingdom.[58]

*Alcuin's Augustinian theory of the Christian emperor.* Discussion of Alcuin's political notions should be of help toward understanding the royal and imperial theocracy of Charlemagne. The absolute religious rule of the Frank seemed to eliminate the differences between Church and State and to effect what has been called by Arquillière *la compénétration du temporel et du*

---

[55] *Epist.* 174 Dümmler 288.17–26, addressed to Charlemagne.

[56] *Epist.* 178 D.295.8; 179 D.297.36; the same phrase also in *Epist.* 111 D.160.11; 177 D.292.34; 243 D.390.33.

[57] Cf. Wallach, "The Roman Synod of December 800 and the alleged trial of Leo III," *Harvard Theological Review* 49 (1956), especially p. 135 f.

[58] *Sententiae* III.51.4, *PL* 83, 723.

*spirituel*,[59] so that Charlemagne's political activities appear to be almost completely dominated by religious functions and intentions. This political Augustinianism is on the surface visible in Charlemagne's work as a ruler, although direct proof based on historical sources is actually lacking.[60] To be sure, Einhard (c.24) noticed Charlemagne's fondness for Augustine's writings, especially for *On the City of God*, but little supporting evidence [61] of much knowledge of this work has come to light in the writings of the men close to Charlemagne. There are, however, some Augustinian traces in Alcuin's idea of peace,[62] and extensive use was made of *De civitate dei* in one of his exegetical treatises.[63] Since this is the only noticeable influence of *On the City of God* in the work of a man so closely associated with Charlemagne, it is an important piece of evidence. Moreover, further traces of *De civitate dei* in Alcuin's thought may be seen, I believe, in his idea of Charlemagne as a Christian ruler.

Charlemagne appears in Alcuin's theories quite clearly as the *rector morum* of the *imperium christianum* in the same fashion that Augustine expected rulers to be *rectores morum*.[64] Like Augustine, Alcuin envisaged a universal church that comprehended all nations [65] and included in the Christian people nations beyond the borders of the Roman empire. With Augustine, Alcuin subordinated the lower purposes of the state to the higher purposes to be realized by the *ecclesia Christi:* it is a

[59] H.-X. Arquillière, "L'essence de l'augustinisme politique," *Augustinus Magister* II (Paris, 1954), 997 f.

[60] See Joseph Ratzinger, "Herkunft und Sinn der Civitas Lehre Augustins," *Augustinus Magister* II (Paris, 1954), 965 n. 6.

[61] Hubert Bastgen lists in his notes to the edition of Charlemagne's *Libri Carolini* (*MGH, Legum Sectio III, Concilia* II, *Supplementum*, Hannover and Leipzig, 1924) a few possible references to the *De civitate dei*; see pp. 77 n. 7; 92 n. 5; 153 n. 3.

[62] Cf. Arthur Kleinclausz, *Alcuin* (Paris, 1948), 109 ff.

[63] See above, nn. 6 and 47.          [64] *De civitate dei* II.20.

[65] XVIII.49: Unitatem catholicae ecclesiae per omnes gentes futuram; XVIII.32 (ed. Hoffmann, pp. 350.7 and 314.12): Gentes...quae non sunt in iure Romano erunt in populo Christiano.

blessing to the *res publica* to be concerned with *praecepta religionis Christi* (*De civ. dei* II.19). It now becomes clear that Alcuin saw in Charlemagne Augustine's ideal Christian emperor, the *felix imperator* (V.24), who uses his power for spreading the worship of God (si suam potestatem ad dei cultum maxime dilatandum maiestati eius famulam faciunt), who loves more that kingdom (regnum) in which he does not need fear any consorts, who lives up to an entire series of qualities (enumerated by Augustine) "not out of vainglory but out of love for everlasting bliss (non propter ardorem inanis gloriae, sed propter caritatem *felicitatis aeternae*). "We say of such Christian emperors," Augustine concludes, "that they are in this life happy in their hope, but destined to be truly happy when that life will come for which we live in hope" (Tales christianos imperatores dicimus esse felices).

In order to conform to this ideal of a Christian emperor, Charlemagne had to propagate the worship of the true God. This was the principal meaning of the word *dilatare*, which occurs so often in Alcuin's writings in phrases such as *nomen domini dei dilatare*.[66] Seeing it in this context, we understand the meaning of the divine gift (*munus*) of the *imperium terrenae felicitatis* ascribed to Charlemagne by Alcuin, an *imperium* that was to lead Charlemagne to the felicity of eternal bliss (ad aeternae beatitudinis felicitatem).[67]

The same Augustinian concept of the *felix* Christian emperor

[66] See n. 34 above; Charlemagne's letter to King Offa of Mercia, *Epist.* 100 Dümmler 146.16:...*quatenus* mitissima superni regis *bonitas regnum* sanctae ecclesiae protegere, *exaltare*, et *dilatare dignetur*. Deus...*longeva prosperitate...desiderantissime* frater; that this letter was probably written by Alcuin may be seen from *Epist.* 101 D.147.32, a letter by Alcuin to King Offa of Mercia: *quatenus* divina clementia in *longeva* te custodiat *prosperitate* et *regnum tuum*, immo Anglorum omnium,...ex suae *bonitatis* gratia *exaltare*, *dilatare*, et coronare dignetur in aeternum, (p. 148.15):...domine...nobisque desiderantissime. See Augustine, *De civ. dei* IV.15.

[67] *Epist.* 178 Dümmler 294.22.—It is important to know that the noun *felicitas* does *not* occur in the Vulgate.

is seen in Alcuin's letter to King Ethelred of Northumbria, where Alcuin speaks of the *felicitas huius saeculi* (the bliss of this present age), and the earthly honors that are to become celestial ones (ut post hos honores terrenos caelestes habere mereamini).[68] And all the passages in Alcuin's letters congratulating the Frankish people as a *beata gens* or a *felix* or *beatus populus* for having a ruler like Charlemagne [69] are suggested by the ideal of the Christian emperor. Those governments are to be called blessed (*felicia* esse *regna*) which are ruled by Plato's philosopher kings, Alcuin wrote to Charlemagne, changing the original *beatae res publicae* of his source—Boethius—in order to conform to Augustine's *felices imperatores*.[70]

Clearly, Chapter 24 of the fifth book of *De civitate dei* entitled, "What Is and How True Is the Felicity of Christian Emperors," was in Alcuin's mind when he wrote a letter to Charlemagne in 799, offering, like Augustine, a list of the ruler's duties. At the end of this list he said that through the performance of those duties the *felicitas regni* (the bliss of rulership) and the beatitude of the heavenly kingdom (caelestis regni beatitudo) might be attained by Charlemagne.[71]

The identification of Charlemagne with Augustine's ideal Christian emperor, in which I see the origin of Alcuin's concept of the *imperium christianum*, borders, in Alcuin's panegyric style, on an apotheosis of the Frankish king and Roman emperor. But this genuine admiration for the greatness of his royal friend never prevented Alcuin from disagreeing with Charlemagne and from expressing his opinion, even when he himself thought that anybody might rightfully ask, "Why does that man meddle in other people's affairs?" [72] Still, none of Charlemagne's other advisers dared to question his governmental

[68] *Epist.* 18 D.49.31, also 51.33: Valde feliciter regnat in terra qui de terreno regno merebitur celeste.

[69] *Epist.* 41 D.84.12; 171 D.281.27; 229 D.373.1.

[70] *Epist.* 229 D.373.2 following Boethius, *Cons. phil.* I.4.5.

[71] *Epist.* 177 D.293.18.          [72] *Epist.* 211 D.352.24.

policies as strongly and frequently as did the man who praised him most. Exasperated at the king's ferocious way of conquest and his enforced conversions of Saxons and Avars, whom he preferred to call Huns,[73] Alcuin inveighed tirelessly against compulsory missionary methods. His open protest against the abuse of royal power in the treatment of conquered nations was something unheard of in his barbaric age; this protest really shows the greatness of the man. His was the only voice raised in the name of humanity in support of those pagan nations. Following his teacher Augustine, he stated realistically, "Fides...res est voluntaria, non necessaria" (Faith is a voluntary matter, not one of coercion).[74] Believing in the Augustinian idea of peace,[75] he had to doubt the necessity of Charlemagne's never-ending wars. Thus he questioned the wisdom of one of Charlemagne's expeditions against the Duchy of Beneventum. "Quid populo profitiat Christiano?" he asked the king.[76] Did the king not know, argued Alcuin, that divine providence was fighting for him against his enemies? For Alcuin had no illusions about the permanence of kings and kingdoms. He knew "in Whose Hands are the powers of all kings and kingdoms." [77] Not the size of states is decisive for their existence, but their moral fiber. "The greatest empires of the world" (maxima mundi imperia) [78] have vanished on account of internal dissensions, whereas the rule of some very small city (civitas) or province (provincia) has flourished, because it had achieved peaceful harmony (pacifica concordia).

While Alcuin ascribed to Charlemagne almost unlimited authority, he certainly never assumed him to be above the law. The king and emperor who made laws was also bound by

---

[73] *Epist.* 107, 110, 111.

[74] *Epist.* 111 D.160.19, 796; 113 D.164.27, 796.

[75] See n. 62 above.          [76] *Epist.* 211 D.352.3.

[77] *Epist.* 107 D.154.6: in cuius manu sunt omnes regum et regnorum potestates; cf. to this *Epist.* 111 D.160.26.

[78] *Epist.* 18 D.52.20.

them; he was not *legibus solutus*. Alcuin expected him to respect the laws of the Church and those of his imperial predecessors (see Ch. VIII).

Yet Alcuin, on his part, was not at all doctrinaire in matters of government and law. When his friend Arno, the bishop of Salzburg, became involved with Charlemagne in disputes over the ownership of church property, Alcuin counseled him to comply *prompta voluntate* with the "wisest prince" and to remember Matt. 22:21, "Reddite Caesari quae Caesaris sunt, et Deo, quae Dei sunt." [79] On the other hand, Alcuin showed the open mind of a truly civilized man when he reminded Charlemagne that humanity toward his subjects (clementia in subiectos suos) is a fitting imperial virtue, so much so that the most noble Roman emperor Titus used to say, "No one [who comes to] an emperor should leave discontented." [80]

[79] *Epist.* 265 D.423.27.18.

[80] *Epist.* 249 D.403.43 following Eutropius VII.21: Titus...ait neminem ab imperatore tristem debere recedere.—

Heinz Löwe, *Göttingische gelehrte Anzeigen* 214 (1962), 144, misinterprets my view of Alcuin's influence on Charlemagne's policies towards the papacy when he states that I consider "Karls Politik gegenüber dem Papst nur als Spiegelung der Ideen Alkuins." I use neither the equivalent of "Spiegelung" nor that of the word "nur" (only) when I say (p. 22, above) that "Charlemagne's autocratic dealings with the Roman See are reflections of Alcuin's ideas on the papacy." The "autocratic dealings" together with the context of the quotation plainly refute Löwe's interpretation of my words. Alcuin's panegyric formulary (above, pp. 15-22) leaves no doubt concerning the primacy of Charlemagne's royal and imperial authority and motivation. Loewe might have conveniently recalled in 1962 what he wrote in 1957 (*Historische Zeitschrift* 183, p. 694): "The influence of Alcuin on Charlemagne had its limits, as W(allach) shows." P. E. Schramm, *Historische Zeitschrift* 198 (1964), 331 n. 2, likewise overestimates my opinion of Alcuin's influence. See now "Alcuin" in the *New Catholic Encyclopedia* I (New York, 1967), 279-80.

*Part One*

# THE *VIA REGIA* OF CHARLEMAGNE: THE *RHETORIC* OF ALCUIN AS A TREATISE ON KINGSHIP

THE *Disputatio de rhetorica et de virtutibus* by Alcuin[1] has been accepted for centuries simply as the exposition of a system of rhetoric. The purpose of this section is to suggest that the treatise contains more than mere rhetorical instruction. Arthur Kleinclausz[2] expresses the generally accepted view that the treatise was composed as a textbook to be used for the study of the art of rhetoric within the system of the Seven Liberal Arts. J. W. H. Atkins[3] assumes that the book was written by Alcuin in 793 on his return from England to France and that it is the author's contribution to literary theory. W. S. Howell,[4] who decides on 794 as the date of composition, considers the treatise primarily as a rhetorical textbook, although he sees in it inci-

[1] Edited by Carl Halm, *Rhetores Latini Minores* (Leipzig, 1863), 523–550.

[2] *Alcuin* (Annales de l'Université de Lyon III,15; Paris, 1948), 57.

[3] *English Literary Criticism: The Medieval Phase* (Cambridge, 1943), 54–58; for an analysis of the *Rhetoric* from the aesthetic point of view see Edgar de Bruyne, *Études d'Esthétique Médiévale* (Rijksuniversiteit te Gent; Brugge, Belgium, 1946), 216–223.

[4] *The Rhetoric of Alcuin and Charlemagne* (Princeton Studies in English XXIII; Princeton, 1941), 5–8, 61–62; G. K. Anderson, *The Literature of the Anglo-Saxons* (Princeton, 1949), 237, unjustly condemns the treatise as "an extremely unconvincing conglomeration of Cicero, Aristotelian theory, and the Bible."

dental value as a work on politics, law, and morals. The importance of rhetoric in the training of students for positions in the medieval chanceries, secular and ecclesiastical, stressed by Professor Harry Caplan in a well-known study,[5] led the present writer to the characterization of Alcuin's *Rhetoric* as a *speculum principis (Fürstenspiegel)*.[6]

No student of history has thus far tried to investigate the literary composition of the *Rhetoric* in the light of Alcuin's entire production. The historical appropriateness of the treatise, its date and sources, as well as its contents and composition, are here examined especially in relation to Alcuin's other treatises and his numerous *Epistles*.[7] This approach will, I hope, throw light upon the forgotten historical background of the *Rhetoric* and subsequently enable us to discover Alcuin's own purpose in writing the work. The uniformity of Alcuin's personal style [8] suggests this procedure.

Our exposition proceeds from the treatment of the sources and the date of the *Rhetoric* to the proof that this treatise possesses the characteristics of a *littera exhortatoria* in conformity with Alcuin's letters and other treatises, and that it was written with the Biblical idea of the King's Highway, the *via regia*, in mind, as a tractate on kingship or good government. A survey of the extant manuscripts of the *Rhetoric* and of various *testimonia* will ultimately permit additional conclusions concerning the trans-

[5] "Classical Rhetoric and the Mediaeval Theory of Preaching," *Classical Philology* XXVIII (1933), 74 f.

[6] First mentioned in *Speculum* XXIV (1949), 588 f.; cf. Heinz Löwe in Wattenbach-Levison, *Deutschlands Geschichtsquellen im Mittelalter* (Weimar, 1953), 230 n. 211 and p. 233.

[7] Edited by Ernst Dümmler, *MGH, Epistolae* IV (1895), 1–493, with additions pp. 614–616, and *Epistolae* V (1899), 643–645. Letters discovered since then are listed in Chapter XIV.

[8] The opinion of H. O. Taylor, *The Medieval Mind* II (4th ed.; Cambridge, Mass., 1949), 202, that Alcuin has "no personal style" is sufficiently contradicted by our investigations.

mission of the text. Finally, the political purpose of the treatise will be investigated in terms of Alcuin's interest in the secular and church legislation of Charlemagne and his acquaintance with certain legal procedures of his age.

Heinz Löwe in Wattenbach-Levison, *Deutschlands Geschichtsquellen im Mittelalter: Vorzeit und Karolinger* II (Weimar, 1953), 234, still questions Alcuin's political importance in the making of Charlemagne's empire, and in a review of the first edition of the present volume which he yet kindly calls "one of the most important contributions to the Alcuin studies of the last decades" (*Göttingische gelehrte Anzeigen* 214, 1962, 144) characterizes him as a *Stubengelehrter*, that is a "bookworm". Löwe unfortunately repeats his evaluation of the Saxon nobleman which he first presented in his book *Die Karolingische Reichsgründung und der Südosten* (Stuttgart, 1937), 102 etc. His assessment of Alcuin's Germanic thinking has been uniformly rejected by F. L. Ganshof, *Revue belge* 17 (1938), 976-78; Philip Grierson, *The English Historical Review* 54 (1939), 525-26; and François Himly, *Le Moyen Age* 49 (1939), 206-208. Says Ganshof: "A vouloir trop expliquer par un facteur unique—il s'agit ici de la *Rasse* et du *Volkstum* germaniques—on fausse ses conclusions." In addition, Hans-Walter Klewitz, *Historische Zeitschrift* 161 (1940), 341-44, records Albert Brackmann's objections to Löwe's thesis of Charlemagne's empire as an expression of Germanic *Selbstbewusstsein*. On Alcuin's acquaintance with the literary tradition of Beowulf see my remarks in *Speculum* 27 (1952), 103. Cf. p. 4, above.

# CHAPTER II

# Sources and Date of the *Rhetoric*

HALM'S edition of Alcuin's *Rhetoric* is still the only critical text. Howell reprints Halm's text with a few emendations of his own. While Halm shows that nearly 60 per cent of the treatise contains borrowed matter, Howell's statistical inquiry into the sources ascribes almost 80 per cent to Cicero's *De inventione*, and Julius Victor's *Ars rhetorica*, with Alcuin depending four times as much on Cicero as upon Julius Victor. It is to be regretted that Eduard Stroebel's textual study of Cicero's *De inventione*[1] escaped Howell's attention, because many of Alcuin's anonymous references to Cicero were already listed by Stroebel in his *apparatus criticus*. Unacknowledged quotations from Cicero and Julius Victor which were overlooked by Halm have also been listed by Paul Lehmann in one of his *Cassiodorstudien*.[2]

Howell finds that certain parts of the *Rhetoric* are original with Alcuin: (i) the versified *Preface*, (ii) several Biblical illustrations of rhetorical doctrine, (iii) a short disquisition on

---

[1] M. Tulli Ciceronis Scripta, Fasc. 2: *Rhetorici libri duo qui vocantur de inventione*, rec. Eduard Stroebel (Teubner, 1915).

[2] Paul Lehmann, "Cassiodorstudien," *Philologus* LXXIV (1917), 365; cf. Josef Martin, "Zu den Rhetores Latini Minores," *Würzburger Jahrbücher für die Altertumswissenschaft* III (1948), 319, whose deductions were anticipated by W. S. Howell, *The Rhetoric of Alcuin and Charlemagne* (Princeton, 1941), 168.

the functions of the accuser, defendant, judge, and witnesses in cases at law, (iv) a specimen of sophistical discourse, (v) an oration in praise of Christian virtues, and (vi) such apparatus as Charlemagne's and Alcuin's interrogations and comments. But even some of these items contain borrowed matter. The sources of items i, iv, and v are readily discernible, and the historical background of item iii and of one Biblical illustration of ii can be shown. Alcuin's various treatises and letters provide numerous parallels to the phraseology of item vi. And newly found sources for other parts of the *Rhetoric* enable us to state that more than 90 per cent of the treatise is borrowed matter. The remaining percentage is accounted for by characteristic elements of Alcuin's style and by borrowings from one of his own treatises.

In the following sections we shall deal with these topics: the codex of Cicero's *De inventione*, excerpted by Alcuin; the influence of Cassiodorus' *Institutiones*, of Aulus Gellius and Boethius, of Alcuin's own treatise *De virtutibus et vitiis*, of Fortunatianus' *Ars rhetorica*, of the *Rhetorica ad Herennium*, the metrical *propositio* of the *Rhetoric*, and the date of the treatise.

*The Cicero codex of Alcuin.* The collation of Alcuin's quotations from Cicero's *De inventione* with Stroebel's critical text provides a number of indications as to the provenience of the Cicero codex which served as Alcuin's source. Since Alcuin's Cicero-*testimonia* are older than any of the extant MSS of *De inventione*, it is to be expected that some of Alcuin's (A) variants are in agreement with the older MSS of the Mutili (M) class, saec. ix–x, whose characteristics are two *lacunae:* I.62–76 and II.170–174. Compare the following readings:

Cicero, *De inventione*, ed. Stroebel, pp.

2,14 artis sive studii...principium) artis initium M; artis vel studii initium A.

86,24 comparanda) comparandum M and A.

94,9 somnus) somnum M and A.

115,8 aliud) aliud crimen H and A.
117,19 aetatis) non habui *add.* H, S, and A.
117,21 imperator) mandavit *add.* H, S, and A.
119,9 posita) deposita M and A.

These variants seem to indicate that Alcuin's codex of Cicero was somehow related to the Mutili class of *De inventione*. The text of this MS is closer to that of the H(erbipolitanus), saec. ix, and to the S(angallensis), saec. x, than to any other extant MS of the M class. The Carolingian origin of M and H is confirmed by the agreement between the variants of M, H, and Alcuin. The question is whether Alcuin used a complete MS of *De inventione*, which belonged to the same tradition from which the M class stems, or whether Alcuin used a MS of the M class. Alcuin's testimonies in the *Rhetoric* do not seem to offer a text portion of *De inventione* which covers the two *lacunae* of the M class. There is nevertheless some reason to surmise that Alcuin had available not only a MS belonging to the incomplete M class, but also an older and complete MS of Cicero's work. For we read in Alcuin's *De dialectica*, xv (*PL* CI, 970D): "*Si, quo* [not qua] *die caedes ista Romae facta est, ego Athenis fui, in caede interesse non potui.*" This is a quotation from *De inventione* I.36.63, a passage which is missing in all M codices. Thus Alcuin probably had at his disposal at some time a complete MS of Cicero's treatise that was older than the oldest MS now extant of the Mutili class but related to the archetype of M.

Since Alcuin anonymously quotes the Commentary on *De inventione* by Marius Victorinus [3] in *De dialectica*, one might expect to find traces of this influence also in the *Rhetoric*. But thus far the only passage which betrays a conscious adoption of one of Victorinus' interpretations seems to be the observation of Alcuin that induction and deduction belong to the domain of

[3] Pierre Hadot, "Marius Victorinus et Alcuin," *Archives d'histoire doctrinale et littéraire du moyen âge* XXIX (1954), 5–19, deals with the traces of Victorinus in two of Alcuin's theological treatises.

the philosopher and not to rhetoric (Halm, p. 540.2–3). This interpretation does not amplify or misread a passage in *De inventione*, as Howell assumes, but renders the comment of Victorinus on *De inv.* I.31 (Halm, p. 240.16): "Verum inductione philosophi utuntur."

*Alcuin's definition of rhetoric.* The definition of rhetoric, "bene dicendi scientia in civilibus questionibus" (H.526.12 f.), is identical with that of Cassiodorus, *Institutiones* II.2.1, and Isidore of Seville, *Etymologiae* II.1.1. Alcuin, however, followed Cassiodorus and not Isidore, as Paul Lehmann [4] has shown. As a matter of fact, the impact on the treatise of Cassiodorus' definition is stronger than has been assumed. It is referred to at the beginning and at the end of the *Rhetoric*. "*Charlemagne*" alludes to it in his introductory speech as well as in his closing words:

Quia te, venerande magister Albine, *Deus adduxit et reduxit*,...Nam te olim memini dixisse,[5] totam eius artis vim *in civilibus* versari *questionibus* (H.525.10);

Sermo iste noster, qui de volubili *civilium questionum* ingenio initium habuit (H.550.33).

The phrase *Deus adduxit et reduxit* is an element of Alcuin's literary style. It appears in the form of a benediction in the *salutatio* and *conclusio* of three letters addressed by Alcuin to Charlemagne and in two letter poems:

Epist. 145 (D.235.8) to Charlemagne in Saxony: Benedictus dominus *Deus, qui adduxit et reduxit* David dilectum cum prosperitate et salute ad servos tuos;

Epist. 229 (D.372.33) to Charlemagne in Italy: Benedictus dominus *Deus*...vos, dulcissime David, prospere *duxit et* pacifice *reduxit;*

Epist. 178 (D.296.5) to Charlemagne in Italy:...divinam hu-

---

[4] *Philologus* LXXIV (1917), 366 f.

[5] For the same phrase see also *Rhetoric* H.546.11 and Alcuin, *Ars grammatica* (PL CI, 891D): Memini te dixisse.

militer obsecrantes clementiam, quatenus vos vestrosque
simul cum omni prosperitate sanos *ducat et reducat* gau-
dentes;

*Carm.* xlvii.11 (*MGH, Poetae* I) to Charlemagne:

> Prospere per terras ignotas *ducat* euntem,
> Gaudentem nobis clemens iterum *reducat;*

*Epist.* 243 (D.392.10) to Arno of Salzburg:

> Per castella, vicos, per fortia flumina terrae,
> Semper ubique, precor, *ducat* simul atque *reducat*
> Gaudentem, sanctae cum prosperitate salutis.

The phrase in these last passages refers to Charlemagne's departure for, and return from, a foreign country. On the other
hand, the fictitious Charlemagne of the *Rhetoric*, using the
language of Alcuin, applies the phrase to Alcuin. Here the phrase
refers to Alcuin's departure from England and his adoption of
Frankland as his new home.[6]

*Alcuin on sophistry.* The specimen of sophistical discourse in
Chapter 35 of the Rhetoric (H.543.22–544.1) is traceable to
Aulus Gellius and Boethius.[7] *Sophistica elocutio* (H.543.23)
appears in the text between the expositions of *inventio* and
*dispositio.* Alcuin deals with the subject in an obvious digression
from the main topic. As rhetorician he thus makes use of the
rhetorical device called *egressio* or *excessus,* which was looked
upon as a special elegance of style.[8]

---

[6] Arthur Kleinclausz, *Alcuin* (Paris, 1948), 145, offers the same interpretation.

[7] Carl Prantl, *Geschichte der Logik im Abendlande* II (2nd ed.; Leipzig, 1927), 19, referred to Gellius, a fact overlooked by Halm and
Howell. G. K. Anderson, *The Literature of the Anglo-Saxons* (Princeton, 1949), 251, unjustly derogates the reasoning of Alcuin, forgetting
that Alcuin himself rejects the cunning way of reasoning. See Luitpold
Wallach, "Alcuin on Sophistry," *Classical Philology* L (1955), 259–261.

[8] See E. R. Curtius, *European Literature and the Latin Middle Ages*
(Bollingen Series XXXVI; New York, 1953), 501 f.

The syllogism *ego homo* and *tu non homo* (H.543.33) is based on Aulus Gellius' *Noctes Atticae* 18.2.9:

> quod ego sum, id tu non es.
> homo ego sum:
> homo igitur tu non es.

"What I am that you are not. I am a man: therefore you are not a man!" To this fallacy is added and rejected the fallacious identification of the meaning of *homo* with its two syllables: "numquid tu duae syllabae" (H. 543.38). The syllogism bears on the subject of *definitio nominis* treated by Alcuin in *De dialectica* (PL CI, 973D), where he states that the meaning of *domus* cannot be derived from its two syllables *do* and *mus*, although both syllables possess meanings of their own. Boethius' discussion in the Commentary on Aristotle's *De interpretatione* (PL LXIV, 304,306) seems to have inspired Alcuin to the inclusion of the second syllogism. Remigius of Auxerre, we note, probably in the wake of Alcuin, mentions the same Gellius passage.[9]

The insertion of this sophistic discourse has a specific historical appropriateness. It was written at a time when Alcuin was no longer connected with the Royal Palace School at the court of Charlemagne. It displays his disapproval of his successor's conduct of the school. Even when still connected with it, Alcuin had had his difficulties with members of the younger Frankish generation, who did not always appreciate and understand the more refined ways of the Saxon scholar. In a letter of March, 798 (*Epist.* 145, D.231.17), he wrote to Charlemagne: "As the ass is whipped for his sluggishness, so perhaps I too have felt, not undeservedly, the whip of Palace School students." He left behind *Latini*, as he says; but now *Aegyptici*, who, according to Jerome, are identical with *tenebrae*, are in control of the

---

[9] Quoted by M. Hauréau, *Notices et Extraits des Manuscrits de la Bibliothèque Imperiale* XX,2 (1862), 11. Gellius is the anonymous *quidam* whose syllogism is cited by Augustine, *De doctr. christ.* 2.48.117, ed. G. M. Green, *CSEL* 80 (Wien, 1963), 67; Alcuin was naturally familiar with this passage.

school. In a letter (*Epist.* 307, D.470.19.24) written between 801 and 804 which deals with the price paid for the salvation of mankind, Alcuin ridicules the sophistry of the arguments used. Only a sophist of the Palace School, he declares, would have dared to pose such a question. In the *Rhetoric* he expresses his disapproval of the school's new course by saying that he would not have dared to answer such sly questions had they been posed by any member of *scola palatii tui* (H.543.23) except the king himself. Nevertheless, he does not refrain from labeling in a rather sarcastic tone this kind of sophistic reasoning as *versutia* (H.543.36), which is elsewhere identified by him with the devil's language (*Epist.* 139, D.221.1). After all, the king ought to know better than to pose *cunning* questions, "because to question *wisely* is to instruct (nam interrogare sapienter est docere—H.543.27)." Thus Alcuin puts in the mouth of Charlemagne the adaptation he himself had made of the aphorism, so frequently repeated in his letters,[10] that *discere* is the foundation of *docere*. About 798, he writes to Charlemagne (*Epist.* 136, D.205.18): "per inquisitiones magis docere, quam ignorata discere agnovi. Quia *sapienter interrogare docere est.*" The same ideas are repeated in another letter (*Epist.* 308, D.471.25), written between 801 and 804: "unde etiam me magis doceri vestris inquistionibus intellego... Nam *sapienter interrogare, docere est.*" The stress put on *sapienter* is not accidental. Among the precepts of style Alcuin reiterates (H.545.30) the injunction to observe decorum also with regard to speech, saying: "As in life, so in speech, nothing is more praiseworthy than to do everything wisely (*sapienter*)." Alcuin had evidently adopted the saying of Jerome, "Vir studiosus et sapiens, etiam si discere aliquid vult, magis docet dum prudenter interrogat." [11]

*The influence of Alcuin's own treatises on the* Rhetoric. I

[10] *Epistles* 19, D.55.21; 31, D.73.9; 88, D.132.30; 117, D.173.6; 168, D.277.1; 243, D.390.30; 270, D.429.6.

[11] Jerome, *Epistolae* 58.3.7, ed. I. Hilberg (*CSEL* 54; Wien-Leipzig, 1910), 449.7.

have discussed elsewhere [12] the relationship between Alcuin's
*Rhetoric* and his treatise *De virtutibus et vitiis*. There are identical portions in the last chapter of this treatise and in the last
section of the *Rhetoric*. Alcuin's borrowings from his own
treatise are designated in the following passages by italics. Compare:

a. *Rhetoric* (H.548.23) and *De virtutibus et vitiis* (PL CI, 637BC);
   *Virtus est animi habitus, naturae decus, vitae ratio, morum*
   nobilitas; [13]
   H.548.30 and *PL* CI, 637BC: *Iustitia est habitus animi unicuique*
   *rei propriam tribuens dignitatem: in hac divinitatis cultus et*
   *humanitatis iura et aequitas totius vitae conservatur;*
   H.549.21 and *PL* CI, 637CD: Temperantia...per quam *totius*
   *vitae modus.*[14]

Halm and Howell refer to Cicero for these passages, but
Alcuin clearly uses the definitions provided in his *De virtutibus*
*et vitiis*. Neither Halm nor Howell adduces any source for the
remainder of the *Rhetoric*. But we can see additional borrowings
(in italics) from the moral treatise in the *Rhetoric*:

b. H.549.30 and *PL* CI, 637C:...cum *haec* nunc *in fide et caritate*
   *observantibus aeternae gloriae ab ipsa veritate, Christo Jesu,*
   *praemia pollicentur;*
   H.549.37 and *PL* CI, 637C: Nonne tibi videtur *sapientia* esse
   *qua Deus secundum modulum* [15] *humanae mentis intellegitur*
   *et timetur et futurum eius creditur iudicium;*
   H.550.3 and *PL* CI, 637D:...numquid non *fortitudinem* esse
   cernis, qua hostis antiquus vincitur et *adversa mundi toleran-*
   *tur.*[16]

[12] Wallach, "Onulf of Speyer," *Medievalia et Humanistica* VI (1950),
40.

[13] *Morum nobilitas* also in *Epistles* 19, D.55.32; 94, D.139.16; 122,
D.180.4; 129, D.191.27; 132, D.180.3.

[14] Cf. *Epist.* 209, D.349.22: Temperantia...quae est via regia totius vitae
nostrae.

[15] See *modulum* in *Epist.* 173, D.286.38; 213, D.354.15.

[16] This is the definition by Isidore of Seville, *Etymologiae* II.24.6; also
quoted by Alcuin, *De animae ratione, PL* CI, 640BC.

The following passage is an example of the manner in which Alcuin rearranges portions (in italics) from the treatise *De virtutibus et vitiis* and pieces them together in the dialogue of the *Rhetoric:*

c. H.550.11–24, and *PL* CI, 637D–638B; Quid facilius est *quam amare species pulchras, dulces sapores, sonos suaves, odores fragrantes, tactus iocundos, honores et felicitates saeculi?* Haecine amare facile animae, *quae velut volatilis umbra recedunt,*[17] et Deum non amare, *qui est aeterna pulchritudo, aeterna dulcedo, aeterna suavitas, aeterna flagrantia, aeterna iocunditas, perpetuus honor, indeficiens felicitas?*... Laboriosior est enim huius mundi amor quam Christi; quod enim in illo anima quaerit, non invenit,[18] id est felicitatem et aeternitatem, quoniam haec infima pulchritudo transit et recedit, vel amantem deserit vel ab amante deseritur: [19] teneat igitur anima ordinem suam.

There is finally the following parallel between the *Rhetoric* and Alcuin's *De animae ratione:*

d. H.550.25:
KARLUS: Quis est ordo animae?
ALBINUS: Ut diligat quod superius est, id est Deum, et regat quod *inferius est,* id est corpus, *et socias animas* dilectione nutriat et foveat;
*De animae ratione (PL* CI, 639C, 641C):

[17] The phrase *umbratilis error* occurs in the following *Epistles:* 18, D.49.31; 44, D.90.19; 167, D.275.9; 228, D.372.11; 251, D.407.11; 297, D.456.15; in Alcuin's *Vita Richarii* x, *PL* CI, 688C; *Carmina, MGH Poetae* I, no. 48,17 (p. 261); in a letter to Beatus of Liébana, ed. Wilhelm Levison, *England and the Continent in the Eighth Century* (Oxford, 1946), 322.14.

[18] An echo of an aphorism by Jerome; see *Epist.* 18, D.49.21: Quia amicitia quae deseri potest numquam vera fuit. Amicus fidelis diu quaeritur, vix invenitur, difficile servatur. Also in *Epistles* 204, D.337.31; 250, D.404.26; 167, D.275.22; 212, D.353.2.

[19] Cf. the proverb in n. 18; cf. *Epist.* 251, D.406.34: nec in incerto divitiarum sperare, quae aut deserunt possidentem, aut a possidente deseruntur; Alcuin, *Ars grammatica (PL* CI, 850A):...deserit possidentem; *ibid.* (851D): Quid de divitiis congregandis studetis, quae vel deserunt vel deseruntur.

> ...et id *quod* sibi *inferius est,* id est carnem, toto regeret studio...
> quia haec est animae summa beatitudo eum diligere a quo est,
> *et socias* beatitudinis diligere *animas.*[20]

With the exception of the section listed under b (H.549.30),
which Alcuin puts in the mouth of Charlemagne, all the passages
just quoted appear in the dialogue between scholar and king
under Alcuin's Latin name *Albinus.* The parallels between the
*Rhetoric* and *De virtutibus et vitiis* are sufficient evidence, if
such proof is at all necessary, that Alcuin is the sole author of
the *Rhetoric,* notwithstanding the fact that the metrical *propositio* refers to the treatise as the work of both friends (unum
opus amborum—H.525). The king's alleged coauthorship is not
a historical fact, but merely a rhetorical expression of the author's endeavor to honor the king and to lend authority to his
own work.

*The influence of Fortunatianus.* The influence of Fortunatianus' *Ars rhetorica* is noticeable in Alcuin's theory of *status.*
The classification of disputes under two categories, *status rationales* and *legales* (H.527.20), and Alcuin's substitution of the
term *status* for the Ciceronian *constitutio* [21] are perhaps traceable
to Fortunatianus I.11 (Halm 89.21–28). Moreover, the same may
be said of Alcuin's enumeration of the "types of issue": "Quattuor, id est facti aut nominis aut qualitatis aut translationis"
(H.527.23). It is obvious, furthermore, that Alcuin does not
only follow the listing of Cicero, *De inventione* I.8.10 (aut
facti aut nominis aut generis aut actionis) but also that of Fortunatianus I.11 (H.89.29): "Rationales status quot sunt?
...quattuor, coniectura, finis, qualitas, translatio." [22] And For-

---

[20] Cf. *Epist.* 264, D.421.39: benefici esse contendant in socias huius laboris
animas.

[21] As used in *De inv.;* but Cicero elsewhere, in treatises unknown to
Alcuin, uses *status.*

[22] This definition also appears in a marginal note of some Mutili MSS
of *De inventione* I.8.10, ed. Stroebel, p. 9,15, which defines the Cicero
passage by using the definitions of Fortunatianus.

tunatianus also provides Alcuin with the example for the type of issue called *finitivus status*, issue of definition; compare *Ars rhetorica* I.13 (H.91.16–21) and Alcuin (H.527.27–35). On the other hand Alcuin's discussion of the theft of a privately owned sacred object combines the arguments of Cicero with those of Fortunatianus.[23] Halm refers to Cicero as Alcuin's source. Cicero, however, does not mention the provision of Roman law that a thief is fined an amount four times the value of the stolen object and that the *sacrilegus* is beheaded. The legal problem in itself was a *cause célèbre* among the classical and medieval rhetoricians. Alcuin adopted the example of Fortunatianus (H.91.17): "Sacrilegus capite plectitur fur quadruplum solvat."

*Alcuin and the Rhetorica ad Herennium.* Paul Schwenke mentions "the occasional use made by Alcuin of the *Rhetorica ad Herennium* not recorded by Halm." [24] The following passages apparently suggested to him the possible influence of this textbook:

Alcuin (H.527.38):...et haec constitutio generalis dicitur, cuius exemplum est: Quidam dux Romanus cum obsideretur ab inimicis nec ullo modo evadere potuisset...;

Alcuin (H.530.28): Conparatio est..., ut in illo exemplo, quod paulo ante posuimus (*vide supra*). Cum dux Romanus ab hostibus *obsideretur*, nec ullo pacto evadere potuit...;

*Rhetorica ad Herennium* I.15.25 (ed. Harry Caplan, Loeb Classical Library, 1954): Ex conparatione causa constat... Ea causa huiusmodi est: C. Popilius, cum a Gallis *obsideretur* neque fugere ullo modo posset, venit cum hostium ducibus in conlocutionem;

[23] See Artur Steinwenter, *"Rhetorik und römischer Zivilprocess,"* *Zeitschrift der Savigny-Stiftung für Rechtsgeschichte,* Roman. Abt. LXV (1947), 105.

[24] "Des Propstes Hadoardus Cicero Excerpte," *Philologus,* Suppl. Bd. V (1889), 404; C. H. Beeson, "The Collectaneum of Hadoard," *Classical Philology* 40 (1945), 201–227, shows that H. excerpted the Florence MS San Marco 257 of the tenth century.

*Ibid.* IV.24.34 (s.v. *subiectio*): Nam quid me facere convenit, cum a tanta Gallorum multitudine circumsederer?... At obsidebamur;

Cicero, *De inventione* II.24.72 (ed. Eduard Stroebel, Teubner, 1915): Comparatio est...ea huiusmodi: quidam imperator, cum ab hostibus *circumsederetur* neque effugere ullo modo posset....

The passages in the *Rhetoric* refer to the example of a Roman general who, surrounded by the Gauls and unable to escape, made a pact with them. Alcuin, who follows Cicero, uses the debacle of Popilius to illustrate "comparison." He lists the same example under *constitutio generalis*, because Cicero (*De inventione* I.11.15), dividing this "issue of quality" into the parts of equity and law, enumerated *comparatio* among the four divisions of the assumptive subhead of the equitable part. The reading *obsideretur* is common to Alcuin's texts and to the *Rhetorica ad Herennium*,[25] whereas Cicero reads *circumsederetur*. But Alcuin may have been quoting Cicero from memory and would naturally use the more common word. Friedrich Marx[26] justly denies Alcuin's dependence on the *Rhetorica*. There is indeed no evidence at all that Alcuin used this textbook. If he had, it would surely have left many traces in his work.

Alcuin's texts contain, however, one significant variant. While Cicero speaks of the defeat of *quidam imperator*, Alcuin

[25] See the edition by Harry Caplan (Loeb Classical Library, 1954), 48.
[26] In his edition of the *Rhetorica ad Herennium* (Leipzig, 1894), 9. Konrad Burdach, *Schlesisch-Böhmische Briefmuster* (Vom Mittelalter zur Reformation V; Berlin, 1926), 63, agrees with Marx.—What Burdach says of *MS Halberstadt*, saec. XII–XIII, published by Moritz Haupt, *Berichte der Kgl. sächsischen Gesellschaft der Wissenschaften* II (Leipzig, 1849), 53–58, must be corrected. Haupt's publication is not a commentary on the *Rhet. ad Her.*, but—without his realizing it—Marbod of Rennes, *De ornamentis verborum*, PL CLXXI, 1687–1692. This edition of the treatise may be added to the editions listed by A. Boutemy, *Bulletin Du Cange* XVII (1943), 34, No. 221.

ascribes it to a *dux Romanus*. Since the *Rhetoric* is dedicated to Charlemagne, the Roman emperor, Alcuin had to take into account the changed meaning of *imperator*. Thus Cicero's *imperator* became a "Roman duke."

*The date of the Rhetoric.* The dating of the *Rhetoric* can now be determined with greater certainty than before. That it was composed during Charlemagne's imperial period (as mentioned above) can be supported by other facts. The *pater mundi* of the *Rhetoric's propositio* (H.525.6) is naturally Charlemagne, the Roman emperor, referred to there as the Frankish *rex Karolus*. The use made by Alcuin of his own treatise *De virtutibus et vitiis* (see above) in the writing of the *Rhetoric* furnishes the years after 800 as *terminus ante quem non*, since the treatise dedicated to Duke Wido was written between 801 and 804 (*Epist.* 305, D.464), i.e., after Charlemagne's coronation as Roman emperor on Christmas Day of the year 800, and, of course, before the death of Alcuin in 804. For these reasons we assign the composition of the *Rhetoric* to the years 801–804.[27]

[27] Max Manitius, *Geschichte der lateinischen Literatur des Mittelalters* I (Munich, 1911), 283, connects the remark in a letter of Alcuin to Angilbert (*Ep.* 97, D.141.21), possibly written in 796, with the composition of the *Rhetoric*. But there is no reason at all for the assumption that Alcuin's "playing with the elegance of rhetoric (rhetorica lepiditate)" refers to the composition of the treatise. Howell, *op. cit.*, pp. 6–8, bases his dating—794—on the formulalike phrase at the beginning of the *Rhetoric* (H.525.10): Quia te, venerande magister Albine, *Deus adduxit et reduxit*. Since the phrase belongs to Alcuin's style, as was shown above, it cannot be used for the dating of the treatise. W. S. Howell, *Logic and Rhetoric in England, 1500–1700* (Princeton, 1956), 32 n. 1, repeats his dating; see my remarks in *Classical Philology* 50 (1955), 260.

# CHAPTER III

# The *Rhetoric* as a *Littera Exhortatoria*

A STUDY of the *Rhetoric* within the body of Alcuin's writings will reveal that the treatise has the characteristics of a *littera exhortatoria* and that it contains the same commonplaces and topics as are found in Alcuin's hortatory *Epistles* and treatises.

The following analysis of the rhetorical topoi [1] *iussio, humilitas, contemptus mundi,* of *cumulatio* and *brevitas,* and of other specific literary elements of Alcuin's speech and style, which are common to the *Rhetoric,* to his treatise *De virtutibus et vitiis,* dedicated to Margrave Wido, and to *De animae ratione,* written for Eulalia, i.e., Gundrada, sister of Charlemagne's trusted adviser Adalhard of Corbie, proves that each of the three treatises was composed as a *littera exhortatoria,* to use the designation Alcuin gave to the tract written for Wido.

## ANALYSIS OF RHETORICAL TOPOI

a. *iussio:* the author writes upon the request of the recipient.

Eulalia wishes to be enlightened *de ratione animae* (*Epist.* 309, D.474.1). Wido requests a tractate of moral exhortations

[1] See E. R. Curtius, *European Literature and the Latin Middle Ages* (Bollingen Series XXXVI; New York, 1953), 83, 407 ff.

(*Epist.* 305, D.464.11). Charlemagne supposedly asks for information in *civilibus questionibus* (H.525.12).

b. *humilitas:* the author feigns humility by making statements of self-deprecation.

This commonplace appears as *excusatio propter infirmitatem* in *De animae ratione* (*Epist.* 309, D.474.4); Alcuin confesses that he is not sure whether he is capable of explaining *tam arduas rationes*. In the form of an *excusatio propter rusticitatem*, Alcuin apologizes for his lack of literary art in Wido's tractate (*Epist.* 305, D.464.16). The same *excusatio* is used in the Rhetoric (H.525.19–25) where the author stresses his ignorance and his feeble intellect in contrast to the great wisdom of the recipient.

c. *contemptus mundi* [2] : the author stresses the contrast between the temporal nature of *ambitio saecularis*, i.e., worldly occupations, and the eternal quality of man's longing for the Kingdom of Heaven.

Eulalia is encouraged to pursue those studies that are detached from earthly matters; she should not be swayed by the present (*Epist.* 309, D. 475.10; 476.2). Wido is told that his military profession and other secular activities are no hindrance to entering the portals of heavenly life (*Epist.* 305, D.464.12; 465.7). Charlemagne's daily work (H.525.16; 526.21) is described as secular (H.550.13), and more specifically as "occupationes regni et curae palatii" (H.525.13).

d. Jerome's pre-Vulgate translation of Job 28:28 (*PL* XXIX, 95A), "Sapientia hominis est pietas, recedere autem a malo scientia," occurs in all three treatises. The passage is directly quoted in *De animae ratione* (*Epist.* 309, D.479.19). In *De virtutibus et vitiis* (*PL* CI, 614 f.) the passage is anonymously referred to when Alcuin says: "Scientia vera est a diaboli servitio,

---

[2] On *contemptus saeculi* see Alcuin, *De dialectica, PL* CI, 952A, which is borrowed either from Cassiodorus, *Inst.* II.5 ed. Mynors, p. 110.18, or else from Isidore of Seville, *Etym.* II.24.9.

quod sunt peccata recedere, et sapientia perfecta est Deum colere." In the *Rhetoric* (H.549.39–550.1), the passage is connected with a Graeca in a combination culled from Augustine (*Enchiridion* I.4).[3]

The analysis of these topoi indicates Alcuin's literary tastes and the conscious application of rhetoric to his prose. The topos *iussio* is closely connected with *captatio benevolentiae*, a device designed to win the good will of the reader by the author's expression of humility (*humilitas*). *Captatio* in the *Rhetoric* proceeds through various stages of increasing glorification, which I call *cumulatio*.[4] Thus the great wisdom of Charlemagne, frequently identified with that of the Biblical Solomon (*Epist.* 309, D.478.11), is designated as *sapientia, pietas,* and *scientia* (see *d* above). The topos, "The absolute wisdom of the Ruler," is apparent in Alcuin's statement that Charlemagne (H. 525.21) is capable not only of imitating the masters (ingenia magistrorum), but even of surpassing them in knowledge. This stage of the *cumulatio* is based on Alcuin's theory that the Frankish king is the wisest of all men, since it behooves the head of the Christian people to know everything—better than anybody else—for the good of his subjects (*Epist.* 257, D.415.5): "...*Neque* enim *quemquam magis decet vel meliora* nosse *vel plura, quam* imperatorem, *cuius doctrina omnibus potest prodesse subjectis. Non quo, imperator invicte* et sapientissime rector, aliquid scientiae vestrae fidei catholicae *incognit*um esse, vel minus exploratum cogitarem." The passages in italics are literally derived from the *Preface* of Vegetius' *Epitoma rei Militaris*, Bk. I.[5] They denote a sentiment willingly

---

[3] See Wallach in *Medievalia et Humanistica* VI (1950), 55.

[4] Cf. also Curtius, *op. cit.,* 162 ff.

[5] This influence of Vegetius on Alcuin has been unknown until now; it supplements the note of C. W. Jones, "Bede and Vegetius," *Classical Review* XLVI (1932), 248 f., who assumes that no evidence is extant for the use of Vegetius by Carolingian writers between the ages of Bede and Hrabanus Maʳʳus.

shared, Vegetius says, by "Octavianus Augustus" and often expressed by the good princes that came after him. Alcuin ascribes
to Charlemagne, the Roman emperor, the qualities of Vegetius'
late Roman Augustus, whose title *imperator invictus* thus sud-
denly appears in a letter of Alcuin addressed to the Frankish
king. Alcuin elsewhere summarizes his theory of Charlemagne's
unsurpassed perfection as a believer, as king, pontifex, judge,
philosopher, and as an ethical model: [6] "catholicus est in fide,
rex in potestate, pontifex in praedicatione, iudex in aequitate,
philosophus in liberalibus studiis, inclytus in moribus, et in omni
honestate praecipuus."

In the *Rhetoric* (H.525.21) the reference to the *magistri* falls
within the *captatio benevolentiae*, because Alcuin is always
thinking of himself as a *magister*, the designation he used for
himself in the *Epistles* and treatises. The climax of the *cumulatio*
is carried into the context of the *Rhetoric* when Alcuin identifies
Charlemagne with that mythical "great man" (H.550.29) who,
according to Cicero (*De inventione* I.2.2) and also according to
Alcuin (H. 525.31–526.1), discovered the potentialities of the
human soul (magnus videlicet vir et sapiens). The question of
Charlemagne (H.550.29), "Magnum quendam virum et vere
beatum praedicas, o magister?" (Master, you predict some great
and truly blessed man), is Alcuin's own idea, rhetorically expressed, of the king's greatness: "magnum te faciat Deus et
vere beatum." *Magnus vir* is furthermore inserted by Alcuin
in an otherwise literally quoted passage from *De inventione*
II.54.162. It is a passage concerning instruments of justice
(H.549.7–10); judicial decisions are defined as a body of opinions rendered by "some great man" or by several men. While
Cicero defines "iudicatum, de quo alicuius [magni viri] aut
aliquorum iam sententiis constitutum est," Alcuin inserts *magni
viri* after *alicuius*, thus clearly referring to Charlemagne as the
highest judge of his royal court. The epithet *vir magnus* is

[6] Alcuin, *Adv. Elipandum Libri Quattuor* I.16, PL CI, 251CD.

applied by Alcuin to Charlemagne alone, with one exception: Angilbert, son-in-law of the king, is once so addressed (*Epist.* 306, D.465.21).[7]

The uniformity between Alcuin's style in the *Rhetoric* and the style of his letters is illustrated by the fact that the *captatio benevolentiae* of the *Rhetoric* consists of a conglomeration of topics employed by Alcuin in the *captatio* of letters addressed to Charlemagne. Compare (H.525.19–25):

Albinus: Deus *te*, domine mi rex Karle, *omni sapientiae* lumine *inluminavit et scientiae claritate* [a] ornavit, ut non solum magistrorum ingenia prompte subsequi, sed etiam in multis velociter praecurrere possis, et licet flammivomo tuae sapientiae lumini scintilla [b] *ingenioli mei* [c] nil *addere possit,*[d] *tamen ne* me aliqui *inoboedientem* [e] notent, tuis *promptulus* [f] respondeo interrogationibus, et utinam tam sagaciter quam oboedienter.

[a] The same *invocatio* in *Epist.* 143, D.224.16 (February, 798), addressed to Charlemagne: Spiritus...qui *te inluminavit* et dilatavit cor tuum in *omni sapientiae et scientiae claritate;* cf. II Cor. 4:6: Deus...qui inluxit in cordibus nostris ad inluminationem scientiae claritatis.

[b] Cf. Alcuin, *Ars grammatica* (*PL* CI, 850B): Naturale itaque est mentibus humanis scientiae lumen...in se quasi scintilla in silice latet; cf. *Epist.* 139, D.220.15: ut flamma caritatis in corde abscondita aliquam fortasse scintillam elicere valeat.

[c] *Epist.* 121, D.177.32 (796–97) to Charlemagne: Ego vero secundum modum *ingenioli mei*...seminare non ero; *Epist.* 155, D.250.4 (798) to Charlemagne: cartam...quam *ingenioli mei* adtingere valuisset humilitas; *Epist.* 261, D.418.37 (798–803) to Charlemagne: *ne ingeniolum animi mei* ...otio torpuisset inani; cf. *Epist.* 137, D.214.9: ingenioli nostri; *Epist.* 265, D.424.7: meum ingeniolum optarem.

[d] *Epist.* 308, D.471.24 (801–804) to Charlemagne: Unde etiam me magis doceri vestris inquisitionibus intellego, quam vestrae aliquid affluentissimae sapientiae ex mea *addi possit* responsione.

[e] *Epist.* 145, D.234.13 (798) to Charlemagne:...ne ad vestrae venerandae dignitatis praecepta tacerem...si inoboediens tantae auctoritati viderer; *Epist.* 296, D.455.11 (796–804) to the monks of St. Vaast at Arras: *Tamen, ne inoboediens* vestrae essem dilectioni, scripsi; *Epist.* 268, D.426.29 (785–

[7] The definition in Alcuin's *De virtutibus et vitiis* xxii, *PL* CI, 630B, Magnus vir est qui invidiam humilitate superat, discordiam charitate destruit, is not original; it is from Jerome, *Epist.* LX.19.5, ed. Hilberg, p. 560.4.

804) to Arno of Salzburg: Aliquid inde, *ne inoboediens* preceptis tuis viderer, brevi sermone dictavi.

*ᵗ Epist.* 229, D.373.14 (804) to Charlemagne:...servulum, quam *promptulum* vestrae oboedire voluntati.

In the *Rhetoric* Alcuin addresses Charlemagne in a fashion that makes it quite obvious that he has in mind the writing of a letter. He uses two technical parts of an epistle, the *invocatio* and the *captatio*. The former is identical with the invocation of *Epistle* 143 addressed to the king. And the same self-depreciatory topoi and locutions which occur in the *captatio benevolentiae* of letters sent to Charlemagne also appear in the *exordium* of the *Rhetoric*. Here Alcuin is indeed the true disciple of Cicero, who finds it advisable for the orator to show submissiveness and humility (*De inv.* I.16.22). Alcuin therefore inserts in the *Rhetoric* (H.534.27–535.34) theories on *captatio* drawn from *De inventione* I.15.20;18.26, which he also used in his letters.

Various topoi are used in the *exordium* of the *Rhetoric*. Alcuin writes only upon the request of Charlemagne; the recipient knows the subject matter better than the author, who, being in the possession of the required information, answers obediently and promptly. Moreover, the same formulas appear in Alcuin's letters, usually in connection with expressions of self-depreciatory and affected modesty, such as apologies for ignorance, inexperience, or lack of style.

Additional authority is lent to one's work if the author writes with the approval of a person of higher station in life, to whom the work is dedicated. This fact is stressed in the *Epistle* (257, D.415.24) that accompanies the treatise *De fide sanctae trinitatis*, offered to Charlemagne: "Nemo iuste mea dicta spernere poterit, quia probantis auctoritas pluris aestimatur quam scribentis voluntas." A similar tactic occurs in the introductory letter (*Epist.* 120, D.175.15) prefacing the *Vita S. Willibrordi*, written upon the order of Beornred of Sens. Apologizing for the style of the work, Alcuin says: "Meum fuit praecipientis non spernere auctoritatem; tuum est oboedientis defendere imperitiam." After Charlemagne had perused one of Alcuin's antiadoptionist treatises, composed upon the king's request, Alcuin assures him that the writer's work could hardly have found a more competent judge: "Nam auctoritas praecipientis oboedientis industriam defendere debet" (*Epist.* 172, D.284.23). Questions from Charlemagne, orally transmitted to Alcuin by their mutual friend Candidus, are answered by Alcuin *inculto sermone* (*Epist.* 163, D.263.11) and submitted to the king's judgment: "Nam oboedientis devotio laudanda est, si auctoritate iubentis probatur."

The topos, "the recipient is better acquainted with the subject than the writer," is used, for example, in a letter to Charlemagne (*Epist.* 145, D.232.29) in which Alcuin answers computistical questions: "Ita etiam parvitas mea non indigenti, sed multum *melius* intelligenti vobis, si quid scribere temptavero, faciendum veraciter agnosco." Monks are admonished by Alcuin (*Epist.* 278, D.435.4): "ex caritatis fonte, non quasi ignorantibus, sed quasi haec omnia *melius* scientibus." A like exhortation is addressed to a Saxon abbot (*Epist.* 67, D.111.33): "Obsecro...dum haec omnia *melius* scientem ammoneo. Caritas me compulit loqui." Alcuin once unequivocally writes Charlemagne (*Epist.* 143, D.227.27): "non ignoranti scripsi, sed ei qui haec omnia *optime* novit. Ideo perpaucis haec praelibavi verbis, quia vobis haec omnia esse *notissima* sciebam."

Another commonplace in the *Rhetoric* and in the *Epistles* is the demand of *brevitas*. It is the practical application of Cicero's request that the *narratio* be brief,[8] a doctrine also incorporated in the *Rhetoric*. A letter to Charlemagne (*Epist.* 308, D.473.4) contains an excuse for *epistolaris brevitas*. Alcuin in two antiadoptionist treatises complains that the heretic Felix of Urgel replied to his *epistola exhortatoria* with a "libellus non epistolari brevitate succinctus" (*PL* CI, 127D,252A). In the *Rhetoric*, the

---

[8] Cicero, *De inv.* I.20.28 and 22.32, i.e., *Rhetoric*, Halm, p. 535.36–536.12 and 536.26–27; cf. Curtius, *op. cit.*, 85 f., 487 ff., on *brevitas* and *fastidium*.

king receives the assurance of Alcuin, "Dicam, et breviter dicam" (H.541.23), and Charlemagne himself allegedly requests that Alcuin be as brief as possible (H.549.35). Alcuin pretends to comply with the demand of brevity (H.542.13), even if it means refraining from the mention of additional ways in which the arguments of a speaker can be refuted. The thoroughly rhetorical nature of Alcuin's feigned interest in brevity may be seen in the following dialogue (H.548.11):

ALBINUS. ...succincta brevitas pauca postulat et res arduas plura desiderat.

KARLUS. ...Tempera te in utrumque, *ne* aut *prolixitas fastidium* aut brevitas ignorantiam *generet*.

The warnings against excessive length of exposition that might cause boredom to the reader and against an author's too concise brevity that could lead to ignorance are topoi of modesty, elsewhere employed by Alcuin in the *exordium* and the conclusions of antiadoptionist treatises. Compare:

> *Adv. Felicem Libri Septem* III.1 (*PL* CI, 161D): Nova proponentes argumentatio, novum libelli poscit exordium, ne confusa sermonis series legenti fastidium faciat, et minus intelligatur quid cui parti conveniat, si non competentibus locis ab alio principio orationis incipiat textus;
>
> *Ibid.* V.11 (*PL* CI, 200C): Sed ne longior libelli series legenti *fastidium generet*, hic sit huius sermonis *finis*, ut ab alio liberius oratio sumat exordium;
>
> *Adv. Elipandum Libri Quattuor* I.22 (*PL* CI, 258B): Sed *ne prolixitas* sermonis mei *fastidium generet* legenti, hic huius libelli faciamus *finem*, et resumptis per Dei gratiam viribus, ab alio exordio, quae dicenda sunt, liberius incipiamus.

Alcuin naturally found the preceding exordial and concluding phraseology in patristic literature.[9]

---

[9] Cf. *brevitas succincta*, Boethius (*CSEL*, XLVIII), ed. S. Brandt, p. 143,8; Gregory the Great, *Dialogi* I.12 (*PL* LXXVII, 216A): Liberius

The merely rhetorical implications of Alcuin's interest in *brevitas* have been mistaken by some scholars for serious statements. Specht and Gaskoin [10] erroneously assume that Alcuin stresses brevity because he expects the reader of the *Rhetoric* to have Cicero's *De inventione* at hand when studying the excerpts from the classical treatise in the *Rhetoric*.

But distinct literary topoi occur also in the dialogue of the *Rhetoric's conclusio* (H.550.33–41):

ALBINUS. "I hope that this dialogue of ours, which began in the ever-changing whirl of civil questions, may have such a consummation of everlasting stability that nobody may charge us with having only uselessly undertaken so long a discussion."

KARLUS. "Could anyone dare say that our discussion has been in vain, whether he be a careful investigator of the honorable arts of the age or a follower [read *servator* for *scrutator*] of the noblest virtues? For myself, I openly confess that love of knowledge only has prompted my inquiries, and I thank you for not declining to answer the question it investigated. I therefore value the good will shown in your answers, and I am convinced that it will be profitable to students, if only the blot of envy does not mislead the reader."

In the *conclusio* Alcuin restates the point of departure of the treatise, which closes in hope for "the Kingdom of Heaven" (ad caelestis regni arcem—H.550.31). The wording and the content of the conclusion, "Sermo iste noster qui...initium habuit, hunc aeternae stabilitatis habeat finem," resemble those of Alcuin's theological treatise *De fide s. trinitatis* (PL CI, 54D):

itaque haec loquemur, si aliud exordium sumamus; Jerome, *Comment. in Dan., Prol.* (PL XXV, 494A):...ne librorum innumerabilium magnitudo lectori fastidium faciat; cf. on *brevitas* in Jerome: Walter Stade, *Hieronymus in prooemiis quid tractaverit et quos auctores quasque leges rhetoricas secutus sit* (Diss. Rostock, 1925), 68–71.

[10] C. J. B. Gaskoin, *Alcuin: His Life and His Work* (London, 1904), 195 f.; F. A. Specht, *Geschichte des Unterrichtswesens in Deutschland* (Stuttgart, 1883), 117.

"Nunc ego qui nobis huius sermonis initium causa fuit, sic etiam perfectio et finis." The concluding words put by Alcuin in the mouth of his fictitious interlocutor reveal a personal style noticeable in letters to Charlemagne. The king's approval of the *benevolentia* is once mentioned by Alcuin in a letter to the ruler as *regalis benivolentia* (*Ep.* 257, D.415.22). And the thanks expressed for not having objected to the inquiry (et tibi gratiam habeo quod *inquisita* non negasti) represent an inverted application of the topoi of *modesty* and *iussio* directly applied in epistles to the king: "Tamen, *ut ad inquisita respondeam,* non sapientiae divitiis suffultus, sed vestrae auctoritatis litteris instinctus" (*Epist.* 145, D.233.12); "Sed *ut ad inquisita respondeam...*quamvis vestrae claritati vix mea aliquid dignum parvitas conferre valeat" (*Epist.* 308, D.472.1).

Three closely connected topoi are employed in the *conclusio:* a rebuke to fault-finders who might question the usefulness of so long a dialogue; the author's hope that the results of the inquiry will be of advantage to the student; and the expectation that the reader of the treatise is not going to be corrupted by jealousy or envy (macula livoris) when studying the treatise.

Censure by the reader caused by envy was criticized by Alcuin in two letters to the royal family. He wrote to Charlemagne (*Epist.* 202, D.335.10) that he answered questions in the hope that the king's "bona voluntas" will protect his reply "ab invidorum linguis." When sending parts of his Commentary on John to Gisla, Charlemagne's sister, Alcuin similarly refuted envious critics (*Epist.* 214, D.358.9–17) who attacked the *dicta* of others instead of publishing their own. Of course, *caritas* makes *invidia* disappear, and it is more important "magis proficere studentes quam curare *invidentes.*"

Alcuin's polemics against his critics were concentrated in his resentment at *invidia, invidi, invidentes,* and *macula livoris,* as he named the topos of envy in the last sentence of the *Rhetoric.*

The author's refutation of anticipated detractions by envious readers was a stock literary formula in the prefaces and conclusions of literary works.

In many of his prefaces and introductory letters to certain books of the Vulgate, Jerome [11] strongly inveighs against the *invidia* of the *latrantes canes*, these *obtrectatores* of his translations. His famous *Praefatio* to the Pentateuch, extensively copied —for example, in Bede's dedicatory letter to Herefridus [12]— with his outcry *contra invidos*, provided medieval authors with this topos.[13] Alcuin, editor of a revised Vulgate,[14] presented by a messenger to Charlemagne on Christmas Day of the year 800 at Rome, was naturally familiar with the topos from his study of Jerome's Vulgate. Sedulius,[15] one of Alcuin's models for verse, wrote on the *macula invidiae* in the prose letter of dedication to the presbyter Macedonius, which Alcuin imitated in one instance in the letter preface of his *Vita S. Willibrordi*,[16] written upon the request of Beornred of Sens. Sedulius feared censure for having dared to write on a significant subject without special learning (nulla veteris scientiae praerogativa suffultus), while Alcuin confesses to having composed the work without being endowed with special eloquence of style (nullo praerogativae munere eloquentiae suffultus—*Epist.* 120, D.175.5). Alcuin's assurance that he feels unequal to the task to be undertaken by

[11] See *Biblia Sacra iuxta Latinam Vulgatam Versionem*, ed. Aid. Gasquet (Rome, 1926 ff.); especially I (Rome, 1926), *Librum Genesis*, ed. H. Quentin, 63–69; X (1953), 4 ff.; VIII (1940), 3–7; VII (1948), 6; V (1949), 9–11; cf. *PL* XXIII, 497,936; XXIV, 313D,680; XXV, 1189C; XXVIII, 85A,772B; *CSEL* 59 (1913), 4,221.

[12] *De tonitruis libellus ad Herefridum*, *PL* XC, 609 f.

[13] Cf. Anton E. Schönbach, "Otfridstüdien III," *Zeitschrift für Deutsches Altertum und Deutsche Litteratur* IXL (1895), 400–402.

[14] See F. L. Ganshof, "La révision de la Bible par Alcuin," *Bibliothèque d'humanisme et renaissance* IX (1947).

[15] Sedulius, ed. I. Huemer, *CSEL* 10 (Wien, 1885), 4.

[16] See the edition of the letter by Wilhelm Levison, *MGH, Scriptores Rerum Merovingicarum* VII (1920), 113 f.

him—"Sed tamen *longe imparem me* petitioni vestrae *con-sideravi*"—is a topos of modesty used also in his letter to Gisla (*Epist.* 213, D.354.11): "*...me*que ipsum *longe imparem* vestrae laudabili devotioni *agnosco.*" [17]

The epistolary style in the *conclusio* of the *Rhetoric* is further illustrated by parallels from Alcuin's letters, listed in the notes to the following section (H.550.27.30):

ALBINUS. ...his enim sacrificiis purgata atque exornata anima ab hac laboriosa vita et aerumnosa [a] revolabit ad quietem et intrabit in gaudium Domini sui.

ALBINUS. Magnum te faciat Deus et vere beatum, domine mi rex, et in hac virtutum quadriga [b] *ad celestis regni arcem* [c] *geminis dilec-tionis pennis* [d] saeculum hoc nequam *transvolare* concedat.

[a] Cf. the *conclusio* in *Epist.* 137, D.216.2: Qui (*scil.* Deus) vos et de huius mortalitatis aerumnosa miseria ad aeternitatis gaudia transire concedat.

[b] *Epist.* 60, D.103.23:...et sanctarum quadrigae virtutum.

[c] *Epist.* 13, D.39.21:...et ea te vehat *quadriga ad celestis regni palatium.*

[d] *Epist.* 198, D.328.13 to Charlemagne: tantum te geminae caritatis indue pennis, ut volare facias, quo victor Christus ascendit; *Epist.* 175, D.290.7: ad volandum caritatis pennis; *Epist.* 83, D.126.5: O si pennae aquilae habuissem et altitudines...*transvolare* voluissem. Sed quia hoc fieri non valet, induamur nos *duplicis caritatis pennis.* Alcuin here follows Sedulius, *Epistula ad Macedonum*, ed. I. Huemer (Wien, 1885), 6: non semper aquila super nubes elata pervolitat, sed etiam remissioribus aliquando pennis discendit ad terram.

Alcuin's style in the original parts of the *Rhetoric*, therefore, is the style which he uses in his correspondence. This fact is an additional reason for characterizing the treatise as a *littera ex-hortatoria*—notwithstanding the dialogue form which compels Alcuin to put his own rhetorical topoi and other elements of his epistolary style in the mouth of his royal interlocutor.

[17] Probably after Sulpicius Severus, *Dial.* III.2: imparem se esse tantae moli fatebatur; cf. I.27: licet impar sim tanto oneri.

# CHAPTER IV

# The *Rhetoric* as a Treatise on Kingship

THE designation of the *Rhetoric* as a *littera exhortatoria* naturally leads to the assumption that Alcuin's purpose in writing the work was identical with that of the letters he called *ammonitiones, litterae ammonitoriae, litterulae,* or *litterae exhortatoriae*.[1] Alcuin frequently expressed his predilection for hortatory epistles. He wrote to Adalhard of Corbie (*Epist.* 175, D.291.1) that he would welcome *exhortatoriae litterae*. A nun was told that Alcuin did not mind writing such letters to King Offa of Mercia (*Epist.* 62, D.105.3) provided that the ruler found time to read them. He took it upon himself to write hortatory letters to every region, parish, province, and state of his world, admonishing the people after the fashion of the Holy Fathers (*Epist.* 179, D.297.4). It is for the *sacerdos*, he said, to issue warnings (*admonere*) to the people, who ought to listen in humility (*PL* CI, 617C). "These are perilous times," complained Alcuin, who then went on to say that there are many who violate the purity of *fides catholica;* therefore the Church

---

[1] Cf. Arthur Kleinclausz, *Alcuin* (Paris, 1948), 112 f.; cf. Alcuin, *Adv. Elipandum* I.16, *PL* CI, 252A: epistola exhortatoria.

is in need of defenders.[2] Thus he exchanged letters of exhortation with his compatriots in Northumbria and Mercia, and with many acquaintances in Frankland. He wrote to the kings of the Anglo-Saxon nations, also to Charlemagne and his sons, Kings Charles and Pippin, and to other members of the royal Frankish family. The moralizing missives went to his friends of the Palace School fellowship, to archbishops of York and Canterbury, to secular and ecclesiastical dignitaries, to abbots and abbesses, to monks and nuns, to noblemen and members of the lower nobility, both on the Continent and in the British Isles. All these letters were similar; those sent to sovereign rulers are not infrequently almost identical. Compare the hortatory self-characterizations in the following *Epistles:*

> *Epist.* 5, Dümmler, p. 30.30 to Bishop Felix of Urgel: eos ammonere de virtutibus;
>
> 10, D.35.12 to Archbishop Arno of Salzburg: ammoneo;
>
> 16, D.42.24 to King Ethelred of Northumbria: vos...verbis...scriptis ammonere non cesso;
>
> 18, D.51.13 to the same king: non solum vos...his meis ammoneo literulis;
>
> 30, D.71.22 to the same king: semper te ammonere non cessabo;
>
> 61, D.104.31 to King Egfrid of Mercia: exhortatoriae litterae;
>
> 67, D.112.34 to an unknown Frankish duke: meae ammonitionis verba;
>
> 108, D.155.8 to King Eardwulf of Northumbria: ammonere;
>
> 119, D.174.25 to King Pippin in Italy: ammonitio;
>
> 122, D.178.24 to Osbert, former official of King Offa of Mercia: litterulae commonitoriae;
>
> 188, D.316.2 to King Charles, son of Charlemagne: ammonitoriae litterae;
>
> 224, D.367.33 to comes Chrodgarius: admonitio litterarum;
>
> 251, D.407.10 to several clerics: ammonerem vestrum nobile ingenium.

[2] Alcuin, *Vita Vedastis*, ed. Bruno Krusch, *MGH, Scriptores Rerum Merovingicarum* III, 415.33 ff.

The famous *Admonitio Generalis* addressed by Charlemagne on March 23, 789, to all secular and ecclesiastical dignitaries of the empire corresponds very well with this type of hortatory letter. The capitulary repeats the verb *ammoneo* fourteen times and *ammonitio* three times and uses *adhortor* and *adhortatio* once each.[3] Alcuin's co-authorship of the *Admonitio* seems to be a fact.

There is hardly any difference in the manner by which Alcuin appeals to Anglo-Saxon and Frankish rulers [4] in his hortatory letters addressed to them. Compare the following passages:

> *Epist.* 30, D.71.26 to King Ethelred of Northumbria (790–795): non decet te in solio sedentem regni rusticis vivere moribus... Misericordia te amabilem faciat...laudabilis in omni opere bono;
>
> *Epist.* 61, D.105.13 to King Egfrid of Mercia (786–796): non decet te rusticum esse moribus...qui natus es in solio regni. Temperantia et honestas vitae te amabilem et laudabilem cunctis efficiat populis;
>
> *Epist.* 119, D.174.10.19 to King Pippin of Italy (796 ex.):...pietas solium regni tui exaltet...et gentes tuae subiciat potestati...Deo te amabilem faciet et hominibus honorabilem efficiet;
>
> *Epist.* 217, D.361.6 to King Charles, son of Charlemagne (about 801):...misericordias,...quae exaltant solium regni et...regiam efficiunt potestatem.

What Alcuin was interested in was the realization of the ruler's moral responsibility toward his subjects, regardless of origin or nationality. The ideal to be achieved by sovereigns he called *stabilitas regni:*

[3] *MGH, Capitularia Regum Francorum* I, ed. Boretius, no. 22, pp. 52–62. Cf. F.-C. Scheibe, "Alcuin und die Admonitio Generalis," *Deutsches Archiv für die Erforschung des Mittelalters* 14 (1958), 221–229.

[4] Gaston Hocquard, "Quelques réflexions sur les idées politico-religieuses d'Alcuin," *Bulletin des Facultés Catholiques de Lyon* 74, N.S. 12 (1952), 20, wrongly contends that there is a difference in the manner of Alcuin when admonishing Frankish and when admonishing Anglo-Saxon nobles.

*Epist.* 174, D.288.13 to Charlemagne:...de stabilitate regni vobis a Deo dati;

*Epist.* 249, D.402.2 to Charlemagne:...pro vestra incolomitate et christiani imperii stabilitate intercedere;

*Epist.* 108, D. 155.8 to King Eardwulf of Northumbria:...quo modo stabilis tibi traditus honor Deo donante permaneat;

*Epist.* 123, D.181.16 to King Coenwulf of Mercia:...et presentis regni stabilitatem.

The expression *stabilitas regni* also occurs in the *formula* of the so-called *indiculum regale*,[5] a royal summons issued by the Frankish king to his subjects, directing them to comply with a court order and to appear before the king's court at law or before that of his representatives, the *missi*. But a distinction in meaning must be made between the political concept of the kingdom's stability and the religious idea of *stabilitas* recommended in Alcuin's letters for popes and Church, abbots and monks.[6] The latter concept is basically the *stabilitas* of the Benedictine vow: "Ego ille promitto stabilitatem meam." [7] The religious connotation in the relevant passages is confirmed by Alcuin's exegesis: "Quid est 'Expecta Dominum' nisi stabili mente expecta, donec tibi veniat dies renumerationis" (*Epist.* 205, D.342.8). This is also the meaning of Alcuin's personal expectation, "ad portum stabilitatis venire." [8] When answering Charle-

[5] *MGH, Formulae*, ed. Karl Zeumer, *MGH, Legum* Sect. V: Marculf I.6 (46, 34): pro stabilitate regni; *Form. Imperiales*, no. 40 (317 f.): et stabilitatem regni a Deo nobis commissi; cf. Heinrich Brunner, *Deutsche Rechtsgeschichte* II (2nd ed., 1928), 186 f.

[6] Cf. *Epist.* 93, D.137.13: pro totius ecclesiae stabilitate; *Epist.* 173, D.286.32 to Arno of Salzburg: in honoris ecclesiastici sublimissima stare stabilitate; cf. *Epistles* 187, D.315.3; 108, D.155.8.

[7] See the *formulas* in *MGH, Libri Confraternitatum*, pp. 111–113, 328 f.; *Regula S. Benedicti*, ch. LXI; *Epist.* 223, D.366.24 Alcuin to Theotgarius: pro stabilitate vitae vestrae et perseverantia boni operis usque in finem; *Reg. S. Ben.* LVIII: si promiserit de stabilitatis suae perseverantia.

[8] *Epist.* 97, D.141.7; the same words in *Vita Alcuini*, ch. IX (*MGH, Scriptores* XV,1, 190).

magne's letters sent to him from the Saxon battlefields, Alcuin referred to the same idea of *stabilitas*,[9] in the sense of an enduring solidity of faith. And a similar *stabilitas* was stressed in the last words of the *Rhetoric* (H.550.34), where Alcuin stated that the treatise comes to a close with *stabilitas aeterna*, so that this evil generation might nevertheless, he hoped, gain the Kingdom of Heaven, *gratia divina donante*.[10]

Another central ideal again and again called for by Alcuin in his hortatory letters is named *honestas morum*, the integrity of ethical deportment in life.[11] The concept occurs also as *morum nobilitas* and *morum dignitas*, though Alcuin was sufficiently realistic to know that *omnis morum dignitas* could not be found in every camp.[12] He told King Ethelred of Northumbria (*Epist.* 16, D.43.22) to watch *mores principum*. The same *mores* are the subject of the *Rhetoric*, as may be deduced from its metrical *propositio* (H.525): [13]

> 1 Qui rogo civiles cupiat cognoscere mores,
>   Haec praecepta legat, quae liber iste tenet.
>   Scripserat haec inter curas rex Karulus aulae
>   Albinusque simul: hic dedit, ille probat.

[9] *Epist.* 149, D.242.11, a passage possibly modeled on Boethius, *Cons. philosoph.* IV.6.7, ed. Wilhelm Weinberger (*CSEL* 67; Vienna, 1934, 96.12). Reto R. Bezzola, *Les origines et la formation de la littérature courtoise en occident* I (Biblioth. de l'Ecole des hautes Etudes, 286; Paris, 1944), 125, misinterprets *stabilitas* as an allusion to Charlemagne's physical toughness!

[10] The same formulation appears often in the *Epistles:* 98, D.142.24; 120, D.115.8; 200, D.331.1; etc.

[11] It occurs in *Epistles* 16, 18, 20, 74, 122, 164, 166, 169, 225, 251, 268, 278, 280, 281; see below, p. 204 n. f.

[12] *Epist.* 272, D.431.12; and *Epist.* 19, D.55.32; 198, D.327.23.

[13] Needless to say, Alcuin was quite familiar with the literary function of the *propositio* as the metrical prologue of the *Rhetoric*. See what he says on the function of the *prologus* of two of his Biblical commentaries, *Epist.* 254, D.412.3 and 214, D.358.2. Cf. the English translation of the *propositio* by W. S. Howell, *The Rhetoric of Alcuin and Charlemagne* (Princeton, 1941), 168.

5 Unum opus amborum, dispar sed causa duorum:
  Ille pater mundi, hic habitator inops.
  Neu temnas modico lector pro corpore librum:
  Corpore praemodico mel tibi portat apis.

1-2 Cf. *Disticha Catonis,* ed. Marcus Boas (Amsterdam, 1952), LXXV.
  5 Alcuin, *Carm.* CII,12 (*MGH, Poetae* I): Unum opus amborum;
    Poem on York, v. 1045 (p. 192): Par opus ambobus vitae, sed et
    exitus unus; Sedulius, *Paschale Carmen,* V.206: sed dispar causa
    duorum.
  7 *Carm.* XXX,2 (248): non spernas nardum, lector, in corpore parvum.
  8 *Carm.* LXX,2 (294): Corpore premodico viscera magna gerens;
    *Carm.* XXX,2 (248): Mel apis egregium portat tibi corpore parvo.

The *mores* illustrated by the rhetorical precepts naturally are
the *mores* of Charlemagne, who felt himself responsible for the
moral conduct of his subjects. This fact is further borne out
by some parallels between Alcuin's treatise *De animae ratione*
and the *Leitmotiv* of the *Rhetoric,* parallels illustrative of Alcuin's myth of Charlemagne as the wisest and morally most out-
standing man of his realm. We read in the *Rhetoric* (H.525.13),
Charlemagne to Alcuin: "As you very well know, on account
of the duties of the State and the affairs of the Palace (propter
OCCUPATIONES REGNI ET CURAS PALATII), we are constantly wont
to be busy with questions of this kind, and it seems absurd not
to know the rules of this art [of rhetoric] when the necessity
of using it confronts us daily." In this instance the daily practice
in *civiles quaestiones* which results from the ruler's activities
illuminates the *mores* of Charlemagne. Other illustrations of
those most noble and consecrated *mores* are to be seen in the
daily expressions of the king's "wisdom" that can be observed
at work in the midst of PALATII CURAE ET REGNI OCCUPATIONES,
as described in the *peroratio* of *De animae ratione* (*Epist.* 309,
D.477.39-478.14): "...sapientissimus imperator...dum inter tantas
PALATII CURAS ET REGNI OCCUPATIONES philosophorum planiter
arcana curavit scire mysteria...Nec tibi a nobis necesse est causas
querere rerum...dum illius clarissima quotidie uteris sapientia...

cernite Salomonem nostrum...IMITAMINI MORES ILLIUS NOBILIS-
SIMOS; *aversamini* [14] *vitia, colite virtutes. Magna vobis* incumbit, *si
dissimulare non vultis, optime vivendi necessitas,* dum apud eum
quotidie conversamini, in quo totius honestatis habetis exemplar,
quatenus per praesentis illius SACRATISSIMOS MORES ad eius cum
eodem pervenire mereamini praesentiam...." The words of this
*peroratio* in italics are copied from the *peroratio* of Boethius'
*Consolatio:* "Hope and prayers are not put on God in vain, and
when they are properly directed cannot lack results. Therefore
*hold back vices, practise virtues,* lift up the soul to right hopes,
offer humble prayers to Heaven. *Great is the necessity* of right-
eousness laid upon you, *if you will not hide it,* since you work
before the eyes of the all-seeing judge."

The parallels between the two treatises are quite obvious.
Charlemagne's MORES are held up as examples to be imitated by
his subjects and by Gundrada. Alcuin admonishes Charles, son
of the king, in a similar fashion (*Epist.* 217, D.361.15):

Examples (*exempla*) are not far to seek. You have in the house in
which you were raised the best examples of all goodness (optima
totius bonitatis exempla).[15] You may expect most certainly to attain,
God willing, to the blessing (benedictionem te consequi) of that
most excellent and in all splendor most noble father of yours (illius
excellentissimi...patris tui), leader and emperor of the Christian
people, if you endeavor to imitate the MORES of his nobility and
piety and entire modesty (et totius modestiae MORES IMITARI niteris).

[14] The words in italics from *aversamini-necessitas* are an unacknowledged quotation from Boethius, *Cons. Philosoph.* V.6.47–48, ed. Weinberger, 127.4–8. The phrase *inter...curas et occupationes* occurs in earlier
and later imperial and papal documents; see Heinrich Fichtenau, *Arenga*
(Wien, 1957), 93 nr. 174.

[15] Alcuin in a letter to Gundrada, then at the court of Charlemagne
(*Ep.* 241, D.386.29), admonishes her to be "totius bonitatis exemplar" to
the other *virgines* at the court: Sint nobiles in moribus...Non serviant
carnali desiderio. Paschasius Radbertus in the Vita of her brother Adalhard of Corbie calls Gundrada, "palma pudicitiae...inter venereos palatii
ardores"! (*MGH, Scriptores* 2 [Hannover, 1829], 527).

Another letter to Charles (*Epist.* 188, D.315.23) resembles the preceding in word and contents. Alcuin suggests that the son follow "the examples of [your] most excellent father (sequens excellentissimi patris tui exempla) in all honesty and sobriety in so far as the divine clemency of Christ the God may allow [him] to possess his blessing by right of inheritance (benedictionem te...possidere concedat)." The ruler's MORES as examples guiding the life of the nation are recommended in an epistle to Osbert, former official of King Offa of Mercia (*Epist.* 122, D.180.8). Alcuin urges the nobleman to exhort the people that they observe the *mores bonos et modestos et castos* instituted in their midst by the laws of the late king. The present incumbent, King Coenwulf, is advised to adorn himself "bonis moribus" (D.180.24).

Closely associated with the theme of the ruler's exemplary *mores* as a guide for his subjects is the concept of the *via regia* after Num. 21:22, "via regia gradiemus," ("We will go by the King's Highway"). In these *via regia* passages the main stress is on the idea of unwavering religious faithfulness and moral restraint. The wording of Alcuin's letters is often like that of Isaiah 30:21, "And thine ears shall hear a word behind thee, saying, This is The Way, walk ye in it, when ye turn to the right hand, and when ye turn to the left." [16] When speaking of the *via regia* Alcuin does not make a clear distinction between ethics and law. This is not very surprising, for his legal philosophy was that of the Church fathers, whose theory of natural law consisted of a mixture of law and ethics.[17]

In a letter to his intimate friend Arno of Salzburg (which also testifies to Alcuin's influence on Charlemagne in legal matters) Alcuin identifies the *via regia* (*Epist.* 186, D.312.30) with

[16] Et aures tuae audient verbum post tergum monentis: Haec est via, ambulate in ea, et non declinetis neque ad dexteram, neque ad sinistram.

[17] Cf. Fritz Kern, *Kingship and Law in the Middle Ages* (tr. S. B. Chrimes; Oxford, 1939), 75, 152.

*via iustitiae.* In another epistle we read that there should be no wavering in the service of the Lord but that we should go by the *via regia* (*Epist.* 184, D.309.35). Arno is further told not to let up but to show everybody the road leading to eternal salvation: "Make haste; this is the *via regia,* this is the *strata publica,* which leads to the palace of Christ, where there is peace, reward, and glory" (*Epist.* 193, D.321.8). Felix of Urgel in the Spanish March is asked to ferret out what is essential for the salvation of souls and then to proceed on the *via regia,* so often traveled by the Apostles, frequented by the fathers, and chosen by the majority of the world (*Epist.* 23, D.64.38). One of Alcuin's pupils, evidently on a pilgrimage to Rome, is assured that if he will go by the *via regia* (*Epist.* 281, D.439.11), he may be found worthy to reach the portal of the Eternal City. Monks are admonished that "no damnation rests heavier on the flock of Christ than a shepherd gone astray. When the leader travels the by-paths how can the simple wanderer find the *via regia?*" (*Epist.* 117, D.172.15). Others are told to walk the open road with the help of the Apostolic doctrine and not to leave the *via regia* (*Epist.* 137, D.211.17). Charlemagne too is admonished to travel by the *via regia* (*Epist.* 41, D.84.8). And in answer to one of Charlemagne's letters from the battlefields of Saxony, Alcuin reminds the king of the unifying quality of the idea of the *via regia* (*Epist.* 149, D.242.19). Elsewhere Alcuin remarks that a magister should neither be too strict nor of a frolicsome nature; he should follow the *via regia* (*PL* C, 696B) and carefully investigate what is best for the salvation of his soul. The *via regia* is mentioned also in Alcuin's *Vita Richarii.*[18] One might add here that the concept is not foreign to the *Libri Carolini,*[19] the manifesto of the Frankish Church against the worship of images (restored by the Seventh Ecumenical Council

[18] Ed. Bruno Krusch, *MGH, Scriptores Rerum Merov.* IV, 392.25.
[19] *Libri Carolini,* ed. H. Bastgen (*MGH, Concilia* II: *Supplementum;* Hannover-Leipzig, 1924), 5 f., 102.

held at Nicaea in 787), an apologetic treatise presumably edited by Alcuin. Moreover, two papal letters referring to the *via regia* are found in the *Codex Carolinus*,[20] a collection of the papal correspondence with Frankish rulers of the eighth century, officially edited at Charlemagne's request in 791. During the Carolingian age the expression gained general recognition as a political idea, so that Smaragdus of St. Mihiel used *Via regia* as the catchy title for a treatise on kingship.

Two occurrences of the concept of the *via regia* in Alcuin's works will be helpful for the interpretation and the proper understanding of a central passage in the *Rhetoric*, a passage which has a decisive bearing on Alcuin's purpose in writing the treatise. Compare:

A. *Rhetoric*, ed. Halm, p. 547.38:

KARLUS. Intellego philosophicum illud[a] proverbium non solum moribus, sed etiam verbis necessarium.

ALBINUS. Quodnam?

KARLUS. *Ne quid nimis.*[b]

ALBINUS. Est et vere est[c] in omni re necessarium, quia *quidquid modum excedit*[d] in vitio est. Ideo virtutes in medio sunt positae, de quibus tuae venerandae auctoritati *plura dicere potuissem,*[e] si non disputatio nostra ad finem festinaret.

B. *Dialogus de dialectica*, xi (*PL* CI, 963C), De contrariis vel oppositis:

CAROLUS. Si aliquando mala malis opponuntur?

ALBINUS. Etiam secundum philosophos, qui virtutes semper medias esse dixerunt, et ex utraque parte habere vitia. Et hoc reor Apostolum significasse, dum dicit: VIA REGIA nobis gradiendum (cf. Num. 21:22), neque ad dexteram, neque ad sinistram declinandum (cf. Is. 30:21), ut plus justum, et minus justum.

[20] Ed. Gundlach, *MGH, Epistolae Merowingici et Karolini Aevi* I (1892), no. 3, 486.36; no. 95, 641.27.—The patristic origin of Alcuin's *via regia* topos is certain; cf., for instance, Jerome, *Contra Pelagianos* I, prol., *PL* 23, 520B.

C. *Epist.* 209, ed. Dümmler, p. 349.22, to clerics in England (about 800):

Et comicus quidam ait: *Ne quid nimis.* In omni re TEMPERANTIA servanda est, quae est VIA REGIA TOTIUS VITAE nostrae, nec ad dextram nec ad sinistram declinans (cf. Is. 30:21), sed honeste et sapienter incedens.[f]

[a] Cf. Alcuin, *Ars grammatica* (PL CI, 850D):...unde philosophicum illud valet elogium: *Ne quid nimis.* Notum est omnia nimia nocere; *Comm. in Eccles.* (PL C, 694D): Idcirco comicus quidam ait, *ne quid nimis,* quia omnis intemperantia cadit in vitium; *Libri Carolini* IV, 8 ed. Hubert Bastgen, p. 188.16: illud philosophicum: *Ne quid nimis.*

[b] Terence, *Andria* I.i.34. Often quoted by the Latin grammarians and in patristic literature. Cf., e.g., Augustine, *De doctrina christiana* II.39 (*PL* XXXIV, 62), *De beata vita* I.32 (*PL* XXXII, 975); *Regula S. Benedicti,* c.64; in the *Praefatio* of the *Libri Carolini,* ed. H. Bastgen, p. 4.13.

[c] Cf. *Rhetoric,* H.550.8: Est et vere est et valde necessaria.

[d] Alcuin, *Ars grammatica* (PL CI, 892A): Saxo to Franco: Necessarium esset, sed modum nostri ludi excederet; see below note *e; Epist.* 181, D.300.20: Si modum excessi, ignoscat quae modum non habet, quae omnia sustinet.

[e] *Epist.* 143, D.227.26: Plurima exhinc dicere potui, sed nolui cartulae excedere modum; *Epist.* 144, D.230.23: De hoc autem...quod plurima hinc dici possint, sed noluisse te excedere modum cartulae; *Epist.* 136, D.210.8: Plurima exinde dici possint; see note *d* above; Alcuin, *Adv. Elipandum* IV.11, PL CI, 293D:...plura potuissem si non. Charlemagne in *Epist.* 144, above, is quoting from Alcuin's *Epist.* 143.

[f] Alcuin, *De virtutibus et vitiis,* c. 35 (PL CI, 637C): Temperantia est totius vitae modus, *ne quid nimis* homo vel amet vel odio habeat; a trace of this definition also in the *Rhetoric,* ed. Halm, p. 549.21: Temperantia ...per quam totius vitae modus.

The identical topics and ideas in these three passages show the close connection between the *via regia* concept and the principle of moderation. And, significantly, Alcuin suggests that the maxim applies not only to the sphere of morals but also to that of speech (verba), i.e., to rhetoric as the art of dealing with questions of government (H.525.11) as moral issues. This explains the occurrence in the treatise of the definitions of the four cardinal virtues. Indeed, the passage from the *Rhetoric* is best commented on by an earlier statement of Alcuin (H.547.26) put in the mouth of Charlemagne: "Necessary in every activity of life, honesty (honestas) is of the greatest importance, especially in discourse (in sermonibus), because a man's speech completely reveals his ethical behaviour (mores)." The interrelationship that exists between *via regia, mores,* and *temperantia,* and Alcuin's adoption of the Aristotelian definition of virtue as the mean between two extremes, can be easily seen in the three parallel passages that supplement each other. The connection of the three concepts is a commonplace of Alcuin's hortatory epistolary style. He therefore requests (*Epist.* 119, D.174.22) of Pippin, king of Italy and son of Charlemagne, what he actually recommends in the *Rhetoric* to the father, namely, "*Sint tibi...* veritatis verba in ore, honestatis exempla in moribus.*" Arno of Salzburg is reminded (*Epist.* 166, D.268.1) that "verborum veritas" in missionary activities contributes to the "honestas morum" of the pagans. A disciple is warned against unbridled speech (*Epist.* 281, D.440.2–4): "*Sint tibi* verba in veritate, mores in honestate. Indisciplinate loquele non adsuescat os tuum. *Sint tibi* verba simplicia sine iuramento, veritate plena.*" Alcuin even finds it necessary to tell a bishop whom he befriended (*Epist.* 40, D.83.22): "*Sint tibi,* fili mi, mores cum honestate et temperantia.*"

What our study has thus far disclosed is that the *Rhetoric* presents the *mores* of Charlemagne as the exemplary expression of the *via regia,* the Christian mean of moderation in Alcuin's view. The *Rhetoric* is made up of rhetorical doctrine, not because Alcuin wanted to write a rhetorical textbook, but because he wished to describe the *mores* of Charlemagne as those that ought to serve as examples to his subjects (H.525.11). It is on the basis of these deliberations that I propose to call Alcuin's work THE VIA REGIA OF CHARLEMAGNE and to designate the *Rhetoric* a treatise on KINGSHIP.

Certain of Alcuin's letters to sovereigns have been previously [21]

[21] By L. K. Born, "The *Specula Principis* of the Carolingian Renaissance," *Revue belge de philologie et d'histoire* XII (1933), 583–612.

characterized as short treatises on kingship, e.g., *Epistle* 18 (D.49–52) to King Ethelred of Northumbria, and the letter to Osbert, former official of King Offa of Mercia (*Epist.* 122, D.178–180). Alcuin's treatise *De virtutibus et vitiis*, written as a manual for Charlemagne's successful general Duke Wido of Brittany,[22] was to serve as a mirror wherein the valiant margrave might find moral guidance. Each one of these hortatory writings sounds like a forerunner of the so-called *Fürstenspiegel* or *Sittenspiegel*, mirrors of princes or mirrors of morals, of the later Middle Ages.[23] Alcuin's *via regia* of Charlemagne inaugurates this species of political treatise, which was so strongly cultivated during the Carolingian epoch.

[22] Cf. Chapter XII.
[23] See W. Berges, *Die Fürstenspiegel des hohen und späteren Mittelalters* (Weimar, 1938).

# CHAPTER V

# Legal Elements of the *Rhetoric*

IN the *Rhetoric* as a *via regia* Alcuin commends to Charlemagne's subjects the exemplary deportment of their king, the highest Frankish judge, who, according to the *Capitulare Missorum Generale* of 802,[1] felt himself personally responsible for the proper conduct of all his subjects. Charlemagne requested that everybody conduct himself in accordance with the Lord's commandments and his oath of fidelity to the emperor, because the sovereign could not devote to every subject of his empire the necessary personal supervision. This notion of responsibility coincides with Alcuin's belief that Charlemagne's imperial dignity entails the task "populo praeesse et prodesse," so that the emperor's "doctrina" may be of advantage to all his subjects (*Epist.* 257, D.414 f.). The obligation Charlemagne felt toward his subjects was reciprocated by their recognition of the sovereign as the master of *all* Christians: this exaggerated claim that he had attained such recognition had previously been made at the Synod of Frankfurt in 794 by the Patriarch Paulinus of Aquileia, as reported in the *peroratio* of the resolution against adoptionism, which Paulinus drew up for the Italian clergy:

[1] *MGH, Capitularia Regum Francorum* I, ed. Alfred Boretius, no. 33, p. 92:...quia ipse domnus imperator non omnibus singulariter necessariam potest exhibere curam et disciplinam.

"...sit omnium Christianorum moderantissimus gubernator." After all, says Alcuin, God "has honored Charlemagne above all other kings and emperors with the splendor of wisdom and exalted him through the power of kingship." This honored station enables the "populus Christanus," his subjects, to live religiously and in security under the shadow of his power (sub umbra potentiae).[2]

Alcuin's intention to picture in the *Rhetoric* the *civiles mores* of Charlemagne (H.525.1) led to his treatment of rhetorical doctrine, which was traditionally connected with "public questions," *civiles questiones*. It has been demonstrated (Ch. III) that in the *Rhetoric* Alcuin thinks of Charlemagne as judge and lawgiver. Additional material in the treatise that does not belong to rhetorical doctrine but represents legal and juridical elements of Frankish procedures of law also has definite bearing on the functions of Charlemagne's kingship.

Alcuin's *questio civilis* is identical with the *causa civilis* (H.526.33), the secular case, in contrast to the *causa ecclesiastica*, the case belonging under the jurisdiction of the Church. Thus the *Rhetoric* treats as parallels *causa civilis* and *negotium seculare;* correspondingly, *iudicium seculare* is once mentioned by Alcuin in a letter to Arno of Salzburg (*Epist.* 254, D.411.7). The *causa civilis* belongs under the jurisdiction of the *iudex civilis*, i.e., the Frankish king, or the *comes palatinus*, who substitutes as the leading judge of the royal court, or the royal *missus dominicus*, the itinerant judge.[3]

The composition and the functions of a law court concerned with the *causa civilis* are briefly described (H.533.13–19). The court consists of a plaintiff and a defendant, the witnesses and the judge, whose respective functions in the practical procedure (officium) of the dispensation of law are accordingly deter-

[2] *Epist.* 211, D.352.27; 41, D.84.19.
[3] See Heinrich Brunner and Claudius von Schwerin, *Deutsche Rechtsgeschichte* II (2nd ed.; Munich-Leipzig, 1928).

mined. The place of the participants in the actual court action is stated and their individual functions are denoted by the insignia of their office (H.534.15–22). This treatment represents an *ordo iudicialis* which seems to be original with Alcuin. It reads as follows:

A. (H.533.13–19, ch. 16):
KARLUS. Quot personae solent in iudiciis esse?
ALBINUS. Quattuor: accusator causae, defensor causae, testes, iudex.
KARLUS. Quo quisque utitur officio?
ALBINUS. Iudex aequitate, testes veritate, accusator intentione ad amplificandam causam, defensor extenuatione ad minuendam causam, nisi forte in laude vel praemii petitione sit causa posita: tunc converso ordine accusatori extenuatione et defensori amplificatione utendum est.

B. (H.534.15–22, ch. 19):
KARLUS. Quia personas causarum dixisti [see above] dic, obsecro, loca singularum.
ALBINUS. Dicam, licet hoc non tantum ad artis [*scil.* rhetoricae] praecepta pertineat, quantum ad officii decorem.
Iudex in tribunali, causa in medio ante eum ad laudem vel ad poenam posita, ut forte patriae defensio vel proditio: accusator ad sinistram causae et defensor ad dextram, testes retro.
KARLUS. An insignia sua singulae ex illis habent?
ALBINUS. Habent. Iudex sceptro aequitatis armandus est, accusator pugione malitiae, defensor clypeo pietatis, testes tuba veritatis.

Section A of the *ordo* is falsely presented as a Carolingian capitulary by Pseudo-Benedictus Levita, *False Capitularies* III.339,[4] which was compiled somewhere in the Frankish empire about the year 847. Emil Seckel[5] has pointed out that the

---

[4] Edited by F. H. Knust, *MGH, Legum* (in folio) II, pars altera (Hannover, 1837), 137; Paul Fournier and Gabriel Le Bras, *Histoire des collections canoniques en Occident* I (Paris, 1931), 155.

[5] Emil Seckel, "Studien zu Benedictus Levita, VIII," *Neues Archiv der Gesellschaft für ältere Deutsche Geschichtskunde* XL (1916), 101–103. Seckel wrongly assumes that the *praecepta*, which are clearly defined as

occurrence of A in the *Pseudo-Isidorian Decretals* and in a forged capitulary of a Frankish Pseudo-Synod of 744, allegedly presided over by Boniface, is traceable to the occurrence of A in Benedictus Levita. Both sections of Alcuin's *ordo* are mentioned in the *Rhetorica ecclesiastica*,[6] a forensic rhetoric for canon law, written in France between 1159 and 1179, and they are also used by Eilbert of Bremen in his *Ordo iudiciarius*,[7] composed between 1191 and 1204. Alcuin's list of insignia in section B (above) is quoted by Geoffrey of Vinsauf.[8]

It is rather significant that Alcuin apologizes to the reader for inserting the treatment of the insignia in his treatise on the art of rhetoric, since the subject "does not so much appertain to the precepts of rhetoric as to the dignity of the office" (H.535.15) of a court at law. Alcuin's excuse cannot be taken seriously; the insertion was made in order to give emphasis to the subject under discussion. His apology is a conscious application of the rhetorical device called *egressio* or *excessus*, a topos also used elsewhere in the *Rhetoric*. That Alcuin indeed had the royal court at law in mind becomes evident from the hypothetical examples of a *causa civilis* concerning *patriae defensio vel proditio* (H.534.18 f.), i.e., a case clearly belonging under the jurisdiction of the Frankish king.

Alcuin used allegory not only to characterize the functions of the participants in a Frankish *causa civilis*, but also to describe the powers invested by the pope in an Anglo-Saxon archbishop

---

rhetorical principles, refer to *praecepta* of the Frankish king in a diplomatic sense. See Isidore of Seville, *Etymologiae* 18.15.6: in omni iudicio sex personae quaeruntur: iudex, accusator, reus et tres testes.

[6] Cf. Emil Ott, *Die Rhetorica ecclesiastica* (*SB. Wien Akademie* CXXV [1892]), 51 and 46; on Eilbert see Heinrich Siegel, *ibid.* LV (1867). Both treatises are edited by Ludwig Wahrmund, *Quellen zur Geschichte des römisch-kanonischen Processes* I, Heft 4 and 5 (Innsbruck, 1906).

[7] Cf. Albert Lang, "Rhetorische Einflüsse auf die Behandlung des Prozesses in der Kanonistik des 12. Jahrhunderts," *Festschrift Eduard Eichmann* (Marburg, 1941), 69–97.

[8] See L. Wallach in *Speculum* XXIV (1949), 418.

through the granting of the pall. Compare the insignia in Section
B of Alcuin's *Ordo* and his *Epist.* 311 (D.480.15) of 802–804,
addressed to Ethelhard of Canterbury, who is told: "Sit tua
dextra *sceptro equitatis* armata et sinistra *clipeo pietatis* honesta."

That Alcuin intended the *Rhetoric* to be used for a practical
purpose becomes quite obvious from his reinterpretation of
Cicero's doctrine of customary law (*De inv.* II.54.162), i.e., law
consisting of such instruments as covenants, equity, and decisions
which have been sanctioned, for instance, by the lapse of time
and continued habit of public approval. Alcuin asks: "How is
justice subserved by the use of custom?" (H.549.5), and then
proceeds to adapt the source to his purpose by making two
significant changes (in capitals) in Cicero's text. Compare:

| Cicero, *De. inv.* II.54.162, ed. Stroebel, pp. 148b–149b: | Alcuin, *Rhetoric,* ed. Halm, p. 549.5–10: |
|---|---|
| ...consuetudine ius est...aut quod in morem vetustas vulgi adprobatione perduxit; | K. Quomodo ex consuetudinis usu iustitia servatur? |
| quod genus pactum est, par, iudicatum. | A. Ex *pacto, pari, iudicato* ET LEGE. |
| *pactum* est, quod inter aliquos convenit; *par*, quod in omnes aequabile est; | K. Plus quaero et de his quoque. |
| *iudicatum*, de quo alicuius aut aliquorum iam sententiis constitutum est. | A. *Pactum est, quod inter aliquos convenit;* |
| lege ius est, quod in eo scripto, quod populo expositum est, ut observet, continetur. | *par, in omnes aequabile est;* |
| | *iudicatum*, QUOD *alicuius* MAGNI VIRI *aut aliquorum sententiis constitutem est;* |
| | LEX est omni populo scriptum ius quid cavere vel quid observare debeat. |

The equating of judicial decisions with opinions issued by
"one great man" or by several men points to Charlemagne as
the highest judge of the royal court at law. Cicero's three instruments of customary law are augmented by a fourth, "law,"

here the codified law to which everybody is subject, and which stipulates what people ought to avoid or to observe. Alcuin's LEX as *ius scriptum*, on the other hand, consists of the contemporary legislation of Charlemagne as the first judge of the empire and the capitularies decreed by him and his Diets. This LEX is also listed as a special department of *iustitia consuetudinaria* in the *schemata* (PL CI, 494 f.), which accompanies a joint edition of Alcuin's rhetorical and dialectical treatises brought out by an unknown editor before the year 821 (see Ch. VI).

The expansion of Cicero's concepts of customary law seems to have been of Augustinian origin.[9] The same portion of Cicero's treatise dealing with the cardinal virtues which Alcuin used in the *Rhetoric* had been inserted by Augustine in *De diversis questionibus* LXXXIII, ch. 31 (PL XL, 20–22), where we read: "...quod genus pactum est, par, lex, iudicatum." Eleven of the fifteen MSS on which Migne's edition of this tractate is based include *lex*, just as Alcuin does. Since Alcuin quotes from Augustine's treatise in one of his apologetic tractates (PL CI, 156B), he was in all probability familiar with Augustine's expansion of the Ciceronian system of customary law.

As one of Charlemagne's councilors *pro tempore* Alcuin occasionally accompanied the itinerant court of the Frankish king, and thus was doubtless somewhat familiar with Frankish procedures of law as well as with the king's current legislation. Moreover, Charlemagne was in the habit of discussing problems of government with his friends and advisers,[10] and Alcuin was not the least intimate of these. We know that he and his friends were interested in the reorganization of the *missi dominici*, the traveling judges, who dispensed law in the name of the Frankish

[9] Cf. Maurice Pallasse quoted supra, Ch. VI, nn. 4 and 8. The Augustinian origin of Alcuin's *lex* is denied by M. B. Crowe, *Medium Aevum* 27 (1958), 118, who assumes that Alcuin used a faulty text of Cicero. On the Cicero codex of Alcuin see above, Ch. II, p. 36.

[10] *Epist.* 162, D.260.26.

king.[11] We know too, that the function of such a *missus* who conducted the *inquisitio* in legal cases was not unknown to Alcuin, who once witnessed the harsh procedures of Frankish law employed in a case in which he himself was seriously involved.[12] In letters to Arno of Salzburg (*Epist.* 107, D.154.30) and to Gisla, Charlemagne's sister (*Epist.* 15, D.41.38), Alcuin mentions *indicula*, i.e., royal summons, by which the litigants in a *causa* were summoned before the king's court.

Alcuin's cherished friendship with Charlemagne—"such a friend is not one to be scorned," he once wrote (*Epist.* 43, D.89.2)—made it possible for him to be of help, as he says, to many people in legal cases brought before the king's court at law. Thus he acted as intercessor (*adiutor*) in the case of certain Italian monks whose petitions he recommends (*Epist.* 90, D.134.20) to Charlemagne (in this instance even with the specially secured support of Queen Liutgarda). For his Abbey of Cormréry, Alcuin himself petitioned the king to permit the monks to operate—duty free—two ships on the Loire, the Sarthe, and some tributaries.[13]

A trace of Alcuin's practical application of an element of rhetorical doctrine is preserved in a letter of Charlemagne to Alcuin in which the king refers to an epistle of Alcuin now lost. Charlemagne tells Alcuin (*Epist.* 247, D.400.16) that the case of the Apostle Paul in Acts 24 and the principle of conducting one's own defense before Caesar "does not at all coincide with the present case" before the royal court, as Alcuin had maintained when speaking in favor of an accused cleric. In the *Rhetoric* (H.527.4-7) Alcuin illustrates the judicial kind of oratory, in which there are accusation and defense, with a refer-

[11] *Epist.* 186, D.312.26–35; Richard Schröder and Eberhard von Künnsberg, *Lehrbuch der deutschen Rechtsgeschichte* (7th ed.; Berlin, 1932), 143.

[12] See below Chapter VII.

[13] DK 192 in *MGH, Diplomata Karolinorum*, ed. Mühlbacher.

ence to the case of the Apostle Paul (Acts 24), who, accused by the orator Tertullus, demands the right to conduct his case before Felix, the Roman governor, "for in judicial oratory what is just is quite often inquired into," says Alcuin.

The treatise on "Kingship" must have followed from Alcuin's interest in the internal order of Charlemagne's empire. *Tempora sunt periculosa*, he repeatedly stated in his letters [14] when complaining about the lawlessness of his days. The lawful dispensation of justice is again and again requested by him in his hortatory epistles.[15] "Iustitia ad omnes" is recommended to Comes Chrodgarius, "iusta iudicia" to Comes Magenharius. King Ethelred of Northumbria is told to be righteous "in iudiciis." The patrician Osbert, former official of King Offa of Mercia, is admonished to urge the native nobles to rule their people justly. The necessity of rejecting bribes is very forcefully impressed on King Charles, son of Charlemagne; Charles ought to engage honest councilors, since "gifts blind the heart of the wise and change the words of the Righteous." [16] The Biblical verse (Exod. 23:8), "Nec accipies munera, quae etiam excaecant prudentes, et subvertunt verba iustorum," was frequently cited in Alcuin's letters in connection with requests for justice; it appears in letters addressed to Charlemagne and his son Charles, to Arno of Salzburg, and in the hortatory treatise dedicated to Duke Wido.[17] Alcuin was convinced that Charlemagne had the best of intentions but lacked incorruptible helpers in the just dispensation of law. "I am quite certain," he wrote to Arno of Salzburg, "of the good will (*bona voluntas*) of the Emperor, who has not as many *iustitiae adiutores* as he has [iustitiae] *subversores*" (*Epist.*

[14] II Tim. 3:1; cf. *Epistles* 193, D.320.10; 206, D.342.29; 116, D.171.17; *MGH, Poetae* I, 261.

[15] *Epistles* 224, D.367.35; 33, D.74.21.26; 18, D.51.19; 122, D.180.14.

[16] *Epistles* 188, D.315.27; 217, D.361.6.

[17] See for Charlemagne *Epist.* 174, D.288.28, not acknowledged by Dümmler; for Charles see n. 16; for Arno *Epist.* 186, D.312.31; 254, D.411.26; for Wido *PL* CI, 628CD.

254, D.411.22).[18] So the loyal friend came to the assistance of his beloved king with his *via regia*.

More than half a century ago, the Abbé Laforêt[19] classified the *Rhetoric* as a treatise on government without fully substantiating this characterization. Today his judgment may be repeated on, it is hoped, better grounds.

Alcuin's treatise must be added to the numerous treatises of the Carolingian age on kingship.[20] This type of political essay addressed to sovereigns and dignitaries of lower rank began with the *Liber exhortationis ad Heiricum*, written before 799 by Alcuin's friend, Paulinus of Aquileia, for Charlemagne's celebrated general, Duke Eric of Friuli. Alcuin's *De virtutibus et vitiis*, addressed to Margrave Wido of Brittany about 800, was followed between 801–804 by what I term his *Via regia*. Smaragdus of St. Mihiel wrote a *Via regia* between 813/4 and 816, probably for Louis the Pious.[21] About 834 Jonas of Orléans dedicated *De institutione regia* to his son Pippin.[22] Sedulius Scottus dealt with Christian kingship in the *Liber de rectoribus Christianis*, which he presented to King Lothar II of Italy. A veritable flood of political essays poured forth from the pen of the versatile Hincmar of Reims, who offered the treatise *De regis persona et de regis ministerio* to Charles the Bald in 873. Of special interest to us is Hincmar's *De ordine palatii*,[23] which was al-

[18] Cf. furthermore *Epist.* 111, D.161.13 ff.: "...propter tempora periculosa (cf. II Tim. 3:1) huius saeculi, quod rariores habet adiutores... quam necesse est."

[19] J.-B. Laforêt, *Histoire d'Alcuin, réstaurateur des sciences* (Namur-Paris, 1898), 38 f.

[20] Cf. L. K. Born, "The Specula Principis of the Carolingian Renaissance," *Revue belge de philologie et d'histoire* XII (1933), 583–612.

[21] M. L. W. Laistner, "The date and the recipient of Smaragdus' Via Regia," *Speculum* III (1928), 392–397.

[22] Jean Réviron, *Les idées politico-religieuses d'un évêque du IXe siècle* (L'église et l'état au moyen âge I; Paris, 1930).

[23] Edited by Viktor Krause, in *MGH, Capitularia Regum Francorum* II (Hannover, 1897), 518–530; Louis Halphen, "Le *De ordine palatii*

legedly based on a treatise (not extant) by Adalhard of Corbie, cousin of Charlemagne and a close friend of Alcuin.

---

d'Hincmar," *Revue Historique* 183 (1938), 1 ff., discounts Hincmar's allegation as designed to provide a legitimate historical background for his ambitious political machinations.—

J. M. Wallace-Hadrill, "The *Via Regia* of the Carolingian Age," in: *Trends in Medieval Political Thought,* ed. Beryl Smalley (Oxford, England 1965), 22-41, agrees (p. 30) with my interpretation of Alcuin's *Rhetoric* as a statement of political theory concerning the royal authority invested in Charlemagne.—Wallace-Hadrill, *The English Historical Review* 76 (1961), 89, unfortunately overlooked that the proof promised on p. 14 n. 35, above, is offered on pp. 23-28.

CHAPTER VI

# The Composition of the *Rhetoric:* Editions, Manuscripts, and Testimonies

THE literary composition of the treatise (Halm, pp. 525–550), whose title in the MSS is properly listed as a *disputatio*, can now be analyzed in the following manner:

A.  LITERARY FRAME OF DISPUTATIO: epistolary elements of a *littera exhortatoria,* A 1–3
D.  Metrical *propositio* .................. p. 525.1–8
A1. Prose *propositio* ................... p. 525.9–19
A2. Exordium: *invocatio* and *captatio bene-volentiae* ......................... p. 525.19–25
B.  RHETORICAL DOCTRINE: B1 and B2
B1. Treatment of the five parts of *ars rhetorica* ........................... p. 525.25–547.18
B2. *Conclusio* of B1 and connecting link with C ......................... p. 547.18–548.5
C.  Disquisition on the cardinal virtues .... p. 548.5–550.33
A3. *Conclusio of littera exhortatoria* ....... p. 550.33–41.

Excerpts of rhetorical doctrine (B) are set in the literary frame (A) of the treatise, which consists of typical elements of an Alcuinian *littera exhortatoria*. The bulk of B treats the traditional five parts of *ars rhetorica* (B1), with a special conclusio (B2) dealing with the concept of moderation and serving as a link with C. The epideictic oration on the cardinal virtues (C) consists of Christian interpretations of Cicero's definitions of the virtues.

The individual literary parts of the treatise were probably written in the order B, C, A, and D. The metrical *propositio* (D), as the poetic transcription of the prose *propositio* (A1), informs the reader of the author's purpose in writing the work. Stylistically, D resulted from Alcuin's awareness of the classical *periphrase*, the turning of prose into poetry and vice versa.[1] This Roman technical practice was continued in Christian literature, the best-known medieval example being Sedulius' double Paschal work. Alcuin found double treatments of the same theme, for instance, in Aldhelm's *De virginitate* and in Bede's *Vita Cuthberti*. His own *Vita S. Willibrordi*, which consists of prose and metrical treatments of the same subject, thus belongs to a literary tradition previously established among earlier Anglo-Saxon scholars. The *propositio* (D) is additional evidence of the same literary tradition. But what is the meaning of *De virtutibus* in the title of the *Rhetoric?*

*De virtutibus* in the title of the treatise does not indicate that C is an appendix to B, as some critics have maintained. The title supports, however, our characterization of the book as a moralizing political treatise. The customary designation of the treatise as a rhetorical textbook is traceable to the later Carolingian legend, which falsely ascribed to Alcuin the composition of textbooks for the study of all the seven liberal arts. But what Alcuin wrote was a hortatory letter in the form of a rhetoric. The tractate is cast in the form of a fictitious dialogue between

[1] See E. R. Curtius, *European Literature and the Latin Middle Ages* (Bollingen Series, XXXVI; New York, 1953), 147 f.

scholar and king, for the Charlemagne of the dialogue always speaks the language of Alcuin.

Two ninth-century editions of the treatise are extant in the MSS and attested by the entries in medieval library catalogues. One of these editions is perhaps representative of, and derived from, the book's archetype, i.e., the copy dedicated and offered by Alcuin to Charlemagne, between 801 and 804. The other edition is a joint edition of the treatise and Alcuin's *Dialogus de dialectica,* the only other work of Alcuin with king and scholar as interlocutors. This second edition must have originated before 821, as we shall see, but at present little is known about its origin. A new critical edition based on the entire MS transmission and the *testimonia,* subsequently collected, might shed some light on this question.

A list of twenty-six MSS of the treatise is provided by W. S. Howell.[2] Three undated MSS mentioned by Howell on the basis of Montfaucon's catalogue are the *Reginenses* 342, 1209, and 1461 of the Vaticana.[3] I add to Howell's list additional extant MSS and testimonies of other codices which are mostly drawn from medieval library catalogues.

Investigation of all available MSS on the basis of their descriptions in modern catalogues indicates frequent transmission of Alcuin's *Rhetoric* (R) with his *Dialogus de dialectica* (D) in the same codex. It seems incorrect to state, as Howell does, that these MSS more or less completely obliterate the line between R and D, allegedly making the second an immediate continuation, if not an integral part, of the first. As a matter of fact, the texts of the two treatises, even when transmitted in the same MS, remain as a rule undisturbed and intact so far as can be ascertained. Only the insertion of a systematic classification of the sciences of the seven liberal arts (S) between the texts

---

[2] *Op. cit.,* 9.

[3] Cf. the description in *Archiv der Gesellschaft für ältere deutsche Geschichtskunde* XII (1874), 275, 314, 320, listed as *Reginenses,* of which MS 342 is now described by André Wilmart, *Codices Reginenses Latini* II (Città del Vaticano, 1945).

of R and D could be understood as a connection linking the two tractates. These *schemata* (S),[4] as they are called in the MSS, present the doctrinal contents of R and D. They are published in Migne, *PL* CI, 945–946, together with the poem (P) "O vos est aetas, iuvenes," on the basis of the *Monacensis* 14377 (see below A: no. 3). An anonymous reviewer[5] of Halm's edition ascribes S and P to Alcuin, but Halm rightly excluded both pieces from his edition of R. The problem is: Are they genuine Alcuiniana and do both actually belong to the text of R?

The location of S and P as the connecting link between the *Rhetoric* and the dialectical treatise does not make sense from an editorial point of view. No author would put the summary (S) of a second treatise (D) in front of a poem (P) which supposedly concludes the preceding (R) treatise! A comparison of P with the metrical *propositio* of R (Halm, 525) also proves that the content of the poem is incompatible with these introductory distichs, which are addressed to adults and express the intention of the author to write on government and kingship. P, however, is addressed to *iuvenes* and presents a strictly didactic educational appeal. But even though internal considerations forbid the acceptance of P as the concluding poem of R, it cannot be denied that the text of P is by Alcuin. Ernst Dümmler prints P among Alcuin's poems as the allegedly concluding poem of R without verifying the authorship of Alcuin. Parallels from other poems by Alcuin, however, do prove that Alcuin wrote the following verses:

> 1 O vos, est aetas, iuvenes, quibus apta legendo,
> Discite: eunt anni more fluentis aquae,
> Atque dies dociles vacuis ne perdite rebus:
> Nec redit unda fluens, nec redit hora ruens.

[4] Discussed by M. Pallasse, "Brève histoire d'un schème cicéronien au moyen âge," *Revue du moyen âge latin* I (1945), 35–42, who apparently takes Alcuin's authorship for granted; see below n. 8.

[5] In *Literarisches Centralblatt für Deutschland* (1864), no. 24, p. 570.

5 Floreat in studiis virtutum prima iuventus,
  Fulgeat ut magno laudis honore senex.
  Utere, quisque legas librum, feliciter annis,
  Auctorisque memor dic: "Miserere Deus."
  Si nostram, lector, festucam tollere quaeris,
10 Robora de proprior lumine tolle prius:
   Disce tuas, iuvenis, ut agat facundia causas,
   Ut sis defensor, cura, salusque tuis.
   Disce, precor, iuvenis, motus moresque venustos,
14 Laudetur toto ut nomen in orbe tuum.[6]

2–4 Ovid, *Ars Amatoria* 3.62–64:
    ...eunt anni more fluentis aquae.
    Nec quae praeteriit iterum revocabitur unda,
    Nec quae praeteriit hora redire potest.
    The same Ovid passage occurs frequently in Alcuin's poems: 76.11
    (p. 297); 93.8 (p. 319); 63.146 (p. 280); 48.25 (p. 261).
5–7 Floreat, Fulgeat, Utere, at the beginning of other verses in Alcuin's
    poems, 75.1.1 (p. 296); 85.4.2 (p. 304); 62.97 (p. 278); *Epist.* 309,
    D.476.24: Floreat in studiis semper ubique sacris.
  7 Read *feliciter* (not: felicibus) *annis* as in other poems of Alcuin:
    83.19 (p. 301); 69.199 (p. 292); *Epist.* 70, D.114.13.
7–8 Cf. Alcuin, *Carm.* 66.16–17 (p. 285):
    In quo quisque legat domini dulcissima verba,
    Sit memor auctoris, illum qui scribere iussit.
9–10 Cf. Sedulius, *Paschal. Carm.* 4.243–244:
    Nec poterat quisquam fistucam uellere parvam
    Ex oculo alterius, proprio lumine, grandem sciret messe trabem.
    Cf. Matt. 7:3–4.
 13 Cf. Alcuin 91.3.1 (p. 318): Surge, precor, iuvenis.
 14 Alcuin 75.5 (p. 297): Nomen ut aeternum toto laudetur in orbe;
    Alcuin, in poem on York, v.612 (p. 183):
    Et celebri fama laeto laudatur in orbe;
    Ovid, *Ars Amatoria* 2.739:
    Me vatem celebrate viri, mihi dicite laudes
    Cantetur toto nomen in orbe meum;
    Ovid, *Amores* 1.15.7:
                                mihi fama perennis
    Quaeritur in toto semper ut orbe canar.

[6] Alcuin, *Carmina*, ed. Ernst Dümmler, *MGH, Poetae* I, no. 80 (p. 299);
quoted by M. L. W. Laistner, *Thought and Letters in Western Europe*
(2nd ed.; London, 1957), p. 338, translation p. 390 f.

The textual history of this "poem" can be reconstructed with the help of Ernst Dümmler's *apparatus criticus*. Some MSS offer the first three distichs as a separate poem; one MS contains the last two verses as an independent poem. Alcuin's authorship of all these verses and the remaining distichs (vv.7–12) can hardly be doubted. Their joint transmission as one poem, supposedly representing the concluding verses of the *Rhetoric*, as Dümmler and Ludwig Traube assume,[7] is traceable to some MSS of the ninth century which offer Alcuin's *Rhetoric* and *Dialectic* in the *same* codex. But the fusion in one poem of at least three little Alcuinian versifications seems to be the work of an editor of the ninth century who brought out a joint edition of both treatises. This edition originated in all probability before 821, since the lists of the Reichenau Library (below, nos. 31-32), which were written between 821 and 822, give two MSS with R and D in one volume. The redactor of this joint edition, who read in the metrical *propositio* of R (H.525.5) about Charlemagne's alleged co-authorship of the book:

Unum opus amborum, dispar sed causa duorum,

apparently tried to indicate Alcuin's and Charlemagne's *joint* authorship by a poem at the very end of R in his version. This could be the reason why some MSS read in verse 8 of P

Auctorumque memor dic: "Miserere Deus,"

and not *Auctorisque*, as other MSS read. Ludwig Traube surmised that *auctorumque* is the correct reading, because he believed P to be the poem at the very end of the *Rhetoric*. But the composite poem does not belong to Alcuin, though its various parts might well constitute separate versifications by Alcuin, formerly attached to some of his other didactic treatises.

The *schemata* (S) [8] placed—like the poem just dealt with—

---

[7] Ludwig Traube, *Karolingische Dichtungen* (Berlin, 1888), 50.

[8] Maurice Pallasse, *Cicéron et les sources de droits* (Annales de l'Université de Lyon, Droit III, 8; Paris, 1945), 119, surmises that Alcuin is the author of S.

between R and D are not by Alcuin, but probably by the unknown redactor of the joint edition of the two treatises. There
is no proof at all that Alcuin wrote them.

The origin of the joint edition in MSS of the ninth century
may be ascribed to the school custom of including the study
of rhetoric and dialectic under the broad heading of *logica*.[9]
In addition, the opening sentence of D (*PL* CI, 951D), which
refers to a preceding "philosophical" treatise, might have lent
encouragement to a joint edition of both treatises, though the
*Rhetoric* cannot have been the philosophical treatise. This joint
edition of Alcuin's treatises evidently reflects their use for the
study of *logica* in monastic schools of the ninth century. The
following lists of MSS and testimonies seem to corroborate
these conclusions.

## A. MANUSCRIPTS

Abbreviations

> pR – metrical *propositio* of R, ed. Halm, p. 525.1–8.
>
> R – *Disputatio de rhetorica et de virtutibus*, ed. Carl Halm,
>     *Rhetores Latini Minores* (Leipzig, 1863), pp. 525–550.
>
> S – *Schemata* of R and D, ed. Migne, *PL* CI, 945–950.
>
> P – composite poem of Alcuinian versifications, *PL* CI, 950,
>     and above.
>
> pD – metrical *propositio* of D, *PL* CI, 951C–D.
>
> D – *Dialogus de dialectica, PL* CI, 951–976.
>
> \* – Incomplete manuscript.

1. Munich 6407 (Frisingensis 207), about 800: R, S, P, pD, D.
2. Munich 13084 (Ratisbonensis civ. 84), s.IX: R, S, P.
3. Munich 14377 (St. Emmeram D.102), s.X: pR, R, S, P, D.
4. St. Gall 64, s.IX: D, pR, R.
5. St. Gall 273 s.IX: D, S, P, R.
6. St. Gall 276, s.IX: pR, R, P, pD, D.
\*7. St. Gall 855, s.IX: pR, R.

[9] Richard McKeon, "Rhetoric in the Middle Ages," *Speculum* XVII
(1942), 15.

*8. St. Gall 820, s.X: R.
*9. St. Gall 62, s.XIII: R.
10. Vienna 2484, s.IX: R, D.
11. Vienna 160, s.XIII: D, R.
*12. Vienna 2269, s.XIII: P, D,* pR, R.*
13. Vienna 5271, s.XVI: R.
14. Wolfenbüttel 579 (Helmstadt 532), s.IX: pR, R.
15. Brussels 1372 (9581–95), s.X: S, R, P, D.
16. Chartres 77, s.X: pR, R, P, pD.
17. Valenciennes 337, s.IX: R, P, D.
18. Valenciennes 404, s.IX: R.
19. Valenciennes 405, s.IX: R, D, pR.
*20. Cambrai 168, s.IX: R.
21. Vatican Urbinas lat. 308, s.XV: R.
22. Vatican Reginensis 342, s.IX in.: R, S, P, D.
*23. Vatican Reginensis 1209, s.IX: D,* R.*
24. Vatican Reginensis 1451, s.X: R, D.
25. Oxford Junius 25, s.IX in.: pR, R, S, D.
26. Berlin 176 (Fleury), s.X: pR, R, S, P, pD, D.
27. Zürich 80 (St. Gall), s.IX: pD, D, pR, R, S, P.
28. Leipzig Paulinus 1493, s.XI(?): pR, R, P, pD, D.
29. Halberstadt Domgymnasium, s.XII/XIII: pR, P, R.
*30. Stuttgart theol. quarto 262, s.XIII: R.

1–3. See Bernhard Bischoff, *Die südostdeutschen Schreiberschulen und Bibliotheken in der Karolingerzeit* I (Leipzig, 1940), 90, 119–120, 149–150, 218. Clm 13084 is a copy of Clm 6407. The content of Clm 6407 is minutely described by Heinz Löwe in *Deutsches Archiv für Geschichte des Mittelalters* VI (1943), 366–369. Clm 14377 offers S and P according to Migne, *PL* CI, 946, a fact not mentioned in *Catalogus Codicum Latinorum Bibliothecae Regiae Monacensis* II,2 (Munich, 1876), 164.
4. Gustav Scherrer, *Verzeichnis der Handschriften der Stadtbibliothek St. Gallen* (Halle, 1875), 29, designates pR as the *conclusio* of D, whereas it is in reality the metrical *propositio* of R; cf. also A. Bruckner, *Scriptoria Medii Aevi Helvetica* III (Geneva, 1938), 62.
5. Scherrer, *op. cit.*, p. 104, again overlooks that pR belongs to R.

13. See *Tabulae Codicum Manu Scriptorum in Bibl. Palatina Vindo-bonensi Asserv.* IV (1870), 81.
25. Cf. F. Madan, H. H. E. Craster, N. Denholm-Young, *A Summary Catalogue of Western Manuscripts in the Bodleian Library at Oxford* II,2 (Oxford, 1937), no. 5137, p. 970.
26. MSS Berlin 138 and 174, listed by W. S. Howell, *The Rhetoric of Alcuin and Charlemagne* (Princeton, 1941), 9, belong among the *testimonia*, since they contain but a few lines from R. See no. 43–44 below.
27. Cf. Cunibert Mohlberg, *Katalog der Handschriften der Zentralbibliothek Zürich* I (1932), no. 112, p. 46; A. Bruckner, *op. cit.*, III, 126.
28. See the description of this MS by Paul Piper, *Die Schriften Notkers* (Freiburg-Tübingen, 1882), XCf.
29. Cf. Moritz Haupt in *Berichte über die Verhandlungen der Kgl. Sächsischen Gesellschaft der Wissenschaften* II (1848), 53, 58–59.
30. Karl Löffler, *Die Handschriften des Klosters Zwiefalten* (Linz a. D., 1931), no. 103, p. 42; Theodor Merzdorf in *Intelligenzblatt zum Serapeum* (1859), no. 6, p. 43.

Sixteen of these MSS are from the ninth century. R and D are jointly preserved in seventeen MSS, of which eleven are from the ninth century. Eleven MSS contain R without D, but of these only three from the ninth century seem to offer the complete text of R. The predominance of ninth-century texts of R together with D is paralleled by their joint occurrence in the catalogues of medieval libraries and other book lists.

## B. TESTIMONIES IN BOOK LISTS AND MANUSCRIPTS

31. Reichenau, 821–822: De dialectica et rhetorica in codice I.
32. Reichenau, 835–842: libri duo Alcuini de rhetorica et dialectica.
33. St. Gall, 841–872:...Albini dialecticam et rhetoricam in volumine I.
34. Murbach, s.IX: de arte rhetorica de arte dialectica.
35. Fulda, s.IX: Alcuini dialectica...eiusdem de rhetorica lib. I.

36. Lorsch, s.IX: Disputatio de rhetorica; Item altera disputatio de rhetorica.

37. Puy, s.XI: Alcuinus de dialectica, rhetorica.

38. St. Amand, s.XII: Disputatio Albini et Karoli de dialectica et rhetorica.

39. Corbie, s.XII: disputatio Karoli et Albini.

40. Arnstein, s.XIII in.: Disputatio Karoli imperatoris et Albini magistri sui in I vol.

41. Prag, s.XIV: Dialogus Albini et Karoli de arte rhetorica.

42. Göttweg, s.XII: Rhetorica Alcvvni.

43. MS Berlin 138 (Fleury), s.X: fragment from R, ch. 47 (Halm, p. 550).

44. MS Berlin 174, s.X/XI: fragment from R, ch. 43 (Halm, p. 547)

45. MS British Museum 12Exxi, s.XIV: fragments from R, chs. 7 and 43 (Halm, pp. 527.38 ff., 547.35–37).

46. MS Munich 15813 (Salzburg), s.IX: fragments from R or S.

47. MS St. Gall 270, s.IX: pR.

48. MS Vienna 116 (Salzburg), s.X, f.1–5, excerpts from R.

48a. MS Trier Dombibliothek, s.IX(?): R. [Lost MS].

31–33. See Paul Lehmann, *Mittelalterliche Bibliothekskataloge* I (Munich, 1918), 250,17 f., 26 f.; 258,25 f.; 89,10 f.; for no. 33 see A. Bruckner, *Scriptoria Medii Aevi Helvetica* III (Geneva, 1938), 31 f.

34–41. Cf. Max Manitius, "Geschichtliches aus mittelalterlichen Bibliothekskatalogen," *Neues Archiv der Gesellschaft für ältere deutsche Geschichtskunde* XXXII (1907), 667 f.; "Nachträge," *ibid.* XXXVI (1911), 766; Max Manitius, *Geschichte der lateinischen Literatur des Mittelalters* I (Munich, 1911), 282.

42. Cf. Theodor Gottlieb, *Mittelalterliche Bibliothekskataloge Oesterreichs* I (Wien, 1912), 12, 16.

43–44. Valentin Rose, *Verzeichnis der lateinischen Handschriften der Kgl. Bibliothek in Berlin* I (Berlin, 1893), 308, 390.

45. *British Museum. Catalogue of Western Manuscripts* II, ed. Warner-Gilson (1921), 57, nos. 3 and 4; the editors overlooked the fact that the excerpt in no. 4 is from Alcuin's *Rhetoric*.

46. See *Catalogus Codd. Lat. Bibl. Reg. Monacensis* II,3 (1878), 35

47. A. Bruckner, *Scriptoria Medii Aevi Helvetica* III (Geneva, 1938), p. 90, refers to pR as *Schreiberverse* without realizing that they are the metrical *propositio*.

48. Cf. Max Manitius, *Geschichte der lateinischen Literatur des Mittelalters* II (Munich, 1923), 801.

48a. Cf. Paul Lehmann, *Erforschung des Mittelalters* (Leipzig, 1941), 237.

Nine of the preceding testimonies are from the ninth century; seven of these clearly refer to MSS which contained R and D in the same codex. A book donation (no. 33) made by Alcuin's pupil, Abbot Grimald of St. Gall, to the library of his abbey has been identified with the *Sangallensis* 276 (no. 6). Manitius identifies MS no. 25 with testimony no. 34; but Paul Lehmann assumes that the *Oxoniensis* came from Reichenau.

Another testimony (no. 49) to the joint transmission of R and D seems to be provided by Ermenrich of Ellwangen,[10] who, coming from St. Gall to Reichenau, wrote between 850 and 855 an abstruse *Epistula* dedicated to his patron Grimald. It is preserved in the *Sangallensis* 265, s.X. Ermenrich draws portions from R, S, and D in the following sequence: R, ch. 46; S, from *Porro sapientiam* (PL CI, 947) to *modum imponit* (col. 950); D, ch. 16 (PL CI, 972). These excerpts might indicate that Ermenrich's source was a MS of the ninth century, which jointly contained R, S, and D. The catalogue of the Reichenau Library of 821/822 (above nos. 31-32) lists two copies of such a MS, but neither has survived. Of the St. Gall MSS, our no. 6 suggests itself as the one perhaps used by Ermenrich, since it is supposed to be the copy given to the library by Grimald; but this codex does not seem to contain S. Thus *St. Gall* 273 (no. 5) is left as the possible source of Ermenrich, though the *variae lectiones* of S and Ermenrich's quotations from S are of little help in determining the probable relationship because of the lack of a critical text of the *schemata*.

[10] *MGH, Epistolae* V, 537-544.

The *Rhetoric* was also used (nos. 50–55) by Hrabanus Maurus,[11] by Notker Labeo,[12] by Benedictus Levita (see above, Ch. V), in two canon law books of the twelfth century, and probably also by Geoffrey of Vinsauf.

The transmission of the treatise in the MSS and testimonies, accordingly, reflects the fact that the treatise was studied during the ninth century, whereas in later centuries it was not so popular. There is, however, no reason at all to surmise with Howell that the large number of well-preserved copies from the ninth century, and the frequent listing of the work in the catalogues of monastic libraries of the ninth century, suggest why MSS of a later date are rare. The codices of the ninth century have come down to the present in such good condition because, first, they were apparently not too frequently used for study purposes, either then or in subsequent centuries. Even during the latter part of the ninth century the use of the *Rhetoric* as a textbook was rapidly declining; this seems to be the actual reason for the small number of MSS of a later date and for the good state of preservation of the extant codices. The composition of the treatise in the form of a simple compilation was no challenge to students of Roman authors, intensified study of whom was already noticeable during the first half of the ninth century. The predominantly Ciceronian character of Alcuin's rhetorical doctrines cannot have escaped their attention. But instead of studying Cicero in the form of Alcuin's excerpts from *De inventione*, they turned directly to Cicero's treatise. In the thirties of the ninth century, Lupus of Ferrières asked Einhard, then abbot of Seligenstadt, for a good copy of *De inventione*, since his own copy was too corrupt for his good taste.[13] About

[11] *De vitiis et virtutibus* III, *PL* CXII, 1253D, 1254BD, 1255A, quotes from the *Rhetoric*, chs. 35, 44–45, ed. Halm, pp. 549.27–28, and 548 f.

[12] See O. A. L. Dieter, "The Rhetoric of Notker Labeo," *Papers in Rhetoric*, ed. Donald C. Bryant (Saint Louis, 1940), 27–33.

[13] *MGH, Epistolae* VI, 7–9; ed. Leon Lévillain (Paris, 1927), whose dating of the letter I follow.

the same time, Paschasius Radbertus of Corbie was sufficiently acquainted with Cicero's treatise to quote from it in his correspondence. Regardless of the veneration accorded by his own age to Alcuin's great educational work of organization, the older tradition of learning connected with the seven liberal arts—to which Alcuin likewise belonged—was naturally still stronger than the individual expression Alcuin gave to it through his *Rhetoric.* Notwithstanding Alcuin's significance, Cicero's *De inventione* continued to be used in the liberal arts program of the monastic schools of St. Gall, Fulda, Corbie, Tours, and elsewhere, rather than Alcuin's excerpts from the treatise. Alcuin's treatise could not find a place in the extensive curricula of the rapidly developing cathedral schools. To understand why Alcuin's *Rhetoric* was not included in the study plans of these episcopal schools, one has only to read the account of Richer [14] of the curriculum followed by Gerbert, later Pope Sylvester II, when he taught at the cathedral school of Reims, or the metrical report by Walther of Speyer [15] on the curriculum of St. Gall, introduced at the Speyer cathedral school by Balderich (970–986), one of the most erudite pupils of the Swabian abbey. In the light of these developments, the doctrinal influence of Alcuin's *Rhetoric,* whose main source—Cicero's *De inventione* —was well known and accessible to students of the ninth century, cannot have been very great, even during that century. Nevertheless, the treatise is an interesting product of learning, considering its author and his purpose in composing it, and as such deserves a modern edition. Halm's edition of 1863 is based on only three *Monacenses* (nos. 1–3 above). Since then Stroebel, Lehmann, and Howell have supplemented the Ciceronian tes-

[14] Richer, *Historiae* III.46–47, ed. Robert Latouche (Paris, 1937), 54–56. Cf. Wallach, "Education and culture in the tenth century," *Medievalia et Humanistica* 8 (1955), 18–22.
[15] See the *Preface* to the *Vita S. Christopheri,* ed. Karl Strecker, *MGH, Poetae* V.

timonia incompletely listed by Halm, who seems to have substituted the classical Latin spellings for the original, medieval spellings of the MSS,[16] and therefore also for Alcuin's spellings. In addition to extant Carolingian MSS, we now have at our disposal for Alcuin's spellings his treatises, *Ars grammatica* and *De orthographia*,[17] which contain his theories and will help a future editor in choosing the proper variants.

[16] See the criticisms of Halm's edition by T. Stangl, "Zur Kritik der lateinischen Rhetoren und Grammatiker," *Xenien: Der 41. Versammlung deutscher Philologen dargeboten vom historisch-philolog. Verein München* (München, 1891), 27–38; cf. also the review of Hermann Sauppe in *Göttingische gelehrte Anzeigen* (1864), 2013–2036, and in Sauppe, *Ausgewählte Schriften* (Berlin, 1896), 410–423.—Stangl's corrections of Halm are not used by Howell.

[17] Cf. Aldo Marsili, *Alcuini Orthographia* (Pisa, Italy, 1952), a critical edition of the treatise.

*Part Two*

---

# ALCUIN'S ACQUAINTANCE WITH

# PROCEDURES OF FRANKISH LAW

ALCUIN'S choice of the *quaestiones civiles* as the sphere in which he would apply the full force (*tota vis*) of the art of rhetoric (H.525.10) was not only determined by his academic knowledge of rhetorical doctrine, but also by his practical experience in matters of law. He considered rhetoric a civil science, probably adopting the definition of Cicero (*De inv.* I.5.6). References to, and quotations from, Roman and canon law books which are found in his correspondence prove his acquaintance with actual law cases and with Frankish procedures of law. This fact is evident from Alcuin's controversy with Theodulph of Orléans and Charlemagne concerning the case of a condemned cleric. Five *Epistles* (nos. 245–249), which testify to the existence of additional documents no longer extant, enable us to reconstruct the various stages and developments [1] of the quarrel between Alcuin and Charlemagne. The twelve documents connected with the case are here given in chronological order; the asterisk indicates that the document is lost.

1.* A letter of Theodulph of Orléans addressed to Charlemagne, reporting the escape of the condemned criminal and invoking the ruler's aid.

[1] Arthur Kleinclausz, *Alcuin* (Paris, 1948), 273–275, misinterprets some of the stages in this development. See below, n. 3.

2.\* *Indiculus commonitorius,*[2] issued by the king's court at law to Theodulph, empowering him to request the return of the fugitive into his custody. This document is referred to in no. 7 (below) as Charlemagne's "first order" ("nostrae primae iussionis" —*Ep.* 247, D.400.2–5).

3.\* A letter of Theodulph, addressed to Alcuin, abbot of Tours, in content probably almost identical with no. 4 (below). This letter is critically discussed by Alcuin in no. 6 (below): "sicut in eius legebatur litteris; in venerabilis episcopi litteris invenimus" (*Ep.* 245, D.394.16.40).

4.\* A letter of Theodulph to Charlemagne, acknowledged by the king in no. 7: "litterae a Theodulfo episcopo missae" (*Epist.* 247, D.399.41 ff.). Theodulph's letter arrived at the royal court one day ahead of no. 5\* (D.399.40).

5.\* A letter of Alcuin to Charlemagne, referred to in no. 7 (below): "a vobis missa venisset epistola" (D.399.40); "ad nos missa... epistola" (D.401.3 f.). The content of this letter was in all likelihood identical with nos. 6 and 6a (below). It included the comparison of the case in question with that of the Apostle Paul (Acts 24).

6. *Epistle* 245 (D.393–398.2) of Alcuin to his friends Witto and Fridugis at the court of Charlemagne, requesting their intervention and outlining to them his theory of the historical development of the right of sanctuary on the basis of Roman and canon law sources.

6a. *Epistle* 246 (D.398–399) of Alcuin to an unknown Frankish bishop, possibly at the court of Charlemagne, in content almost identical with no. 6.

7. *Epistle* 247 (D.399–401) of Charlemagne to Alcuin and the Brethren of Tours. Actually it is a *placitum (Gerichtsurkunde),*[3]

[2] See on these documents Heinrich Brunner, *Deutsche Rechtsgeschichte* II (2nd ed.; Munich-Leipzig, 1928), 186 f. On the law of the Frankish empire see generally Hermann Conrad, *Deutsche Rechtsgeschichte* I (Karlsruhe, 1954), 94–205; Jacques Ellul, *Histoire des Institutions* I (Paris, 1955), 709–773.

[3] Not listed by Rudolf Hübner, *Gerichtsurkunden der fränkischen Zeit* I (Appendix to *Zeitschrift der Savigny-Stiftung für Rechtsgeschichte* XII

reporting the decision of the royal court at law, severely repri-
manding the actions of the addressees reported to the king with
the documents nos. 3*, 4*, and 5*, and announcing an impend-
ing *inquisitio per testes* by an especially appointed royal *missus*
and judge (see no. 8*).

8.* *Indiculus inquisitionis,*[4] citing *fratres* of St. Martin at Tours before a royal court, "ad placitum nostrum" (D.401.2), presided
over by the *missus ad hoc* Teotbertus (D.402.25).

9. *Epistle* 248 (D.401) of Alcuin to Arno of Salzburg, recommend-
ing to his care one of his fratres, surreptitiously removed from
the scene, and out of the reach of Theodulph. In *Epistle* 270
(D.428 f.) Alcuin seems to admonish some "innocent lamb"
(*vitulus*) to lead a virtuous life.

10.* Report of Teotbertus (see no. 8*, above) to Charlemagne on the
facts established by his investigation as to the origin and the
participants in the riots at Tours.

11. *Epistle* 249 (D.401–404) of Alcuin to Charlemagne, assuring him
of his and his brethren's innocence, notwithstanding the accusations that came to light during the *inquisitio,* and imploring the
emperor's forgiveness, favor, and mercy for himself and the
*fratres.*

---

(Germanist. Abt., 1891). W. von den Steinen, *Karl der Grosse: Leben und
Briefe* (Breslau, 1928), 99–101, correctly designates the letter as a
*Gerichtsurkunde.* Kleinclausz, *op. cit.,* 274 f., wrongly states that this letter
was written after the *inquisitio* had taken place; on the contrary, it an-
nounces the *inquisitio* and clearly precedes it. Cf. also Cesare Manaresi,
*I Placiti del "Regnum Italiae"* (Fonti per la Storia d'Italia; Roma, 1955).

[4] On these documents see Brunner, *op. cit.* II, 690.—Von den Steinen,
*Historische Zeitschrift* 191 (1960), 367, and after him Heinz Loewe, *Göttingische gelehrte Anzeigen* 214 (1962), 147, identify the *vitulus* in No. 9
(*Epist.* 248) with one of Alcuin's young *fratres* (see pp. 103-106). Loewe's
designation of *Epist.* 247 (p. 100, No. 7, above) as a mandate is incorrect,
notwithstanding his reference to Harry Bresslau, *Handbuch der Urkundenlehre* I (3rd ed.; Berlin, 1958), 52 n. 3, because certain essential
*formulae* of this type of document are missing in the letter. It is indeed a
*placitum,* as also von den Steinen (above, n. 3) recognized long ago.

# CHAPTER VII

# The Quarrel with Charlemagne
# concerning the Law
# of Sanctuary

A CLERIC under the jurisdiction of Theodulph of Orléans had been found guilty of some crime in a publicly conducted court action and was subsequently retained in the custody of the bishop of Orléans. He somehow escaped from prison and fled to the Basilica of St. Martin at Tours, claiming the ancient right of sanctuary. Theodulph reported the incident to Charlemagne (no. 1*), whose court empowered Theodulph through an *indiculus commonitorius* (no. 2*) to seek the extradition of the criminal from his refuge. The fugitive was subsequently turned over (D.393.37; 398.14) to messengers sent from Orléans to Tours. But the menacing attitude of the *fratres* of St. Martin toward the Orléanists on their way through the church and the atrium forced the visitors to abandon their captive in front of the basilica. Thus Theodulph's men arrived empty-handed at Orléans. They returned to Tours reinforced, and as Alcuin thought, in larger numbers than the occasion warranted. On the Sunday after their return, eight of Theodulph's men (D.394.1;

398.20) led by Joseph, the local bishop of Tours, entered the Basilica of St. Martin in order to remove the fugitive from his refuge—with the consent, to be sure, of the residing bishop. But the *fratres* of St. Martin expelled the intruders from the church (D.394.5; 398.23), only to be forced afterward to rescue them from the wrath of the "common mob" (*vulgus indoctum*).[1] This is Alcuin's derogatory designation of the assembled townspeople and peasants who, misunderstanding the proper legal procedures, were excited by the appearance of strange, armed men and, incited by rumors that the men of Orléans were desecrating the sanctuary of their patron saint, warded off the alleged invaders by force. The crowd went for its cudgels (*ad fustes*, D.403.20) and engaged in a brawl with Theodulph's representatives. These, however, were extricated by some of the less excited *fratres* and led to safety into the monastery of St. Martin under the guidance of one *Amalgarius* (D.403.30–33), the only *vassus* of St. Martin then on the premises, who upon Alcuin's request helped to quell the riot and to rescue Theodulph's men. Theodulph thereupon quickly informed (no. 4*) Charlemagne of the riot which frustrated the ultimate execution of the royal request (no. 2*) and obviously accused Alcuin (see no. 3*) of being the instigator of, and the *fratres* of being participants in, the local riots. The emperor also received from Alcuin a report on the events (no. 5*) which undoubtedly was, by and large, identical in content and tenor with letters no. 6 and 6a. Alcuin, not relying solely on his own presentation of the case, however, at the same time wrote a detailed *Epistle* (no. 6) on the happenings and the motivation of his own actions to his friends at the court, whom he asked to intervene in his own and his brethren's behalf. An almost identical *Epistle* (no. 6a) went to an unknown cleric, also at the court, who probably wielded some influence with

[1] An Augustinian expression, *De civitate dei* IV.1.

Charlemagne. The reports of Theodulph and Alcuin on the riots at Tours (nos. 4* and 5*) were read at a session of the royal court, probably presided over by Charlemagne or by his substitute as the highest judge, i.e., the *comes palatinus*. The decision of this court at law was couched in rather irate and harsh words that might well mirror Charlemagne's anger at Alcuin and the congregation at Tours. They were severely reprimanded (D.400.2.26) for disregarding the emperor's first expression of authority (no. 2*) in the case. Though Alcuin's letter to Charlemagne (no. 5*) cleared himself and his *fratres* from the charge of sedition (D.401.3), some of the brethren had to stand trial before a special royal court under the *missus ad hoc* Teotbertus on the charge of inciting a riot, or—as Alcuin repeatedly terms it—a *tumultus* or *concursus*.[2] The emissary's investigation into the origin and the most likely instigators of the riot produced evidence unfavorable to Alcuin and the *fratres*, some of whom suffered, probably on account of contradictory statements, the punishment of lashes and chains. Considering the close relationship between the emperor and Alcuin, the royal judge probably informed (no. 10*) Charlemagne of the court's findings. Alcuin also sent a detailed report (no. 11) to the emperor, in order to offset the results of the investigation, attacking the judicial procedure of Teotbertus and passionately questioning the testimony elicited by force. Alcuin repeatedly assured his friend of his own innocence and belittled the proved participation in the brawl at Tours of some of the *fratres*, who allegedly acted not with intent, but on impulse and without much thought.

The name of the culprit who caused the disagreement between the three friends and the nature of the crime committed by him are unknown. The inexorable attitude of Theodulph, however, and his merciless prosecution of the case might suggest

[2] D.394.10; 398.27.31; 402.18.41; 403.9.16.26.27.31.32.

some capital offense. The fugitive apparently stayed at the basilica up to the time of the arrival at Tours of Charlemagne's court order (no. 7), which requested his delivery into the hands of Theodulph. It seems that, at this very moment, Alcuin made another contribution to the controversy by surreptitiously sending one of his infantes to his friend Arno of Salzburg, introducing him as an "innocent lamb" (*vitulus*) which must be torn from the grasp of its enemies, especially from the hands of Theodulph of Orléans (no. 9). Remembering Alcuin's predilection for the analogy, one may well believe that his characterization of a young monk as a *vitulus* harks back to the passage from Cicero's *De inventione* II.31.95 referring to the law "that no one should sacrifice a *vitulus* to Diana," a passage inserted verbatim by Alcuin in the *Rhetoric* (H.525.8).

There is little doubt that the emperor's decisions (nos. 2* and 7) correspond to the then current law of the Frankish capitularies. On the other hand, Alcuin's opposition to Charlemagne's concept of the right of sanctuary, based by him on certain canons of councils held at Orléans during the sixth century and on the Roman law of the *Breviarium Alaricianum*, correctly represents—as we shall see—the Church's traditional interpretation of the law of sanctuary. The actual origin of the controversy is thus the result of a clash between the Church's, i.e., Alcuin's, and Charlemagne's opposing views with regard to the refuge to be accorded to a condemned fugitive from justice. How much these views are at variance with one another will become more evident in the course of the following treatment of various aspects of the case: Charlemagne's court order (no. 7), Alcuin's arguments against the emperor's interpretation of the law of asylum, the *inquisitio per testes* of a royal court conducted at Tours, and finally the reception of the *Breviarium Alaricianum* as the code of Roman vulgar law used at the court of Charlemagne.

The historical importance of Charlemagne's court order (*Epistle* 247, D.399–401) sent to Tours warrants the insertion of a translation of the document: [3]

In the name of the Father and of the Son and of the Holy Ghost. Charles [Most Serene Augustus, crowned by God, great peace-making Emperor, governing the Roman Empire, and also by the mercy of God King of the Franks and of the Lombards] to the Venerable Magister Alcuin and the entire congregation of the Monastery of St. Martin [at Tours].

The day before your letter [no. 5* above] reached our presence, a letter was brought to us from Bishop Theodulph [no. 4*], containing complaint of dishonor done to his men, or rather to the bishop of your own city [Tours], and in contempt of the order of our Empire. Which order we caused writ under the authority of our name for the delivery of a certain cleric, escaped from the bishop's custody, and in hiding in the Basilica of St. Martin, a confirmation of which you have sent to us. In it we think that we did not decree anything unjustly, as you have thought we did.

We have had both letters [nos. 4* and 5*] read to us again, yours and Theodulph's. Your letter appears to us to be much harsher than Theodulph's, and to have been written in anger, without any seasoning of charity toward him, in defense of the fugitive, and in accusation against the bishop. Under cover of a concealed authority it maintains that the accused person could and should be allowed to bring an accusation, whereas both divine and human law forbids to allow a criminal to accuse another person. For this reason he was defended and protected by you, under pretext of the authority of our name; as though one who had been accused and judged in sight of the people of his own city of Orléans should have an opportunity of bringing an accusation by appeal to the Emperor, after the example of the blessed Apostle Paul [Acts 24–25]. But Paul, when accused by his

[3] See G. F. Browne, *Alcuin of York* (London, 1908), 235–238; I have occasionally changed Browne's translation. The last sentence of the charter is mistranslated by him; "inustum crimen" is not the "unjust crime," but "the crime with which you have been branded."

own nation before the princes of Judea, but not as yet judged, appealed to Caesar, and by the princes he was sent to Caesar to be judged. That does not at all coincide with the present case. For this cleric of evil repute was accused, and judged, and sent to prison, and thence escaped, and contrary to law entered the basilica, which he ought not have entered till after he had done penance, and still—it is said—ceases not to live perversely; this man you say has appealed to Caesar in the same manner as Paul. But he certainly is not coming to Caesar as Paul did.

We have given orders to Bishop Theodulph, by whom he was judged and sent to prison, and from whose custody he escaped, that he be brought back; and the bishop must bring him to our audience, whether he speaks truth or falsehood; for it consists not with our dignity that for such a man as this there should be any change of our original order.

We greatly wonder that to you alone it should seem fit to go against our authoritative sanction and decree, when it is quite clear, both from ancient custom, and from existing law, that [imperial] ordinances must be obeyed and that no one is permitted to disregard edicts and statutes. And herein we can not sufficiently marvel that you have preferred to yield to the entreaties of that criminal fellow, rather than to our authoritative commands, since by now it is perfectly obvious that through his breach of charity a spirit of dissension —so to say—emanates from this place [Tours].

Now you yourselves, who are called the congregation of this monastery and the servants of God—I only hope true ones—know how your way of life is now frequently spoken of by many, and not without cause. You declare yourselves sometimes to be monks, sometimes canons, sometimes neither. And we, acting for your good and to remove your evil repute, looked for a suitable master and rector for you and invited him to come from a distant province. He [Alcuin] by his words and admonitions, and—for that he is a religious man— by his example of good conduct, could have amended the manner of your life. Unfortunately, all has turned out the other way, and the devil has almost found in you his servants for sowing discord among those to whom it is least becoming, namely, the sages and doctors of the Church [i.e., between Alcuin and Theodulph]. And you drive those who ought to correct and chastise sinners into the sin of envy and wrath. But they, by God's mercy, will not lend an ear to your evil suggestions.

And you, who stand out as condemners of our command, whether you be called *canonici* or monks, know that you are arraigned before our royal court at law, as our present *missus* will indicate to you; and although your letter sent to us here excuses you of actual sedition, you must come and wash off by suitable amends your crime with which you have been branded.

This document is very strongly phrased and undoubtedly mirrors Charlemagne's personal anger about the entire affair. The analysis of the letter's legal contents will reveal some clues concerning its author.

The disregard shown by Alcuin to the first order of the emperor is severely criticized by the author, who stresses the irrevocability of imperial decrees and the crime of ignoring them, "nec cuiquam permissum illorum edicta vel *statuta contemnere*" (D.400.29), having in mind the *interpretatio* [4] of the *Breviarium Alaricianum* I.1.2 (*Codex Theodosianus* I.1.2), *De constitutionibus principum et edictis:* "Leges nescire nulli liceat aut quae sunt *statuta contemnere*." [5]

The reference to the lost no. 2* in the passage "quam iussionem...sub nostri nominis auctoritate *conscribere iussimus*" (D.400.2) is identical with the formula—used in Charlemagne's diplomata—called the *Beurkundungsbefehl*, i.e., the expression of the ruler's command to issue a charter in his name. This

---

[4] The text of the *Breviarium Alaricianum* is used in the edition of the *Codex Theodosianus* by T. Mommsen and Paul M. Meyer, I,2 (Berlin, 1905). The references are always to the *interpretatio,* not to the *Legaltext* of the Code. Cf. also Gustavus Haenel, *Lex Romana Visigothorum* (Leipzig, 1849); Max Conrat (Cohn), *Breviarium Alaricianum: Römisches Recht im Fränkischen Reich* (Leipzig, 1903).

[5] The same *interpretatio* is quoted by Hincmar of Reims, *De ordine palatii,* ed. Victor Krause, *MGH, Capitularia Regum Francorum* II (Hannover, 1897), 520.25.

formula belongs to that part of the charter called the *dispositio*, the legal expression of the king's authority. Its formularized wording in many of Charlemagne's charters is "propter hanc praeceptionem auctoritatis nostrae *conscribere iussimus*." [6] This diplomatic formula, used otherwise only by scribes of the imperial capella, here indicates that an *indiculus commonitorius* (see no. 2\*) was issued by Charlemagne's court to Theodulph after the arrival of the latter's complaint (no. 1\*) reporting the frustration at Tours of the king's command. According to the formulary of such an *indiculus*, no. 2\* must have contained the request that Alcuin and the *fratres* of Tours comply with the demand of Theodulph and return the fugitive to his custody. In case of a refusal, the party who refused to execute the royal request had to appear before the king and give his reasons. The formulary of the *indiculus* expressly provides for such a negation of the royal request: "...si...aliquid contra hoc habueritis ...ad nostram veniatis praesentiam." [7] This procedure was adopted in the case under consideration. In the end, Charlemagne (D.400.24–26) clearly refers to it when stating that the fugitive, regardless of whether he is telling the truth or whether he is lying, should be brought by Theodulph before the king's court (ad nostram audientiam), since it is not proper that for the sake of such a criminal any change be made in the king's first order (quia non decet ut propter talem hominem nostrae primae iussionis ulla fit immutatio)! Had there not been a riot at Tours,

[6] See Harry Bresslau, *Handbuch der Urkundenlehre für Deutschland und Italien* II (2nd ed.; Leipzig, 1915), 96; cf. *MGH, Diplomata Karolinorum* I (ed. E. Mühlbacher; Hannover, 1906), DK.81 of 774 (p. 117.21); DK.83 (p. 120.2); DK.104 (p. 149.1), etc., frequently in various types of charters. The same formula occurs in the *Formulae Imperiales*, ed. K. Zeumer, *MGH, Formulae Merovingici et Karolini Aevi* (Hannover, 1886), no. 40 (p. 318); no. 53 (p. 326).

[7] Cf. Heinrich Brunner, *Die Entstehung der Schwurgerichte* (Berlin, 1872), 78 f.; Brunner, *Deutsche Rechtsgeschichte* II (2nd ed.; Munich-Leipzig, 1928), 186 f.; *Formulae Marculfi* I, nos. 26–29, ed. Zeumer, pp. 59–61.

but a peaceful presentation of the refusal before a royal court, as provided for in the formulary of the *indiculus*, the events of the case would have run a different course. Although the disregard of a royal command was a legitimate procedure to bring the accused party of an *indiculus commonitorius* before the king as the highest legal judge, this disregard could not find its expression in the breaking of the king's peace. Since, in this case, the peace was broken, a new, even more serious point was added to the already existing issues.

The fact that each of the letters received from Alcuin and from Theodulph (nos. 4* and 5*) was written by its respective author *cum iracundia* (D.400.7), each undoubtedly hurling accusations against the other, must have weakened Charlemagne's trust—and that of his court at law—in the reliability of the evidence submitted by both parties. His observation is reminiscent of the *Brev. Alaric.* IX.1.3 (*CTh* IX.1.5), which rejects the validity of a charge made by one person against another when in an angry and excited frame of mind (Si quis iratus...). Such accusations, if not repeated in writing, *post iracundiam*, are to be ignored. The request that the accusations be made without *iracundia* also appears in the capitularies. The subjects of a bishop, for instance, are advised not to act "iracundia commoti" (*MGH, Cap.* I.110.82).

The charge that Alcuin advocated the *licentia criminandi* of a criminal, suggesting that the fugitive is entitled, and should be permitted, to level accusations against Theodulph (vel posset *vel admitti* ad accusationem *deberet*), clearly refers to the denial of this *licentia* in the *Brev. Alaric.* IX.1.7 (*CTh* IX.1.12): "The allegations made against others by accused criminals shall not be given credence until they should prove themselves innocent, because their statement against anyone is dangerous, and must not be permitted" (*et admitti non debet* rei adversum quemcumque professio). And to accuse the bishop of Orléans, as Alcuin does, was especially prohibited (specialiter prohibetur), since nobody should dare to accuse a bishop before secular judges (apud publicos iudices—*Brev. Alaric.* XVI.1.2.; *CTh* XVI.2.12).

The statement that the criminal had been publicly tried by Theodulph at Orléans (in conspectu populi civitatis suae—D.400.13), again conforms to the interpretation of the *Brev. Alaric.* XVI.1.3 (*CTh* XVI.2.23), which decrees that the cleric involved in a criminal allegation should be brought to the attention of the judge of his municipality (ad notitiam iudicis in civitate, qua agitur, deducatur). Thus the criminal was not tried by an ecclesiastical court, though one might at first think he had been, since Theodulph, then the bishop of Orléans and shortly afterward, i.e., after April, 801, the city's archbishop,[8] loomed so prominently in the case. The criminal was at first tried by a secular court, probably presided over by Theodulph as special imperial *missus* [9] and not as ecclesiastical judge. This secular trial was then followed, in accordance with current practice,[10] by a second trial of the cleric before an ecclesiastical tribunal, *secundum canones*, with Theodulph presiding this time in his capacity as bishop of Orléans and superior to the criminal. The "canonical penitence" imposed by this court is referred to in one of Alcuin's letters (D.398.15). Charlemagne's *placitum* mentions the fact that the fugitive entered the Basilica at Tours, contrary to law, before he had done proper penitence (quam nisi post poenitentiam ingredi non debuerat, contra legem ingressus—D.400.20). The competence of the secular court in criminal cases involving members of the clergy is repeatedly mentioned in the *Lex Romana Curiensis*, a version of the Visigothic Code, which was strongly imbued with elements of Frankish court procedures of the eighth and ninth centuries.[11]

[8] See Alcuin's congratulatory letter, *Epist.* 225 (D.368).

[9] See Edgar Loening, *Das Kirchenrecht im Reiche der Merowinger* II (Strassburg, 1878), 531 n. 1.

[10] *Ibid.*, 530.

[11] See Elisabeth Meyer-Marthaler, "Das Prozessrecht der Lex Romana Curiensis," *Schweizerische Zeitschrift für Geschichte* III (1953), 23.

The public riots at Tours were looked upon as *seditio* (D.401.3) in accordance with *Brev. Alaric.* IX.23.1 (CTh IX.33.1), which deals with persons who, contrary to imperial command (iussio), attempt to incite people against the established order and thus disturb the king's peace (Si quis populum ad seditionem concitaverit). Indeed, sedition was the charge leveled against Alcuin and his *fratres* (D.403.9; incitatores) by the investigating judge of the royal court. Though Alcuin was cleared of the charge of *seditio* (D.403.4) on the basis of the *deperditum* no. 5,* some of his *fratres* and *canonici* had to stand trial on the charge of having participated in a public riot.

There is finally in the *Gerichtsurkunde* (D.401.1) the formulalike parallelism between *canonici sive monachi*, who are summoned before the royal *missus* in order to expiate their crime (condigna satisfactione) and the recommendation of the *Capitula de examinandis ecclesiasticis* of 802 (*MGH, Cap.* I.110.2.5): *canonici vel monachi...condigna satisfactione.*

The analysis of legal elements in Charlemagne's *placitum* (*Epist.* 247, D.399–401) makes it clear that the court charter hardly represents Charlemagne's dictation, though its brash bluntness probably runs true to the anger he felt for the violators of his laws. The charter must have been written by a scribe of the court, i.e., a *Gerichtsschreiber*, and not by a member of Charlemagne's *capella*, who acted as his chancery staff. This court scribe was not only familiar with some legalistic formulas and the Roman vulgar law of the Visigothic Code, but also, as we shall see, with the Frankish legislation of the capitularies. The latter background of the *placitum* may be shown through an analysis of Alcuin's arguments in favor of his interpretation of the case as expressed by him in two letters to friends of his at the court of Charlemagne (nos. 6 and 6a).

Alcuin summarized his position in the case by listing three points under the headings *si iustum sit,...et an aequum sit,...et utrum fas sit* (D.394.17–23; 398.36–39). He suggested to his friends at the court of Charlemagne that they beg the emperor to arrange a meeting between Theodulph and himself in order to provide him with an opportunity to dispute with Theodulph *"whether it is just* that an accused person should be taken by force from a church and subjected to the very punishments from which he has fled; *whether it is right* that one who has appealed to Caesar should not be brought to Caesar; and *whether it is lawful* to spoil of all his goods, down to his shoe-lace,[12] a man who is penitent and has confessed his sin." There was no denying the misdeeds and vicious crimes of the fugitive (D.399.1), who had properly confessed his sins to Christian and Adalbert, two presbyters of Tours, before he suffered the penalties of arrest and chains. Alcuin's further statement that the criminal *poenis torqueretur* (D.399.1–5) can hardly mean that the fugitive was punished with the rack, since torture was, as a rule, not applied to members of the clergy. On the contrary, Alcuin argued, the penitent criminal had suffered the penalty of his crime and therefore had every right to enter a church. This opinion was, strangely enough, not shared by Theodulph, who rather unceremoniously called the fugitive a *devil* (D.394.40). Against such an attitude Alcuin counseled that nobody is so great a sinner as not to find redemption in the Church (D.394.40–395.24). "Be zealous," he says, "but moderately fanatical" (sit zelus, sed moderate saeviens).

The points at issue as stated by Alcuin in the *deperditum* no. 5* were rejected in the decision of the court (*Epist.* 247). The first question, whether an accused person should be taken by force from a refuge, was answered in the affirmative, because the fugitive entered the Basilica at Tours *contra legem* (D.400.20), before having done proper penitence. This decision of the royal court conforms, if not in letter at least in spirit,

---

[12] D.394.21 (cf. D.398.38):...spolietur omnibus bonis usque *corrigiam* calciamenti; cf. Isa.5:27 nec rumpetur *corrigia calceamenti (scil.* inimici); Gen.14:23...ad corrigiam caligae, non accipiam.

to title 8 of the *Capitulare Haristallense* of 779 (*MGH, Cap.* I.48), according to which the punishment of condemned criminals was not annulled in case they should gain refuge in a church. The second question (D.394.20), whether a person's request to be brought before Caesar can be denied, was again confirmed by the court, because the *ius reclamandi* did not apply to persons found guilty by a court. Title 8 of the *Capitulare missorum* of 805 (*MGH, Cap.* I.123 f.) states that this *ius* must be claimed in writing to the king *before* the judgment of a court has been found and spoken. If the appeal was submitted after the judgment, the appeal was looked upon as a subterfuge and therefore held invalid.[13]

The court decision unequivocally states that a criminal convicted in accordance with divine and human laws cannot accuse another person (D.400.10): "et divina et humana lege sanccitum sit *nulli criminoso alterum accusandi dari licentiam.*" This is the law of title 36 in the Capitulary of Frankfurt of 794 (*MGH, Cap.* I.77), which stipulates that criminals do not have the privilege of leveling accusations against persons of higher station or against the bishops in whose territory they reside: "DE CRIMINOSIS: *ut non habeant vocem accusandi* maiores natu aut episcopos suos." This law seems to be a combination of title 35 of Charlemagne's *Admonitio Generalis* of 789 (*MGH, Cap.* I.56) with the previously mentioned law of the *Brev. Alaric.* IX.1.7 (*CTh* IX.1.12) concerning the *licentia accusandi* of a condemned criminal. Furthermore, the interpretation of the *Brev. Alaric.* IX.1.11 (*CTh* IX.1.19) determines that the testimony of a confessed criminal shall not be credited when he accuses another person.

Alcuin's comparison of our case with that of the Apostle Paul in Acts 25:11, who, accused by the orator Tertullus, had demanded the right to state his case in person before Felix, the

---

[13] Heinrich Brunner, *Forschungen zur Geschichte des deutschen und französischen Rechtes* (Stuttgart, 1894), 138.

Roman governor, was vehemently rejected in the court order
"quod nequaquam praesenti negotio convenit" (D.400.16).
Paul's request was granted because at the time it was made the
Apostle had not yet been found guilty (nondum iudicatus),
while the *infamis clericus* (D.400.18) had already been properly
sentenced (iudicatus) in public court action before making his
appeal to Charlemagne. This is the reason why the criminal
could not be granted free access to the emperor. He could be
brought before him only upon official request and as the prisoner of his first judge (cf. *MGH, Cap.* I.123 f.), i.e., of Theodulph. The refusal of Charlemagne's court to accept an appeal
from a sentenced criminal is analogous to the provisions of the
*Brev. Alaric.* XI.11.1 (*CTh* XI.36.1): If persons should be
convicted or should confess that they are guilty of certain
crimes and then should wish to appeal the sentence, the delay
prescribed by law for an appeal against the execution of the
sentence shall be denied. The wording of the court order proves
that Alcuin himself argued in favor of the fugitive by pro-
ducing the case of the Apostle Paul as an analogous precedent.

In the *Rhetoric*, Alcuin illustrates judicial oratory, which
includes accusation and defense, by referring to the case of the
Apostle Paul (Acts 24), who was permitted to plead his case
before the representative of Caesar (H.527.4–7): "The judicial
[kind of oratory] is that kind in which there is accusation and
defense, as in the Acts of the Apostles [Acts 24] we read how
the Jews through a certain orator, Tertullus, accused Paul before Felix, the governor, and how Paul defended himself before
the same governor. For in judicial oratory *what is just* is more
often inquired into" (Nam in iudiciis saepius *quid aequum sit*
quaeritur). We note that here and in Alcuin's letters addressed
to his lobby at the imperial court (D.394.20; 398.37) one of the
three arguments listed by him is *"an aequum sit."*

It can hardly be maintained that the example of Paul in the
*Rhetoric* and Alcuin's attempt to find in Acts 24 a legal prece-

dent are accidents. One could well argue that our case, involving three friends, must have appeared to Frankish contemporaries as a scandal of major proportions with strong suspicions of lese majesty. And taking into account the number of documents written and issued during the controversy, the case must have been in the public eye for at least a year. Alcuin's longstanding friendship with Charlemagne must have received quite a jolt, and his basic disagreement with the emperor might well have been the ultimate reason for the writing of the *Rhetoric*. He would wish to show the king that legal procedure is based on an established system whose theory finds expresson in the art of rhetoric and that this system includes accusation *and* defense, plaintiff *and* defendant, and the witnesses of both parties. This purpose in writing the *Rhetoric* probably accounts for the insertion in the book of an *ordo iudicialis* (see Ch. V). For Alcuin was puzzled by the legal procedures observed by the royal judge at Tours, who—so Alcuin bitterly complains to Charlemagne—acted arbitrarily, without questioning Alcuin and his witnesses and without paying heed to Alcuin's defensive arguments. But Alcuin's resentment against the judge's employment or nonemployment of witnesses was unjustified; it reveals to us the exact nature of Alcuin's misunderstanding of the royal judge's activities.

Alcuin here confused the position of the *testes* in the typically Germanic *inquisitio testium* with the quite different nature of the *testes* in a specifically Frankish *inquisitio per testes*, the latter being the procedure employed by the *missus* Teotbertus when investigating the happenings at Tours. While in the former procedure accusation, defense, and witnesses were provided by both parties of the case, the *testes* in the *inquisitio* of the royal *missus* were not called by the plaintiff and the defendant but chosen (testes rogati) by the *missus* himself from among the *boni homines*, i.e., the honest, well-known, established residents of the locality and its neighborhood where the court action took place. The testimony of these free men was the basis of the *missus'* findings, which were in no way influenced by any other type of witness.

Charlemagne's rejection of Alcuin's analogy between our case and that of the Apostle Paul was justified. Alcuin's use of such an analogy proves either his inability to grasp the legal mechanics of the typically Frankish *inquisitio per testes* or else his refusal to recognize royal jurisdiction in such an investigation over members of the clergy. We must stress the fact that the request of a cleric to be judged before a secular court, i.e., a royal tribunal, and not by an ecclesiastical court, is as such not rejected[14] by the decision of the court (D.400.23–26), if this request is submitted to the royal court by the metropolitan[15] under whose jurisdiction the cleric stands. An analysis of the activities of the royal court that convened at Tours shows them to be typical of a Frankish *inquisitio*.

## THE *INQUISITIO PER TESTES* AT TOURS

A special royal court (placitum nostrum) was held at Tours upon Charlemagne's command (D.401.2), and the *missus ad hoc* Teotbertus (D.402.25) conducted the *inquisitio* into the origin of the riots which prevented Theodulph's men from carrying out legal actions ordered by the authority of the Frankish king. The names of some of the persons who had to appear before this missatic court are listed in Tironian notes in the Paris MS B. N. 2718[16] at the very end of Charlemagne's court order: several clerics from the Basilica of St. Martin at Tours, a deacon and a provost, also Giraldus the son of Gislarius, the presbyters Gislefridus and Sifridus, and other *fratres*, and six old retainers

[14] Cf. Georges Lardé, *Le Tribunal du cleric dans l'empire roman et la Gaule Franque* (Moulins, 1920), 156 f.

[15] See Johann Adam Ketterer, *Karl der Grosse und die Kirche* (München, 1898), 171 f.

[16] See Guilelmus Schmitz, *Monumenta Tachygraphica Codicis Parisiensis Latini 2718* I (Hannover, 1882), 35 to no. 45.

of the monastery. The complaints of Alcuin (*Epist.* 249) addressed to Charlemagne describe the activities of the court proceedings.

The investigation lasted for nineteen days (D.402.25), which would indicate that a large number of persons were interrogated by the judge. The *inquisitio* opened with a promissory oath on the Bible and the Cross made by those of the congregation of St. Martin who were chosen (upon the *missus'* own discretion) to be questioned: "...the holy gospel was brought; there was laid upon it the wood of the holy Cross; they made such of the brethren as they chose, swear by that" (sanctum allatum est evangelium, ligno sanctae crucis superimposito; quoscumque iusserunt iurare ex fratribus, fecerunt—D.403.23). Alcuin resentfully mentions the presence at the proceedings of "accusatores nostri" (D.402.26; 403.22), probably the eight men of Theodulph who were chased from the basilica when they attempted to carry off the fugitive. These and some *fratres* were undoubtedly questioned by the royal emissary. Since the charge to be investigated was sedition (D.401.3), the interrogation of *testes* sought the ringleaders of the riot, the "incitatores...huius tumultus" (D.403.9) and the circumstances that led to the riots. The *missus* discovered that the alarm bells of the basilica were rung—not, as one might have expected, by the *fratres* of the monastery, but by "the ignorant people, always doing thoughtlessly inconvenient things" (vulgus indoctum—D.403.19–22), who mistakenly believed that the invaders had come to carry off the criminal by force. This fact was confirmed even by Theodulph's men, "immo et ab ipsis accusatoribus nostris" (D.403.22). The bells drew the monks from the refectory to the scene of the brawl, since they were alarmed by them (D.403.25). The testimony also apparently produced some evidence and some statements pointing to Alcuin as the wirepuller behind the scene, the one who actually instigated the opposition against the royal court orders. The fact that such charges were brought out against Alcuin by some of the interrogated persons must be deduced from Alcuin's vehement denial of having had anything to do with the *concursus* or *tumultus* (D.402.18). It happened— he states—without his instruction, premeditation, or intent (nec me exhortante vel praesciente vel etiam volente factus est). The investigation further revealed that those of the *fratres* who actually participated in the brawl were mere children (infantes), as Alcuin contemptuously reports (D.403.27). They declared that they acted on their own, upon nobody's advice, but, as Alcuin explains, on the spur of the moment from sheer foolishness (ex impetu stultitiae). Alcuin stresses the fact that only one of the many vassals of St. Martin actively participated in the riot. The *vassus* Amalgarius (D.403.30 ff.) happened to be visiting with Alcuin when the turmoil started. Upon his abbot's request, and aided by some *fratres*, he rescued Theodulph's eight men and Joseph, the local bishop of Tours, from the cudgels of the mob (ad fustes cucurrerunt—D.403.20), leading them through the free-for-all to the safety of the monastery.

The judge's procedure of investigation and the punishment meted out are angrily summarized by Alcuin in the letter to Charlemagne (D.402.27): "Whom he wished, he whipped; whom he wished, he put in chains; whom he wished, he questioned under oath; whom it pleased him, he called before your presence" (i.e., the royal court). In this fashion Alcuin registers his dislike for the procedure of the judge who acted, as Alcuin suggests in a completely arbitrary manner, citing persons before his tribunal, interrogating them after having administered to them an oath on the Bible and the Cross, and finally punishing some on the basis of the evidence collected and judged by him.

The *missus* seems to have been empowered, however, not only to conduct a special *inquisitio*, i.e., to investigate and to report to the royal court, but also to judge the findings of the investigation. He must have received a *mandatum ad inquirendum et definiendum*, not only a *mandatum ad inquirendum et referen-*

*dum.*[17] Though his judgment constituted the *definitiva sententia*, Teotbertus in all probability also reported the outcome of the inquiry and the sentences he had imposed to Charlemagne. An appeal against such a judgment was impossible, since, contrary to a mistaken assumption of scholars, the Frankish king and his court did not dispense justice on the basis of the law of equity.[18] The ruler, however, possessed and exercised the right of amnesty and mitigation. Alcuin made use of the privilege of appeal and reported to Charlemagne his disagreement (*Epist.* 249) with the *missus'* procedures of law, which he characterized as high-handed and arbitrary. Simultaneously, he apologized for the participation in the riot by some of his brethren, and he countered the accusations against their bad way of life expressed in Charlemagne's court decision (*Epist.* 247) by citing the opposite findings of the royal *missus* Wido, margrave of Brittany, "a gentleman and incorruptible judge" (D.402.6), to whom Alcuin had dedicated the treatise *De virtutibus et vitiis* (*Epist.* 305, D.464). In addition, Alcuin assured the king that he himself had not been remiss in teaching "the honesty of monastic life" (honestas morum—D.402.8).

Alcuin argues throughout his letter against the procedure of the royal court which, it seemed to him, used only accusation and not, as he obviously expected, accusation *and* defense. He

---

[17] Heinrich Brunner, "Zeugen- und Inquisitionsbeweis der karolingischen Zeit," in *Forschungen zur Geschichte des deutschen und französischen Rechtes* (Stuttgart, 1894), 197 f.

[18] Cf. Paul Kirn, "*Aequitatis iudicium* von Leo dem Grossen bis zu Hinkmar von Reims," *Zeitschrift der Savigny-Stiftung für Rechtsgeschichte* 52 (Germ. Abt., 1932), 53–64. That *aequitatis iudicium* does not mean "Billigkeitsgericht" but a just sentence may be deduced also from the occurrence of the term in Charlemagne's letter to Offa of Mercia (*Epist.* 100, D.145.27); Alcuin uses the expression in the same manner in *Epist.* 249 (D.404.4) and 305 (D.464.26); cf. also Alcuin, *De virtutibus et vitiis*, ch. 20 (*PL* CI, 628C) following Isidore of Seville's *Sententiae;* see further *Epistles* 17, D.47.11; 119, D.174.19; 288, D.447.7; 124, D.183.4.

complains that the testimony of the *fratres* was not readily accepted (si quis eorum testimonio credendum putat—D.402.9), while on the other hand the plaintiffs from Orléans seemed to have had the ear of the court (D.402.26; 403.22). Though Alcuin and his friends helped Charlemagne reorganize (in or before 802) the institution of the Frankish *missus* (*Epist.* 186, D.312.26), Alcuin seems to misunderstand the function of the so-called *testes rogati* in the missatic *inquisitio per testes*. For the "testes" of this inquiry were neither procured nor selected by the plaintiff or the defendant. They were selected at will by the royal emissary from the trustworthy men—called in the sources *boni homines* or *optimi pagenses*—of the place where the events to be investigated had occurred. Their report was irrefutable. The accused party could not call his own witnesses. The position occupied by the witnesses (testes) selected by the *missus* was not just that of ordinary witnesses, but more like that of jurors who were expected to answer truthfully the questions put to them by the royal judge, because they were loyal subjects of their sovereign. They promised to tell the truth not only on their promissory oath (D.402.27;403.24), which lent more authority and credence to their replies, but also on the strength of the oath of allegiance sworn as subjects of their king and emperor. The intentional withholding or concealment (celare) of truthful information was thus looked upon as a violation of one's loyalty toward the ruler, since it might have been of help to violators of royal laws. The personal relationship between subject and king was the basis of the judge's expectation that the questions of his court would be answered truthfully by the interrogated persons. The scribe of Charlemagne's court order had in mind this concept of the basic loyalty of a king's subject when he reproached Alcuin for referring in a letter to the king to something "sub velamine quodam *celati* nominis" (D.400.9). The official Frankish commentary of the *Capitulare Missorum Generale* of 802 (*MGH, Cap.* I.92.40) on the oath of allegiance forbade anyone "to abstract or conceal" information from the courts (neque abstrahere vel *celare* audeat). If, for instance, someone knew of the activities of poachers in royal forests (*Cap.* I.98.c.39), "let him not dare to conceal this (nullus hoc *celare* audeat), in order that he may preserve the fidelity which he has promised to us."

The fact remains that Alcuin was indeed guilty (in his *Epistle* 249) of concealing his part in the outbreak of the riots at Tours. The evidence is rather overwhelming, notwithstanding his re-iterated assurances to the contrary. To be sure, he emphatically denies all knowledge of, and participation in, the riots (D.402.19), but the extant documents—all except one from his own pen—contradict his allegations. At the same time, he can hardly escape the accusation of sanctimoniousness. In order to obscure his share of responsibility in the riots that were to him such an "impious crime" (D.402.30.37), he uses as alibis his long service in the Church (D.402.30.36), his old age (twice mentioned), his physical weakness, and his retirement (D.402.39) upon Charlemagne's advice from the "tumult" of this world. Not for the gold of all *Francia* (D.402.31) would he have lent his support to such a dangerous undertaking, Alcuin maintains.

Alcuin's final account of the origin and the originators of the riots must have appeared to Charlemagne and the members of his court at law an insult. Ignoring the information known to the king from letters he had received from Alcuin and from Theodulph (nos. 1*–5*), from Alcuin's own lobby at the court (nos. 6 and 6a), and from Teotbertus' report of his findings, Alcuin now offered "without blushing" his version of the "truth" (D.402.41), summarized in three points and to nobody's disadvantage.

Alcuin argued that the real sinner in the case was Theodulph, the bishop of Orléans, who was actually responsible for all the evil because his negligence enabled the criminal to escape. Not the fugitive but Theodulph ought to be put in irons, an opinion which Alcuin—on the basis of a rather arbitrary Biblical exegesis —considered to be "Domini roboratus sermone" (D.403.6). He might also have thought of the interpretation of the *Brev. Alaric.* IX.2.2 (*CTh.* IX.3.5), which states that "if the negligent prison guard is not able to produce the escaped prisoner, he shall know that he will undergo either the fine or the punishment which the escaped prisoner would have undergone."

Secondly, the instigators of the riots (incitatores—D.403.9) were Theodulph's armed men, who entered Tours in numbers larger than warranted by the occasion and thus incited the people to rise and defend the *patrocinia* of their patron saint.

And, finally, the riots broke out (instigatio—D.403.16) as the result of the open co-operation of Joseph, the local bishop of Tours, with the armed men of Theodulph, who on a Sunday unwisely entered the basilica with them in order to remove the fugitive from the sanctuary. The presence of Joseph drove the ignorant and misinformed mob to violent action against the intruders. The brethren of St. Martin, who upon Alcuin's request got involved in the riots, saved the bishop and Theodulph's men from the fury of the incensed mob. And yet, Alcuin whined, the rescued men, once safe within the protecting walls of the monastery, full of hatred for him, ungratefully accused him of feeding them (D.402.34) with malicious joy (obprobium; D.403.34)—in view of their precarious situation.

Alcuin's version of the events at Tours is diametrically opposed to the actual facts of the case as we know them from the extant documents. Theodulph's men, he says, and not the *fratres* of St. Martin, incited the mob to riot and to defend the peace of their patron saint's *patrocinia*. In this fashion the accusations leveled by Theodulph against Alcuin and his brethren were diverted by Alcuin toward Theodulph and his emissaries. This feat of sophistry was achieved by the application of the rhetorical concept called *remotio criminis*, as described in Alcuin's *Rhetoric* on the basis of Cicero's *De inventione* (H.531.10):

"What is known as the shifting of the crime (evasion) occurs when the formal complaint made by the plaintiff is diverted by the defendant towards some other person, or towards some other antecedent fact. This shifting of the complaint may be accomplished in two ways. Sometimes the motive, sometimes the deed itself, is shifted." [19]

Alcuin's assertions (D.402.29–40) that the record of his past life gives the lie to his inciting the riots corresponds to the method recommended in his *Rhetoric* (H.538.18) for defending an accused person by showing the spotlessness of his reputation:

The defendant should show first, if he can, that his life has been most honorable and most steadfast . . . and that his deeds, if they must be mentioned at all, are to be praised for having been done well and faithfully and bravely; and that it is a sorry spectacle indeed if such marks of good conduct are darkened by so insignificant an accusation. Or he should show that the deed was done not as a result of covetousness or malice or disloyalty, but rather by accident or in ignorance or at the instigation of another.

*Purgatio*, "denial of intent," the first of the principles of "open acknowledgement" (concessio), is applied by Alcuin when he belittles the proved participation in the riots of some young *fratres* of St. Martin (D.403.25). He calls them disdainfully *infantes*, who acted upon nobody's suggestion, *ex impetu stultitiae*, on an impulse of naïveté or ignorance. This argument is clearly the application of the concept of *purgatio* (H.532.5): "Denial of intent occurs where the intent of him who is accused, and not his act itself, is made the subject of the defense; and this has three aspects, ignorance, chance, and necessity. Denial of intent through ignorance occurs when he who is indicted denies that he understood something or other."

Alcuin's use, in his letter to Charlemagne (*Epist.* 249), of

[19] See W. S. Howell, *The Rhetoric of Alcuin and Charlemagne* (Princeton, 1941), 85; the translations in the two following sections see *ibid.* 109 and 89.

rhetorical doctrines of defense dealt with in the *Rhetoric* may therefore be taken as additional evidence for our thesis that Alcuin pursued practical purposes in writing the treatise. We note as the especially significant feature of this letter the absence of any explicit mention of the law of sanctuary, which looms so significantly in two of Alcuin's letters (*Epistles* 245 and 246) sent to members of his lobby at the court of Charlemagne.

# CHAPTER VIII

# Alcuin's Theory of the Law of Sanctuary and the "Reception" of the *Breviarium Alaricianum*

ALCUIN'S outline of his theory of asylum in a church (*Epist.* 245–246) was designed to supply his friends at the Frankish court with his point of view as opposed to that of Theodulph of Orléans, with whom Charlemagne and his royal court at law evidently had sided. The text compiled by Alcuin consists of instances of canon law and Roman law sources interspersed with historical and pseudohistorical references, dealing, directly and indirectly, with the main topic under consideration. The partly academic nature of the texts cited can hardly have escaped the attention of the compiler. For Alcuin must have realized that the only valid law of asylum in the Frankish empire was the law actually promulgated in Charlemagne's capitularies. The method applied by Alcuin to his catena is akin to the one he previously had used so successfully in the official Frankish white papers against the heresy of adoptionism, documents which he had written upon the express request of Charlemagne. But while the texts in these political pamphlets were drawn— for the most part—from patristic sources, the texts document- ing the law of sanctuary were taken mainly from legal sources. Though Alcuin's collection *in asylis* indeed offers some of the most important sources concerning the history of the law of sanctuary in the Latin West,[1] its relevance to the alleged viola- tion of the law at St. Martin's of Tours is rather doubtful, if not altogether mistaken. For that case—as has been pointed out—concerned the secular Frankish law and did not represent the theological treatment of a problem historically documented by Alcuin. What we have before us is Alcuin's expert opinion on the subject, an opinion repeatedly requested by Charlemagne in theological controversies, but this time given without solicita- tion. Alcuin's disagreement with Theodulph's execution of established Frankish law was fundamentally responsible for the disagreement among the three friends.

The analysis of this collection of texts will plainly show the historical reasoning that was such an important part of Alcuin's independent personality. There is ample reason to look upon these texts as the result of one of Alcuin's endeavors at reform —an endeavor in which he failed. The principle to be proved by Alcuin was the inviolability and the preservation of the *honor ecclesiarum* (D.397.33), the freedom or peace of churches, in their role as places of refuge. He found support for this in the canons of earlier synods and in imperial laws. A brief synopsis[2] should be of help in the subsequent discussion of the texts.

---

[1] See Pierre Timbal, *Le droit d'asile* (Paris, 1939), 181 n. 2; for the Frankish period see Willibald M. Plöchl, *Geschichte des Kirchenrechts* I (Wien-München, 1953), 225 f., 379 f.; Hans Erich Feine, *Kirchliche Rechtsgeschichte* I (2nd ed.; Weimar, 1954), 66. The best outline is still that by Paul Hinschius, *Das Kirchenrecht der Katholiken und Protes- tanten in Deutschland* IV (Berlin, 1888), 380–387.

[2] Alcuin, *Epist.* 245, D.395–397.

CANONES "De fugitivis ad ecclesiam"

I Orléans 511, c.1: Criminals who take refuge in a church may be taken from this refuge only (eos abstrahi omnino non liceat... nisi) if the injured person or his relatives promise on oath to abstain from vengeance and to be satisfied with penance. (The punishment for breaking this oath is excommunication.) [3]

IV Orléans 541, c.21: The violation of the law of asylum resulting in the removal of the fugitive by means of force or deception (seu vi seu dolo abstrahere aut sollicitare fortasse praesumpserit) entails excommunication, the lifting of which depends upon the return of the abducted person to his refuge in the church.[4]

V Orléans 549, c.22: If a slave takes refuge in a church he may not be handed over to his master until the latter has forgiven him on his oath. Should the master violate this promise, and in some way torture the slave, he is to be excommunicated.[5]

Agde 506, two apocryphal canons, ascribed to the Synod of Agde,[6] but culled from the *Collectio Hibernensis*, c.38.3 and 38.9a,

---

[3] Dümmler's text is corrupt; we must read with *Conc. Aurelianense* of 511, c.1 ed. F. Maassen, *MGH, Concilia Aevi Merovingici* (Hannover, 1893), 2 f.: "eos abstrahi omnino non liceat; sed nec aliter [not alteri!] consignari, nisi...sint securi (ita ut ei, cui reus fuerit, criminosus de satisfactione conveniat)." This first canon of I Orléans 511 is missing in the *Collectio codicis Laureshamensis* (see below, n. 4), which offers the canons of IV Orléans 541, c.21, and V Orléans 549, c.22; I Orléans 511, c.1, is, however, contained in the *Collectio Hibernensis* (see below, n. 7).

[4] Dümmler 396.1 reads "eo tamen qui *a se raptus*, prius ecclesiae restituto"; see F. Maassen, *op. cit.*, 92.7: "eo tamen, qui abstractus est,...] *a se raptus* N = Cod. Vaticanus Palatinus 574, s. IX, the so-called *Collectio codicis Laureshamensis*.

[5] According to Alcuin D.396.2, titulus 21. This fact indicates that Alcuin's transmission is related to that of the *Coll. codicis Lauresh.* (see above, n. 4), where c.22 precedes c.21; see F. Maassen, *op. cit.*, 107.

[6] Not contained in the acts of the Council of Agde 506, written by Caesarius of Arles, ed. Germain Morin, *Sancti Caesarii Opera* II (1940), 36–89.

*De civitatibus refugii:* [7] Murderers are not to be driven from the protection of a church in which they are protected against any kind of punishment, provided that they give satisfaction to the injured party; . . . no faithful Christian who takes refuge in a church should be expelled; he should do penance there according to the decision of a judge.

Appendix (historical example): Apocryphal law of Emperor Constantine the Great, drawn from the *Actus Sylvestri*,[8] the basic source of the notorious *Constantine Donation:* On the fifth day after his baptism Constantine decreed a law automatically granting the law of asylum to every church.

## IMPERIAL LAWS FROM THE *LEX ROMANA VISIGOTHORUM*, THE *BREVIARIUM ALARICIANUM*

*Brev. Alaric.* IX.34.1 (*Codex Theodosianus* IX.45.4),[9] *De his qui ad ecclesias confugiunt* (On those persons who flee for sanctuary to the churches), Constitution of Emperors Theodosius II and Valentinian III, 23 March 431, with Intitulation and date line (but without *Legaltext*) and the pertinent INTERPRETATIO: "Churches and places dedicated to God shall so shelter accused persons who flee to them driven by fear that nobody shall dare to bring force and violence to holy places in order to seize accused persons; but we decree that whatever space belongs to the church either in the colonnades, or in the halls, in the houses, or in the courtyards adjacent to the church, shall

---

[7] See Timbal, *op. cit.*, 118 n. 2; Herrmann Wasserschleben, *Die Irische Kanonensammlung* (2nd ed.; Leipzig, 1885). Cf. Paul Fournier and Gabriel Le Bras, *Histoire des collections canoniques en Occident* I (Paris, 1931), 62 ff., on the *Hibernensis.*

[8] Ed. Bononius Mombritius, *Sanctuarium seu Vitae Sanctorum* II (2nd ed.; Paris, 1910), 513.19; Dümmler reads 369.13 *Quarta die*, but Mombritius' text, like Dümmler's MS S1, offers *Quinta*. Wilhelm Levison, *Aus Rheinischer und Fränkischer Vergangenheit* (Düsseldorf, 1948), 397, assigns Alcuin's excerpt to the version A1 of the *Actus*. See also Eugen Ewig, "Das Bild Constantins des Grossen im abendländischen Mittelalter," *Historisches Jahrbuch der Görresgesellschaft* 75 (1956), 38.

[9] See Chapter VII n. 4; cf. Clyde Pharr, *The Theodosian Code* (Princeton, 1952), 266, and 230 for the following item.

be looked upon just as the inner parts of the temple, so that the drive of fear may not constrain criminals to remain around the altars or to defile places deserving of reverence."

*Brev. Alaric.* IX.2.3 (*Cod. Theod.* IX.3.7), *De custodia reorum* (On the custody of accused persons), Constitution of Emperors Honorius and Theodosius II, 25 January 409, with Intitulation and date line (but without *Legaltext*) and the pertinent INTERPRETATIO: "On every Lord's Day judges shall provide that accused persons shall be led out from prison under trustworthy guard, in consideration of religion. If any of the judges should neglect to fulfill this regulation, he shall be compelled to pay the penalty which the law itself has established."

*Brev. Alaric., Pauli Sententiae* V.28.1, Sententia [10] (entitled by Alcuin, D.396.18, *De eis qui caesarem appellant vel ad principem se duci flagitant*): The person who is responsible, directly or indirectly, for the death, torture, whipping, and public chaining of a *civis Romanus*, who has appealed to the emperor (ad imperatorem), makes himself punishable under the *Lex Iulia de vi publica*.

*Brev. Alaric., Pauli Sententiae* V.28.2, INTERPRETATIO: The *Lex Iulia* decrees that every judge is punishable on the charge of public violence (pro violentia publica), if he is responsible for outrages listed in *Pauli Sententiae* V.28.1 and inflicted on a Roman citizen who has appealed to, and requested to be led before, the *princeps*; on this charge persons of lower station suffer capital punishment, those of higher station are deported to an island.

Appendix (historical example): Alaric I, this "paganus rex" (Alcuin D.397.8), plundering Rome on 24 August 410, ordered his soldiers to spare those who had fled to churches and to restore abducted cult objects. Orosius, *Historiae adversum paganos* VII.39.1: "Alaric appeared, laid siege to trembling Rome, and broke into the confused city, after first, however, giving orders that particularly those who had taken refuge in

---

[10] In the edition by Johannes Baviera, *Fontes Iuris Romani Antejustiniani* II (Florence, Italy, 1940), 412: *Pauli Sententiae* V.26.1.

sacred places, especially in the basilicas of the holy Apostles
Peter and Paul, should be left unharmed and unmolested";
VII.39.4–6: "all the vessels just as they were, should be
brought back immediately to the basilica of the apostle" (qui
continuo *reportari* ad...).[11]

The genuine and apocryphal *canones* here listed were taken
by Alcuin from a collection of canons related to the so-called
*Collectio codicis Lauresbamensis*[12] of the *Vaticanus Palatinus*
574, saec. IX, and from the *Collectio Hibernensis*, which
originated in all probability in Brittany. The imperial laws and
the *Sententiae* of Paulus were drawn from the *Breviarium
Alaricianum*, the two historical examples from the *Actus
Sylvestri* and from Orosius.

The first three canons, from synods held at Orléans during
the sixth century, should have convinced the *pontifex* of
Orléans—Theodulph—that he could not act contrary to the
synodal decisions. Furthermore, Alcuin asks (D.395.31), is it
lawful and honest that the pontiff of the *civitas* of Orléans
should dare to infringe upon the *auctoritas* of his own city?
The first canon of I Orléans of 511, which decrees the adoption by the church of the *Lex Romana* (Visigothorum), might
well have induced Alcuin to thumb through the *Breviarium
Alaricianum* (perspectis cautissimis Romanorum libris *or* legibus
—D.396.17) and then to cite the two constitutions of Roman
emperors and the sections from Paulus' *Sententiae*. The alleged

---

[11] Alcuin's quotation may be added to the Orosius *testimonia* listed by
C. Zangemeister in his edition, *CSEL* V (Wien, 1882), 707. On the historical accuracy of Orosius see Pierre Courcelle, *Histoire littéraire des
grandes invasions germaniques* (Paris, 1948), 217 f. Cassiodorus, *Variae*
XII.20, ed. T. Mommsen, *MGH, Auct. Antt.* XII, 376, uses Alaric's rescue
of *vasa sacra* as a historical example in a letter to Roman treasury
officials, thus justifying the return of cult objects pawned by Pope Agapit
I. Erich Caspar, *Geschichte des Papsttums* II (Tübingen, 1933), 206,
seems to overlook the fact that Cassiodorus' illustration is from Orosius.

[12] See above, nn. 3, 4, 5, 7.

imperial law of Constantine is cited to prove the protection of churches ordered by one of Charlemagne's predecessors.

In case the quoted sources from canon and Roman laws were not sufficient to prove the inviolability of the law of asylum [13] in churches, since they were considered only lesser authorities (minores...auctoritates—D.397.16), then one could refer to the Biblical laws *de fugitivorum civitatibus*, that is, to the cities of refuge in Exod. 21:13, Num. 35:11–15, Deut. 4:41–43, 19:1–13.

Thinking of the asylum said to have been established by Romulus [14] at Rome, Alcuin continues to argue that even the pagan Romans, in order to mitigate the severity of their laws, instituted an asylum at Rome and cities of refuge elsewhere in the world.

The train of argument in favor of unrestricted asylum in churches is here also presented under the influence of the imperial laws of Charlemagne's predecessors, Constantine the Great, Theodosius II, Honorius, and Valentinian III (ut antecessores sui statuerunt—D.397.36). Alcuin fervently believes that the "christianissimus et serenissimus imperator domnus Carolus" [15] will abide by the decisions of canon and Roman laws.

Alcuin clearly indicates his belief in the Biblical origin of the Christian law of asylum in churches, but argues that the law must be preserved, because even pagans honored such a law. With like reasoning he stresses the freedom accorded churches during the sack of Rome by Alaric I, who, being an Arian Christian, is unceremoniously called by him a "Barbarian King." Since Theodulph and the Frankish king have violated the basic

[13] Cf. Leopold Wenger, "Asylrecht," in *Reallexikon für Antike und Christentum* I (Stuttgart, 1950), 836 f.

[14] Cf. *Thesaurus Linguae Latinae* II (1906), 990, s.v. De asylo a Romulo constituto; Augustine, *De civitate dei* 1.34, 2.29, 5.17.

[15] Alcuin, *Epist.* 245, D.397.34; the same intitulation also in *Capitulare Missorum Generale* of 802, *MGH, Capitularia* I no. 33, p. 91.41: Serenissimus igitur et christianissimus domnus imperator Karolus.

freedom of a Christian church at Tours, as Alcuin mistakenly believes, their disregard of this fundamental *honor ecclesiae* is contrasted by him with the pagan Roman practice and observance of the law of asylum in their holy places. With feeling he asks: [16]

Is it right that the Church of Christ receive less freedom (minoris esse honoris) among Christians than the Temple of Jupiter (templum Iovis) had received among pagans?

And is it right that the House of Blessed Mary, Mother of God, be held in lower esteem (inferioris venerationis haberi) than the sanctuary of impious Juno (impie Iunonis asylum, [Virg. *Aen.* 2.761])?

And is it right that the Blessed Martin himself (the Patron Saint of Tours), true servant of God, be less revered (minus venerari) in the Christian Empire (in christiano imperio, [of Charlemagne]) than the imposter Aesculapius in the realm of the pagans?

The trend of Alcuin's thought is quite obvious. He argues *a minore ad maius:* since the law of asylum was recognized and honored even in pagan temples by pagan Romans, all the more should the *honor ecclesiarum* (D.397.33), the freedom or peace of the churches, be respected by Christians. This argument again shows that Alcuin adhered to the fundamental concept of the Church, according to which the law of asylum was ordained for all Christian churches on the analogy of the Biblical cities of refuge (D.397.15–18), to which Alcuin allots—as we have seen—an authority greater than that of canon and secular laws. He held that the Christian law of asylum did not necessarily depend on special secular sanction and laws, as was the case among the pagan Romans. He assumed an independent origin of the Christian law, in no way inspired by the pagan Roman idea of sanctuary, though the comparison of both institutions appears among the topics of early Christian apologetics against the Roman pagans.

[16] Alcuin, *Epist.* 245, D.397.21–25

Augustine, in *De civitate dei* I.4, for instance, develops the contrast between the asylum of Juno at Troy (Virgil, *Aen.* 2.761), which was "not the holy place from which it was forbidden to remove captives, but a prison house to encage them," and the basilicas of the apostles at Rome, which protected all who took refuge in them from the barbarian hordes of Alaric.

The theme that one cannot deny to Christian asylums what had been granted to those of the pagans occurs in the acts of councils.[17] One example must suffice. The First Synod at Macon, 585, c.8, complained of pseudo-Christians who, regardless of previously tendered oaths, violated the law of asylum and abducted persons (*fugitivos subtrahere*) who had sought sanctuary in sacrosanct churches. The author of the synodal acts asks: Since secular rulers have decreed immunity for anybody who should flee to their statues (ut, quicumque ad eorum statuas fugiret, inlesus habeatur), how much more should those remain unpunished who are heirs of the patrocinia of the Kingdom of Heaven?

Alcuin had in mind a restoration of the Biblical law of asylum guaranteeing impunity to those who fled to churches, regardless of their guilt. This concept of the Christian law of sanctuary was actually at the bottom of his quarrel with Theodulph. Had this not been the case, he would hardly have failed to quote among his texts, together with the *sententia* of *Pauli Sententiae* V.28.1 and the *interpretatio* of V.28.2, the sententia of V.28.2, which expressly excludes persons who had been found guilty by a court and those who had already confessed their crimes (*iudicati etiam et confessi*) from the possibility of appealing to the emperor, a provision that clearly applies to the case of the criminal illegally sheltered and defended by Alcuin.

The cumulative comparison between the *honor* respectively

---

[17] See J. Gröll, *Die Elemente des kirchlichen Freiungsrechtes* (Kirchenrechtliche Abhandlungen 75–76, 1911), 255; for the Synod of Macon see F. Maassen, *MGH, Concilia Aevi Merovingici* (Hannover, 1893), 168.

accorded to pagan and to Christian asylums also appears, quite significantly, as a point of argument in a Frankish capitulary. Charlemagne decreed in the *Capitulatio de partibus Saxoniae* of 785 [18] that "the churches of Christ [in Saxony] may have no less *honor* [freedom or peace], but greater and better *honor* than the vanities of the [Saxon] idols had enjoyed." The wording "*...ecclesiae Christi...non minorem habeant honorem* sed maiorem et excellentiorem quam vana habuissent idolorum," is reminiscent of the rhetorical question posed by Alcuin (D.397.20): "*An fas est apud Christianos minoris esse honoris ecclesiae Christi* quam templum Iovis apud paganos?" The decisive element in Charlemagne's order is that the freedom, the *honor*, of the churches in Saxony is plainly connected with the freedom formerly inherent in the pagan places of worship, and not at all with the tradition of the Church's law of asylum. The reason for this is to be seen in Charlemagne's role as defender and protector of the Church, since he himself was the only authority actually disposing of the *honor ecclesiae*,[19] that is, the freedom of the churches, because all churches in his realm were protected by the *bannum* of the Frankish king and as such were automatically under the protection of the king's peace, the *pax regis*.

The quotations from the *Breviarium Alaricianum* in Alcuin's list of legal texts, together with our proof (in Ch. VII) that the *Alaricianum* was also used by the unknown court scribe of Charlemagne's *placitum* (*Epist.* 247), enables us now to arrive at certain conclusions with regard to the disputed "reception" of the Visigoth Code by Charlemagne and the use made of it in Carolingian judicial practice.

Alcuin's citations from the lawbook clearly presupposed the

---

[18] *MGH, Capitularia* I no. 26, p. 68, c.1; on 785 as the proper date as suggested by Louis Halphen see F. L. Ganshof, *Wat waren de Capitularia?* (Brussel, 1955), 106.

[19] See the references in the capitularies collected by Martin Siebold, *Das Asylrecht der römischen Kirche mit besonderer Berücksichtigung seiner Entwicklung auf Germanischen Boden* (Münster, 1930), 104 f.

recognition and "reception" of the code by Charlemagne, by his councilors, and by Alcuin's friends at the court; otherwise Alcuin's citations would have been meaningless. And Alcuin, who had an intimate knowledge of the emperor's acquaintance with legal procedures, doubtlessly knew best how to conduct his own case with some reasonable expectation of success. As a matter of fact, Alcuin seems to have been so certain of the authoritative legality of the code that he even conformed with the technical provision of the *Brev. Alaric.* I.1.1, an edict by Constantine the Great from the *Codex Theodosianus* I.1.1,[20] which determined that the legal validity of imperial constitutions depended on the presence in such documents of the date line and the names of the consuls in office. For this reason Alcuin included in his excerpts these parts of the two imperial constitutions. Thus the scribe of the court charter (*Epist.* 247) and Alcuin (D.396.18) depended on *lex scripta,* as was requested in the *Capitulare Missorum Generale* of 802, c.26, "that judges lawfully judge in accordance with written law (*secundum scriptam legem*), and not at their own discretion." [21]

The question remains whether Charlemagne ever decreed the formal reception of the law book which, by the ninth century, had acquired widespread legal authority in the Frankish empire. Heinrich Brunner [22] surmises that the care known to have been extended by Charlemagne to the written law codes of his realm was also accorded to the *Lex Romana Visigothorum,* of which the Frankish king had had official copies made for practical use. The *Breviarium* [23] was the law code for persons of Gallo-Roman

---

[20] Mommsen, *Theodosiani Libri XVI* I,2 (Berlin, 1905), 27: INTER-PRETATIO: Quaecumque leges sine die et consule fuerint prolatae, non valeant.

[21] *MGH, Capitularia* I no. 33, p. 96.19 f.; the *Annales Laureshamenses* ad a. 802 (see *MGH, Concilia Aevi Karolini* I.230) follow the Cap. of 802 and read:...ut iudices per scriptum iudicassent.

[22] *Deutsche Rechtsgeschichte* II (2nd ed.; Leipzig, 1906), 515.

[23] See A. von Wretschko in Mommsen's *Theodosiani Libri XVI* I,1 (Berlin, 1905), CCCVII ff., especially CCCXIII ff.; Hans von Schubert,

origin, for the remnants of Spanish Visigoths in Septimania, Aquitania, and the Spanish Marches, as well as for the Frankish Church. Since Charlemagne upheld the legality of the codes of the various Germanic tribes within his empire, legal procedure was, theoretically at least, personal and local. But it is open to question how much the actual dispensation of justice corresponded with this legal theory in the case, for instance, of a non-Frankish ethnic minority living in the midst of a completely Frankish environment. After all, by the time of Charlemagne, the assimilation of such groups into the Frankish ruling majority must have largely solved this problem in certain regions of Frankland despite the theory that Frank, Bavarian, Burgundian, and Lombard was each supposed to be judged—and probably usually was—in conformity with his own respective national law book. The more or less transitional character of this legal theory is also evident from Charlemagne's intention to amend the Barbarian Codes [24] in accordance with the changed social and political conditions.

Neither Charlemagne nor any member of his court could have been familiar with each one of the national codes used in the empire. Hence the presence of legal experts at his court was an administrative necessity.[25] The special status of the *Romanus* in the Salian and Ripuarian Codes of the Franks and the adoption by the Church (see below) of the Visigoth Code must have required also the services of experts in Roman law—experts

---

*Geschichte der christlichen Kirche im Frühmittelalter* (Tübingen, 1921), 41–46; Max Conrat (Cohn), *Geschichte der Quellen und Literatur des Römischen Rechts* I (Leipzig, 1891), 41 ff.; Rudolf Buchner, *Die Rechtsquellen* (Beiheft to Wattenbach-Levison, *Deutschlands Geschichtsquellen im Mittelalter;* Weimar, 1953), 9 f.; J. Gaudemet, "Survivances romaines dans le droit de la monarchie franque du Vème au Xème siècle," *Tijdschrift voor Rechtsgeschiedenis* 23 (1955), 149–206. J. Imbert, "Le droit romain dans les textes juridiques carolingiens," *Studi in onore di Pietro De Francisci* 3 (Milano, 1956), 61–67.

[24] Cf. Einhard, *Vita Caroli,* c.29.
[25] Cf. Joseph Calmette, *Charlemagne* (Paris, 1945), 201.

familiar with the *Lex Romana*—among the councilors and legislators of Charlemagne. A Roman jurist at the Frankish court would have been in line with the historical tradition which testifies to the employment of such specialists by Germanic rulers.[26] So, too, administrative needs must have necessitated the presence of a Roman jurist in Charlemagne's *capella* and palatine court. This jurist was probably a *Romanus*, that is a Gallo-Roman, versed in the Roman law of the *Breviarium*. Hincmar of Reims seems to refer to the presence at the palatine court of informed lawyers who were experts in the *leges mundanae* or the *lex saeculi* and in the *lex Dei* and who knew both (utramque legem).[27]

At the outset, historical precedent suggests the formal "reception" of Alaric's code by Charlemagne through some capitulary, a reception comparable to the confirmation of the Ripuarian and Salian Frankish Codes through *Capitularia Legibus Addenda*. Despite this precedent, however, such formal reception was never decreed for the Visigoth Code. To be sure, Charlemagne's merely tacit recognition of the *Lex Romana* was not designed to please the small number of Gallo-Romans who, about 800, had survived his policy of Frankization, or the people of Visigothic extraction who had been resettled by Charlemagne, or even the Church, which, especially since the days of Isidore of Seville,[28] had canonized the *Breviarium*. But by the time of Charlemagne, the Code was not and could not be

[26] See the beginning of our Part III, below; K. F. Stroheker, *Der senatorische Adel im spätantiken Gallien* (Tübingen, 1948), nos. 212, 284, 358, 369; F. Beyerle, "Die süddeutschen Leges und die Merowingische Gesetzgebung," *Zeitschrift der Savigny-Stiftung für Rechtsgeschichte* 49 (Germ. Abt. 1929), 392–397; M. R. Madden, *Political Theory in Medieval Spain* (New York, 1930), 37 following Karl Zeumer; T. Mommsen, *Reden und Aufsätze* (Berlin, 1905), 139–141.

[27] *De ordine palatii*, c.21, ed. Victor Krause, *MGH, Capitularia Regum Francorum* II (Hannover, 1897), 524 f.

[28] P. Séjourné, *Saint Isidore de Séville: Son rôle dans l'histoire du droit canonique* (Paris, 1929), 104.

looked upon any longer as the national code of the Germanic people, who, we may recall, had dispensed with it during the seventh century, when Visigothic kings tried to accelerate the amalgamation of their Gothic and Roman subjects by a new combination of both law systems. The disappearance of the Visigoths as a potential body politic and as a distinct Germanic tribe obviated the need for the official "reception" of one of their outdated law books by Charlemagne. He did, however, tacitly recognize the Roman law of the Visigoth Code, since by the ninth century this had acquired the status of customary law, which was utilized especially by the Church, as we saw in the case of Alcuin. Charlemagne had to reckon with the Roman law of the code also because the above mentioned Frankish codes took into account the special status of the *Romanus* and his gradual assimilation into a predominantly Germanic environment.[29]

We can safely maintain the tacit "reception" of the *Breviarium Alaricianum* by Charlemagne as the authoritative code of Roman law in his empire. Since the code was used (see Ch. VII) in a *placitum* of the royal court at law, we leave the question open whether the *Lex Romana Visigothorum*[30] was looked upon as a *codex* or as a *lex*.

---

[29] Cf., for instance, Heinrich Mitteis, *Der Staat des Hohen Mittelalters* (3rd ed.; Weimar, 1948), 64 f.; Hermann Aubin, "Vom Absterben antiken Lebens im Frühmittelalter," *Antike und Abendland* 3 (ed. Bruno Snell, Hamburg, 1948), 98 f.

[30] See Leopold Wenger, *Die Quellen des römischen Rechts* (Wien, 1953), 558 n. 289.

*Part Three*

# ALCUIN IN THE SERVICE OF

# CHARLEMAGNE

LEGISLATIVE documents from the rulers of Germanic states established in former Roman territories are frequently the work of men of Roman descent. Thus Leo of Narbonne was probably the main helper of the Visigothic King Euric, and the Gallo-Roman Syagrius, of the Burgundian Gundobad. The Ostrogoths had Roman jurists in their service; one of these wrote the *Edictum Theoderici*. Cassiodorus is the author not only of the *Variae*, a selection of documents composed by him as chancellor of Theodoric the Great, but also of the *Edictum Athalarici*. The Merovingians Chlodewig and Childebert I employed Gallo-Roman administrators; the patrician Parthenius was an official of the Austrasian King Theudebert I. But the need for Roman officials in Germanic governments largely disappeared with the growth of genuine Germanic political and legal institutions. Charlemagne's leading helpers were, therefore, no longer descendants of the old senatorial nobility which survived in Gaul and Italy, but primarily men of Germanic origin. On the other hand, of all the brilliant scholars of Saxon, Lombard, Spanish-Gothic, and Italic origin in Charlemagne's cosmopolitan entourage, one man alone achieved great political prominence before 800: Alcuin. A little known phase of his activities in the empire of Charlemagne will be investigated here.

It has been said that some of the letters of Charlemagne,[1] unlike his charters, were composed not by notaries or scribes— clerics of his *capella* who served on the staff of his chancery— but by confidential advisers and friends allied with the royal court.[2] Of these, Angilbert, the son-in-law of the Frankish king, is probably mentioned by Alcuin as *secretarius*.[3] Sickel[4] assumes that Alcuin himself served his royal friend in this capacity, be- cause certain letters of Charlemagne are transmitted in the man- uscripts of Alcuin's voluminous correspondence. Although the charters of Charlemagne are available—thanks to the highly developed science of modern *Kaiserdiplomatik*[5]—in a critical edition,[6] the diplomatic origin of the king's letters, their com- position, and their redactors remain subjects inviting research. To be sure, historians have often spoken of Alcuin as Char-

[1] The letters of Charlemagne are published in various volumes of the *MGH: Epistolae* 4 and 5; *Concilia* 2.1; *Capitularia* 1; for the letters ad- dressed to Amalarius of Trèves, see now the edition by I. M. Hanssens, in his *Amalarii Episcopi Opera Liturgica* I (Studi e Testi 138; Città del Vaticano, 1948); for his letter to Pope Hadrian I, see the ed. by E. Mun- ding, *Königsbrief Karls d. Gr. an Papst Hadrian* (Texte und Arbeiten, ed. Erzabtei Beuron 1.6; Leipzig, 1920; cf. also Wilhelm Levison in *Neues Archiv der Gesellschaft für ältere deutsche Geschichtskunde* 43 [1920], 464 ff.; W. Erben, *ibid.* 46 [1926], 11-13, and *Historische Zeitschrift* 127 [1923], 289-291). Cf. also W. von den Steinen, *Karl der Grosse: Leben und Briefe* (Breslau, 1928).

[2] Harry Bresslau, *Handbuch der Urkundenlehre für Deutschland und Italien* I (2nd ed.; Leipzig, 1912), 381-382; C. Paoli, *Diplomatica* (ed. G. S. Bascape; Florence, 1942), 34-35; F. L. Ganshof, "Charlemagne et l'usage de l'écrit en matière administrative," *Le moyen âge* 57 (1951), 18.

[3] Alcuin, *Epist.* 27 regiae voluntatis secretarius (ed. Ernst Dümmler, *MGH Epistolae* 4 [1895] 69.15).

[4] T. Sickel, "Alkuinstudien," *Sitzungsberichte Wien Akademie* 79 (1875), 532-533.

[5] Carl Erdmann, *Archiv für Urkundenforschung* 16 (1939), 184; we are better informed on later collections of letters. See Erdmann, "Brief- sammlungen," in Wilhelm Wattenbach, *Deutschlands Geschichtsquellen im Mittelalter* I (ed. Robert Holtzmann; Tübingen, 1948), 415-542, 836- 837.

[6] E. Mühlbacher, *MGH Diplomata Karolinorum* I (1906).

lemagne's secretary, but none has provided reliable proof of Alcuin's authorship of a single document issued in the name of Charlemagne. Thus Mabillon, and after him many other scholars, assigned to Alcuin Charlemagne's famous *De litteris colendis,* addressed to Baugulf of Fulda. Recent investigation proves, however, that all Alcuin contributed to this royal mandate is a preliminary note, which was used by the unknown notary of the Carolingian *capella* who wrote the document.[7] Furthermore, three letter poems sent by Charlemagne to Paul the Deacon and Peter of Pisa,[8] and also Charlemagne's epitaph for Pope Hadrian I,[9] seem to be products of Alcuin's pen. To these we add for the first time a letter of Charlemagne written by Alcuin, namely, the king's letter sent in 794 from the Synod of Frankfurt to the metropolitan Elipand of Toledo. Alcuin also wrote the synodal letter of the Frankish clergy assembled at Frankfurt. This is additional proof of Alcuin's important role at the Synod as adviser to Charlemagne and as spokesman of the Frankish Church.

In the light of these discoveries, the attendance at Frankfurt of clergy from England, hitherto assumed, turns out to be unfounded. And the problem of Alcuin's share in the composition of the *Libri Carolini,* Charlemagne's manifesto against the worship of images restored by the seventh Ecumenical Council of Nicaea, 787, can now be placed in a new historical context.

[7] See Chapter XI.

[8] P. Neff, *Die Gedichte des Paulus Diaconus* (München, 1908), nos. 33, 34, 41.

[9] See Chapter X.

# CHAPTER IX

# Alcuin as the Author and Editor of Official Carolingian Documents

## I. A LETTER COMPOSED FOR CHARLEMAGNE BY ALCUIN

TWO major theological issues were decided by the national synod of the Frankish Church over which Charlemagne presided at Frankfurt-am-Main in June, 794.[1] The worship of images (see Pt. IV) and the adoptionist heresies of Felix of Urgel in the Spanish Marches and of Elipand, metropolitan in Moslem Toledo, were publicly condemned.[2] As far as the con-

[1] H. Barion, "Der kirchenrechtliche Charakter des Konzils von Frankfurt 794," *Zeitschrift der Savigny-Stiftung für Rechtsgeschichte*, Kanon. Abt. 19 (1930), 139–170; id., *Das Fränkisch-Deutsche Synodalrecht des Frühmittelalters* (Bonn-Köln, 1931); F. L. Ganshof, "Observations sur le synode de Francfort de 794," *Miscellanea historica in honorem Alberti de Meyer* I (Brussels, 1946), 306 ff.

[2] Cf. J. F. Rivera, *Elipando de Toledo: Nueva aportación a los estudios*

demnation of adoptionism is concerned, four documents are available,[3] in addition to the the Frankish Capitulary of 794: a letter by Charlemagne sent to Elipand and the Spanish clergy; the papal excommunication of the adoptionists in the form of a letter by Pope Hadrian I; and two separate synodal resolutions of the Italian and the Frankish clergy assembled at the synod. Both *synodicae* were drawn up at the request of Charlemagne during the time the synod was in session, the Italian one by Paulinus of Aquileia, the Frankish—as we shall prove—by Alcuin. Charlemagne's letter accompanying these three documents sent to Elipand displays a thorough acquaintance with the theological issues under consideration as well as an obvious familiarity with the proceedings of the synod. But the king himself is hardly the author of the dogmatic epistle, in spite of the fact that he was the indisputable leader of the Frankish Church and quite capable of discussing [4] theological questions with his leading clerics. Notwithstanding the intellectual capacity of Charlemagne, one cannot ascribe to him, for instance, a composite and exegetical treatment of the *Niceno-Constantinopolitan* Creed, interspersed with refutations of adoptionist theories. A theologian must have written the letter for him. Authorship by one of his ecclesiastical friends, be it Paulinus of

---

*Mozárabes* (Toledo, 1940); C. S. de Robles, *Elipando y San Beato de Liébana* (Madrid, 1935); Emile Amann, "L'adoptionisme espagnol du viiie siècle," *Revue des sciences religieuses* 16 (1936), 281–317; R. de Abadal y de Vinyals, *La batalla del adopcionismo en la disintegración de la Iglesia visigoda* (Real Academia de Buenas Letras de Barcelona 1949); cf. also Augusto Pascual in *Revue d'histoire ecclésiastique* 45 (1950), 339–340; and Jesús Solano, "El concilio de Calcedonia y la controversia adopcionista del siglo VIII en España," *Das Konzil von Chalkedon* 2 (Würzburg, 1953), 841–871.

[3] *MGH Concilia* 2 (ed. A. Werminghoff = *Conc. aevi Karolini* 1; 1906), nos. 19 A–G, pp. 110–171.

[4] L. Halphen, *Charlemagne et l'empire carolingien* (Paris, 1947), 213 ff.; K. Voigt, *Staat und Kirche von Konstantin dem Grossen bis zum Ende der Karolingerzeit* (Stuttgart, 1936), 320, 344.

Aquileia,[5] Theodulph of Orléans,[6] or Alcuin himself, suggests itself at the very outset, since all three men wrote occasionally about theological matters upon the express wish of the king. Yet a comparison of the letter with the prose of Theodulph and of Paulinus excludes their authorship. Style and diction of the epistle, however, frequently coincide with the language of Alcuin as it appears in his three antiadoptionist treatises [7] and in his letters.[8] The following parallels between Charlemagne's letter and Alcuin's writings prove that the letter was written by Alcuin.

C = Charlemagne, *Epistle* to Elipand of Toledo (ed. A. Werminghoff, *MGH Concilia* 2.157–164):

C 158.30–31, 40–43:...an quasi ex auctoritate magisterii nos vestra *docere* disposuistis an *ex humilitatis discipulatu nostra discere* desideratis;...

*Nec* pigeat Christianum ubi hesitet querere nec pudeat ubi nesciat discere, quoniam pia *humilitas discendi* sapientiae intrat secreta, et melius est *discipulum esse veritatis, quam doctorem existere falsitatis.* Ille ad altiora semper provehitur, iste ad inferiora semper dilabitur et inde *magister efficitur erroris,*[9] unde auditor contempsit esse veritatis.

Alcuin, *Epist.* 278 (ed. E. Dümmler, *MGH Epistolae* 4.434.33): Unusquisque alteri sit magister in opere bono, et unusquisque alteri *discipulus in humilitatis oboedientia;*

---

[5] He participated at Frankfurt and edited the Italian *synodica,* the "Libellus Sacrosyllabus Episcoporum Italiae," *MGH Concilia* 2, no. 19D, pp. 130–142. He wrote against Felix of Urgel, *PL* 99; cf. A. Wilmart, "L'ordre des parties dans le traité de Paulin d'Aquilée contre Félix d'Urgel," *Journal of Theological Studies* 39 (1938), 22–37.

[6] *De Spiritu Sancto, PL* 105.239–276.

[7] Cf. Alcuin, *Libellus adversus Felicis haeresin, PL* 101.85–119, written in 797; *Libri septem adversus Felicem* (of 798), col. 127–230; *Adversus Elipandum libri quattuor* (about 800), col. 243–300.

[8] Alcuin's letters to Felix of Urgel, ed. Ernst Dümmler, *MGH Epist.* 4, nos. 5 and 23; to Elipand, no. 166, with Elipand's answer, no. 182; Felix to Charlemagne, no. 199, and Elipand to Felix, no. 183.

[9] Cf. Leo the Great, *Epistola dogmatica ad Flavianum,* ed. August

Alcuin, *Epist.* 280, to Paulinus of Aquileia (438.29 Dümmler): singuli *humilitatem* habeant *in discendo et* devotionem *in docendo;*

Alcuin, *Epist.* to Beatus of Liébana (ed. W. Levison, *England and the Continent in the Eighth Century* [Oxford, 1946]), 321.20–322.1: *Nec* serpentinos invidorum dentes pertimesco, dum *humilitas discendi* defendat me ab errore pertinaciae, *magis* optans *esse veritatis discipulus quam falsitatis magister;*

Alcuin, *Adversus Elip. lib. quat.* 1.15 (*PL* 101.251C): *Disce prius, et postea doce, ne magister efficiaris erroris.* Melior est *humilitas discendi* quam temeritas *docendi; ibid.* 3.12 (*PL* 101.279B): Habete *humilitatem discendi* et desiderium ecclesiasticae veritatis.

These parallels in thought and style speak for themselves. The main argument invoked by C against Elipand is the traditional principle of abiding by the doctrines and testimony of the Church fathers—not deviating from the *via regia*, the King's Highway, either to the right or to the left. This concept is characteristic of Alcuin; it occurs in ten of his *Epistles* and in three of his treatises.[10] Compare, for instance,

C 159.2–5.9: *Discamus quae* scribserunt (sc. patres), credamus quae docuerunt et *non declinemus ad dexteram neque ad sinistram,* sed per *viam regiam* ad regem et redemptorem...concordi fidaei et veritatis curramus professione...*Sequamur sanctorum patrum venerabilia* in caritate *praecepta.*

Alcuin, *Epist.* 23, to Felix of Urgel (64.35–40 Dümmler): His et huiusmodi *venerabilibus sanctorum patrum sententiis* non credere impium esse putamus.... *Discite quae* ad salutem animarum vestrarum pertinent, et *viam regiam* ab apostolis

---

Hahn, *Bibliothek der Symbole und Glaubensregeln der alten Kirche* (3rd ed.; Breslau, 1897), no. 36, p. 322: et ideo *magistri erroris* existunt, quia *veritatis discipuli* non fuerunt; ed. E. Schwartz, *Acta Con. Oecum.* II.ii.1 (Berlin-Leipzig, 1932), no. 5, p. 25.4; JK 423.

[10] *MGH Epist.* 4, nos. 23, 41, 117, 137, 149, 184, 186, 193, 209, 281; *Comment. in Eccles. PL* 100.696B; *Dialogus de dialectica* c. 11, *PL*

tritam, a patribus frequentatam,...pleno catholicae fidei
pede incedite;

Alcuin, *Epist.* 137 (211.18 Dümmler): Sanctorum patrum in fide
sequimini vestigia...per apostolicae doctrinae publicam per-
gite stratam, *nec* per diverticula cuiuslibet novitatis *in dexteram vel in sinistram a via regia declinate.*

The following antirationalistic passage is typical of Alcuin's
thinking: it provides one of his main arguments against adoptionism.

C 161.29–31: nec *ratiotinando humano ingenio divina vos mysteria
investigare* arbitremini, sed magis credendo honorate quae *humana fragilitas* temere perscrutando invenire *non valeat.*[11]

Alcuin, *Epist.* to Beatus of Liébana (ed. W. Levison, 320.18):
Stultissimum est altissima *Dei mysteria humanis ratiunculis
investigare* velle et nostrae infirmitatis dicioni subicere;

Alcuin, *Adv. Fel. libri septem* 3.2 (PL 101.164C): Concede igitur Deum aliquid posse, quod *humana non valeat infirmitas*
comprehendere; *nec nostra ratiocinatione* legem ponamus
majestati aeternae.

Compare also the following parallel passages to be found in
Alcuin's antiadoptionist treatises:

*Adv. Fel. libri septem* 7.3 (PL 101.215C): sed revera...Filium Dei
secreto illo *mysterio* quod ipse solus novit... Quod tu omnino
oblitus conaris illud *ratione investigare* quod fide venerari de-
buisses;

*Ibid.* 6.9 (211A): Quid enim *ratione humanae* consuetudinis *investi-
gandum* est quod divinae potestatis miraculo factum esse probatur?

---

101.963D; *Vita Richarii,* ed. Krusch, *MGH Scriptores Rerum Merovingicarum* 4.392.25–27.

[11] See the anonymous ninth-century credo, ed. Hahn, p. 353: neque ullo
modo *humana fragilitas* debet *nec valet* ejus originem perscrutari. Levison refers for *humanis ratiunculis* to Augustine, *De civ. dei* 20.1.1; see
further Ambrose, *De officiis ministrorum* I.125 (PL 26): omnibus igitur
hominibus inest secundum naturam humanam verum investigare.

*Ibid.* 6.10 (213D–214A): *Humana* quippe *ratio investigare* non poterit quomodo qui fecit omnia factus est inter omnia;

*Ibid.* 7.10 (222C): *humanaque ratiocinatione* divinae bonitatis ineffabile sacramentum scrutari niteris;

*Ibid.* 3.6 (166B): Salvatorisque nostri mirabilem nativitatem *humanis ratiunculis* desinat aestimare;

*Ibid.* 3.2 (164A): nec infirmis *humanae conjecturae ratiunculis*...comprehendi poterit;

*Adv. Elip. libri quattuor* 4.10 (*PL* 101.294A): Sed vos...praeponentes *humanae conjecturae* fribulosas *ratiunculas* fidei soliditati, volentes prius intellegere et secundo loco credere;

*Ibid.* 4.14 (298A–B): scientes certissime quod laudanda sunt *mysteria Dei, non ratione discutienda.*

The lengthy profession of faith in Charlemagne's letter [12] is of special interest. It is a mosaic of quotations from various creeds with (I) the *Niceno-Constantinopolitan Creed* [13] as the basis. Some quotations are culled verbatim from the symbol *Quicumque*, the *Athanasian Creed* (II),[14] the *Libellus fidei* of Pelagius [15] of 417 (III), and from (IV) the symbol of the Synod of Toledo of 675.[16] The main sources are indicated by the Roman numerals I–IV in the left margin. Parallels from Alcuin's writings and some comments are given in the notes *a–h.*

---

[12] In addition to Hahn (n. 9) see H. Denzinger and I. B. Umberg, *Enchiridion Symbolorum* (Freiburg i. Br., 1932).

[13] Cf. I. Ortiz de Urbina, "La struttura del simbolo Constantinopolitano," *Orientalia Christiana Periodica* 12 (1946), 275–285; *El Simbolo Niceno* (Madrid, 1947); A. d'Alès, "Nicée-Constantinople: Les premiers symboles de foi," *Recherches des sciences religieuses* 26 (1936), 85–93.

[14] C. H. Turner, "A critical text of the *Quicumque vult*," *Journal of Theological Studies* 11 (1910), 408.

[15] During the Middle Ages ascribed to Jerome and Augustine; cf. W. Levison, *England and the Continent in the Eighth Century* (Oxford, 1946), 237.

[16] J. Madoz, *Le symbole du XI^e Concile de Tolède* (Spicilegium Sacrum Lovaniense 19; Louvain, 1938).

C 163.19–164.38 passim:

I    *Credimus in unum Deum patrem omnipotentem, factorem caeli ac terrae, visibilium omnium et invisibilium....filium Dei unigenitum, natum ex patre ante omnia secula* [a] et ante omnia tempora,[b] *lumen de lumine,*...

III   *non adoptivum,*...*et unius substantiae cum patre.*

I    *Credimus et in Spiritum sanctum,* Deum verum, *vivificatorem omnium, a patre et filio procedentem, cum patre et filio coadorandum et conglorificandum.* Credimus eandem sanctam trinitatem...Spiritum sanctum procedentem ex patre et filio,

III   *nec patrem aliquando coepisse,* sed sicut semper est Deus, ita *semper et pater est,*

IV   quia *semper habuit filium.*

II   *Aeternus pater, aeternus filius, aeternus et Spiritus sanctus ex patre filioque procedens,*[c]... In qua sancta trinitate nulla est

III   persona vel *tempore* posterior vel *gradu* inferior vel *potestate* minor,... Alius [d]... in persona pater, alius in persona filius,... Spiritus sanctus....

II   *perfectus* in divinitate *Deus, perfectus* in humanitate *homo; Deus ante* omnia *secula; homo in* fine *seculi;*...

IV   in *forma Dei aequalis patri,* in *forma servi minor patre;*...

II   *Haec est fides catholica,* et ideo nostra,...quia una est fides et *unum baptisma* et unus dominus noster... Hanc fidem vos, karissimi fratres, firmiter tenere in commune deprecamur...contentiones nominum *novitatesque vocum* [e] devitate, quia iuxta apostolum *non est hereticus nisi ex contentione.*[f]... Habetote nos cooperatores [g] salutis vestrae, *catholicae pacis* [h] auxiliatores,...

---

[a] Alcuin, *Adv. Felicem* 1.9 (*PL* 101.134 f.), and in the *Epist.* to Beatus of Liébana (ed. Levison, 320 n. 3) quotes the NC creed but with variant readings, which also occur in the *Irish Stowe Missal,* ed. Warner (HBS 32; London, 1915), 8. See the unique variant "natum ex patre ante omnia saecula" in our letter and in Alcuin's writings. Dom B. Capelle, "Alcuin et l'histoire du symbole de la messe," *Recherches de théologie ancienne et médiévale* 6 (1934), 255–256, was the first to point out the connection between Alcuin and the variants of the *Stowe Missal.* Cf. his newest summary referred to below in n. 57.

ᵇ Alcuin, *Adv. Elipandum* 4.15 (*PL* 101.290A) reads:...qui *ante omnia tempora* ex Patre natus est.

ᶜ On the *Filioque* see Emile Amann, *L'époque carolingienne* (Histoire de l'Eglise, ed. A. Fliche and V. Martin 6; Paris, 1936), 173–184. Paulinus of Aquileia inserted it in his version of the Symbol; see *Concilium Foroiuliense* of 796–797, *MGH Conc.* 2.187.11–12; W. von den Steinen, *Neues Archiv der Gesellschaft für ältere deutsche Geschichtskunde* 49 (1930–1932), 228–232. Cf. V. Rodzianko, "Filioque in patristic thought," *Studia Patristica* II (Berlin, 1957), 295–308.

ᵈ Alcuin, *De fide s. trinitatis* (*PL* 101.57C): Sed alius est Pater in persona, alius Filius in persona, alius Spiritus sanctus in persona; the same words in *Epist.* 166, to Elipand (Dümmler 269.28).

ᵉ Cf. I Tim. 6:20 devitans profanas vocum novitates, often used by Alcuin in connection with antiadoptionist expressions: *Ep.* 166, to Elipand (Dümmler 272.1); *Adv. Felicem* (*PL* 101.129, 199, etc.).

ᶠ Alcuin, *Epist.* 23, to Felix of Urgel (Dümmler 61.13), written in 793: *non est hereticus nisi ex contentione.*

ᵍ *Ibid.*, Me enim *habebis* in Christi tuae *salutis* fidelem, quantum valeo *cooperatorem.*

ʰ *Pax catholica* is a favorite expression of Alcuin, as has been pointed out by Levison, *op. cit.*, 320 n. 1.

The composite structure of this section is obvious. When Alcuin was in the process of compiling this creed, he evidently used a manuscript collection of various creeds.[17] The profession of faith is presented as Charlemagne's personal creed: "Haec est fides catholica, et ideo *nostra.*" This then is the *Symbolum* used in the liturgy of the Mass at the royal collegiate church at Aix-la-Chapelle. Since its basis is the *Niceno-Constantinopolitan* symbol, we must assume that the latter [18] is also the credo referred to in section 33 of the Frankfurt Capitulary of 794. The custom of singing the symbol in the Mass was introduced at Aachen in all probability by Alcuin.[19] Permission for this litur-

[17] Comparable to the one edited by K. Künstle, *Eine Bibliothek der Symbole* (Mainz, 1900), from a MS of the ninth century.

[18] And not the *Athanasian* Creed, as is stated by Hefele-Leclerq, *Histoire des Conciles* 3 (Paris, 1910), 1059 n. 1.

[19] Dom B. Capelle, *loc. cit.* (note *a* above), 249–260; Levison, *op. cit.*, 159, 320.

gical innovation was granted by Leo III as late as 809—with the exhortation, however, to omit the disputed *Filioque.*[20]

Charlemagne's creed was used at Aix-la-Chapelle until 798, when it was replaced by the *symbolum* promulgated by Paulinus of Aquileia at the Synod of Friuli in 796 (*Conc.* 2.187). This profession of faith was adopted by Charlemagne upon the initiative of Alcuin, who had openly expressed his interest in a letter of congratulation addressed to Paulinus on the occasion of the latter's publication of a commentary on the new creed. Lauding its desirability, Alcuin stated (*Epist.* 139 Dümmler 220.27) that he had long advocated the necessity of a libellus on the creed and often counselled Charlemagne in the matter (quod diu optavi et saepius domno regi suasi). A reference to Paulinus' creed is contained in a letter of 809 sent by a monk to Pope Leo III. He reported that he had heard—probably in 799—in the Chapel of Charlemagne *in symboli fidei* the disputed *qui ex Patre Filioque procedit.*[21]

To the passages listed thus far as evidence for Alcuin's authorship, I add as further proof the following parallels between C 158–164 and Alcuin's treatises and letters.

C 158.5: *Gaudet* pietas Christiana...*per lata terrarum spatia;*
> Alcuin, *Epist.* 121 (Dümmler 176.17): *per* multa *terrarum spatia* dilatare *gaudeat;*
> Alcuin, *Vita Vedastis* ed. Krusch, *MGH SS. Rer. Merov.* 3.416.19: *lata terrarum spatia.*

C 158.13: intra murum catholicae fidei;
> Alcuin, *Adv. Felicem* (PL 101.209D, 217A, etc.).

C 158.34: inter *fluctivagos* huius seculi aestus, *Spiritu sancto navigium nostri* cursus regente, *ad portum...pervenire* mereamur;

[20] Cf. J. A. Jungmann, *Missarum Sollemnia* 1 (2nd ed.; Wien, 1949), 578–579; Gustave Neyron, "Charlemagne, les Papes et l'Orient," *Orientalia Christiana Periodica* 13 (1947), 260–263. On Charlemagne's creed see J. N. D. Kelly, *Early Christian Creeds* (London, 1950), 420 ff.

[21] *MGH Epist. Karol. Aevi* 5, *Epist.* 7, 65.33.

*Adv. Elipandum* 3.1 (*PL* 101.271A): dum *spiritu sancto* guber-
nante orationis nostrae *navigium...ad portum perveniret;*
*Epist.* 97 (Dümmler 141.7):...*ad portum...venire.*

C 158.37: precibus *mentis acies* inlustranda, ut...;
*Epist.* 155 (Dümmler 250.26): turbatae *mentis aciei* occurrere
potuit; 257 (Dümmler 415.16): devota *mentis acie.*

C 159.29: desiderantes. *vos socios habere;*
*Epist.* to Beatus of Liébana (Levison 322.5): obsecro ut *me so-
cium habeas.*

C 160.1: veritas catholicae fidei investigaretur et probatissimis *sanctorum patrum* hinc inde *roborata testimoniis absque ulla dubi-
tatione* teneatur;
*Epist.* 201 (Dümmler 334.7): Tamen firmiter *absque ulla dubi-
tatione sanctorum* sequimini vestigia *patrum;* et catholicam
fidem quam multis *roboratam testimoniis* aspicitis, tenete
et praedicate.

C 160.19: *ne paucorum...*consentirem, *sed plurimorum* testimoniis;
*Epist.* 23, to Felix of Urgel (Dümmler 65.10): *Nolite* vestrae
amatores esse sapientiae cum *paucis, sed* veritatis adsertores
sitis cum *plurimis.*

C 160.24: et catholicis traditionibus *tota* me *mentis intentione, tota
cordis alacritate* coniungo;
*Epist.* 166 (Dümmler 269.3): ut catholicam doctrinam...*tota
mentis intentione* consequi studeas; 309 (D.475.12);
229 (D.374.9): *tota* meae *mentis intentio;*
Alcuin, *Vita Willibrordi* 1.7 (ed. W. Levison, *MGH SS. Rer.
Merov.* 7.122.13): *tota cordis alacritate.*

C 160.35: Cuius (*scil.* civitatis Christi) antemurale est fides catholica
...et *propugnacula divinarum* testimonia *scripturarum...Huius*
vero *civitatis...;*
*Adv. Felicem* 1.7 (*PL* 101.133C): *Huius civitatis propugnacula
sanctae* sunt *scripturae.*

C 160.39: *regali* praesidet *potentia;*
*Epist.* 171 (Dümmler 281.23): et *regalis* pietatis *potentia*
splendescere probetur.

C 161.16: *non opus est mihi;* the same phrase in *Epist.* to Offa of

Mercia (ed. W. Levison, *England and the Continent*, 245.24) and *Adv. Felicem* 3.19 (*PL* 101.160B); *Epist.* 149 (D.244.22); 69 (D.113.11); 70 (D.114.6).

C 161.27: nec *vos doctiores* aestimetis;

> *Adv. Felicem* 2.7 (*PL* 101.152D): Numquid igitur *vos doctiores* illo estis?

C 161.37: et quoscunque *ex filiis* sanctae matris ecclesiae valeo, *mihi* in hac petitione *adiutores convoco;*

> *Epist.* 207 (Dümmler 344.5): *adiutores mihi...ex filiis* elegi; 229 (D.373.11): *ex* diversis mundi partibus *adiutores convocare.*

C 162.4: *ne* callida *antiqui hostis versutia* sensus vestros in *aliqua parte* corrumpat;

> *Epist.* 139 (Dümmler 221.1): *ne antiqui hostis versutia aliqua ex parte.*

C 162.14: si catholicae fidei *unanimitate adiungere* curetis;

> *Epist.* 137 (Dümmler 211.14): et universalis ecclesiae sanctissima vos *adiungite unanimitate.*

C 162.29: *divina auxiliante gratia;* also *Ep.* 23 (Dümmler 65.4); 168 (D.277.19); *Adv. Felicem* 1.7 (*PL* 101.133C).

C 163.15: adhuc enim *pia mater* ecclesia quae revocat vos;

> *Epist.* 23 (Dümmler 62.6): *Pia* est *mater*, te ipsum recollige.

C 164.28: quia iuxta apostolum (Titus 3:9–10) *non est hereticus nisi ex contentione;*

> *Epist.* 23, to Felix of Urgel (Dümmler 61.13): *non est hereticus nisi ex contentione.*

C 164.29: *Vos* igitur *pauci* estis;

> Alcuin, *Epist.* 23, to Felix of Urgel (Dümmler 61.42): Cognoscite...quam *vos paucos;*
>
> *Adv. Felicem* 2.3 (*PL* 101.148C): cum *paucis* Hispaniae, non dico doctoribus, sed veritatis desertoribus;
>
> *Adv. Elipandum* 1.13 (*PL* 101.249D): si in sola Hispania perpauci musitatores.

The numerous parallels are ample proof that Alcuin is indeed the author of the royal epistle. This is not too surprising because we know from statements in his own letters that he wrote upon the request of Charlemagne against the adoptionism of Felix of Urgel and Elipand of Toledo.[22]

Charlemagne's letter has been characterized as a significant document,[23] "a truly royal letter of genuine wisdom and sincerity."[24] Erich Caspar calls it "the most important document of the Frankfurt Synod."[25] Menéndez y Pelayo[26] and Gaskoin[27] seem to be the only scholars who have considered Alcuin as the possible author. The Spanish scholar says "y puede atribuirse con fundamento á Alcuino." The "gentle tone" of the letter suggested to Gaskoin the hand of Alcuin. With his authorship definitely established, the importance ascribed to the letter becomes illustrative of Alcuin's position as adviser to Charlemagne and of his influence on the royal government. This fact constitutes new evidence for the leading role of Alcuin[28] in the political growth of the Frankish empire.

## II. ALCUIN AS THE AUTHOR
## OF THE FRANKISH SYNODICA OF 794

Alcuin's authorship of Charlemagne's letter (= C) suggests that he collaborated in the resolution of the Frankish clergy against adoptionism[29] drawn up during the time the Synod of

---

[22] See the references collected by W. von den Steinen, *Neues Archiv* 49 (1930–1932), 217; Bastgen, *ibid.* 37 (1912), 516–524.

[23] A. Hauck, *Kirchengeschichte Deutschlands* 2 (3rd–4th ed.; Leipzig, 1912), 313.

[24] H. von Schubert, *Geschichte der christlichen Kirche im Frühmittelalter* (Tübingen, 1921), 387.

[25] "Das Papsttum unter fränkischer Herrschaft," *Zeitschrift für Kirchengeschichte* 54 (1935), 307; in the book edition (Darmstadt, 1956), 107.

[26] *Historia de los Heterodoxos Españoles* 1 (Madrid, 1880), 209.

[27] C. J. B. Gaskoin, *Alcuin* (London, 1904), 87.

[28] See the summary by F. L. Ganshof, *The Imperial Coronation of Charlemagne: Theories and Facts* (Glasgow University Publications, 1949).

[29] *MGH Conc.* 2.143–157, no. 19E.

Frankfurt was in session. Gaskoin[30] and de Clercq[31] ascribe to Alcuin such a co-authorship on the basis of the leading part he played at the synod. "Certain ideas and formula-like expressions" of the document led Kleinclausz (who did not, however, list them specifically) to surmise that Alcuin, if he did not edit the letter, might yet have worked on it.[32] Amann assumes that Alcuin is the editor of the document.[33] Is there sufficient evidence to link Alcuin with the origin of the synodal letter? As in the case of C so here we list parallels of style and diction between the Frankish *synodica* (= S) and Alcuin's epistles and treatises. Additional parallels to be found in S and C are listed in a special section.

S = *Epistola synodica episcoporum Franciae* (ed. A. Werminghoff, *MGH Concilia* 2.143–157):

S 143.9: et *ad praedicandam* orthodoxae *fidaei veritatem;*
>    Alcuin, *Epist.* 23, to Felix of Urgel (Dümmler 65.12): *ad...praedicandam fidei veritatem.*

S 143.37: *Sed tempus est, ut* ad *discutiendos* sensus libelli vestri veniamus, in quo sanctorum patrum per loca *testimonia* invenimus posita;
>    *Adv. Felicem* 1.4 (PL 101.130C): *Sed tempus est, ut dicutiamus* sermones praefati viri et sententias sanctae scripturae, quas ad sui sensus nititur trahere *testimonium.*

S 144.1: sensus per intermissiones aliquorum verborum *masculare nitimini;*
>    *Adv. Elipandum* 2.5 (PL 101.261C): prava interpretatione *maculare niteris; Epist.* 43 (D.89.7) maculari nititur;

[30] Gaskoin, *op. cit.,* 87.

[31] C. de Clercq, *La législation religieuse franque de Clovis à Charlemagne* (Louvain, 1936), 185.

[32] A. Kleinclausz, *Alcuin* (Paris, 1948), 89.

[33] Émile Amann, *L'époque carolingienne* (Paris, 1936), 143; *Revue des sciences religieuses* 16 (1936), 230; Edmund Bishop, *Liturgica Historica* (Oxford, 1918), 171, sees the hand of Alcuin in the reference to "noster vero Gregorius" (*scil.* Gregory the Great), (*Conc.*I.145) following the example of Bede in referring to Gregory I as "noster Gregorius."

*Epist.* 74 (Dümmler 117.13): impiis adsertionibus *maculare ni-tuntur;* cf. 2 Tim. 3:1 and 2 Pet. 2:1.

S 153.27–37: Tu vero, quisquis es, qui Christum praedicas adoptivum, unde tibi iste sensus venisset, voluissem scire: ubi hoc nomen didicisses, ostende.... *Forte in tertium caelum raptus fuisti et ibi audisti* archana *verba* (2 Cor. 12:2), quae hucusque sanctae Dei ecclesiae ignota essent, si tu in tertium caelum raptus non esses.... Aut per choros angelorum te ducens agnus hoc tibi nomen ostendit? Aut tibi *leo de tribu Iuda librum septem sigillis* (Apoc. 5:5–7) clausum *aperuit,* unde haec mysteria intellegeres et *nomina proferres,* quae quattuor animalibus *incognita* mansissent, immo toto *mundo inaudita,* nisi tu *novus doctor* ad declarandum *tuum nomen* venisses? Dicis enim:...

> Alcuin, *Adversus Felicem libri septem* 2.2 (*PL* 101.147A–B): Dicis itaque quod *novus homo novum nomen* habere debeat. Dic, rogo, quis hoc *novum nomen* Spiritus vestris insonuit auribus? *Forte* Deus tecum loquebatur in turbine...ut *inaudita* a saeculis *nomina* mundo *proferre* valuisses: vel cum Apostolo (cf. 2 Cor. 12:2) *raptus fuisti ad tertium coelum, et ibi audisti* ineffabilia *verba;* vel cum beato evangelista vidisti et legisti *librum* sigillatum *septem sigillis,* quem nemo potuit *aperire, nisi leo de tribu Iuda,* cuius potestati infeliciter Felix derogare non metuis; cf. Apoc. 5:5–7.

> *Adv. Elipandum* 4.13 (*PL* 101.296B): *nisi tu* aliquid per te invenires, unde *tuum nomen* celebrares *in mundo* (see the parallels adduced below to S 156.8).

S 154.3: *Plurimae* vero sunt in sanctis scribturis appellationes domini nostri Iesu Christi sicut *leo,* agnus, *lapis, vermis,* et multa *talia, quae* omnia certas habent et mysticas *significationes,* cur ita dicantur;

> Alcuin, *Epist.* 166 (Dümmler 274.2): *Significativa nomina* sunt propter quasdam actiones, quae complete sunt in illo: *leo, lapis,* ovis, vitulus, *vermis,* et *talia* (not: alia) *plurima,* quae ratione discernenda sunt.

S 156.8: Intellegite, fratres, quae legitis et *nolite nova et incognita nomina fingere*...;

*Adv. Felicem* 1.2 (*PL* 101.129C): *nova* inferre, *et incognita; Ibid.* 1.3 (131A): contraria toti orbi *fingunt nomina; Epist.* 23 (Dümmler 61.17): non *nova fingentes nomina;* 166 (D. 269.5): nec *nova nomina* permittas inseri traditionibus; *Adv. Elipandum* 2.10 (*PL* 101.267A): ita *novas* siquidem ex *nominibus* sanctorum patrum *fingis* tibi epistolas.

S 156.19: Desinite fratres vestros per aures populi Christiani *diffamare parentes* (the comma belongs after *parentes,* and not after *diffamare*);
*Adv. Elipandum* 2.8 (*PL* 101.266B): *maculare nomen parentum.*

S 156.21:...et nolite *per diverticula* errorum discurrere..., sed per *viam regiam*...festinate;
*Epist.* 137 (Dümmler 211.18): nec *per diverticula* cuiuslibet novitatis a *via regia* declinate; cf. Num. 21:22.

S 156.21: et nolite...*cisternas*...dissipatas *fodere,* quae aquas non tenebunt, sed...ad...*fontem* festinate...quatenus...*fluant aquae vivae* salientes in vitam eternam;
Alcuin, *Epist.* to Beatus of Liébana (ed. Levison 322.17):
Nec placet illorum mentibus alma fides,
Sed sibi *cisternas fodiunt* sine luminis unda,
In quibus haud ulla est *vivida fontis aqua.*
Cf. Jer. 2:13, John 4:14, 7:38; Alcuin, *Epist.* 295 (Dümmler 452.30).

S 156.28 (and 157.2): *doctores* in fide et *ductores* ad vitam; the same play on words *Adv. Felicem* 6.8 (*PL* 209D); *Liber de virtutibus et vitiis* (*PL* 101.617A); *Epist.* 17 (Dümmler 49.1).

S 156.25: Tenete vos *intra terminos* sanctorum *patrum;*
Alcuin, *Epist.* to Beatus of Liébana (ed. Levison 319.4); *Adv. Felicem* (*PL* 101.130D; 131A, etc.).

S 157.26: *eterna beatitudo et beata eternitas;*
Alcuin, *De fide s. trinitatis* 22 (*PL* 101.54C); *Epist.* 43 (Dümmler 88.24). *Epist.* 111 (Dümmler 162.6); 214 (D.358.31); 250 (D.404.27); 255 (D.413.13).

The traces of Alcuin's style and diction are plainly noticeable in S, which in itself is the reply of the Frankish clergy to an epistle (*libellus*) they had received from the Spanish clergy

(*MGH Concilia* 2.111–119 No. 19A). This *libellus*, in all likelihood composed by Elipand of Toledo, was read publicly at the opening session of the Synod of Frankfurt and refuted at a later session after the theologians had had time to study the Spanish heresies. S claims to present the *joint* opinion of the Frankish clergy, although Alcuin must be the *sole* author, and not just the editor, of the letter. This fact we deduce from the nature of the following parallels in diction between S (143–157) and C (158–164):

S 143.8: cum consilio *pacificae unanimitatis;*
C 158.26 (161.26, etc.): *pacifica unanimitate.*
S 143.10: quae *una decet esse omnium Christianorum* dicente beato apostolo (Eph. 4: 5–6) Unus dominus, *una fides, unum baptisma...* Iustus enim *ex fide vivit* (Rom. 1: 17)...quia sicut per fidem iustitia, ita etiam per fidem veram vita obtinetur aeterna;
C 159.6: attestante Paulo apostolo (Rom. 1: 17) *Iustus* autem *ex fide vivit.* Si iustus ex fide vivit, quomodo qui fidem non habet rectam se vivere aestimet? *Decet* enim, ut *omnium Christianorum una* sit *fides* (cf. Eph. 4: 5–6) et unus animus.
S 143.19: domni regis nostri...sapientia *adsedente;*
C 161.23: Ecce ego [*scil.* Carolus]...auditor et arbiter *adsedi.*
S 143.20: *libellum....* Qui cum a notario nobis diligentius adtendentibus sub *distinctione sententiarum* et proprietate sensuum *perlegeretur* ad finem;
C 161.14: eundem *libellum* a capite calcetenus per *distinctiones* uniuscuiusque *sententiae* et per interrogationes vel responsiones, prout cuique libuit, *perlegere* iussimus.
S 143.22: audivimus in eo *novas* quasdam *assertiones* exaratas, non tam *antiquis* sanctorum doctorum *traditionibus* convenientes *quam* vestris *nuper inventionibus;*
C 159.36: *quam nuper novis adsertionibus* et sanctae dei universali ecclesiae *antiquis temporibus* inauditis vos ex vestris scriptis intulisse cognovimus...de hac *nova inventione.*
S 143.27: numquid *sagatiores* sumus ad inveniendam viam veritatis quam apostolici doctores;

C 161.27: nec vos *doctiores* aestimetis universali...ecclesia.

S 143.40: *ut* difficilius error vester *investigaretur;*

C 160.1: *ut* veritas catholicae fidei *investigaretur.*

S 145.37: Nec *vos* in illis *exaudiri* putamus;

C 161.6:...*vos* efficiat *exaudiri.*

S 147.37: sanctae *scripturae tractatores;*

C 160.29: sacrae *scripturae tractatores.*

S 153.30: sancti *tractatores*...tacuerunt, *doctores fidaei* nostrae non
  docuerunt;

C 160.29:...*tractatores* et precipue Christiani *fidaei doctores.*

S 155.12:...dicere in confessione catholicae fidaei quod sancti *patres*
  dixerunt et sic *simbolum* tenere;

C 161.27: Eandem fidem tenete, quam orthodoxi *patres* in suis *simbolis*
  scribtam reliquerunt.

S 156.33: *ut...consortium...habere;*

C 163.10: *ut...consortium,...habere.*

S 156.39: *Intellegite* in hac professione vestra duplices *diabolicae*
  *fraudis* latuisse dolos...(S 157.2) considerate, quale est hoc
  *scandalum;*

C 162.41: Ante igitur quam huius sepedicti *scandali* offensio...(C
  163.3) fraudatis vosmetipsos, non *intellegentes* vos *fraude dia-*
  *bolica* esse deceptos.

S 157.25: *ad* eius beatissimam visionem *pervenire mereamur;*

C 158.34: *ad* portum perpetuae tranquillitatis *pervenire mereamur.*

These parallels are of a nature to point definitely to a close
relationship between the two documents, and this not merely
in the sense that C copies passages in S, but also that both letters
must be ascribed to the same author. The identity of diction in
S and C is additional proof of Alcuin's authorship of S. He
must have first prepared for the Frankish clergy a tentative
refutation (= S) of the Spanish *libellus*. S was then used by the
Frankish clergy as the basis of their discussions during the
synodal proceedings, and finally approved by them officially. A
few days later Alcuin wrote C. Hence both letters may be
added to the *corpus epistolarum Alcuini*.

Alcuin's authorship of both C and S poses the question: How could he occupy at Frankfurt such an important position as adviser to the Frankish king and simultaneously also to the Frankish clergy? His double role can be understood only as the result of his friendship with Charlemagne, who presided at the synod and also secured special permission for the Saxon foreigner from Northumbria to attend a national synod of the Frankish Church, as we learn from c. 56 of the Frankfurt Capitulary of 794. C and S are therefore accounts of events at Frankfurt drawn up not merely by an observer or neutral eyewitness, but by the person who largely determined the direction of the theological decisions which were ultimately endorsed by the synod. Since the subscriptions of the Frankfurt Capitulary are not extant, it cannot be determined whether Alcuin also participated in the public discussions of the synod and in the voting on the dogmatic decisions which he had prepared. Alcuin's ecclesiastical rank as a deacon who framed a synodal resolution for assembled bishops corresponds—*mutatis mutandis*—to the role of nonepiscopal theologians and canonists in the framing of the decrees of later medieval councils. By 794, however, Alcuin's fame as a scholar of European reputation was so well established that it is difficult to see him at Frankfurt only in the role of an anonymous "dictator" of Charlemagne, composing some important documents for his employer. I rather assume that Alcuin's rank as a deacon hardly influenced his actual position at the meeting, because he did not attend the synod, as we shall see (Pt. III), as a representative of the English Church, but upon the special invitation of Charlemagne, the head of the Frankish Church. So much is quite certain: the king's confidence in the foreigner from the British Isles as royal councilor and as theological adviser to the Frankish clergy at Frankfurt is without parallel in the entire reign of Charlemagne.

Although we are primarily interested in the historical and literary aspects of Alcuin's fight against adoptionism, one specific theological issue of the controversy must be mentioned here:

Alcuin's question about the origin of the term *adoptivus*, the occurrence of which in earlier Christian tradition he denies emphatically. Compare:

S 153.27: Tu vero quisquis es, qui Christum praedicas *adoptivum*....
     *Ubi hoc nomen* didicisses, ostende;
       Alcuin, *Adv. Elipandum* 4.2 (*PL* 101.286C): Ubi latuit, *ubi*
          dormivit *hoc nomen adoptionis* vel nuncupationis de
          Christo?
S 153.38: nec sancta Dei et catholica ecclesia consuetudinem habuit
     sic *eum appellare*, immo nec credere eum *adoptivum* esse;
       Alcuin, *Epist.* 202, from the year 800 (Dümmler 336.11): Quid
          enim prodest ecclesiae Dei *Christum appellare adoptivum*
          filium vel Deum nuncupativum?

Harnack assumes that Alcuin "sagt zu viel" when raising this question about the origin of adoptionism; he himself finds its roots in the christology of Ambrose and Augustine (so did adoptionists of the twelfth to the fourteenth centuries), and in some formulations of the Mozarabic liturgy.[34] But this approach seems to be colored by a preference for Augustine as the father of all possible deviations from "Roman" dogma. Remarkable in any case is Alcuin's interest in the question, which remains unchanged even six years (see *Epist.* 202) after the Synod of Frankfurt. For he himself rather impatiently cuts short his own argumentation against the adoptionist heresy when he finally states in forceful simplicity (S 156.43): "...Deum colimus et adoramus."

## III. THE ALLEGED ATTENDANCE OF CLERGY FROM BRITAIN AT THE FRANKFURT SYNOD OF 794

Alcuin's authorship of C and S provides the clue to the question of the attendance of clergy from Britain at the Synod of

---

[34] A. Harnack, *Lehrbuch der Dogmengeschichte* 3 (4th ed.; Tübingen, 1910), 281; J. Turmel, *Histoire des dogmes* 2 (Paris, 1932), 447–448; J. Tixeront, *Histoire des dogmes* 3 (Paris, 1922), 526 ff.

Frankfurt. Haddan-Stubbs,[35] Hauck,[36] von Schubert, de Clercq, Levison, and Ganshof assume such attendance, Alcuin supposedly being a delegate of the English Church. Boehmer-Mühlbacher,[37] Hefele-Leclercq, and others speak of the attendance of British "scholars." Amann[38] finds it strange that the British Church should have been represented at Frankfurt at all, since the controversy on adoptionism was an internal problem of the Frankish Church. Official English participation is indeed unlikely because of the national[39] Frankish character of the Frankfurt assembly, which was held simultaneously with a Frankish Diet. Alcuin's recent biographer, Kleinclausz, concludes: "La présence des membres du clergé de Grande-Bretagne est mentionnée dans un seul texte, mais en termes formels et par Charlemagne luimême."[40] He thus questions the historical reliability of the source under consideration. On the basis of Alcuin's authorship of Charlemagne's letter, which mentions British participation at Frankfurt, we now know that it is Alcuin himself who is responsible for the appearance of men from *Brittannia* as alleged participants at the synod. He writes in

C 159.40–160.1: *Necnon et de Brittanniae partibus* aliquos ecclesiasticae disciplinae viros convocavimus;

C 160.13–16: et virorum venerabilium fidem, qui in Germaniae, Galliae, Equitaniae, et *Brittanniae partibus*...

---

[35] Haddan and Stubbs, *Councils and Ecclesiastical Documents Relating to Great Britain and Ireland* 3 (Oxford, 1871), 481–482; what is said on p. 483 must be corrected after Ernst Dümmler, *MGH Epistolae* 4.316–317, no. 189.

[36] Hauck (above, n. 23), 311; von Schubert (n. 24), 387; de Clercq (n. 31), 185; Levison (n. 15), 112; Ganshof (n. 1), 310.

[37] *Regesta Imperii* (2nd ed.; Innsbruck, 1908), no. 326; *Histoire des Conciles* 3 (Paris, 1910), 1046 also Voigt (above, n. 4), 319; A. Kleinclausz, *Charlemagne* (Paris, 1934), 238.

[38] Amann (above, note 33), 142.

[39] Barion, "Der kirchenrechtliche Charakter" (above, n. 1), especially pp. 161–165.

[40] Kleinclausz, *Alcuin* 87 n. 74.

The latter passage refers to S, whose *inscriptio* enumerates *Germania*, *Gallia*, and *Aequitania*, but not *Brittannia*, although Alcuin wrote the document. Nor is British attendance mentioned in the official Capitulary of Frankfurt, the last section of which gives Alcuin merely the epithet *vir in ecclesiasticis doctrinis eruditus*. The same sequence of countries as in C 160.13 ff. also appears in Alcuin's *Adversus Felicem* 1.6 (*PL* 101. 133A).

There was then, contrary to all previous statements made by historians, no official representation of the English Church at Frankfurt. And Alcuin did not attend as representative of his native Church but as representative of Charlemagne, who had recalled [41] him in 793 from the British Isles in order to combat the Spanish heresies on the Continent. The references in C to the participation of learned *men* from Britain are Alcuin's rhetorical expressions, by which he records his own work at Frankfurt which he, as author of Charlemagne's letter to Elipand, could not very well express openly in the singular. Even if some of his Saxon disciples had gone with him to the synod, none of them represented the English Church.

Alcuin's authorship of C and S explains, if not completely, at least partially, the fact that he never mentions [42] in any of his writings his own considerable contribution to the synod, whereas he provides, as if by contrast, ample information about the Synod of Regensburg on the Danube,[43] held in July or August, 792, at a time when he had not yet returned [44] from England to Charlemagne.

---

[41] Alcuin, *Epist.* 43 (Dümmler 38.4–6); *Adversus Elipandum* 1.16 (*PL* 101.251C–D); Alcuin to Charlemagne, *Epist.* 229 (D.373.11) of Sept. or Oct. 801: atque *ex diversis mundi partibus* amatores illius vestrae bonae voluntati *adiutores convocare* studuistis; cf. *Epist.* 220 (D.322.28).

[42] Gaskoin, *Alcuin* 87; Kleinclausz, *Alcuin* 88–89, 302.

[43] Correctly mentioned by Kleinclausz, p. 79; Alcuin left England between April and June, 793.

[44] Alcuin, *Adv. Elipandum* 1.16 (*PL* 101.251–252), says clearly that he did not attend the Frankish Synod of Regensburg which was held in 792:

It is, however, erroneous to assume, as Gaskoin, Kleinclausz, and other scholars do, that the Synod of Frankfurt is not at all mentioned in Alcuin's writings. Dümmler [45] points out one indirect reference to the synod, and a second can be found in one of Alcuin's letters.[46] There is, naturally, a very plausible reason why Alcuin is silent about his own great influence on the decisions of the synod. As synodal councilor to the Frankish king and clergy he could not very well make public in written form his personal share in the resolutions. After all, he himself repeatedly stresses in C and S the importance of the *catholica* and *pacifica unanimitas* of the synod. Had he openly claimed the authorship of Charlemagne's letter, he would have belittled the official author of the document, who to him was friend and sovereign and to the world was the ruler of an empire. Nor could Alcuin claim publicly the authorship of the Frankish synodal letter without insulting the Frankish clergy, in whose name the document was sent to Spain. It must have been for his own satisfaction as the unnamed author that he recorded in C "his" participation at Frankfurt by the two references to the attendance of learned "men" from Brittannia, thus also giving vent to his lifelong love for the land of his birth. Charlemagne accorded public recognition to Alcuin's position at the synod by including his name in the last section of the official Frankish Capitulary of 794. Contemporaries were undoubtedly aware of Alcuin's leadership at Frankfurt, but *raisons d'état* required Alcuin to remain silent about it.

---

*Antequam* ego rege Carolo iubente venissem in Francia (from England); see above, note 43, and Boehmer-Mühlbacher, *Regesta Imperii* no. 318a.

[45] *MGH Epistolae* 4, no. 137 (D.211.18) written in 798: *ex auctoritate synodali* habetis responsum, a reference to the Frankish *synodica*.

[46] Alcuin to Arno of Salzburg, *Epist.* 208 (D.346.10) from the year 800: Nam quidam Elipandus, Toletanae civitatis—nomine non dignitate episcopus in *damnata synodali auctoritate* et apostolica censura herese permanens; Kleinclausz mentions *Epist.* 208, on p. 233, without realizing that it contains a reference to the Frankfurt Synod.

## IV. CHARLEMAGNE'S *LIBRI CAROLINI* AND ALCUIN

The leading position of Alcuin in the condemnation of adoptionism forces us to re-examine his possible share in the simultaneous rejection by the Synod of Frankfurt of the veneration of the images of saints, restored at Nicaea in 787 by the Seventh Ecumenical Council. Nothing connected with this veneration (subsequently always referred to as image worship), obviously misunderstood in the *Libri Carolini* as adoration, is ever mentioned by Alcuin in his writings. He observes complete silence about image worship, which the Franks rejected as being peculiar to the Eastern Church. Taking into account Alcuin's presence at the Synod of Frankfurt, it seems inconceivable that he should not also have had a share in its condemnation. We here face a problem that has occupied historians since the days of the Reformation: the much-disputed authorship of Charlemagne's *Libri Carolini* (= LC), a manifesto against the "Greek" veneration of images. The LC mistook for "Greek" what was Catholic in origin, and some of its theological allegations are undoubtedly traceable to the fact that its polemic is based on the poor Latin translation of the Greek Acts of II Nicaea.

A manuscript of the LC survives incompletely in *Vaticanus Latinus* 7207. Hubert Bastgen, the modern editor of LC,[47] believed that this MS had been written for Charlemagne. And Wolfram von den Steinen[48] who also traces the involved textual history of the treatise, ascribed to the king the comments in

---

[47] *Libri Carolini sive Caroli Magni Capitulare de Imaginibus*, ed. H. Bastgen (*MGH Concilia* 2: *Supplementum;* Hannover and Leipzig, 1924); see also Bastgen in *Lexikon für Theologie und Kirche* 6 (1934), 553–554.

[48] W. von den Steinen, "Karl der Grosse und die Libri Carolini," *Neues Archiv* 49 (1932), 207–280; "Entstehungsgeschichte der Libri Carolini," *Quellen und Forschungen aus italienischen Archiven und Bibliotheken* 21 (1929–1930), 1–70.

marginal Tironian notes contained in the codex. But Charlemagne's alleged oral authorship of these notes has been convincingly disproved by Heinrich Fichtenau.[49] The assumption that the LC was approved by the Frankish Synod held in 792 at Regensburg on the Danube is historically as unfounded as is the allegation, made by some historians, that the tractate was confirmed by the Synod of Frankfurt. Bastgen assumes that Alcuin is the author of the LC, while von den Steinen ascribes the work to Theodulph of Orléans.[50] Kleinclausz does not accept Alcuin's authorship because of the haughty tone of the LC, which he considers incompatible with the (allegedly) conciliatory nature of the Saxon.[51] But Alcuin's language in his anti-adoptionist writings is anything but meek; on the contrary, it is rich in original invectives and strong vilifications of Felix of Urgel and Elipand of Toledo, who are often mercilessly ridiculed. As a well-versed rhetorician, Alcuin could easily use various styles as might befit his momentary personal temper and his interest in the subject.

A new link between Alcuin and the LC is provided by his authorship of Charlemagne's letter to Elipand ($= C$) and of the Frankish synodal letter of 794 ($= S$). Bastgen has listed many parallels in word and thought between LC and Alcuin's writ-

[49] Heinrich Fichtenau, "Karl der Grosse und das Kaisertum," *Mitteilungen des Instituts für Oesterreichische Geschichtsforschung* 61 (1953), 276–287.

[50] Von den Steinen expressed this assumption in 1929 (see n. 48), but never supplied the evidence. On the other hand, Dom De Bruyne, "La composition des Libri Carolini," *Revue Bénédictine* 44 (1932), 227 ff., has shown that the argument advanced for the authorship of Theodulph of Orléans by Arthur Allgeier, "Psalmenzitate und die Frage nach der Herkunft der Libri Carolini," *Historisches Jahrbuch der Görresgesellschaft* 46 (1926), 333–353, rests on a wrong premise. Ann Freeman, "Theodulf of Orleans and the Libri Carolini," *Speculum* 32 (1957), 663–705, has not succeeded in proving the authorship of Theodulph, as I shall show elsewhere. Cf. H. Schade, "Die Libri Carolini und ihre Stellung zum Bild," *Zeitschrift für katholische Theologie* 79 (1957), 69–78.

[51] Kleinclausz, *Alcuin* 295–305.

ings.[52] To these we can now add a number of topics—all of them typical Alcuinisms—which are common to C and S, and also occur in LC, as well as in the antiadoptionist writings of Alcuin. Very important new links can also be shown between LC and Charlemagne's credo in C, and between the synodal theory of LC and the corresponding doctrine of C and S. Furthermore, the same presuppositions on the proper method of theology are expressed in the rejection of image worship by LC (see chart below) and in the refutation of adoptionism by C and S: the Spanish heresy originated in man's arrogance (C 159.1 *elatio*) and in his presumptuous rationalizations of divine mysteries beyond the bounds of human ken (see Pt. I above, parallels to C 161.29). The false doctrine disregards the truth, the Sacred Scriptures, and the Catholic tradition of the *patres ecclesiae*. The Spaniards' innovations are "foolish," "ridiculous," and "abhorrent to Catholic ears" (S 148.12–13). All three documents urge that their addressees return to the *via regia* (Num. 21:22), the Biblical King's Highway, as the road leading to salvation. The following chart lists some of the topics which are identical in LC, S, and C:

| Topics | LC | S | C |
|---|---|---|---|
| *Via regia*, Num. 21:22 and Is. 30:21 | *Praef.* 5.28–6.1; II.31 p. 102.17 | 156.22 | 159.4 |
| Reference to Is. 26:1 | *Praef.* 1.21 | — | 160.35 |
| Charlemagne's Credo | III.3 p. 110–13 | *passim* | 163–164 |
| Refutation of overjudicious reasoning | III.3 p. 113.15 | 143.30 | 161.29 |
| Disrespect for parents | IV.7 p. 187.33 *parentes inhonorare* | 156.19 *diffamare parentes* | — |
| Papal advice sought in doctrinal matters | I.6 p. 20.1–3 | — | 159.37 |
| Charlemagne's synodal theory | IV.28 p. 227.27–35 | 143.5 | 162.32 |

[52] H. Bastgen, "Der Verfasser des Capitulare über die Bilder," *Neues Archiv* 37 (1912), 491–533.

Especially revealing is the unique relationship between Charlemagne's profession of faith (F) in C,[53] and the important *Filioque* chapter of LC III.3. For the disputed procession of the Holy Spirit, F offers three formulas which are traditionally connected with the question (C 164.25; 30; 32): "a patre et filio procedentem; procedentem ex patre et filio; ex patre filioque procedens." Of the parallels between F and LC III.3 compare the following two:

[a] LC III.3 (110.37 Bastgen): neque quasi *posterior tempore* aut *minor potestate* aut alterius substantiae procedit, sed ex Patre et Filio;

[b] F (C 163.34): In qua sancta trinitate nulla est persona vel *tempore posterior* vel gradu inferior vel *potestate minor;*

[c] LC III.3 (113.20 Bastgen): Sufficiat hoc credere...*Patrem ingenitum, Filium genitum, Spiritum* vero *Sanctum...ex Patre et Filio procedentem;*

[d] F (C 163.29):...*patrem ingenitum, filium genitum, Spiritum sanctum procedentem ex patre et filio.*

The comments listed in the *Vaticanus* 7207 of the LC are: [54]

     *catholice* to: *aut minor potestate* (see *a*),
     *summe* to: *Sufficiat hoc credere* (see *c*).

The same two passages are distinct formulations of the king's creed (see *b* and *d*) in C. The formulations of *a* and *b* are based on corresponding passages of the *Libellus fidei* of Pelagius and the dogmatic epistle of Leo the Great (*Tomus Leonis*) addressed to Flavian.[55] The unique reading *potestate minor* occurs in F

---

[53] *MGH Concilia* 2.163–164. Max Buchner, "Rom oder Reims: Die Heimat des Constitutum Constantini," *Historisches Jahrbuch der Görresgesellschaft* 53 (1933), 161–164, assumes a connection between F and the notorious forgery.

[54] Listed by von den Steinen, *Neues Archiv* 49 (1932), 211. I read *summe* (instead of *summa*) as suggested by A. Mentz, "Die Tironischen Noten," *Archiv für Urkundenforschung* 17 (1942), 262.

[55] Pelagius: ut nec tempore nec gradu nec potestate possit esse inferior; Leo the Great: non posterior tempore, non inferior potestate (see above, n. 9).

*and* in the LC. The formulation commended with the remark *summe* is found *verbatim* in the king's personal profession of faith (*d*). The identity of Charlemagne's concept of the *Filioque* and related parts of the symbolum in LC III.3 *and* his personal credo (= F) in C naturally points to the same author of the creed, i.e., Alcuin. F and LC also close in a similar fashion:

LC III.3 (113.20 Bastgen): Sufficiat hoc credere, hoc *firmiter tenere...* ita duntaxat, ut in confessione fidei *omnes opinationes, omnes verborum novitates caveantur,...taxaverunt;*

F (C 164.25): Hanc fidem vos, karissimi fratres, *firmiter tenere in* commune deprecamur...et *contentiones nominum novitatesque vocum devitate.*

In this text of LC,[56] the passage from *ita* to *taxaverunt* (Bastgen 113.22–24) is written in the Vatican MS as a correction to replace a canceled, original section of considerable length (B. 113.28–47). There is an obvious discrepancy between LC III.3, on the one hand, which argues against the older *ex patre procedentem* in favor of the insertion of the disputed *filioque*, and LC.III.1, on the other, which offers in its present, corrected version the *Libellus Fidei* of Pelagius with the rejected *ex patre procedentem.* This contradiction results from the fact that the original profession of faith of LC III.1, of which only the title is preserved in the Vatican MS (B. 106.9–10), was in part deleted and in part removed from this codex by an editor of the eighth century, who substituted for an original version of the credo that of Pelagius. The first articles of the latter, i.e., the text of fol. 117ᵛ of the Vatican MS (B. 106.11–28), is written on erasure after the text of Charlemagne's original credo (X) had been deleted. The newly inserted fols. 118 and 119, which contain the remaining portions of the Pelagian symbol, replace two original leaves which must have contained the rest of X. The first articles of Charlemagne's credo discussed in LC III.3

[56] See the remarks by von den Steinen, *Quellen und Forsch.* 21 (1929–1930), 74 n. 1; *Neues Archiv* 49 (1932), 230–231.

are therefore probably preserved as palimpsest on fol. 117$^v$ of the Vatican MS.

The relationship [57] between LC III.3 and F may be added to the evidence produced by Bastgen for Alcuin's authorship of the LC, although I believe that Alcuin is not the author, but rather the final editor of the treatise, the larger part of which was probably drawn up for Charlemagne by another theologian. The cursory character of the vestiges of Alcuin's diction and speech in LC seems to indicate this state of affairs. The occurrence, for instance, in the *Praefatio* [58] and in LC II.31 of the idea of *via regia*—a typical Alcuinism, often mentioned in his epistles and treatises [59]—suggests Alcuin's editorial work on an already extant draft of a treatise against image worship. The same motives that prevented him from recording openly his significant contribution to the condemnation of adoptionism at the Synod of Frankfurt of 794 must have forced him to observe complete silence about his personal share in the simultaneous rejection of image worship, a step prepared by Charlemagne through the compilation of LC by one of the trusted theologians of his entourage.

Since the LC were never published officially, it is unlikely that they were ever submitted for endorsement to any of the Frankish synods. Alcuin, as the king's most trusted theological adviser, seems to have put the treatise in its final form and shape after its content was discussed, revised, and approved by the court theologians in the presence of Charlemagne. The fact remains, however, that in all the writings of Alcuin no substantive trace is found of what was to be the main object of the LC,

[57] This interdependence remained unknown to Dom B. Capelle, "L'introduction du symbole à la messe," *Mélanges Joseph de Ghellinck* 2 (Gembloux, 1951), 1009–1015, who suggests Alcuin's possible authorship of F on the basis of the occurrence of the identical, unique (even incorrect) variants in the text of the symbol and in that of the *Irish Stowe Missal*, which had been adopted by Alcuin.

[58] Ed. Bastgen 5.29–6.1; 102.16.          [59] See above, n. 10.

the question of images. But on the strength of the evidence collected by Bastgen for Alcuin's alleged authorship of the LC and the important internal proximity between the *Filioque* chapter LC III.3 and Charlemagne's personal credo in the letter to Elipand (C), I must assume that Alcuin *edited* LC some time before a Frankish Synod and a Frankish Diet convened at Frankfurt on June 1, 794.

Such a connection is further supported by the relation of S and C to the last chapter of the LC, concerning the concept of an ecumenical council. LC IV.28 rejects the claim of the Eastern Church that the Second Council of Nicaea was a universal synod. Two kinds of church assemblies are distinguished in the discussion: the geographically universal, i.e., formally ecumenical synod, and the meeting that consists of just "two or three" provinces. Even such a synod can be called universal, provided that the participants remain within the bounds of traditional, i.e., universal Catholic doctrines. Councils which deviate from this principle, such as the Second Council of Nicaea of 787, are neither Catholic nor universal. Ecumenicity in the formal sense, i.e., any geographically universal character, is implicitly denied to this council. A similar synodal theory is alluded to in S and C, a fact which might point to a common originator of the following texts, namely, Alcuin.

S 143.5: *Ubi sunt duo vel tres congregati in nomine meo, ibi sum in medio eorum* (Matt. 18:20), congregatis nobis *in unum conventum*, praecipiente et praesidente piissimo...domno nostro Carolo rege, ad renovandum cum consilio *pacificae unanimitatis* sanctae Dei ecclesiae statum;

C 162.32: Ad multitudinem populi Christiani et *ad concilii sacerdotalis unanimitatem* revertimini. Si enim duorum vel trium (cf. Matt. 18:20) sancto pioque consensui secundum suam promissionem Dominum esse presentem non dubitamus, quanto magis ubi tot sanctissimi patres...in nomine illius *pacifica conveniunt unanimitate*, eum adesse medium non dubitamus;

LC IV.28 (Bastgen 227.27–31): Cum ergo duarum et trium provinciarum praesules (cf. Matt. 18:20) *in unum conveniunt,* si antiquorum canonum institutione muniti aliquid praedicationis aut dogmatis statuunt, quod tamen ab antiquorum Patrum dogmatibus non discrepat, catholicum est, quod faciunt, et fortasse dici potest universale; quoniam, quamvis non sit ab universi orbis praesulibus actum, tamen ab universorum fide et traditione non discrepat.

Bastgen overlooks the fact that the synodal theory of LC IV.28 contains a verbal echo of Matt. 18:20, a passage directly quoted in S and in part used also in C. The similarities in these three texts cannot be denied, though LC shifts from persons to provinces and adds the key principle of material congruity with tradition.

The references to the synodal theory in S and C sound as if they presuppose the LC. S and C thus refer to the "universal" character of the Synod of Frankfurt and its unanimous condemnation of the heretical doctrines of the adoptionists. Both documents stress the universality (S 143.25,36; C 159.36; 164.30) of the Catholic faith, represented in the *unanimitas synodalis* (S 143.8; 163.11), from which only the few (C 164.27) Spanish heretics are separated (S 156.19,40; C 162.32), because they deem themselves wiser (S 143.27; C 161.27) than the tradition of *universalis ecclesia.* In C, Charlemagne thus claims, in conformity with the synodal theory set forth in LC IV.28 (B. 227.27), the universal validity of the decisions of the Synod of Frankfurt. The same claim is made by the Frankish bishops in S, written for them by Alcuin. It must be stressed, however, that neither Charlemagne, nor the Frankish bishops, nor Alcuin proclaim that the Frankfurt Synod is a universal council. Thus the synodal theory of S and C again conforms to that of LC IV.28, which does not categorically identify the Catholicity of a council with its uncertain (*fortasse*) ecumenical character. We are therefore confronted with the paradoxical fact that a synod which was actually a national council of the Frankish Church claims the prerogative of an ecumenical, universal council, because the Frankish king, as the absolute leader of a national Church and clergy, establishes his own principle and interpretation of synodal law, counseled and advised by the Saxon Alcuin.

The present writer is not alone in questioning the validity of Miss Freeman's notions (above, p. 170 n. 50). A reviewer in the *Archiv für Liturgiewissenschaft* VIII (1963), 219 no. 337, expresses the opinion that future studies must show whether her argumentation is entirely sound and valid: "ob die Beweisführung ganz stichhaltig ist . . .". Her conclusions were rejected in my study, "The unknown author of the *Libri Carolini:* Patristic exegesis, Mozarabic antiphons, and the *Vetus Latina,*" in: *Didascaliae: Studies in Honor of Anselm M. Albareda,* ed. Sesto Prete (New York, 1961), 469-515. M. Cappuyns, *Revue d'histoire ecclésiastique* LIX (1964), 693, in his review of this study concludes: "M. W. n'a pas de peine à énerver cette argumentation." Heinrich Fichtenau, *Mitteilungen des Instituts für oesterreichische Geschichtsforschung* LXX (1962), 112 speaks of the "Zerstörung" of Ann Freeman's thesis. Heinrich Weisweiler, *Scholastik* IXL (1964), 241-42, reports on my rejection of her assumptions —*eine sehr wertvolle Arbeit*—. See furthermore my most recent studies: "The Greek and the Latin Versions of II Nicaea and Hadrian I's Synodica of 785 (JE 2448): A Diplomatic Study," *Traditio* XXII (1966), 103-25; also: "The *Libri Carolini* and Patristics, Latin and Greek: Prolegomena to a critical Edition," in: *The Classical Tradition: Literary and Historical Studies in Honor of Harry Caplan,* ed. Luitpold Wallach (Cornell University Press: Ithaca, New York 1966), 451-98; Part II of the *Prolegomena* will appear in the near future, and will include, among other topics, also the following: "Theodulf of Orléans' alleged authorship of the *Libri Carolini:* Fictions and Facts."

On the official position of Alcuin occupied at the Frankfurt Synod of 794 (above, pp. 147-68) see now H. B. Meyer, "Zur Stellung Alkuins auf dem Frankfurter Konzil (794)," *Zeitschrift für katholische Theologie* 81 (1959), 455-60.

# CHAPTER X

# The Epitaph of Hadrian I
# Composed for Charlemagne
# by Alcuin

ALCUIN is the author of many metrical inscriptions (*tituli*) for the altars and walls of churches and monasteries and for epitaphs [1] and book dedications. None of his biographers has paid proper attention to this aspect of his work; yet even in the role of epigrapher the versatile Anglo-Saxon is deserving of our interest. Edmond Le Blant [2] initiated the critical appraisal of Alcuin's epigraphic work, but since 1856 the subject has been neglected. Available material entitles us to speak not only of the much discussed Scriptorium of Tours but also of the Epigraphic School of Tours. [3] The best-known inscription of the school is

[1] Cf. J. B. de Rossi, "Tituli et epitaphia vetera mixta carminibus Alcuini," *Inscriptiones Christianae Vrbis Romae Septimo Saeculo Antiquiores* II, 1 (Rome, 1888), 280–282.

[2] *Inscriptions chrétiennes de la Gaule antérieures au VIIIe siècle* I (Paris, 1856), cxxxiii–iv.

[3] Wilhelm Köhler, *Die karolingischen Miniaturen*, Text I, 1 (Berlin, 1930), 87, questions the Turonian provenance of the epitaph (suggested by de Rossi) and assumes the East-Frankish origin of the black marble

the epitaph of Pope Hadrian I (772–795), placed on his tomb at Rome upon the request of Charlemagne. J. B. de Rossi [4] concludes that the lapidary workmanship and the style of the inscription are without equal among contemporary epigraphic products of Rome or elsewhere. Its well-executed Roman square capital is fashioned after older Roman inscriptions, many of which were undoubtedly still extant at Tours during the time of Alcuin (796–804).[5]

The metrical epitaph consists of thirty-nine elegiacs and one dateline. There are never more than forty full-sized capitals to a verse. The space-saving ligatures of two letters (*litterae contiguae*) [6] are identical with those in inscriptions of the early Roman empire. In addition to the ordinary capital T, we thus encounter the archaic form of the letter as used during the empire, the heightened T, which extends above the upper rim of the letters so that its transverse line is above the preceding and the following capitals. The same form of the letter is used for the ligature of T and R, in which case the rounded arch of R is below the right branch of the elevated crossbeam, while the normal-sized T is used for the ligature of T and E. Other space-saving devices are the insertion of a small capital in the cavity of a rounded, large capital (*litterae insertae*) such as v in Q and C, and a in C, and finally the small capitals a, o, i, suspended halfway between two normal-sized letters. The *nomina sacra* of

plate. I believe that the evidence for de Rossi's thesis here presented speaks for the existence of the Epigraphic School of Tours.

[4] "L'inscription du tombeau d'Hadrien I, composée et gravée en France par ordre de Charlemagne," *École Française de Rome, Mélanges d'Archéologie et d'Histoire* VIII (1888), 478–501.

[5] See J. Boussard, "Étude sur la ville de Tours du Ier au IVe siècle," *Revue des Études Anciennes* L (1948), 312–329; H. Auvray, "La Touraine Gallo-Romaine," *Bulletin de la Société Archéologique de Touraine* XXVII (1938).

[6] See the lists of ligatures in Réné Cagnat, *Cours d'épigraphie latine* (4th ed.; Paris, 1914), 24–26; J. E. Sandys, *Latin Epigraphy* (2nd ed., by S. G. Campbell; Cambridge, 1927), 52.

the inscription are identical with those occurring in manuscripts from the Scriptorium of Tours.[7] The significance of the use by the engraver of two different ways of writing KAROLVS seems to have escaped the attention of de Rossi. The name is written KAROLVS (v. 24) and KARoLVS (v. 17). The occurrence of the second spelling in an inscription which originated, literally and technically, at the request of the Frankish king, possesses more than a merely epigraphic meaning. The monogram spelling resembles the legend on the coins of Charlemagne.[8] The public display of such a *nomisma nominis nostri* was an exclusive royal prerogative, a fact which was undoubtedly known to the engraver of the inscription.

The question that interests us is the disputed authorship of the inscription. Some scholars ascribe it to Charlemagne, relying on v. 17:

POST PATREM LACRIMANS KAROLVS HAEC
CARMINA SCRIBSI,

others assume Alcuin's authorship or reserve their judgment. Orazio Marucchi ascribes it to the king,[9] Arthur Kleinclausz to Alcuin.[10] The Bollandist Ianning suggested the authorship of Alcuin on the basis of seven locutions in the epitaph for which he adduced parallels from the poems of Alcuin.[11] L. Duchesne mentioned Alcuin with reservation,[12] while E. K. Rand concluded with de Rossi that the Anglo-Saxon is indeed the author of Ha-

---

[7] E. K. Rand, *Studies in the Script of Tours* II (Cambridge, Mass., 1934), 44–45.

[8] See the reproductions of Carolingian coins in *Dictionnaire d'archéologie chrétienne et de liturgie* III (Paris, 1913), 685; Anatole de Barthélemy, "Les monnaies de Charlemagne," in A. Vétault, *Charlemagne* (3rd ed.; Tours, 1888), 523–530; *Capitulare Francofurtense* of 794, MGH, *Concilia* I, 166, art. V: nomisma nominis nostri.

[9] *Christian Epigraphy* (tr. by J. A. Willis; Cambridge, 1912), 455.

[10] *Alcuin* (Paris, 1948), 248.

[11] *Acta Sanctorum Junii* VII, 2 (1867), 98–100.

[12] *Le Liber Pontificalis* I (Paris, 1886), 553.

drian's epitaph.[13]  Ernst Dümmler, who noticed three stylistic parallels between the inscription and Alcuin's poetry, but not those previously listed by Ianning, did not include the metrical inscription among the poems of Alcuin.[14]  His edition of the epitaph is not based on the epigraphic evidence, but on the transmission of manuscripts. One of these contains a revision of the original text. Dümmler accordingly reads v. 14:

> *Urbis et orbis* honor, inclyta Roma, tuas,

while the inscription offers:

VRBS CAPVT ORBIS HONOR INCLYTA ROMA TVAS.

The scribe of the manuscript used by Dümmler in this instance revised Alcuin's words after the epitaph of Hadrian I composed by Alcuin's friend Theodulph of Orléans,[15] *Super Sepulchrum Hadriani Papae*, v. 9:

> Tu decus ecclesiae, fax splendens *urbis et orbis*.

The following edition of Hadrian's epitaph [16] endeavors to prove the authorship of Alcuin on the basis of the numerous parallels between the inscription and Alcuin's poetry.[17]

---

[13] *Studies in the Script of Tours* I (Cambridge, Mass., 1929), 41.

[14] *MGH, Poetae* I, 112–113.      [15] *Ibid.*, pp. 489–490, no. XXVI.

[16] See de Rossi, *op. cit.*, pp. 478–479, and the facsimile of the inscription provided by him; L. Duchesne (n. 12), p. 523; Fedor Schneider und Walther Holtzmann, *Die Epitaphien der Päpste und andere stadtrömische Inschriften (Texte zur Kulturgeschichte des Mittelalters*, VI [Rome, 1933]); Ferdinand Gregorovius, *Le Tombe dei Papi* (sec. ed. ital. riv. et ampl. da C. Hülsen; Rome, 1931); H. Leclerq, "Epitaphe d'Hadrien Ier," *Dictionnaire d'archéologie chrétienne et de liturgie* VI (Paris, 1925), 1964–1967; also XIII (1937), 1255–1264; an English translation of Hadrian's epitaph is offered by Jacob Isidor Mombert, *A History of Charles the Great* (New York, 1886), 337–338; see ch. xiii n. 2.

[17] Abbreviations used in the commentary:

*CLE—Carmina Latina Epigraphica*, ed. Buecheler and Lommatzsch;

de Rossi—J. B. de Rossi, *Inscriptiones, Christianae Vrbis Romae* I–II, 1 (Rome, 1888);

### The Epitaph of Pope Hadrian I (772–795)

(today in the Portico of St. Peter's at Rome)

1  Hic pater ecclesiae, *Romae decus, inclytus auctor*
    Hadrianus requiem papa beatus habet.
    Vir cui vita Deus, pietas lex, gloria Christus,
      *Pastor apostolicus, promptus ad omne bonum,*
5  *Nobilis* ex *magna genitus* iam *gente parentum,*
      *Sed* sacris longe *nobilior meritis,*
    *Exornare stud*ens *devoto pectore* pastor,
      *Semper ubique* suo *templa sacrata Deo,*
    *Ecclesias donis,* populos et dogmate sancto
10    *Imbuit et* cunctis pandit *ad astra viam.*
    *Pauperibus largus, nulli pietate secundus,*
      Et pro plebe *sacris pervigil in precibus,*
    Doctrinis, opibus, muris erexerat arces,
      *Urbs caput orbis honor, inclyta Roma,* tuas.
15  *Mors cui nil nocuit,* Christi quae *morte perempta* est,
    *Ianua sed vitae* mox *melioris* erat.
    Post patrem lacrimans Karolus *haec carmina scribsi,*
      *Tu mihi dulcis amor, te* modo *plango,* pater.
    *Tu memor esto mei, sequitur te mens mea semper,*
20    *Cum Christo teneas regna beata poli.*
    Te clerus, populus *magno dilexit amore,*
      Omnibus *unus amor,* optime praesul, eras.
    Nomina *iungo* simul titulis, clarissime, nostra,
      Hadrianus Karolus, rex ego tuque pater.
25  *Quisque legas versus, devoto pectore supplex:*
    "Amborum mitis," dic, "miserere Deus."
    Haec tua nunc teneat requies, carissime, membra,
      Cum sanctis anima gaudeat alma Dei.
    *Ultima* quippe tuas *donec tuba clamet* in aures,

---

Diehl—Ernestus Diehl, *Inscriptiones Latinae Christianae Veteres* I–III
    (Berlin, 1926–1931);
Fortunatus—Venantius Fortunatus, ed. Friedrich Leo, *MGH, Auctores*
    *Antiquissimi,* IV.1; IV.2, ed. Bruno Krusch;
Ianning—*Acta Sanctorum Junii* VII, 2 (1867), 99;
Dümmler—*MGH, Poetae* I.112.

30      Principe cum Petro *surge* videre Deum.
     *Auditurus eris vocem,* scio, *iudicis almam:*
     "*Intra nunc domini gaudia magna tui.*"
     *Tunc memor esto tui nati, pater optime, posco:*
     "Cum patre," dic, "natus pergat et iste meus."
35      O pete *regna,* pater felix, *caelestis* Christi;
     Inde tuum *precibus auxiliare* gregem.
     Dum *sol ignicomo rutilus splendescit ab axe,*
      *Laus tua,* sancte pater, *semper in orbe manet.*
     Sedit beatae memoriae Hadrianus papa
40      Annos XXIII menses X dies XVII obiit VII Kalendas Ianuarias.

1   *Romae decus*] Cf. Publ. Optat. Porfyrius, *Carmina,* X.21, ed. Elsa
Kluge (Teubner, 1926): Concordi saeclo *Romae decus;* II.19:
    Alme, salus orbis, *Romae decus, inclyta fama;*
cf. Alcuin in Poem on York, v. 455 (p. 179):
    *Inclyta fama* viri nec solum iure Britannos
    inlustrat populos. Cf. Bede, *Hist. Eccl.,* III, 13.
*inclytus auctor*] Alcuin, *Epit. Pauli Monachi Turonensis,* CXIII.17
(p. 344), cited by Ianning;
    Mox Martinus amor rapuit me *inclitus auctor;*
*Vita Willibrordi,* II.3.1 (p. 210):
    Crescere Pippinus dum viderat *inclytus auctor;*
in Poem addressed to Paulinus of Aquileia, XVII.14 (p. 239), cited
by Ianning:
    O laus Ausoniae, *patriae decus, inclytus auctor;*
*Epit. Civitatis Papiae, MGH, Poetae,* I, 102, no. I.1.3:
    Et pater et pastor, *patriae decus, inclitus auctor;*
cf. Virgil, *Aen.,* VII.134: Dardanus...pater urbis et auctor.

4   *Pastor apostolicus*] Alcuin, XLV.69 (p. 259); *Vita Willibrordi* II.3.6
(p. 210).
*promptus ad omne bonum*] *Vita Willibrordi* II.34.38 (p. 219), cited
by Dümmler; in two epitaphs: XCIX.13.4 (p. 325), and XCII.2.6 (p.
319): Hic decus ecclesiae, *promptus in omne bonum;* Alcuin's model
is Fortunatus, II.11.19–20:
    Ecclesiae fultor, laus regum, pastor egentum,
    Cura sacerdotum, *promptus ad omne bonum;*
the locution occurs in the following Carolingian epitaphs: *Ep. Folradi,*
ed. *MGH, Poetae,* I, 404, no. XII.14, cited by Dümmler; *Ep. Grimo-
aldi,* p. 430, 16; *Ep. Godefridi, MGH, Poetae,* II, 652, no. IV.6; Diehl,
4766, 4 (Rome), without reference to Fortunatus.

5–6   Alcuin, *Vita Willibrordi* II.33.1–2 (p. 218), cited by Dümmler:
      *Nobilis* iste fuit *magna* de *gente* sacerdos,
         *Sed* magnis multis *nobilior meritis;*
      in the Poem on York, vv. 752–754 (p. 186):
      Accepit sponsam Adiltrudam nomine dictam,
      Nobilium genitam regali stirpe parentum,
      Nobilior longe casta quae mente manebat;
      *ibid.*, vv. 1250–1251 (p. 197):
      Hic fuit Ecgbertus regali stirpe creatus,
      Nobilium coram saeclo radice parentum,
      Sed domino coram meritis praeclarior almis.
      Alcuin uses consistently the figure of *antimetabole* in these characteri-
      zations; see also Otto Weinreich, "Ueber einige panegyrische Topoi
      der Schönheits- und Charakterschilderung," *Würzburger Jahrbücher
      für die Altertumswissenschaft* I (1946), 121–123. Alcuin's source is
      Fortunatus IV.8.11–12:
      *Nobilis* antiquo veniens de germine patrum,
         *Sed* magis in Christo *nobilior meritis;*
      Nobilis et merito nobiliore potens (IV.13.4);
      Nobilis antiqua decurrens prole parentum,
         Nobilior gestis nunc super astra manet (IV.2.5);
      Nobilitas in gente sua cui celsa refulsit
         Atque suis meritis additur alter honor (IV.26.37).

7   *Exornare studens*] Alcuin in the Poem on York, v. 1027 (p. 192):
      *Exornans* ovibus Christi *studiosus* alendis;
      *devoto pectore*] Alcuin, *ibid.*, v. 1256 (p. 197):
      Pauperibus tribuens *devoto pectore gazas;*
      Alcuin, LXVIII, 22 (p. 287); Sedulius, *Carm. Pasch.*, V.350; Iuvencus,
      *Evang. Libri Quattuor*, I.610; Diehl, 611, 1 (Rome).

8   *Semper ubique*] A favorite locution of Alcuin; cf. CXIII.30 (p. 344),
      cited by Ianning;
      Vosque valete mei *semper ubique* deo;
      Atque dies nostros precibus rege *semper ubique* (XCIX.12.11);
      *Semper ubique* vale, dic dic, dulcissime David,
         David amor Flacci, *semper ubique* vale (XXXVII.7–8, p. 252);
      *Semper ubique* deo, peto, vos estote fideles (X.16, p. 236);
      cf. *Acts*, 24:3: *Semper* et *ubique* suscepimus.
      *templa sacrata deo*] Alcuin, LXIX.118 (p. 290); Ovid, *Fasti*, I.706:
      templa dicata deis.

9   Alcuin in the Poem on York, v. 275, p. 175;
> Extruit *ecclesias donisque* exornat opimis;

*ibid.*, v. 1228, p. 196:
> *Ecclesias* alias *donis* ornavit opimis.

10   Alcuin in the Poem on York, v. 1652 (p. 206):
> *Imbuit et* primis utcumque verenter ab annis;

Alcuin, XC.13.4 (p. 315):
> clementem nobis *pandat ad astra viam;*

cf. *Miracula Nynie Episcopi*, v. 498, *MGH, Poetae*, IV:
> *Pandit ad astra* volans meritis celestibus aures.

Alcuin had received a copy of the *Miracula Nynie* from his native York, which he acknowledged in a letter, *MGH, Epistolae* IV, no. 273, p. 431. The *Miracula* are preserved in Cod. Bamberg. B.II.10, a sylloge ascribed to Alcuin. Mr. R. Toussaint of Bois-Colombes (France) calls my attention to Elpis, *Hymnus* I, v. 4, *PL* 63, 537:
> Reisque in astra liberam pandit viam;

see furthermore *CLE*, 669, 2 (Rome): fecit *ad astra viam.*

11   *Pauperibus largus*] Alcuin, *Versus ad Leonem Papam*, XV.6 (p. 238):
> *Pauperibus largus,* clarus honore pio;

*Ad Friducinum*, XLVI.14 (p. 259):
> *Pauperibus largus* seu miserisque pater;

in the Poem on York, v. 269 (p. 175):
> *Pauperibus largus,* parcus sibi, dives in omnes;

*ibid.*, v. 1018 (p. 192):
> *Pauperibus largus,* sibimet sed semper egenus;

cf. Epitaph of Pope Felix IV, Diehl, 986, 5 (Rome):
> *Pauperibus largus,* miseris solatia praestans;

epitaph of Marea, Diehl, 989, 9 (Rome):
> *Pauperibus largus* vixisti, nulla reservans;

sylloge of Tours, ed. de Rossi, II.1, p. 67, no. 25, 3–4:
> Pauperibus larga distribuere manu;

sylloge of Verdun, Diehl, 1135, 7 (Rome):
> *Largus pauperibus* dives tibi carus amicis;

Diehl, 1678, 11 (Vienne):
> Semper devota suis, pauperibus larga;

epitaph *Siconis principis* of 832, *MGH, Poetae*, II.648, no. 2, 36:
> *Largus* et in cunctis *pauperibus*que pius;

epitaph of Hugo Lausannensis episcopus (d. 1038), *MGH, Scriptores*, XXIV, 799, 25:
> *Pauperibus largus* fuerat viduisque maritus;

Pseudo-Turpin, epitaph of Roland, *MGH, Poetae*, I.110, 10:
> *Largus pauperibus,* prodigus hospitibus.

Cf. Arator, *Act. Apost.*, I.835: pauperibus quae larga fuit; Bede, *Hist. Eccl.*, III.6: pauperibus et...largus.

11 *nulli pietate secundus*] Alcuin, CIX.24.11 (p. 340), cited by Ianning:
   Vir pius et prudens, *nulli pietate secundus;*
Alcuin, *Vita Willibrordi*, II.4.3 (p. 210):
   Vir bonus et prudens, *nulli pietate secundus;*
cf. Alexander Riese, *Anthologia Latina*, I (1894), no. 1, p. 8, cited by Dümmler:
   Vir magnus bello, *nulli pietate secundus;*
epitaph of Louis the Pious of 840, *MGH, Poetae*, II.654, 5:
   Hic fidus, fortis, *nulli pietate secundus;*
cf. Fortunatus, IV.9.11–13:
   Egregius, nulli de nobilitate secundus;
Virgil, *Aen.*, XI.441: ulli veterum virtute secundus.

12 Alcuin, XCI.2.3 (p. 317):
   *Pervigiles precibus* iam, vos insistite *sacris;*
in the Poem on York, v. 1196 (p. 195):
   At *vigil in precibus* perstabat nocte sacerdos;
XCI.3.7 (p. 318):
   Pervigil idcirco magnum tibi conde triumphum.

13 Alcuin, XXV.1.1–3 (p. 245), cited by Ianning:
   Salve, *Roma* potens, mundi decus, *inclyta* mater;
   Et *caput orbis*, honor magnus, Leo papa valeto.
XXI.5 (p. 242), cited by Ianning:
   *Urbs, caput orbis*, habet te maxima *Roma* magistrum;
XLV.31.63 (p. 258), IX.37 (p. 230):
   Roma, caput mundi, mundi decus, aurea Roma;
*Vita Willibrordi*, I.32, ed. Wilhelm Levison, *MGH, Scriptores Rerum Merovingicarum*, VII, 139, 7: Roma urbs, orbis caput; cf. Ovid, *Fasti*, V.93: hic, ubi nunc Roma est, orbis caput; *Amor.*, I.15.26: Roma triumphati dum caput orbis erit; *Met.*, XV.435; *Trist.*, III.5.46. The Roman Church is called by Hadrian in letters to Charlemagne: caput totius mundi; see *Codex Carolinus*, ed. Gundlach, *MGH, Epistolae Meroving. et Karolini Aevi* I, 72, pp. 602–603, no. 94, p. 636, 5.
*inclyta Roma*] Virgil, *Aen.*, VI.781; Prudentius, *Contra orationem Symmachi*, I.553; II.357; Alcuin was familiar with Prudentius; see CXXIII.13 (p. 350):
   Cur Tyrio *corpus inhias vestirier ostro,*
and Prudentius, *Peristephanon*, 388: corporisque piis inhias; *Psychomachia*, 39: floribus ardentique iubet *vestirier ostro;* cf. Virgil, *Georg.*, III.17: Ego Tyrio conspectus in ostro; Ovid, *Ep.*, XII.179; *Met.*, X.211.

15   Alcuin, XXII.3.7 (p. 319):
     Sed quem Christus amat, illi *mors nulla nocebit;*
     cf. I Cor. 15:54–55; Diehl, 64, 7 (Rome): nil tibi mors nocuit; Diehl,
     244,9 (Rome): non multum, mors dira, noces; Diehl, 170,7 (Salerno):
     sed tibi nil potuit mors haec tam saeva nocere; *Epitaph. Marii episcopi
     Aventicensis*, ed. T. Mommsen, *MGH, Auct. Antt.*, XI.227:
     Mors infesta ruens quamvis ex lege parentis,
     Moribus instructis nulla nocere potest;
     *CLE*, 1361, 8 (Ansa, Lugdunensis): mors nihil est; *Epit. Grimoaldi*
     of 807, *MGH, Poetae*, I.43,37:
     Mors tibi non nocuit;
     cf. Lucretius, III.830 on the folly of the fear of death:
     Nil igitur mors est ad nos neque pertinet hilum.
     *morte perempta*] Dracontius, *De laudibus Dei*, I.649:
     Ac sine morte tamen vitali in *morte perempta;*
     Virgil, *Aen.*, VI.163: indigna morte peremptum.

16   Alcuin, IX.147 (p. 232):
     *Sed* magis ad studium *vitae melioris* abundet;
     CVII.2.13 (p. 334): ianua vitae; XCIX.22.3 (p. 327): vitae melioris
     amator; cf. Alcuin in *Epistle* 266, p. 424.33: novi...et renovetur vita mea
     in melius (i.e., after death).

17   Alcuin in the Poem on York, vv. 1653–1654, p. 206:
     *Haec* idcirco cui propriis de patribus atque
     Regibus et sanctis ruralia *carmina scripsi;*
     cf. *CLE*, 1988, 35 (Rome): hos tibi dat versus *lachrimans* sine fine
     patronus; Einhard, *Vita Caroli*, ch. 19, reports: Nuntiato sibi Adriani
     Romani pontificis obitu, quem in amicis praecipium habebat, sic flevit
     acsi fratrem aut filium amisisset carissimum. On references in the letters
     of Alcuin on the death of Hadrian see Bernhard Simson, *Jahrbücher
     des Fränkischen Reiches unter Karl d. Gr.* II (Leipzig, 1883), 109 n. 4.

18   Alcuin, LV.1.10 (p. 266):
     Dulcis amor lacrimis absentem plangit amicum;
     Tu requies mentem, *tu mihi dulcis amor;*
     IX.191 (p. 234):
     *Tecum plango* tuos casus, karissime frater.

18–19   Alcuin, XXIX.3–4 (p. 248):
     *Tu mihi dulcis amor*, cordis tu carmen in ore,
     *Tu memor esto mihi*, tu sine fine vale;
     *Tu mihi dulcis amor* (already cited by Ianning) is a favorite locution

of Alcuin; see XLI.1 (p. 253), XXXV.3 (p. 251), XC.6 (p. 313). Cf.
Bede, *Vita S. Cuthberti*, XLV.924, ed. Werner Jaager (*Palaestra* 198;
Leipzig, 1935): Hoc te, dulcis amor; Sedulius, *Hymnus*, I.2: Dulcis
amor; Ovid, *Fasti*, V.653: dulci...amore.

19   Alcuin, *Versus ad Leonem Apostolicum*, XLIV.1 (p. 255):
         *Te mea mens sequitur*, carissime Candide, triste;
     *Ad Amicos*, LII.3 (p. 265):
         *Te mea mens sequitur*, magno cum corde amore;
     *Versus ad Carolum Imp.*, XLV.17 (p. 257):
         *Te mea mens sequitur*, sequitur quoque carmen amoris;
     Hrabanus Maurus, Alcuin's pupil, repeats this locution in his *Carmina*,
     *MGH*, *Poetae*, II.188, no. XXV, 7, p. 170, no. VI. 15; cf. Virgil, *Aen.*,
     X.182: mentes omnibus sua sequendi.

20   Alcuin, *Versus ad Carolum Imp.*, XLV.14 (p. 257):
         *Cum Christo teneat regna beata poli;*
     Alcuin in letter to Beatus of Liébana, ed. Wilhelm Levison, *England
     and the Continent in the Eighth Century* (Oxford, 1946), 323, 18:
         *Cum* sanctis *teneas regna beata poli;*
     cf. Ovid, *Ep.*, I.106: regna tenere potest; *Ep.*, XII.24: regna beata.
     Alcuin, LXIX.176 (p. 292):
         Vel praecepta dei, aut *regna beata poli;*
     Diehl, 1043, 2 (Milan):
         Aurelius penetrans *regna beata poli.*

21   Cf. *CLE*, III.2107, 3 (Madaura): non inmerito *magno dilexit amore;*
     Virgil, *Aen.*, I.344: et magno miserae dilectus amore.
     Alcuin, XCII.2.9 (p. 319):
         Iste pios patres *magno dilexit amore;*
     Alcuin, XCIX.12.4:...*dilexit amore.*

22   Alcuin, *De fide s. trinitatis*, XX (Migne, *PL*, CI.54B): *Unus amor
     omnibus;*
     Alcuin, LXV.4a.18 (p. 285):
         *Unus amor*, lector, qui sit tibi semper in aevum;
     cf. *Epit. Pippini*, *MGH*, *Poetae*, I.405, 13–15:
         *Unus amor* populi, virtus, pax omnibus una,
             Dilexit cunctos, unus amor populi;
     cf. *CLE*, 491, 2 (Faventia):
         *Unus amor* mansit, par quoque vita fidelis,
     cf. Fortunatus, VI.1.68: amor populi; VI.1.139: *unus amor.*

23–24  This idea of friendship is the same as that expressed by Alcuin,
LII.17–18 (p. 265):

> Quos caritate pia terris coniunxit amicos,
>> Gaudentes pariter iungat in arce poli;

on the close friendship between king and pope see Erich Caspar,
"Hadrian I und Karl der Grosse," *Zeitschrift für Kirchengeschichte*
LIV (1935), 150–214. Hadrian calls the Frankish king *compater
spiritalis* in the *salutatio* of many letters; cf. *MGH, Epistolae Merov.
et Carolini Aevi*, I, 594 ff.; also *MGH, Epistolae Karolini Aevi*, III, 6,
16.

25  *Quisque legas versus*] Alcuin in the two inscriptions LXXXVII.14.5
(p. 308); XCIX.44 (p. 324); the locution expresses the wish that
travelers will read the inscription; see the examples collected by
Ewald Lissberger, *Das Fortleben der Römischen Elegiker in den Carmina Epigraphica* (Tübingen diss., 1934), 134.
*devoto pectore supplex*] Alcuin, LXV.Ia.17 (p. 285):

> Quae pater Albinus *devoto pectore supplex;*

Diehl, 1810, 2 (Vienne):

> Tu quaecumque (venes) *devoto pectore supplex.*

27  Alcuin, CXXIII.12 (p. 350): me tenet hic requies.

29  *Ultima...*a possible reminiscence of Virgil, *Ecl.*, IV.4–7:

> Ultima Cumaei venit iam carminis aetas.

29–30  Alcuin, CXXIII.20–23 (p. 350) in his own epitaph, written by
himself shortly before 804:

> Personet angelica *donec* ab arce *tuba:*
> Qui iaces in tumulo, terrae de pulvere *surge,*
>> Magnus adest iudex milibus innumeris;

XV.9–13 (p. 338), *In Cimiterio S. Amandi:*

> Donec ab aetheria *clamet* pius angelus arce:
> Surgite nunc prumptim terrae de pulvere, fratres,
>> Vos vocat adveniens iudex ex culmine caeli;

cf. I Cor. 15:52: tuba: canet enim, et mortui resurgent incorrupti;
cf. I Thess. 4:16; Matt. 24:31.

31–33  Alcuin, L.27–30 (p. 263):

> Felix ille dies, *vocem* qua *iudicis* almi
>> *Auditurus eris,* proque labore tuo.
> Tunc gaudens: 'Intra, nimium me serve fidelis

Aeterni aeternus regna beata patris.'
*Tunc memor esto mei* et dic...
LXXXVIII.2.9–10 (p. 309), *Ad Corpus Sancti Vedasti:*
   *Audiet* idcirco *vocem* mox *iudicis almi:*
   'Intra nunc domini gaudia sancta tui';
cf. Ovid, *Met.*, VI.548: *Audiet* haec aether et si deus ullus in illo est;
cf. Lestocquoy, "Notes sur l'épigraphie de l'abbaye de S. Vaast: Les
Inscriptions d'Alcuin," *Commission départmentale des Monuments
Historiques du Pas-de-Calais, Bulletin*, N.S. VII (1941); Alcuin imi-
tates Fortunatus, V.2.57–60:
   Ecce *tui domini* modo gaudia laetior *intra*
   Proque labore brevi magna parata tibi.
   *Auditurus eris vocem*, Martine, beatam,
   Sed Fortunati *sis memor* ipse *tui*.                    Cf. Ps. 94:8.

32  Cf. Matt. 25:21 (Luc. 19:17); Ovid, *Amor.*, II.9.44: Gaudia magna
    feram.

33  Alcuin, *Versus ad Paulinum*, XX.40 (p. 241):
    Qua *memor esto tui nati*, te *posco* per illum;
    *pater optime*] Alcuin, CII.14 (p. 329) and in letter to Hadrian of 794,
    *MGH, Epistolae*, IV.27, p. 68, 15.

35  Alcuin, XX.41 (p. 241):
    Ut tibi cum sanctis tribuat *caelestia regna;*
    also X.19 (p. 236); LXII.4 (p. 275); v. 994, p. 191; cf. Ovid, *Ex Ponto*,
    IV.8.59: caelestia regna; *CLE*, 671, 3:
    confessus Christum caelestia regna petisti;
    cf. *CLE*, 1400, 1 (Rome).

36  Alcuin, *Epit. Monachi Pauli Turonensis*, CXIII.9–10 (p. 344):
    *Auxiliare* piis, te precor, et *precibus;*
    also LI.6.7 (p. 264), CIX.16.1 (p. 338), L.36 (p. 263), II.34, 82 (p.
    220), IX.178 (p. 233).

37  Alcuin, XCV.7 (p. 320):
    *Sol rutilans* radiis domibus *splendescit* in altis;
    Alcuin's source is Iuvencus, *Evang. Libri Quattuor*, IV.149–51, 158:
       Abscondet furvis *rutilos* umbris radios *sol*,
       Amittet cursum lunaris gratia lucis
       Ignicomaeque ruent stellae caelumque relinquent;
                                        ...*ab axe;*
    Iuvencus, III.1:
    Fuderat in terras roseum iubar *ignicomus sol*.

38  Alcuin, *Ad Leonem apostolicum urbis Romae*, XLIII.11–12 (p. 255):
    Ut laus et merces maneat tibi, sancte sacerdos,
        Tempore perpetuo pacis in orbe sacro;
  XXI.33 (p. 243):
    Sic tua laus crescit, merces sic magna manebit
        Pastori summo sedis apostolicae;
  IV.19 (p. 221):
    Dic: *Tua laus* mecum *semper*, dilecte, manebit;
  Since Alcuin connects *sol* (v. 37) and *laus* (v. 38), it seems that he
  imitates Fortunatus, *Ad Justinum et Sophiam Augustos* (p. 276, 47):
    Haec *tua laus*, princeps, *cum sole* cucurrit *in orbe;*
  Hrabanus Maurus, *MGH, Poetae*, II.161, no. III, 17, addressing Pope
  Gregory IV (827–844), seems to copy Alcuin:
    Ut tua laus maneat, merces et gloria semper.

40  Bernhard Simson, *Jahrbücher des Fränkischen Reiches unter Karl
    dem Grossen*, II (Leipzig, 1883), 108 n. 2, assumes that VIII Kal. Ian.
    is the correct date.

The numerous parallels in Hadrian's epitaph with the phraseology and the diction in Alcuin's metrical inscriptions and in
his occasional poetry which we adduce in the notes of the commentary provide, as we hope, ample evidence that Alcuin is
indeed the author of the inscription. Its unity of composition
and spontaneity of expression cannot be the work of a versifier
who imitated the style of Alcuin's poetry.

Alcuin's interpretations of death, immortality, and resurrection pose a problem.[18] Death is pictured as the separation of
body and soul by which another life (16) better than the earthly
is introduced; death therefore does not cause harm to man (15).
The body is held in the tomb (21), while the soul makes for the
stars (10), *spiritus astra petit* (see below), joining with the
saints (28). He believes in the immortality of the soul and the
disintegration of the body in dust, as may also be deduced from

[18] On the contents of epitaphs see Richmond Lattimore, *Themes in
Greek and Latin Epitaphs* (*Illinois Studies in Language and Literature*,
XXVIII, nos. 1–2 [Urbana, 1942]), 301–340, especially pp. 309–311, on
heretical concepts in Christian inscriptions.

his own epitaph, where the traveler (*viator*) is asked (CXXIII.9–10, p. 350):

> Quapropter potius animam curare memento
> Quam carnem, quoniam haec manet, illa perit?

References in Hadrian's and Alcuin's epitaphs reveal their author's belief in an immortal soul freed of its body. "The soul returns to the judgment of Him who gave it," Alcuin wrote to his friend Arno of Salzburg;[19] "I tremble with terror at the thought of Judgment Day...lest it find me unprepared." His vision of an incorporeally immortal soul is a remnant of ancient Greek thought that is not exactly the orthodox Christian point of view of a corporeal resurrection of the flesh from the dust of the grave. But this specific concept is also found in other epitaphs of the early Middle Ages. Both concepts of resurrection appear simultaneously in Alcuin's epitaph written by himself shortly before 804. Not only the resurrection of the soul (see above), but also the resurrection of the body is mentioned in the same epitaph (CXXIII.21, p. 350):

> Qui iaces in tumulo, terrae de pulvere surge.

The idea of the harmlessness of death (15) and the belief in the immortality of the soul determine Alcuin's expression of consolation in Hadrian's epitaph. They make it rather futile to deplore the loss of the departed; instead the *consolatio* is directed toward the living. This results in the panegyric and didactic praise of the virtues of Hadrian (3–6, 11–12), and the laudatory description of his achievements (7–9, 13–14). The inscription appears accordingly as a biographical *encomium* whose climax in the concluding *laudatio*[20] of v. 38,

---

[19] Alcuin, *Epistle*, 239, p. 384, 29–33: Spiritus revertatur ad iudicium illius qui dedit eum. Huius vero iudicii terrore totus contremesco...ne me minus paratum dies illa per omnia inveniat.

[20] On the classical *laudatio* see Marcel Durry, "Laudatio funebris et Rhétorique," *Revue de philologie* LXVIII (1942), 105–114; cf. Konrat

LAVS TVA SANCTE PATER SEMPER IN ORBE MANET,

is inspired by Virgil's famous phrase (*Ecl.*, V.78 = *Aen.*, I.609):

Semper honos nomenque tuum laudesque manebunt,

a verse which is literally quoted by Alcuin in the epic poem on his native York (v. 1595, p. 205).

The extremely literary character of Hadrian's epitaph is obvious from the use made of Roman and Christian literary sources. The influence of Porfyrius (1), Iuvencus (37), and Prudentius (14), is surpassed by that of Fortunatus [21] (4, 5–6, 11, 14, 31–33), a favorite author of Alcuin. There are a few quotations and possible traces of Virgil and Ovid. A faint echo of the *Fourth Eclogue* [22] (29)—the messianic eclogue of the Middle Ages which foretold the birth of Christ and the return of Saturn's golden age of peace—may be contained in verse 29 in connection with the belief in the resurrection.

*Formulae* of medieval epigraphy are the traditional HIC... REQUIE[SCIT] (1–2), PROMPTVS IN OMNE BONVM (4), PAVPERIBVS LARGVS (11), NVLLI PIETATE SECVNDVS (11); literary topoi are the obligation to top noble birth by a nobler life (5–6), the harmlessness of death (15) as the portal leading to a better life (16), and the incorporeal resurrection of the immortal soul (27–30).

A third source used by Alcuin seems to be a *sylloge* (or several collections) of inscriptions which furnished him with some of those locutions for which parallels from Carolingian epitaphs,

---

Ziegler, "Panegyrikos," *R.-E.*, XVIII, 1 (1949), 559–581; on *consolatio* see Skutsch in *R.-E.*, IV, 933 ff.; thus far, the literary genres in medieval epitaphs and in the panegyric Latin poetry from Fortunatus to Alcuin have not been investigated; they frequently continue the corresponding classical traditions.

[21] On Alcuin's use see D. Tardi, *Fortunat* (Paris, 1927), 277; Max Manitius in *MGH, Auctores Antiquissimi*, IV.2, pp. 137–138.

[22] Karl Strecker, "Iam nova progenies caelo demittitur," *Studi Medievali* V (1932), 167–186. Cf. Pierre Courcelle, "Les exégèses chrétiennes de la quatrième églogue," *Revue des études anciennes*, 59 (1957), 294–319.

prior and posterior to Hadrian's, are adduced in our commentary (4, 11, 15, 20). Wilhelm Levison[23] has already called attention to the use made by Alcuin of the *Sylloge Cantabrigiensis*, a collection of papal epitaphs and inscriptions.[24] Alcuin was, in all probability, also familiar with the *Sylloge of Tours* (cf. 11). The use of the locution *iustitiae cultor*, for instance, which occurs in Roman and Christian inscriptions, becomes understandable if we assume Alcuin's possible familiarity with some sylloge. Compare the following examples: Alcuin, *Inscriptio in Monasterio Nobiliacensi*, XCIX.22.3–4 (p. 327):

> *Iustitiae cultor,* vitae melioris amator,
>    Providus ingenio, cautus in eloquio;

*Versus ad Leonem Papam*, XV.5–6 (p. 238):

> *Iustitiae cultor,* verae et *pietatis amator,*
>    Pauperibus largus, clarus honore pio;

*Versus ad Paulinum* (of Aquileia), XVII.15 (p. 239):

> *Iustitiae cultor,* sacrae *pietatis amator;*

*Versus ad Leonem Apostolicum*, XLIII.5 (p. 254):

> *Iustitiae cultor,* sancte et *pietatis amator,*[25]
>    Firmus in officiis, verus in eloquiis;

In the Poem on York, v. 138 (p. 172):

> Qui fuit ore simul verax et pectore prudens,
>    *Iustitiae cultor, verus pietatis amator.*

[23] *England and the Continent in the Eighth Century* (Oxford, 1946), 162, n. 2.

[24] Edited by Wilhelm Levison, "Englische Handschriften des Liber Pontificalis," *Neues Archiv* XXXV (1910), 350–366. See Angelo Silvagni, "La silloge epigrafica di Cambridge," *Rivista di archeologia cristiana*, XX (1943), 49–112.

[25] *Pietatis amator* is often used as *Versschluss*, also by Paul the Deacon, *MGH, Poetae*, I.68, no. XXXIV, 10; Fortunatus, III.22.5; Dracontius, *De Deo*, III.16; *iustitiae cultor*, see also in Diehl, 1011, 7; 1051, 6; Fortunatus, VI.1a.21; *Epit. Marii Episc. Aventicensis*, ed. T. Mommsen, *MGH, Auct. Antt.*, XI, 227.

The last verse is identical with the third in a poem by Alcuin's teacher Aelbert or Koaena of York attached to a letter addressed to Lullus of Mayence.[26]

The unknown Carolingian author [27] of the epic poem *Karolus Magnus et Leo Papa* [28] says of his hero:

> *Iustitiae cultor*, cultores diligit omnes.

The original source of *iustitiae cultor* is Lucan, *Pharsalia* II.389:

> *Iustitiae cultor*, rigidi servator honesti,

a passage frequently referred to in Roman and Christian epitaphs. It appears in the *Sylloge of Tours* (Diehl 1195, 9–10).

> *Iustitiae cultor*, vitae servator honestae,
> Pauperibus dives, sed sibi pauper erat.

Occasionally, the passage from Lucan is connected with Martial, IX.84.4:

> ille tuae *cultor* notus *amicitiae*,

as in the following epitaphs of two Roman senators: Diehl, 243, 7–8:

> purus *amicitiae cultor, servator honesti*,
> eloquio miseros vel pietate iuvans;

Diehl, 135, 11–12:

> fidus *amicitiae* custos, ambitor *honesti*,
> *iustitiae cultor*, pacis *amator* eras.

The identification of *cultor* with *amator* in the last inscription is traceable to another interpretation of the passage from Lucan with the help of Ovid, *Ars amatoria* I.722:

> Qui fuerat *cultor*, factus *amator* erat,

---

[26] *MGH, Poetae*, I.201, n. 1.

[27] D. Tardi, "Fortunat et Angilbert," *Bulletin Du Cange* II (1925), 30–38, ascribes the fragment to Angilbert; Otto Schumann, "Bernowini episcopi carmina," *Historische Vierteljahrsschrift* XXVI (1931), 226, denies Angilbert's authorship.

[28] *MGH, Poetae*, I.367, no. VI, 31–32.

as for instance in Diehl, 1024, 3:

> *Cultor iustitiae*, doctrine et pacis *amator*,

and in the examples adduced from Alcuin's poetry.

Alcuin employs *iustitiae cultor* not only for epigraphic but also for merely literary purposes. In the same way he used the epigraphic formula *spiritus astra petit* (Diehl, 990, 3), *Vita Willibrordi*, II.28.4 (p. 216):

> *Spiritus astra petit* meritis vivacibus alta;

in the Poem on York, v. 739 (p. 186):

> sub quo
> *Spiritus astra petit* [29] sancti terrena relinquens.

Alcuin's method conforms to the custom, followed by Carolingian writers, of fashioning dedicatory verses, for instance, after the inscriptions of a sylloge. A good example is found in the *Versus Godescalci in Carolum*, *Poetae*, I.94, no. VII, 2, 6–9:

> 6  *Praelatus multis, humili pietate superbus,*
>    Providus ac sapiens, studiosus in arte librorum.
> 8  *Iustitiae custos rectus* verusque fidelis,
>    *Pauperibus largus, miseris solacia praestans.*

Ernst Dümmler, the editor of these verses, overlooks the fact that vv. 6 and 9 are from the epitaph of Pope Felix IV (Diehl, 986, 3, 5) and v. 8 is from that of Boniface III (Diehl, 992, 9–10):

> *Iustitiae custos, rectus* patiensque benignus,
>    Cultus in eloquiis et pietate placens.

---

[29] Cf. *Hymnus Nynie Episcopi*, MGH, *Poetae*, IV.962, v.18:
   *Spiritus astra petit* casto de corpore latus
   angelicis manibus, *spiritus astra petit.*
See above the commentary on line 10 of the epitaph. On the influence of Arator on the *Miracula* see Wallach, *Speculum* 29 (1954), 146.

The same verses are inserted in an epitaph by Alcuin's pupil Hrabanus Maurus, *Poetae*, II.237, 7–8:

> *Iustitiae custos, rectus patiensque benignus,*
> Fidus *in eloquiis et pietate placens.*

A study of the epitaphs and the other metrical inscriptions collected in the four volumes of the *Poetae Latini Aevi Carolini* not only reveals the survival of Roman and early Christian epigraphic elements in Carolingian epigraphy, but also bears out the assumption that a sylloge of model inscriptions [30] was often used by Carolingian writers. The use of such a literary manual for the composition of various types of inscriptions parallels that of professional handbooks [31] of Roman and medieval stonecutters and engravers as an aid in the technical fabrication of lapidary and bronze inscriptions.

[30] Karl Strecker, *MGH, Poetae*, IV.1020, assumes for instance that Flodoard of Reims (saec. X) used such a sylloge of papal inscriptions; cf. also Scheffer-Boichorst, "Zur Kritik Flodoards von Rheims und päpstlicher Epitaphien," *MIOEG*, VIII (1887), 423–430; cf. A. Silvagni in *Diss. della Pontificia Accademia Rom. di Arch.*, II, 15 (1921), 181–226; A. Silvagni, *Monumenta epigraphica Christiana saeculo XIII antiquiora quae in Italiae finibus adhuc exstant*, I (Rome, 1938); on new discoveries cf. the report by Attilio DeGrassi, "Epigrafia Romana," in *Doxa, rassegna critica di antichità Classica*, II (1949), 111–119: *Iscrizioni sepolcrali-cristiane.*

[31] Cf. Edmond Le Blant, "Sur les graveurs des inscriptions antiques," *Revue de l'art chrétien*, 1859; Réné Cagnat, "Sur les manuels professionnels des graveurs d'inscriptions romaines," *Revue de philologie*, XIII (1889), 51–65. See also the discussion of the problem by Ewald Lissberger, *Das Fortleben der Römischen Elegiker in den Carmina Epigraphica* (Tübingen diss., 1934), 9-13.—The origin of Hadrian's epitaph as a Carolingian work of art produced at Aix-la-Chapelle is the subject of Johannes Ramackers, "Die Werkstattheimat der Grabplatte Hadrians I.," *Römische Quartalschrift für christliche Altertumskunde und Kirchengeschichte* 59 (1964), 36-78.

# CHAPTER XI

# Charlemagne's *De litteris colendis* and Alcuin

THE famous letter addressed by Charlemagne to Abbot Baugulf of Fulda is not only one of the most often quoted educational documents of the Carolingian Renaissance, but also, I believe, one of the most frequently misinterpreted historical sources of the period. Usually referred to as *Epistola de litteris colendis*, the letter was known for a long time only from the eleventh- or twelfth-century transmission of Metz MS 226,[1] until Paul Lehmann published an older version from the Oxford Laudianus Misc. 126, probably of the eighth century.[2]

[1] *MGH, Capitularia Regum Francorum*, I, ed. Alfred Boretius (Legum Sectio II; Hannover, 1881), no. 29, p. 79. A Vatican MS of the letter is listed in *Neues Archiv* 9 (1884), 653, but investigation shows that Emil von Ottenthal, *MIOEG* 5 (1884), 135 refers correctly to Charlemagne's *Epistola generalis* (no. 30, p. 80), and not to no. 29. Cf. F. L. Ganshof, "Recherches sur les capitulaires," *Revue historique de droit français et étranger* 35 (1957), 33–87, 196–246. In 1955, Professor Ganshof kindly sent me the first edition of this study, *Wat waren de Capitularia?* (Brussel, 1955).

[2] "Fuldaer Studien. Neue Folge," *Sitzungsberichte, Bayerische Akademie* (Phil.-Hist. Klasse, 1927, Abh. 2), pp. 4–13. F. Madan and H. H. E. Craster, *A Summary Catalogue of Western Manuscripts in the Bodleian Library at Oxford*, II, 1 (Oxford, 1922), p. 67, write: no. 1556 (2801)

The appraisals of the epistle by historians before and after Lehmann's study show a surprising variety of interpretations at variance with one another. Lehmann concludes that the letter is a personal epistle addressed to Baugulf which was afterward forwarded by Charlemagne to an unknown archbishop with the request to send copies to his suffragan- and co-bishops and to the monasteries within their dioceses. Abel-Simson,[3] Boehmer-Mühlbacher,[4] Kleinclausz,[5] Amann,[6] Lesne,[7] and Bresslau,[8] characterize it as a circular letter addressed to archbishops.[9] Like Amann, West [10] speaks of a capitulary sent to the abbots of monasteries. Calmette [11] says it is a circular addressed to cathedral and monastic schools. According to Levison,[12] the circular went first to monasteries and afterwards to the metropolitans to be forwarded to their suffragans. Laistner [13] seems to be the only scholar who took notice of Lehmann's publication, which has remained unknown to Calmette, Kleinclausz, Amann, Lesne, and

---

on f. 1: "A letter of Charles the Great commanding the study of letters; A.D. 787." Thus Madan and Craster recognized this transmission of the letter; their dating of the document (787) was long ago rejected by Abel and Simson (see n. 3). On the Oxford MS see E. A. Lowe, *Speculum* 3 (1928), 3–15.

[3] *Jahrbücher des fränkischen Reiches unter Karl dem Grossen,* II (Leipzig, 1883), 566–568.

[4] *Regesta Imperii,* I (2nd ed.; Innsbruck, 1908), no. 292, p. 121.

[5] Arthur Kleinclausz, *Eginhard* (Paris, 1942), p. 28.

[6] Emile Amann, *L'époque carolingienne* (Histoire de l'église, ed. A. Fliche and V. Martin, Paris, 1937), 102.

[7] Emile Lesne, *Histoire de la propriété ecclésiastique en France,* V: *Les écoles de la fin du VIIIᵉ siècle à la fin du XIIᵉ* (Lille, 1940), 15–23.

[8] Harry Bresslau, *Handbuch der Urkundenlehre für Deutschland und Italien,* II, 1 (Leipzig, 1915), 341–342.

[9] Abel-Simson (n. 3 above), p. 567, n. 1: also to bishops.

[10] A. F. West, *Alcuin* (New York, 1901), 49.

[11] Joseph Calmette, *Charlemagne* (Paris, 1945), 255, 271.

[12] Wilhelm Levison, *England and the Continent in the Eighth Century* (Oxford, 1946), 152.

[13] M. L. W. Laistner, *Thought and Letters in Western Europe* (London, 1931), 153; in 2nd ed. (1957), 196 f.

Carlo de Clercq.[14] It is quite clear that Charlemagne's letter cannot be simultaneously a *circular letter* addressed to schools (n.
11), a *double circular letter* addressed to archbishops and bishops
(n. 3–8), a *triple circular letter* sent to monasteries (n. 12), a
*personal letter* addressed to Baugulf subsequently used as a circular letter (n. 2, 13), and a *capitulary* sent to abbots (n. 10).
None of the historians mentioned refers to the document as a
mandate, its correct "diplomatic" classification. West and Amann
designate it falsely as a capitulary, although it does not possess
the legal and diplomatic characteristics of this type of royal legislation. The authenticity of the document has been questioned
by Julius Harttung,[15] but nobody has accepted his argument. It
is unwarranted to dub the letter a mere *dictamen* or a forgery,
since its literary structure conforms in many details with the
*formulae* of charters written by the scribes and notaries of Charlemagne's chancellery staff. A diplomatic investigation will reveal the true character of the letter and its place within the charters of the Frankish king, and lead to a probable solution of the
vexing old problem of Alcuin's connection with the epistle.

The similarities in educational ideals and in style between the
mandate and the writings of Alcuin, Charlemagne's close asso-
ciate in educational matters, induced the great French diploma-
tist Jean Mabillon [16] to suggest that Alcuin may have been the
author of the letter. This assumption has been repeated frequently,[17] but nobody has proved it. Hubert Bastgen [18] never

[14] *La législation religieuse franque de Clovis à Charlemagne* (Université
de Louvain, 1936), 180–181.

[15] *Diplomatisch-Historische Forschungen* (Gotha, 1879), 338–342, rejected by W. Diekamp, *Historisches Jahrbuch der Görresgesellschaft* 5
(1884), 259, and by F. Kaltenbrunner, *MIOEG* 1 (1880), 452.

[16] *Annales Ordinis S. Benedicti* II (Lucca, 1739), 260, no. lxiv.

[17] J. B. Mullinger, *The Schools of Charles the Great* (London, 1877),
99; A. F. West, *Alcuin* (New York, 1901), 52; C. B. Gaskoin in Hoops,
*Reallexikon der germanischen Altertumskunde*, I (Strassburg, 1911–1913),
61; Richard Stachnik, *Die Bildung des Weltklerus im Frankenreiche*
(Paderborn, 1926), 37–38; Arthur Kleinclausz, *Alcuin* (Paris, 1948), 68;

submitted his promised proof of Alcuin's authorship. Modifying Mabillon's original idea, I hope to determine the Anglo-Saxon's possible share in the origination of the document by adducing parallels between Alcuin's numerous letters and the text of Charlemagne's epistle.

## I

*Charlemagne's mandate addressed to Baugulf of Fulda, 794–800.*

MS transmission:

*M*   Metz Stadtbibliothek 226, *saec.* xi/xii, a copy of the original text.

*L*   Oxford Laudianus Misc. 126, *saec.* viii, a copy of Baugulf's circular letter.

Editions:

*M*   *MGH, Capitularia Regum Francorum*, i, ed. A. Boretius, no. 29, p. 79.

*L*   Paul Lehmann, "Fuldaer Studien. Neue Folge," *Sitzungsberichte, Bayerische Akademie* (Phil.-Hist. Klasse, 1927, Abh. 2), 8–9.

English translations:

*L*   M. L. W. Laistner, *Thought and Letters in Western Europe* (London, 1931), 152–153; in 2nd ed. (Ithaca, N.Y., 1957), 196 f.

*M*   Dana C. Munro, *University of Pennsylvania Translations and Reprints* VI (1900), no. 5, pp. 12–14.

    F. A. Ogg, *A Source Book of Medieval History* (New York, 1908), 146–148.

In anticipation of the results of our investigation (Pt. II), the letter is here reprinted after *M*. Since *L* is a re-edition of the archetype of *M*, the more important discrepancies between the two "versions" do not constitute actual "variants," but literary characteristics of two different letters whose contexts are almost

---

E. K. Rand, *The Building of Eternal Rome* (Cambridge, Mass., 1943), 245.

[18] "Alkuin und Karl der Grosse in ihren wissenschaftlichen und kirchenpolitischen Anschauungen," *Historisches Jahrbuch der Görresgesellschaft*, 32 (1911), 816–817.

(yet not completely) identical. In a few instances, we follow the orthography of the older *L*, which in all probability gives the more authentic spelling of words that are identical in *M* and *L*, but were modernized by the scribe of the younger *M*. We read "rel*e*gionis" (sentence 2) with *L* and Alcuin (see commentary, n. *b*), and not "rel*i*gionis" with *M*. The same holds true of the following readings of the Oxford manuscript which we adopt for our edition:

> negl*e*gant (2a; 7a; 10) *L;* negl*i*gant *M;*
> condem*p*naberis (3) *L;* condemnaberis *M;*
> rec*e*dat (14) *L* and Alcuin (f'); r*e*deat *M;*
> spiritaliter intell*e*git (11) *L* and Alcuin (x);
> spirit*u*aliter intell*i*git *M*.

We print Carolus and not Karolus (Boretius and Lehmann), because the king's name is spelled with a *C* in the *intitulatio* of extant original charters of Charlemagne, and with a *K* only in the documents of the imperial period after 800.[19] The punctuation of Boretius has been supplemented in one instance; we put commas after *fidelibus, oratoribus nostris,...*(1). Finally, it seems advisable to set aside in special paragraphs sentence 14 and, together, sentences 15 and 16. The *formulae* of the mandate which are also used by the notaries of Charlemagne's chancellery in other letters and charters are printed in *italics*.

1     *Carolus, gratia Dei rex Francorum et Langobardorum ac patricius Romanorum*, Baugulfo abbati *et omni congregationi, tibi* etiam *commissis fidelibus,* oratoribus nostris, *in omnipotentis Dei nomine amabilem* direximus *salutem.*

2     *Notum igitur sit* Deo placitae devotioni vestrae, *quia nos una cum fidelibus nostris consideravimus utile esse, ut* episcopia et monasteria ᴬ nobis *Christo propitio* ad gubernandum commissa praeter regularis vitae ordinem ᵃ atque sanctae relegionis ᵇ conversationem etiam in litterarum meditationibus ᶜ eis qui donante

[19] E. Mühlbacher, *MGH, Diplomata Karolinorum*, I (1906), 77.

Domino discere possunt secundum uniuscuiusque capacitatem
2a docendi studium [d] debeant impendere, *qualiter,* sicut regularis
norma [e] honestatem morum,[f] *ita quoque* docendi et discendi [g]
instantia [h] ordinet et ornet seriem verborum, ut, qui Deo placere
appetunt recte vivendo, ei etiam placere non neglegant recte
3 loquendo.[i] Scriptum * est enim: 'Aut ex verbis iustificaberis,
4 aut ex verbis tuis condempnaberis.' Quamvis enim melius sit bene
5 facere quam nosse, prius tamen est nosse quam facere.[k] Debet
ergo quisque discere quod optat implere, ut tanto uberius quid
agere debeat [l] intellegat anima, quanto in omnipotentis Dei lau-
6 dibus † sine mendaciorum offendiculis cucurrerit lingua. Nam
cum omnibus hominibus vitanda sint[f] mendacia,[m] quanto magis [n]
illi secundum possibilitatem [o] declinare debent, qui ad hoc solummodo probantur electi, ut servire specialiter debeant veritati.[p]
7 Nam cum nobis in his annis a nonnullis monasteriis saepius scripta
dirigerentur, in quibus, quod pro nobis fratres ibidem commo-
rantes in sacris et piis orationibus decertarent, significaretur, cognovimus in plerisque praefatis conscriptionibus eorundem et
7a sensus rectos et sermones incultos [q]; quia, quod pia devotio interius fideliter dictabat, hoc exterius [r] propter neglegentiam discendi ‡ lingua inerudita exprimere sine reprehensione [s] non vale-
8 bat. Unde factum est, ut timere inciperemus, ne forte, sicut minor
erat in scribendo prudentia, ita quoque et multo minor esset quam
recte debuisset in sanctarum scripturarum ad intellegendum sa-
9 pientia.[t] Et bene novimus omnes, quia, quamvis periculosi sint
errores verborum, multo periculosiores sunt errores [u] sensuum.
10 *Quamobrem* hortamur vos litterarum studia non solum non neglegere, verum etiam humillima [v] et Deo placita intentione ad hoc
certatim discere, ut facilius et rectius divinarum scripturarum
11 mysteria valeatis penetrare. Cum autem in sacris paginis [w] sce-
mata, tropi et caetera his similia inserta inveniantur, nulli dubium
est, quod ea unusquisque legens tanto citius spiritaliter [x] intellegit,
quanto prius in litterarum magisterio plenius instructus fuerit.
12 Tales vero ad hoc opus viri eligantur, qui et voluntatem [y] et pos-
13 sibilitatem discendi et desiderium habeant alios [z] instruendi. Et
hoc tantum ea intentione agatur, qua devotione a nobis praecipitur.

14 Optamus enim vos, sicut decet ecclesiae milites, et interius devotos et exterius ᵃ′ doctos castosque bene vivendo ᵇ′ et scolasticos bene loquendo,ᶜ′ ut, quicunque vos propter nomen Domini et sanctae conversationis nobilitatem ad videndum ᵈ′ expetierit, sicut de aspectu vestro aedificatur ᵉ′ visus, ita quoque de sapientia vestra, quam in legendo seu cantando perceperit, instructus omnipotenti Domino gratias agendo gaudens redeat.ᶠ′

15 Huius itaque epistolae exemplaria ad omnes suffragantes tuosque coepiscopos et per universa monasteria dirigi *non neglegas,*

16 *si gratiam nostram habere vis.* Et nullus monachus foris monasterio iudiciaria teneat, nec per mallos et publica placita ᵍ′ pergat. [Legens valeat.] ʰ′

*Matt. 12:37   †Cf. Acts 24:16   ‡Cf. Isa. 50:4
14 line 6: perciperit instruatur auditus et qui ad videndum solummodo venerat visione et auditione instructus L
15 So M, not in L
16 Hoc ut fieret ortamur (*or:* optamus) ut n. monachorum foras m. iu. t. neque per placita et mallos discurrat L

ᴬ See Charlemagne, *Admonitio Generalis* of 789, c. 72 *MGH, Capitularia* I, 60.4: per singula *monasteria vel episcopia.*

ᵃ Cf. Alcuin, *MGH, Epistolae,* IV, ed. Ernst Dümmler, *Epist.* 54, p. 98, 23–24: *regularis vitae...ordinem; Epist.* 19, p. 53, 16–17, the same phrase. On the many occurrences of *regularis vita* in the letters of Alcuin see *MGH, Epistolae,* IV, p. 633, s.v.

ᵇ *Epist.* 171, p. 281, to Charlemagne: et *sanctae relegionis* fervore omnibus praecellis; cf. 179, p. 296, 25: et constantiam *relegionis sanctae* in eo; 177, p. 293, 8; 195, p. 323, 10–11.

ᶜ *Epist.* 161, p. 260, 16–17: quia tibi decet *meditatio* divinae legis, ut dicatur de te (Ps. 1:2): In lege Domini meditabitur die et nocte; 120, p. 175, 3: in Domino studium et diuturnam in lege eius *meditationem.* Cf. *Regula Benedicti,* cc. 8, 48, 58.

ᵈ *Epist.* 289, p. 447, 37: *docendi studio;* cf. 121, p. 117, 29 to Charlemagne: ad hanc omni studio discendam; 19, p. 55, 24: discendi studium.

ᵉ *Reg. Ben.,* c.73: *norma* vitae humanae; Alcuin, *Epist.* 67, p. 111, 25–27: *regularis vita* in hac terra cadit *normula;* Charlemagne, *Capitulare Missorum Generale,* c.13, *MGH, Capitularia,* I, no. 33, p. 91: regulari(s) *norma;* Aldhelm, *De virg.,* c.58: contra...*regularis vitae normam.* See Bernhard Bischoff in *Zeitschrift für Kirchengeschichte* 66 (1954–1955), 176, on *norma rectitudinis.*

ᶠ *Reg. Ben.,* c.73: *honestatem morum;* often used by Alcuin in his letters in many combinations: pp. 268, 1; 278, 13; 437, 39; 266, 13; 368, 18; 406, 25; 51, 22; 58, 1; 117, 8; 179, 6; 179, 31; 50, 24; 440, 3; 83, 22–23; etc., etc.; Alcuin, *Rhetoric*, ed. C. Halm, *Rhetores Latini Minores* (Leipzig, 1863), 547: Cum in omni parte vitae *honestas* pernecessaria sit, maxime in sermonibus quia fere cuiusque *mores* sermo probat, nisi tibi, magister, aliud videatur.

ᵍ Alcuin, *Epist.* 289, p. 447, 36–448, 1 (793–804), addressed to Fridugis, later abbot of St. Martin at Tours: sed magis laudo hanc praedicantis *instantiam* quia parum prodest *discendi* devotio sine *docendi* studio... quocirca tota debet esse cura bene intellegenti in *docendo*, ne frustra laboret in *discendo;* 280, p. 437, 18–19 (792–804) to monks in Ireland: ubique inter vos *discenda* est et *docenda*, (p. 438.29): singuli humilitatem habent in *discendo* et devotionem in *docendo; discere* and *docere* also in the following letters of Alcuin: pp. 73, 9–10; 132, 30–31; 173, 6–7; 277, 1; 390, 30–31; 429, 6; 205, 18–19; 471, 25–27; 444, 9–11.

ʰ Very often used by Alcuin; cf. pp. 83, 21–22; 105, 8; 150, 34; 133, 17–18; 382, 5; 278, 14; 447, 36; 111, 19; 334, 24; 347, 36–37; 294, 20; 479, 39.

ⁱ Alcuin, *Ars grammatica* (*PL*, CI, 857D): Grammatica...est custos *recte loquendi* et scribendi; see the discussion in our context.

ᵏ Alcuin, *Epist.* 309, p. 475, 23–24: nec aestimas tibi tantum sufficere, *nosse* quid *facere* debeas, nisi etiam opere impleas quae nosti; 124, p. 183, 38: Scio se haec omnia *melius nosse* et perfectius operari; 128, p. 191, 5: melius est ea facere, quae suadeo, quam omittere; 205, p. 342, 1: melius est non vovere, quam vota non *implere;* cf. Eccles. 5:4: melius est non vovere quam non reddere, also quoted in Charlemagne's *Admonitio Generalis* of 789, c.73 (*MGH, Capitularia*, I, p. 66, 11); *Missi cuiusdam admonitio* (*ibid.*, p. 240, 16–17).

ˡ Alcuin, *Epist.* 281, p. 440, 4: in quo *agere debeas;* 305, p. 465, 1: *quid agere debeas.*

ᵐ Alcuin, *Epist.* 309, p. 475, 15: Haec in Virgiliacis non invenietur *mendaciis*, sed in evangelica affluenter repperietur *veritate;* cf. note ᵖ below.

ⁿ Very often used by Alcuin: pp. 95, 35; 101, 32; 133, 21; 144, 3; 165, 40; 437, 16; 447, 5; etc.

ᵒ Alcuin, *Epist.* 259, p. 417, 24–25: *secundum possibilitatem* vestram.

ᵖ I.e., *catholicae fidei veritatem*, as in Alcuin's epistle to Charlemagne, no. 203, p. 337, 1; also 41, p. 84, 9–10; 280, p. 437, 18–19: ipsa catholica fidei *veritatis* ubique inter vos *discenda* est et *docenda;* cf. 166, p. 269, 17, and p. 271, 23.

�q Alcuin, *Epist.* 163, p. 263, 10–11 to Charlemagne: in *inculto* notavi *sermone.*

ʳ *Epist.* 265, p. 423, 13–14: vel *exterius*...vel *interius;* 253, p. 409, 26–27: me vero scito saecularibus propemodum *exterius* negotiis liberatum, sed male *interius* multis fatigatum occupationibus; 19, p. 55, 2: propter *interiores* hostes *exteriores* potestatem habent; see below note a'.

ᵍ *Epist.* 287, p. 446, 12: *sine reprehensione* estote omnibus; Phil. 2:15: ut sitis...*sine reprehensione.*

ᵗ Alcuin, *Epist.* 309, p. 475, 16–18: Quidquid enim *recte per sapientiam intellegitur;* 43, p. 89, 15–16, nostros studiose adulescentes in *sapientia sanctarum scripturarum* instruite; 31, p. 73, 2–3, 9: ideo necessaria est sanctarum lectio librorum, qui non discit, non docet; cf. 117, p. 173, 5–7; 166, p. 271, 17, si humiliter legeris *sanctarum scripturarum* series; *Ars grammatica* (*PL*, CI, 853): ad culmina *sanctarum scripturarum* perveniat.

ᵘ *Epist.* 169, p. 278: quia in nullo loco periculosius erratur.

ᵛ Alcuin, *Epist.* 280, p. 438, 32–33: singuli *humilitatem* habeant *in discendo* et devotionem *in docendo;* Alcuin, *Epist.* to Beatus of Liébana, ed. Wilhelm Levison, *England and the Continent in the Eighth Century* (Oxford, 1946), 321, 22: dum *humilitas discendi* defendat me ab errore pertinaciae; 280, p. 437, 27–31, nec tamen saecularium litterarum contempnenda est scientia...quatenus quibusdam sapientiae gradibus ad altissimum evangelicae perfectionis culmen ascendere valeant; cf. 121, p. 177, 18–19.

ʷ Cf. J. de Ghellinck, "Pagina et Sacra Pagina," *Mélanges Auguste Pelzer* (Louvain, 1947), 23–59.

ˣ Alcuin, *Exposit. in Psalm. CXVIII* (Migne, *PL*, C, 597A): In Christo *spiritaliter* debet *intellegi;* cf. Bastgen in *Neues Archiv*, 37 (1912), 494.

ʸ Alcuin, *Epist.* 257, p. 415, 19 (802), to Charlemagne: si Dominus, qui *voluntatem discendi* dederat; 214, p. 358, 12–13, qui habet *desiderium discendi* dabitur ei gratia intellegendi.

ᶻ *Epist.* 264, p. 421, 37: *aliosque erudire* studeas, ut fidem discant catholicam; 282, p. 441, 12–13, vel quomodo *alios doceas* quae tu ipse non facis?; 19, p. 55, 21, discant pueri scripturas sacras, ut aetate perfecta veniente *alios docere* possint; Charlemagne, *Admonitio Generalis* of 789, *MGH, Capitularia*, I, p. 61. 27, aliosque instruite.

ᵃ' See note r above.

ᵇ' Alcuin, *De virtutibus et vitiis* (*PL*, CI, 615AB): Vere beatus est qui et *recte credendo* bene vivit, et *bene vivendo* fidem rectam custodit; cf. Isidore, *Etym.* II.24.1.

ᶜ' See note i above.

ᵈ' Alcuin, *Epist.* 213, p. 355, 42 *ad videndum* Deum; *Ars grammatica* (*PL*, CI, 853C), vobis *ad videndum* ostendam; Tob. 13:20 ad videndum.

ᵉ' Cf. *Reg. Ben.*, c.47: *Cantare* autem et *legere* non praesumat, nisi qui potest ipsud officium implere ut *aedificentur audientes.*

ᶠ' So M; recedat L.

ᵍ′ Cf. F. N. Estey, "The meaning of *placitum* and *mallum* in the Capitularies," *Speculum*, 22 (1947), 435–439.

ʰ′ Marginal endorsement of a chancellery official (see Pt. II, C).

Many parallels to the text of Charlemagne's letter appear in the more than 250 letters of Alcuin's correspondence that have survived. Although some of the parallels are common generalities of medieval Latin style, their frequent use in Alcuin's epistles still makes them elements of his personal style and diction. There are unmistakable Alcuinisms, as may be deduced from the examples listed in the commentary. Alcuin's favorite saying that *discere* is the foundation of *docere*—he uses it in twelve letters—occurs in the king's epistle in a formulation resembling the wording in one of Alcuin's. In the latter the aphorism appears also in connection with *instantia*, a term for which Alcuin displays special fondness, since we find it in about fourteen of his epistles. No author before Alcuin—and none of his contemporaries—uses the aphorism as consistently in the identical exhortatory context of his letters. Peculiarities of his diction are the frequent use of comparative constructions such as *melius-quam, quanto-magis, interius-exterius*, the emphasis put on the necessity that "others" (*alios*) be instructed by qualified teachers, and the parallels adduced in the notes *x*, *y*, and *z*. Rhetorical over- and understatement is produced by the use of comparatives such as *melius, prius, facilius, rectius, saepius, plenius*, and *quanto prior*. Examples of *paronomasia* are *ordinet et ornet* and *docendi et discendi*. Repetition of antithetical expressions in two clauses, i.e., *antimetabole*, appears in the fourth sentence. Instances of the enthymeme *a maiore ad minus*, a merely rhetorical, not logical, inference are: *omnibus* hominibus...quanto magis illi...qui...*selecti* (6); sicut *minor* erat...ita quoque *multo minor* (8); qui Deo placere appetunt *recte vivendo*, ei etiam placere non neglegant *recte loquendo* (2a).

The rhetorical element of the letter is strengthened by passages of metrical prose which seem to be the result of deliberate construction, since some of the *clausulae* betray acquaintance with the *cursus*. The *cursus* is, however, not systematically applied in accordance with Wilhelm Meyer's law, namely, that there must be an interval of two or four unaccented syllables between the last two accented syllables in the sentence.[20] Of the most often employed medieval *clausulae* we mention *cursus planus* (*récte loquéndo; gaúdens recédat*) and *cursus velox* (*débeant veritáti; álios instruéndi*).

Paul Lehmann's contention[21] that metrical prose in this letter is more systematically employed than in the letters of Alcuin is not borne out by our investigation. Of extant letter mandates of Charlemagne[22] which belong to the same diplomatic type as the one addressed to Baugulf, not one is written in metrical prose, though *homoioteleuton* occurs occasionally. Many of Alcuin's letters, however, contain smaller and larger sections of metrical prose, though scarcely one is completely written in this vein. But there are obvious instances which testify to Alcuin's conscious endeavor to produce metrical prose in his letters.[23] Alcuin was quite capable of writing the kind of prose we find in the letter addressed to Baugulf. In fact, the small portions of metrical prose we find in this document are supporting evidence, though of a somewhat lesser cogency, for Alcuin's participation

[20] *Gesammelte Abhandlungen zur mittellateinischen Rhythmik,* II (Berlin, 1905), 236 ff.; Karl Polheim, *Die lateinische Reimprosa* (Berlin, 1925), 70 ff.

[21] *SB., Bayerische Akademie* (1927), p. 12.

[22] *MGH, Capitularia,* I, nos. 75; 76; 103; 122; 124; 125; no. 76 is also printed as *DK,* 88 (see below n. 41). Charlemagne's private letters (See Pt. III, Introd., n. 1) are published in *MGH, Epistolae,* IV, nos. 85, 87, 92, 93, 100, 144, 247; pp. 528 ff.: nos. 20, 21, 32, 35, 37; and *Epistolae,* V, 242 ff.: nos. 1, 2. This private correspondence was written by trusted members of the royal household and not by official notaries or scribes of the royal *capella;* see Harry Bresslau, *Handbuch der Urkundenlehre,* I (2nd ed.; Leipzig, 1912), 381–382.

[23] On Alcuin's metrical prose see Bastgen, *Neues Archiv* 37 (1911–1912), 511–513; Karl Polheim, *Die lateinische Reimprosa,* pp. 328–329.

in the composition of the letter. This is true since four pieces written by him for Charlemagne are poetical creations: three letter poems [24] addressed to Paul the Deacon and Peter of Pisa and the epitaph of Hadrian I.[25] A dictation in metrical prose was no challenge at all to a versifier of Alcuin's dexterity, who composed not only many hundreds of verses, mainly in pure, and to a lesser degree in leonine, hexameters,[26] but also *carmina rhythmica*.[27] It would have been a mere exercise of the pen after the nature of a dictamen, in the writing of which the teacher of grammar trained his students.[28]

Not only the literary elements of Charlemagne's letter but also its contents point to Alcuin's influence. Of interest is the apparent use of the *Regula Benedicti*,[29] parts of which became royal laws for the clergy of Charlemagne's empire.[30] The king's church legislation abounds in references to the *Rule*. The statement that "the monastic rule [directs] purity of conduct" (regularis *norma* [ordinet] *honestatem morum*) is a conscious adoption of one of the basic principles of the manual, summarized in its closing Chapter 73, where we read "honestatem morum" and "*norma* vitae humanae." References to the *regularis vita*, the life in accordance with the *Benedictine Rule*,[31] appear in about twenty-five letters of Alcuin, and variations of *honestas*

[24] Karl Neff, *Die Gedichte des Paulus Diaconus* (Munich, 1908), nos. xxxiii, xxiv, xli; the last no. is ascribed to Alcuin also by Ernst Dümmler.

[25] See our Chapter X.

[26] Karl Strecker, "Studien zu karolingischen Dichtern," *Neues Archiv*, 44 (1922), 220.

[27] Ed. K. Strecker, *MGH, Poetae*, IV, 903–910. On the *Stabreim* in Alcuin's poetry see Ingeborg Schröbler in *Beiträge zur Geschichte der deutschen Sprache und Literatur* 79 (1957), 17 f., 23, 41; on the *Ecloga de cuculo* see the fine study by Walther Bulst in *Zeitschrift für deutsches Altertum und deutsche Literatur* 86 (1955–1956), 193–196.

[28] *MGH, Epistolae*, IV, Alcuin's *Epist.* 172, p. 284, 25.

[29] See our commentary notes *a, e, f, e'*.

[30] See Carlo de Clercq (n. 14 above), pp. 176–177 and *passim*.

[31] Cf. *Reg. Ben.*, cc. 32, 54, 60, 70. Albert Hauck, *Kirchengeschichte Deutschlands*, II (3rd and 4th eds.; Leipzig, 1912), 130, n. 4.

*morum* [32] in at least eighteen. Although Alcuin was not a monk,[33] he was thoroughly familiar and in accord with many precepts of the *Rule*. Some allusions to the *Rule* (not recognized by Dümmler) can be detected, e.g., in *Epistle* 19,[34] which contains a reference to the last sentence of Chapter 66, on the porter of the monastery. In another letter [35] Alcuin even puns on the "wandering" porter,[36] saying: Qui Deo *vacare* debuerunt *vagari* per terras.

Charlemagne's appeal to attain the highest degree of wisdom by the study of the Sacred Scriptures is again and again reiterated by Alcuin. The doctrine that "in the sacred pages are found embedded phrases, figures, tropes, and other like forms of speech," puts the epistle in the well-known tradition of the *artes liberales*,[37] so important for the study of the Bible, which was propagated by Augustine, Cassiodorus, and Bede, all of whom suggest that the *colores rhetorici* can be found in the Bible. Alcuin defines *schemata* and *tropi* in his *Ars grammatica* (*PL*, CI, 858C). In a letter to Charlemagne,[38] he ascribes to the emperor familiarity with the figure *synekdoche* and awareness that the *tropica loquutio* may be found in the Bible. The old definition of *ars grammatica* as the science of speaking and writing well is clearly contained in Charlemagne's letter. In his *Rhetoric*, Alcuin gives a recommendation similar to that in the

[32] Cf. M. Rothenhaeusler, "Honestas Morum: Eine Untersuchung zu cap. 73, 3 der Regula S. Benedicti," *Studia Benedictina* (Città del Vaticano, 1947), 127–156.

[33] The arguments of W. Delius, *Theologische Studien und Kritiken* (1931), 103, do not convince me that Alcuin was a monk; see also W. Pückert, *Aniane und Gellone* (Leipzig, 1899), and the review in *Le moyen âge*, 15 (1902), 54.

[34] *MGH, Epistolae*, IV, p. 54, 22–23.

[35] *Ibid., Epist.* 253, p. 409, 20.

[36] Cf. Suso Brechter, "Der umherschweifende Pförtner: Eine Textkorrektur an der Regula Benedicti," *Benedictus* (Munich, 1947), 475–504.

[37] See E. R. Curtius, "Das mittelalterliche Bildungswesen und die Grammatik," *Romanische Forschungen*, 60 (1947), 6–15; it seems that Curtius did not know Lehmann's study (n. 2 above).

[38] *MGH, Epistolae*, IV, no. 143, p. 225, 25–30; cf. *Epist.* 137, p. 212, 29.

letter: nam bonus modus est in loquendo. Alcuin seems to have applied the words of Bede: Unde et genti suae et illis in quibus exulabat,...*exemplo vivendi*, et *instantia docendi* multum profuit (*Hist. Eccles.* III.27), to Charlemagne, when we read that "as monastic rule (directs) purity of conduct," "ita quoque *docendi* et discendi *instantia* ordinet et ornet seriem verborum, ut qui... *recte vivendo*, ei etiam...*recte loquendo*." And Alcuin's proverb that *discere* is the foundation of *docere* is reminiscent of Bede's confession: Semper aut discere, aut docere, aut scribere dulce habui (*ibid.* V.24).

Charlemagne's letter, then, contains elements of Alcuin's style and educational ideas which, like those of Alcuin, belong to the tradition of Anglo-Saxon humanism.

## II

The final edition of Charlemagne's letter could hardly have been the work of Alcuin. Only a scribe of the royal *capella*,[39] whose members wrote and verified the king's official documents, would have possessed the technical knowledge required for editing Alcuin's dictation within the framework of that type of royal charter which is called a mandate.[40]

[39] An independent royal or imperial chancellery did not exist under Charlemagne. Members of his *capella* acted as his chancery staff. We ask the reader to keep this in mind when we refer for the sake of brevity to the chancellery of the king. Cf. H.-W. Klewitz, "Cancellaria," *Deutsches Archiv für Geschichte des Mittelalters*, 1 (1937), 44–79, and "Kanzleischule und Hofkapelle," *ibid.*, 4 (1940), 224 ff.; Heinrich Fichtenau, *Grundzüge der Geschichte des Mittelalters* (2nd ed.; Vienna, 1948), 96. Calmette, *Charlemagne: Sa vie et son oeuvre* (Paris, 1945), p. 209, still repeats the wrong assumption that *capella* and *cancellaria* are two different institutions.

[40] On the differences between *mandate, capitulary,* and *diplomatum,* see Harry Bresslau, *op. cit.*, I, 53–54; Erben, *Urkundenlehre*, in *Handbuch der mittelalterlichen und neueren Geschichte*, ed. Below and Meinecke, Abt. IV (1907), pp. 182 ff.; A. Giry, *Manuel de diplomatique* (Paris, 1894). The "diplomatic" terminology used in this chapter is that used by Bresslau and Erben and not Giry's terminology (which differs in certain

The document has, in contrast to those royal charters which are called *diplomata*,[41] a limited legal significance. It is an expression of the king's will concerning educational matters which cannot be enforced by law. Its formalistic legality rests basically on the fact of the *fidelitas* [42] which the addressees of the mandate owe to their king, on the immunity charter granted by Charlemagne to Fulda in 774 (*DK*, 85), and on another charter of the same year which guarantees to the monastery the free election of its own abbot (*DK*, 86). Baugulf and his congregation, subjects of the Frankish king, are admonished by their sovereign to heed his suggestions and requests. The legality of the document, designated by its scribe as an *epistola*,[43] is expressed in a hortatory fashion. From the diplomatic point of view the letter is a mandate of transitory validity which does not establish any new legal relationship between the king and the addressees beyond those already in existence before the writing of the document.

Like the *diplomata* of Charlemagne and some of his mandates, the letter consists of the *formulae* of (*A*) the *protocol* and (*B*) the *context* which characterize its structure as that of a royal *mandate*.

---

instances from theirs). An introduction to modern diplomatic studies is provided by Leo Santifaller, *Urkundenforschung: Methoden, Ziele, Probleme* (Weimar, 1937); cf. also Hans Hirsch, "Methoden und Probleme der Urkundenforschung," *MOEIG* 53 (1939), 1–20. On Frankish charters, formulas, and laws, see R. Schröder and E. Frh. von Künnsberg, *Lehrbuch der deutschen Rechtsgeschichte* (7th ed.; Berlin-Leipzig, 1932), paragraphs 32–34, pp. 280 ff.; Emile Chénon, *Histoire générale du droit français*, I (Paris, 1926), under the relevant headings.

[41] Referred to in our context as *DK* after *MGH, Diplomata Karolinorum*, I, ed. Engelbert Mühlbacher (1906). Cf. *Diplomata Karolinorum: Recueil de réproductions*, ed. F. Lot, P. Lauer, G. Tessier, I (Toulouse-Paris, 1936), 1 ff.

[42] Cf. Heinrich Mitteis, *Lehnsrecht und Staatsgewalt* (Weimar, 1933), 50 ff., on *Treupflicht*.

[43] On this category of documents see Theodor Sickel, *Acta Regum et Imperatorum Karolinorum*, I (Vienna, 1867), 396–404.

*A.* The introductory *protocol* consists of the following *formulae:*

*a. intitulatio,* the name and titles of Charlemagne.

*b. devotio (gratia Dei),* which is expressive of the thought that the king owes his earthly position to divine grace.

*c. inscriptio,* the names of the addressees:...Baugulfo abbati *et omni congregationi, tibi* etiam *commissis fidelibus,* oratoribus *nostris,*...salutem. The form of this *inscriptio* is identical with that in Charlemagne's letter addressed to Alcuin (*Epist.* 247 D.399.38–39):...Albino venerabili magistro *et omni congregationi...*; and in Charlemagne's letter mandate of 805, addressed to Bishop Ghaerbald (*Capitularia,* I, no. 124, p. 245, 2–3):...Ghaerbaldo episcopo cum universis *tibi* omnipotente Deo et nostra ordinatione *commissis* in Domino salutem. The attributive designation *fidelibus...nostris* conforms with the *inscriptio...fidelibus nostris* of Charlemagne's charters for Fulda of 774 (*DK,* 85, 86).

It is evident from the parallelism between the *tibi commissis* of the *inscriptio* and the same formulation in the mandate for Ghaerbald that the *formula* of the Metz MS is the original one, and not that of the Laudianus:...⟨Baugu⟩lf⟨o abbati ⟨nec⟩ non et omni congrega⟨tioni fidelibus nostris⟩.

*d. invocatio,* the verbal invocation of the divine name: in omnipotentis Dei nomine. The *invocatio* usually opens the *protocol,* but in our case it is placed after the *inscriptio,* as in Charlemagne's mandate for Ghaerbald (see *c*).

*e. salutatio,* the personal greeting of the king: amabilem direximus salutem.

The *formula* of (*a*) is identical with the corresponding one in the diplomata of Charlemagne as king, but not with those of the imperial period after 800; (*c*) and (*e*) are characteristic of his mandates.[44] The *salutatio* renders a traditional *formula* which

---

[44] Erben, *Urkundenlehre,* 345, assumes that the *inscriptio* of a mandate is a substitute for its *publicatio.* This is not borne out by our document, nor by other mandates which have both *formulae.*

also occurs in a private letter [45] sent by Charlemagne from the battlefields of Saxony to Queen Fastrada in 791: *Salutem amabilem* tibi mittere studuimus et...ceteris *fidelibus nostris*.

The *oratores* of the *inscriptio* (*c*) are not ambassadors,[46] as Munro and Beeson assumed, but teachers or preachers. Alcuin and Odilbert of Milan [47] both refer to themselves in letters addressed to Charlemagne as *orator vester*. In a letter addressed to Charlemagne between 774 and 800, an abbot refers to himself and his congregation as *oratores vestri*. The same designation is used by bishops for the same purpose in reports of 820 and 829 sent to Louis the Pious.[48] *Oratores* are defined by Hrabanus Maurus and Walafrid Strabo [49] as teachers and preachers. Since the letter is addressed to a cleric, and also stresses the importance of *recte loquendo* as an important part of the educational process, we see that these *oratores* were teachers.

The characterization of Baugulf and his congregation as the *fideles* [50] of the Frankish king presupposes on the part of the scribe a familiarity with the legal relationship between Charlemagne and Fulda that can be expected only from a professional scribe of the king's chancellery.

The customary concluding parts, the so-called *eschatocol* of royal charters, consisting of the signature of the king, the subscriptions of his *capella* official who supervised the scribe's cor-

---

[45] *MGH, Epistolae*, IV, no. 20, p. 528, 10–11.

[46] Used first by D. C. Munro, *University of Pennsylvania Translations and Reprints* 6 (1900), no. 5, p. 12; repeated by C. H. Beeson, *A Primer of Medieval Latin* (Chicago-NewYork, 1925), 152.

[47] *MGH, Epistolae*, IV, no. 177, p. 292, 9; *MGH, Capitularia*, I, no. 126, p. 247, 27.

[48] *MGH, Formulae*, p. 331, no. 5; *MGH, Capitularia*, I, p. 367, 39; II, p. 46, 16.

[49] *De institutione clericorum*, c.19 (PL, CVII, 307C); *De exordiis et incrementis rerum ecclesiasticarum*, ed. *MGH, Capitularia*, II, 485.

[50] Cf. Engelbert Mühlbacher, "Die Treupflicht in den Urkunden Karls des Grossen," *MIOEG*, Erg. Bd., 6 (1901), 871–883.

rect execution of the document, and the date line, are missing in the document, since the *salutatio* designates the mandate as an *epistola*, a characterization expressly referred to by the scribe in the *sanctio* (*B, e* below). *Legens valeat* at the very end of the letter is not the final greeting of Charlemagne but the marginal endorsement of the mandate by a chancellery official (*C* below).

B. The *formulae* of the *context* are:

*a. publicatio*, also called *promulgatio* or *notificatio*, the general announcement of the royal will (To Whom It May Concern): *Notum igitur sit...*devotioni vestrae, *quia nos* una *cum fidelibus nostris* consideravimus *utile esse.* The same *formula* is used in Charlemagne's letter mandate of 805, addressed to bishop Ghaerbald: [51] *Notum sit* dilectioni vestrae, *quia nos cum fidelibus nostris...*invenimus necessarium *esse.* This is the formulation of the *publicatio* characteristic of the charters of Charlemagne [52] which was also adopted by the *Formulae Imperiales.*[53] The *useful* purpose of the king's expression of will is stressed in a similar manner in Charlemagne's *Admonitio Generalis* of 789 (*Capitularia* I, p. 57, 42):...quae nobis *utilia huic...*ammonitione subiungere visa sunt; also in a letter of Alcuin addressed to Charlemagne (*Epist.* 118 D.173, 31): "Vos enim ipsi optime scitis quod *utile* est regno vobis a Deo dato."

The occurrence of *consideravimus* points to a professional scribe and to a formulalike phrase also used in other legislative documents of Charlemagne. Compare: *Capitulare Missorum Niumigae* of 806, c. 18 (*Cap.*, I, 46, p. 132, 28): *Consideravimus itaque...quia...,ut* omnes...*qui...*; *Pippini Capitulare Papiense* of 787, c. 9 (*ibid.*, no. 94, p. 199, 29): *Consideravimus, ut* vias...; and *Admonitio Generalis* of 789 (*ibid.*, no. 22, p. 53, 26): *Con-*

---

[51] *MGH, Capitularia,* I, no. 124, p. 245, 4–5; now dated 805 (not 807) by Wilhelm A. Eckhardt, *Die Kapitulariensammlung Bischof Ghaerbalds von Lüttich* (Göttingen, 1955), 47–49.

[52] Erben, *Urkundenlehre*, 342.

[53] *MGH, Formulae,* ed. Karl Zeumer, for instance, no. 48, p. 323.

*siderans...una cum* sacerdotibus et consiliariis nostris...et quam *necessarium* est....

The last-quoted *publicatio* of the royal law parallels the same *formula* in our letter: *una cum* fidelibus nostris *consideravimus*. It is expressive of the "consent" of some of the great of Charlemagne's entourage to the king's legislative activities (see Pt. III).

*b. arenga*, a general motivation indicative of the meritoriousness of good works to which the king is pledged by divine command. This *formula* usually opens the context of the royal charter.[54] An exception is *DK*, 187,[55] in which the *arenga* follows the *publicatio* (*a*), as seems to be the case also in our mandate: monasteria nobis Christo propitio ad gubernandum commissa...*qualiter...ita quoque* (*ideoque: DK*, 187).

It is possible that the scribe included in the *formula* the entire section including sentence 6. If on the other hand "Christo propitio," which appears, for instance, in the *arenga* of *DK*, 96, is to be taken as a substitute for the *arenga*, then part of the section, especially sentence 6, "Nam cum omnibus hominibus...," could belong to the following *formula*.

*c. narratio*, an account of the circumstances leading up to the matter dealt with in the mandate, "Nam cum nobis" (sentence 7).

*d. dispositio*, the expression of the king's will to act upon his suggestions, exhortations, and requests: *Quamobrem* hortamur vos..., *ut* (sentence 10); Optamus enim vos..., ut (14); *Et hoc* tantum ea *intentione* agatur, qua *devotione* a nobis *praecipitur* (13).

The same traditional formulations of the *dispositio* occur in other mandates by Charlemagne. Compare:

---

[54] Cf. Martin Granzin, *Die Arenga in frühmittelalterlichen Urkunden* (Halle-Wittenberg diss., 1930), 56–61.

[55] Georg Kleeberg, *Untersuchungen zu den Urkunden Karls des Grossen* (Berlin diss., 1914), 41.

*Epistola ad Ghaerbaldum* of 805 (*Capitularia*, 1, no. 124, p. 246, 1–2):
*Quamobrem* bonum nobis omnino videtur, ut...and *Et haec* debet esse
praemissa orationis *intentio*, ut...; *Praeceptum pro Hispanis* (*ibid.*,
no. 76, p. 169, 25-*DK*, 217, p. 290, 14): *Quam ob rem* iussimus..., ut...;
*Epistola ad Fulradum* of 806 (*ibid.*, no. 75, p. 168, 29, 20): Quapropter
*precipimus* tibi, ut and *Et hoc* omnino *precipimus*, ut.

e. *sanctio*,[56] the loss of the king's favor in the case of negligent
execution of the royal will: Huius itaque epistolae exemplaria
ad omnes suffragantes tuosque coepiscopos et universa monasteria
dirigi *non neglegas, si gratiam nostram habere vis.*

This part of the mandate is to be found in the Metz MS but
not in the Laudianus. It is, no doubt, an original part of the
document. The scribe of the mandate must have had a predilection for the *non neglegas* of his *sanctio*, since he uses the negative formulation in other parts of the mandate: non neglegant
(2a), non neglegere (10).

The identical sanction is used in other mandates by Charlemagne: *Epistola ad Fulradum* (p. 168, 39–40): Vide ut *nullam
neglegentiam* exinde habeas, *sicut gratiam nostram velis habere;*
*Praeceptum pro Hispanis*, (p. 169, 35–37 = *DK*, 217):...omnia
in loco restituere faciatis, *sicuti gratiam* dei et *nostram vultis
habere* propiciam.

The same formulation of the *sanctio* in the letter mandates
for Baugulf and Fulrad also occurs in three charters by Charlemagne: [57] *DK*, 66, 88, 91. But whereas the *sanctio* of the mandates speaks to the recipient of the respective documents, that
of the three charters and of the *Praeceptum pro Hispanis* (*DK*,

[56] Cf. J. Studtmann, "Die Pönformel der mittelalterlichen Urkunden,"
*Archiv für Urkundenforschung* 12 (1932), 291; on later occurrences of
the same sanction see Carl Erdmann, *ibid.*, 16 (1939), 196–198; R. Köstler,
*Huldentzug als Strafe* (Kirchenrechtliche Abhandlungen 62, 1910).

[57] Erben, *Urkundenlehre*, 361–362, overlooks the *sanctio* of the two
letter mandates and that of *DK*, 88; also *MGH, Capitularia*, I, no. 85, p.
184, c.1:...et *nullam exinde neglegentiam habeatis.*

217) is addressed to the third person in order to enforce the rights and privileges of the recipients.

The identical sanction appears furthermore in Merovingian charters [58] of Chlodewig III in 692 and Chilperich II in 716; also in the *Formulae Marculfi*, I, 11, the *F. Senonenses* 18, and the *Formulae Imperiales* 15.[59]

The discrepancies in the classification of the letter by the historians listed in our introduction can be traced to their interpretations of the meaning implied in the reference to the "suffragantes tuosque coepiscopos." The mention of these co-bishops accounts for the assumption that an archbishop was the actual recipient of Charlemagne's mandate and that this unknown metropolitan forwarded copies of the letter to bishops and abbots. But the abbot of the politically powerful and exempted monastery of Fulda, under the direct protection of Rome and not under the authority of a metropolitan, could very well be called an *episcopus*. Although the identification of abbot and bishop is not found very frequently in the sources, it occurs in Charlemagne's immunity charter of 772 for St Mihiel de Marsoupe (*DK*, 68).

*f.* The concluding sentence of the mandate reads like a continuation of the *sanctio* (*e*):

*M* (p. 79, 44–45): Et nullus monachus foris monasterio iudiciaria teneat, nec per mallos et publica placita pergat;

*L* (p. 9, 23–26): Hoc ut fieret ortamur: Ut nullus monachorum foras monasterio iudiciaria teneat, neque per placita et mallos discurrat.

The assumption of Boretius [60] that this statement is not a genuine part of the letter is contradicted by its occurrence in

---

[58] *MGH, Diplomatum Regum Francorum E Stirpe Merowingica*, ed. K. A. F. Pertz (Hannover, 1872), nos. 61, 82.

[59] *MGH, Formulae Merovingici et Karolini Aevi*, ed. Karl Zeumer (*Legum Sectio*, v, 1); *Form. Imp.* 15 is identical with *DK*, 88.

[60] *MGH, Capitularia*, I, 79.

both manuscript transmissions. Its formulation and contents correspond with several capitularies. Compare:

*Admonitio Generalis* of 789, c. 73 (*Capitularia*, 1, p. 60): Sacerdotibus.... Et ut monachi ad saecularia placita non vadant;

*Capitulary* of 789, c. 30 (*ibid.*, p. 64): Ut monachi et qui in sacerdotali gradu constituti sunt ad saecularia negotia non transeant;

*Capitulare Missorum Generale* of 802, c. 17 (*ibid.*, p. 91): Foris monasterio nequaquam progrediendi licentiam habeant (monachi).

The hortatory request of our mandate seems to extend to monks, as lower clerics, the regulation of cap. 7 of the *Capitulare Francofurtense* of 794 (*ibid.*, p. 75), namely, that higher clerics such as bishop, presbyter and deacon, may not leave their churches. The same capitulary, cap. 11, decrees for monks specifically: Ut monachi ad saecularia negotia neque ad placita exercenda non exeant.

The initial request that no monk may hold judicial powers (*iudiciaria*) is worded in accordance with the immunity formula [61] of Charlemagne's charters, which forbids representatives of the law to enter properties exempted by royal immunity in order to transact legal business. Its basic formula opens with "..., ut nullus...," and closes with "...audeat" or "praesumat." The corresponding formula, which also occurs, of course, in Charlemagne's immunity charter for Fulda of 774 (*DK*, 85), is always fashioned after the older Merovingian immunity of the *Formulae Marculfi*, 1, 2 (and others):..., ut...nulla iudiciaria potestas...non presumat ingredere.

It is obvious that the exhortations of the last sentence in our mandate presuppose already *existing* royal legislation. Their wording and content, coinciding with the *Capitulare Francofurtense* of 794, suggest this year as the *terminus ante quem non* for the date of Charlemagne's letter to Baugulf.

C. *Legens valeat*, the concluding *formula* of the letter in the

[61] Maurice Kroell, *L'immunité franque* (Paris, 1910), 282 ff.

transmission of MS *M*, is deserving of special interest. *Valeat* does not mean "Farewell" as D. C. Munro would have it, although the scribe of *M* obviously considered the words to be the final greeting of the epistle. But the *formula* is not an original part of the letter. It is a vestige of an older Merovingian chancery custom that survived under the first Carolingians but became extinct under Charlemagne's rule.

*Legens valeat* corresponds to *Bene valiat* in Merovingian and *Bene valeat* in Carolingian charters.[62] The latter *formula* is not an expression of well wishing nor is it addressed to the recipient of the document. It signifies the endorsement of a charter by the chancellery's *referendarius* or his Carolingian counterpart, a notary or scribe of the Royal Chapel. In Merovingian documents *Bene valiat* is usually covered by the wax of the seal. Under Charlemagne, the *formula* became superfluous because permission to affix the seal was granted through the so-called *corroboratio* of the context, a *formula* which does not occur in the context of *De litteris colendis*. The question whether *Legens valeat*, like the Carolingian *corroboratio*, stands for the official order to seal the letter after inspection by a member of the chancellery may be answered in the affirmative, though the original of the mandate is not preserved. Alcuin in a letter addressed to Charlemagne (no. 172, p. 285) mentions the fact that an epistle he received from the king was sealed. Now if a private letter of Charlemagne was sealed, we cannot go amiss in assuming that a letter containing an expression of the royal will was also closed with the royal seal. A member of Charlemagne's chancellery who read (*Legens*) the letter confirmed its formal and legal validity (*valeat*) before the seal was put on it.

The occurrence of an older Merovingian chancery custom in

[62] For the following see Léon Levillain, "La formule Bene valiat et le sceau dans les diplômes Mérovingiens," *Bibliothèque de l'Ecole des Chartes* 92 (1931), 5–15, *passim*, and P. Classen in *Archiv für Diplomatik* 2 (1956), 48 f.

the process of releasing a document from the royal chancellery is not an unusual feature for Charlemagne's notaries and scribes. The *sanctio* (above, B, *e*) is likewise of Merovingian origin. Thus *Legens valeat* is not a part of the authentic text of the mandate, but the marginal endorsement of the letter by an official of Charlemagne's chancellery.

The diplomatic investigation reveals that Charlemagne's letter to Baugulf was an official document of his chancellery and that it was written by a scribe who edited Alcuin's preliminary note (*Konzept*) within the formulary of a mandate which consists of the following *formulae* that are characteristic of similar documents of Charlemagne:

*A.* protocol: *intitulatio, devotio, inscriptio, invocatio,* and *salutatio;*

*B.* context: *publicatio, arenga, narratio, dispositio,* and *sanctio.*

*C.* Marginal endorsement of chancellery official.

The letter is a mandate cast in the customary subjective fashion of a royal charter. The king thus speaks in the *pluralis maiestatis:* "Carolus...direximus salutem." Everything belonging to him is referred to as *noster (nostris, nobis).* Baugulf is addressed in the second person in the negative part of the *dispositio,* i.e., the *sanctio,* which speaks to him alone: *tuos coepiscopos, neglegas, vis.*

Vestiges of the scribe's personal style seem to be the repetitious use of *ita quoque* (2a, 8, 14), *non neglegere* (10, 2a, 15), *quamvis* (4, 9), and the divine name in the form of liturgical and Biblical phrases: *donante Domino, Deo placere, Dei laudibus, omnipotenti Domino, propter nomen Domini.* It cannot be decided whether *interius-exterius* (7a, 14) may be ascribed to Alcuin's share in the context (cf. r), or whether the antithesis, which also occurs in Charlemagne's letter of 805 addressed to Bishop Ghaerbald,[63] is traceable to the same scribe who wrote this mandate.

A comparison of the identical *formulae* used by the scribe who

[63] *MGH, Capitularia,* I, no. 124, pp. 245–246.

wrote the letter to Baugulf and those of the mandates and diplomata adduced in our investigation does not permit us definitely to identify this man as one of the scribes of Charlemagne's Chapel whose names are known to us from the recognition lines of royal charters. But we can state that the *formulae* of the *inscriptio* (*A*, *c*), *invocatio* (*A*, *d*), *publicatio* (*B*, *a*), and *dispositio* (*B*, *d*) reveal the use by the scribe of the letter of a mandate form which resembles the one used also by the unknown scribe of Charlemagne's letter mandate of 805 for Bishop Ghaerbald.

The relationship between the diverse transmissions of the letter in the Metz (*M*) and Oxford (*L*) manuscripts is explained by Lehmann and Laistner, according to chronological considerations, by assuming that the older *L* (*saec.* IX) offers the original text and *M* (*saec.* XI/XII) an expanded version of the same letter. But the relationship is just the reverse; the younger *M* offers the original text and the older *L* the text of a circular which is a somewhat shortened version of the original. Minor discrepancies in spelling between the two manuscripts are traceable to their scribes, other discrepancies to the fact that the manuscripts transmit two different documents: a personal letter (*M*), and a circular letter (*L*). The original text of the mandate is not preserved by the older manuscript, but by the later, because:

*a*. the *inscriptio* of *M* and not that of *L* (*A*, *c*) is the original one, since it is identical with a *formula* used also by the scribe of another letter mandate by Charlemagne.

*b*. the *sanctio* of *M* (*B*, *e*), which is missing in *L*, is an original part of the mandate, because the same *formula* occurs in other documents issued by Charlemagne's chancellery.

*c*. *M* reads *episcopia et monasteria*, *L* *monasteria* alone, because it must have been addressed to a monastery.

*d*. *M* alone preserves the marginal endorsement of the lost original by a chancellery official of Charlemagne.

These four text elements are not real "variants" but special features which distinguish the circular (*L*) from its source, the personal letter (*M*). They are traces of Baugulf's re-edition of Charlemagne's personal letter as a circular letter by omitting those parts that have a merely personal connotation relating solely to the abbot of Fulda. Thus the *inscriptio* was made less personal and put in a more general formulation. The *sanctio* is missing in *L* because it refers to Baugulf alone and a repetition would have been meaningless. The marginal endorsement of the document was copied by the scribe of *M;* it does not occur in *L* since it is not a part of the mandate. The failure to mention *episcopia* characterizes the recipient of *L* as the abbot of a monastery. The re-edition of Charlemagne's letter to Baugulf as a circular which is a shortened version of its source may be compared with the emperor's personal letter of 802–805 addressed to Bishop Ghaerbald and the bishop's circular, based on this mandate, addressed to his clergy.[64] In this instance the circular letter is not a literal copy, as in our case, but a transcript of its contents.

The diplomatic investigation proves that Lehmann's publication is not of the original version of Charlemagne's letter to Baugulf, but is a copy of Baugulf's circular letter addressed to a monastery. The edition of Alfred Boretius presents the original text of the king's letter to the abbot of Fulda, urging him to promote religious education within his orbit of influence. Under Charlemagne, Fulda was a royal missionary monastery of considerable independence and power in church affairs, whose resources were used on a large scale to missionize the territories acquired during the wars with the Saxons.[65] In 781, when the king arrived in Saxony, he divided the territory into *octo episcopatus.*[66] The present writer considers the letter a personal

[64] *Ibid.*, no. 122, pp. 241–242; for the dating see Eckhardt, above, n. 51.

[65] Hans Götting, "Die klösterliche Exemtion," *Archiv für Urkundenforschung* 16 (1939), 111.

[66] *Annalista Saxo* ad a. 781, *MGH, Scriptores*, VI, 542; cf. E. Müller, *Die Entstehung der sächsischen Bistümer unter Karl d. Gr.* (Quellen und Darstellungen zur Geschichte Niedersachsens 47; Hildesheim und Leipzig, 1938).

mandate addressed to the abbot of Fulda, not only on the basis of the diplomatic evidence but also on these historical grounds. Under Baugulf, Fulda occupied as royal monastery a dominating position in the eastern part of Charlemagne's empire,[67] especially guiding and influencing the religious educational work in the young Saxon dioceses and monasteries.

## III

What we have learned thus far enables us to suggest a more definite date for Charlemagne's letter to Baugulf. Hitherto it was assigned to the last two decades of the eighth century because Baugulf was abbot at Fulda from 780–802, and Charlemagne is not referred to as emperor (as he was after Dec. 25, 800). Internal evidence seems to point to the year 794 as *terminus ante quem non* (Pt. II, B, f). Alcuin's share in the text of the mandate provides the *terminus post quem non*.

The *consent*[68] of Charlemagne's councilors (*fideles nostri*), mentioned in the *publicatio* (Pt. II, B, a), offers internal evidence for the fact of Alcuin's contribution of a "preliminary note" used by the scribe of the letter. The Anglo-Saxon was indeed a *fidelis* of the Frankish king. Charlemagne's charter for the monastery of Corméry of June 2, 800 mentions the petitions *fidelis nostri Albini* (*DK*, 192), who thus at one time must have taken the oath of allegiance[69] to the king. Additional internal evidence is provided by Alcuin's editorship of Charlemagne's *Libri Carolini*,[70] the manifesto of the Frankish church against image wor-

[67] See the paragraph at the end of Pt. II, B, e, s.v. *sanctio;* Arthur Kleinclausz, *Eginhard*, 28; K. Lübeck, "Die Exemtion des Klosters Fulda," *Studien und Mitteilungen OSB.* 55 (1937), 132–153; K. Lübeck, "Der Primat der Fuldaer Aebte im Mittelalter," *Zeitschrift der Savigny-Stiftung für Rechtsgeschichte*, Kan. Abt. 33 (1944), 244 ff.

[68] Cf. Bresslau, *Handbuch der Urkundenlehre*, II, 1 (Leipzig, 1915), 37; T. Sickel, *Acta Regum*, 1 (Vienna, 1867), 66.

[69] Cf. C. E. Odegaard, "Carolingian Oaths of Fidelity," *Speculum* 16 (1941), 284–296.

[70] Ed. Hubert Bastgen, *MGH, Legum Sectio III, Concilia, Suppl.* (1924), 92–100.

ship, which contains in Bk. ii. 30, a treatise on the *artes liberales* with special emphasis on the *schemata* and *tropi* and their significance for the study of the Vulgate. Similar stress is displayed by the mention of these *colores rhetorici* in Charlemagne's mandate to Baugulf. Since the *Libri Carolini*, which were never [71] published officially, originated about 791,[72] we have gained some contemporary evidence for the historical background of the letter, whose mention of the *colores* as an allegedly unique suggestion of Charlemagne has thus been overrated by De Ghellinck.[73]

Charlemagne's interest in the *regularis vita* at Fulda under Baugulf is paralleled by a letter [74] of Alcuin addressed to Fulda after 800. He asks the *fratres* to be lenient when judging "Baugulf, my dearest friend, who, because of old age, is unable to abide by the strictness of the *Benedictine Rule*." Charlemagne's charter for Fulda of 774 (*DK*, 86) expresses the same thought, namely, that the congregation must live at all times "secundum ordinem vel regulam sanctam." Since Alcuin and the king mention "regularis vitae ordinem" in their letters to Baugulf, we are inclined to believe that there is some connection between the conditions hinted at by both. Baugulf's difficulties, which seem to have necessitated the writing of both letters, must have begun some time before Alcuin wrote his letter sent from Tours to Fulda. On these and other grounds we assign Charlemagne's letter addressed to Baugulf to the period between the Synod of

---

[71] Wolfram von den Steinen, "Entstehungsgeschichte der Libri Carolini," *Quellen und Forschungen aus italienischen Archiven und Bibliotheken* 16 (1929-1930), 87; Erich Caspar, "Das Papsttum und die fränkische Herrschaft," *Zeitschrift für Kirchengeschichte* 54 (1935), 200. Ernst Kantorowicz, *Laudes Regiae* (Berkeley, 1946), 62, wrongly assumes that the *Libri Carolini* were published in 792; they were never published.

[72] W. v. d. Steinen, "Karl der Grosse und die Libri Carolini," *Neues Archiv* 49 (1930), 207.

[73] J. de Ghellinck, *La littérature latine du moyen-âge*, II (Paris, 1939), 185-186.

[74] *MGH, Epistolae*, IV, no. 250, p. 405, 12-13 (801-802).

Frankfurt in June 794 and the year 800. This dating of *De litteris colendis* would well fit other measures decreed by Charlemagne [75] for the Saxon territories from 794 to 797.

[75] F. L. Ganshof, "Charlemagne," *Speculum* 24 (1949), assumes that *De litteris colendis* was issued after 789—"a little later" (p. 522, n. 7). I have abandoned the dating "794–796" proposed in *Speculum* 26 (1951), 305.—My interpretation of the document coincides with that offered by A. J. Macdonald, *Authority and Reason in the Early Middle Ages* (London, 1933), 23, who, stressing the influence of Alcuin, writes that copies of Charlemagne's letter to Baugulf "are to be sent to all the bishops and monasteries in the abbot's neighborhood." E. E. Stengel, *Urkundenbuch des Klosters Fulda* I, 1 (Marburg, 1956), 251–253, has not proved Alcuin's alleged authorship of *De litteris colendis*, as is pointed out by F.-C. Scheibe in *Deutsches Archiv für die Erforschung des Mittelalters* 14 (1958), 222 n. 18. Professor Stengel, op. cit. I, 3 (Marburg, 1958), 539 f., offers additional comments.

Heinz Loewe, *Göttingische gelehrte Anzeigen* 214 (1962), 151, and *Deutsches Archiv* 18 (1962), 282 f., mistakenly believes that I reversed the sequence of *L* and *M*. On the contrary, it is Stengel who advocates— if I may use Loewe's words—an interrelationship, "die das Verhältnis der beiden Fassungen einfach auf den Kopf stellt," since he apparently assumes that the text of the older *L* represents the original of the mandate, and *M* a later copy. But this assumption is clearly contradicted by the diplomatic investigation (above, pp. 217-21) of the *sanctio* and the *Legens valeat*, both of which are missing in *L*. The personal character of Charlemagne's mandate addressed to Baugulf may well account for the fact that the *sanctio* was not repeated by him in his circular letter. I never questioned the fact that the mandate was indeed used by Baugulf as a circular letter, as is assumed by F. L. Ganshof, *Recherches sur les Capitulaires* (Paris, 1958), 45 n. 173, and *Was waren die Kapitularien?* (Weimar, 1961), 74 n. 173. Ganshof, "Charlemagne et les institutions de la monarchie franque," in *Karl der Grosse I: Persönlichkeit und Geschichte*, ed. Helmut Beumann (2nd.; Düsseldorf, 1966), calls our Chapter XI, first published in *Speculum* 26 (1951), 288-305, an "édition excellente avec commentaire" (p. 391 n. 336) as well as (p. 358 n. 64) a "meilleure édition que Boretius" (above, p. 198 n. 1). See also Bernhard Bischoff and Josef Hofmann, *Libri Sancti Kyliani* (Würzburg, 1952), 97 n. *12.

*Part Four*

# THE LITERARY METHOD

# OF ALCUIN

ONE of Alcuin's many interests [1] was to develop in the leaders among the laity of a barbarian age [2] a sense of moral responsibility and a personal culture fit for the commanding positions which these men held. Many of the letters sent by Alcuin [3] to Charlemagne and other members of the royal household, to the kings of Mercia and Northumbria, to Frankish and British nobles and government officials, overflow, as we have seen, with advice and requests to mend their ways. With this aim he wrote special works for some of these persons—for one example, the Rhetoric [4] as a *via regia* for Charlemagne, a work which must be classed [5] as the oldest Carolingian *speculum principis*,[6] preceding

[1] See Chapter IV.

[2] Cf. the censure of barbarian procedures of law by Alcuin's friend, Theodulph of Orléans, as described by P. M. Acari, "Un goto critico delle legislazioni barbariche," *Archivio Storico Italiano* 110 (1952), 3–37; some of Arcari's interpretations of the *Lex Salica* are, however, mistaken.

[3] Edited by Ernst Dümmler, *MGH, Epistolae* IV (1895).

[4] This thesis is developed in Part I, Chapters II–V.

[5] Heinz Löwe in Wattenbach-Levison, *Deutschlands Geschichtsquellen im Mittelalter* (Weimar, 1953), 230, n. 211, and p. 233, accepts in principle my interpretation of the Rhetoric as a *speculum principis*, as first suggested in *Speculum* 24 (1949), 588 f.

[6] Cf. Lester Born, "The Specula Principis of the Carolingian Renaissance," *Revue belge de philologie et d'histoire* 12 (1933), 483–612, which

that of Smaragdus of St. Mihiel (written for Louis the Pious), that of Jonas of Orléans (for Pippin of Aquitania), that of Sedulius Scottus (for Lothar II), and that of Hincmar of Reims (for Charles the Bald). Related to these *specula* is the treatise *De virtutibus et vitiis*,[7] which Alcuin wrote in the years after 800 for Wido, Margrave of the Marca Britanniae, who during the year 799 overcame the resistance of this territory to Charlemagne. In type, this ethical manual resembles the *Libellus exhortatorius*,[8] compiled between 796 and 799 by Alcuin's friend Paulinus of Aquileia for Duke Eric of Friuli, one of Charlemagne's best generals. We recall also the *Liber manualis* of Dhuoda,[9] wife of Bernard of Septimania, written between 841 and 843 for her son William, who was then attached, probably as a page, to the Court of Charles the Bald. An analysis of the contents, purpose, philosophy, and literary composition of Alcuin's treatise should reveal the author's way of thinking and his method of writing and enable us to assess the historical significance of the tractate.

---

lists neither the *Rhetoric* nor *De virtutibus et vitiis* among the Carolingian *specula*.

[7] Migne, *PL* 101, 613–638.

[8] Migne, *PL* 99, 197 ff.; Dom Rochais lists in the *Revue bénédictine* 63 (1953), 251, the extant MSS of this treatise.

[9] Ed. E. Bondurand, *Le Manuel de Dhuoda* (Paris, 1887); see the fine study by A. Burger, "Les vers de la Duchesse Dhuoda et son poème De temporibus suis," *Mélanges J. Marouzeau* (Paris, 1948), 85–102; and André Vernet, "Un nouveau manuscrit du Manuel de Dhuoda (Barcelone Biblioteca central 569)," *Bibliothèque de l'école des Chartes* 114 (1956), 18–44.

# CHAPTER XII

# Alcuin on Virtues and Vices

THIS treatise [1] of thirty-five chapters may be divided into four parts distinct in style and content. A dedicatory letters opens the treatise, and a brief epistolary peroration (ch. 36) brings it to a close.[2] The first twenty-six chapters deal with the following topics: wisdom, faith, charity, hope, the reading of the Bible lesson, peace, mercy, forgiveness, patience, humility, remorse, confession, repentance, the return to God, the fear of God, fasting, almsgiving, chastity, freedom from conceit, judges, bearing false witness, envy, pride, wrath, deceit, and perseverance in good works. Chapters 27–34 provide a catalogue of eight principal vices. The last chapter, 35, is a disquisition on the four cardinal virtues—wisdom, justice, courage, and temperance—which, together with the term "virtus," are defined and described. The division into thirty-five chapters is confirmed by the title, dating from the ninth century, found in the catalogue of the library at St. Gall: "Alchvvini ad Vitonem comitem capitula xxxv." [3] The

---

[1] Ch. 36, *PL* 101, 638B–C, is not an original chapter of the treatise; see below n. 3.

[2] The introductory letter and the peroration are critically edited by Dümmler, *MGH, Epistolae* IV, *Epist.* 305, p. 464 f.

[3] Paul Lehmann, *Mittelalterliche Bibliothekskataloge* I (Munich, 1918), 79.

letter peroration (chap. 36 in Migne) was therefore not counted by Alcuin as a separate chapter.

The four parts of the treatise are obviously composed in different styles. The epistolary sections conform to the personal style of Alcuin, as known from his many epistles. But while the section on virtues is written in a homiletic vein, that on the *vitia* is factual and descriptive. And chapter 35 contains elements of both styles. That this variety results from Alcuin's use of different sources (see below) is clear.

Alcuin allegedly wrote upon the express request of the recipient. Wido, busily absorbed *in bellicis rebus*, receives a handbook (*manualis libellus*) which is to tell him what to do and what to avoid in his daily life.

The treatise is presented as a *breviarium*,[4] composed, as expected, *brevi sermone*. It was intended to teach a "homo laicus, qui adhuc in vita activa consistit," how to pray and make the best use of his time.[5] The layman Wido is not to be perturbed; his military profession will not prevent him from entering the portals of heaven. Heaven is open to all without distinction of sex or age or station in life, if only they perform good works (cf. Gal. 3:28; Col. 3:11).

Alcuin's purpose in writing can be deduced from certain topics used in the introductory letter and the peroration. His initial allegation that he wrote upon Wido's request cannot be taken seriously, since this is one of the many topics of modesty in his arsenal of rhetorical over- and understatements so abundantly drawn upon in his writings. Further, the pretense of writing upon request was supposed to lend authority to a work.[6]

---

[4] Letter and peroration are always referred to in Dümmler's edition.

[5] *Breviarium* is also the term used for the pseudo-Alcuinian *Officia per ferias. MGH, Epistolae IV, Epist.* 304, p. 462,30. A. Wilmart, *Revue bénédictine* 48 (1936), 262 f., assumes that this collection of prayers is of post-Alcuinian origin; also F. X. Haimerl, *Mittelalterliche Frömmigkeit im Spiegel der Gebetbuchliteratur Süddeutschlands* (Munich, 1952), p. 6.

[6] E. R. Curtius, *European Literature and the Latin Middle Ages* (Bollingen Series 36; New York, 1953), 85.

Similar commonplaces occur, for example, in the dedicatory epistle addressed to Beornred of Sens which accompanies Alcuin's *Vita S. Willibrordi:* that Alcuin has written upon request of the recipient (*petitioni*), that the style of the work is not an eminent example of eloquence (*eloquentia*), and that it is *caritas* which has spurred the author to write. Let us compare these passages: Alcuin writes to Wido (*Epist.* 305 D.464):

> Cui tam honestae *petitioni* libenter me annuere fateor, optans meae devotionis apices tibi ad perpetuam proficere salutem. Quos etiam, quamvis minus *eloquenter* videantur esse compositi, tamen certissime scito sanctae *caritatis* vigore eosdem esse dictatos.

Alcuin writes to Beornred of Sens (*Epist.* 120 D.175):

> Sed tamen longe imparem me *petitioni* vestrae consideravi, utpote nullo praerogativae munere *eloquentiae* suffultus, ad implendum quod iussisti; ac nisi me *caritas* urgeret, quae nulla negare solet, non auderem ultra meae paupertatis vires negotium attingere.

Other topics in Alcuin's letter are the same as those occurring in epistles to high-ranking clerics, in which it is recommended that they read the *Cura Pastoralis* of Gregory the Great, which Alcuin calls a *speculum* [7] of pontifical life.

The main topics employed in the letter to Wido are as follows:

a. Read the treatise frequently,[8] so that
b. your mind, wearied by outward vexations, may have something to turn to in which it can take pleasure;[9]
c. memorize individual chapters of the treatise;[10]

[7] *Epist.* 116, p. 171,27 (Dümmler): Speculum est enim pontificalis vitae et medicina contra singula diabolicae fraudis vulnera, a reference overlooked by R. Bradley, "Backgrounds of the Title *Speculum* in Mediaeval Literature," *Speculum* 29 (1953), 100–103. On *speculum* as a book title see Paul Lehmann, *Mittelalterliche Büchertitel* (SB. Bayer. Akademie der Wiss., 1953, Heft 3), 30–44.

[8] *Epist.* 305, p. 464,24:...litterulas, ita te humiliter deposco, ut easdem saepius legere digneris.

[9] *Ibid.*, p. 464,22:...ut animus exterioribus fatigatus molestiis, ad se ipsum reversus habeat, in quo gaudeat.

[10] *Ibid.*, p. 464,19:...memoriae haec mea dicta inhaerere.

d. study the work as a handbook which teaches you what to avoid and what to do.[11]

The same commonplaces occur also in letters addressed by Alcuin, approximately between 793 and 797, to Eanbald II, archbishop of York (*Ep.* 116); to Arno of Salzburg (*Ep.* 113), to Higbald of Lindisfarne (*Ep.* 124); and to an unknown ecclesiastic (*Ep.* 39). We again find the topics *a-d* in the following letters:

*a* and *d* in *Epist.* 116, p. 171, 25: Sepius illum [*scil.* Liber S. Gregorii Pastoralis] legas et relegas, quatenus te ipsum et tuum opus cognoscas in illo; ut, qualiter vivere vel docere debeas, ante oculos habeas;

*a*, *b*, and *c*, in *Epist.* 113, p. 166, 12: ...ut illum [see above] saepius quasi enchiridion habeas in manibus et in corde reteneas...sanctorum doctorum scio libros habere legere et firma tenere memoria;

*a*, *c*, and *d*, in *Epist.* 124, p. 182, 30: Iste liber [see above] tuis saepius inhereat manibus, illius sensus tuae firmiter infigantur memoriae; ut scias, qualiter quisque...se ipsum circumspicere debeat; et quibus exemplis vivere necesse sit;

*a* and *b*, in *Epist.* 39, p. 83, 2: Sed et pastoralem beati Gregorii papae saepissime perscrutare. His aepulis animam tuam pasce, ut habeas, unde alios quoque reficere valeas.

The dedicatory epistle is typical of Alcuin's style and not indebted to the letter preface of Defensor's *Liber scintillarum*[12] for any of its topics.

Alcuin clearly looked upon his treatise *De virtutibus et vitiis*

---

[11] *Ibid.*, p. 464,31:...ut habeas cotidie quasi manualem in conspectu tuo libellum, in quo possis te ipsum considerare, quid cavere, vel quid agere debeas. This passage is modeled after Alcuin, ch. 5, *De lect. studio* (PL 101, 616C): Sanctarum lectio Scripturarum divinae cognitio beatitudinis. In his enim quasi in quodam *speculo* homo seipsum considerare potest, qualis sit, vel quo tendat.

[12] Dom Rochais, *Revue bénédictine* 63 (1953), 264, seems to assume such an influence.

as something akin—*mutatis mutandis*—to Gregory's *Pastoral Rule*, and as a handbook to guide the soldier Wido in moral conflicts that might occur in the everyday affairs of a military man and royal judge. A letter of Alcuin (*Epist.* 249, p. 402, 5) addressed to Charlemagne praises Wido as "a perfect man and incorruptible judge." Obviously Alcuin's essay continues the continental tradition of Gregory the Great, not a British tradition presented "im insularen Raum" [13] by pseudo-Cyprian's treatise *De duodecim abusivis saeculi*. [14]

In philosophy the treatise is simple. Life is mirrored as a conflict between the virtues and the eight vices which are the root of all evil. Thus Alcuin writes to a correspondent: "Tu vero pacem cum omnibus habeas, *bellum cum vitiis*" (*Epist.* 209 D.349.10). The vices are overcome by their opposites among the virtues: pride is defeated by humility, gluttony by abstinence, fornication by chastity, avarice again by abstinence, anger by patience, sloth by good works, ungodly sorrow by spiritual pleasure, and vainglory by godly charity. In this battle of contraries, the virtues are victoriously led by the four cardinal virtues, the *duces gloriosissimi*, against the *duces impietatis* and their armies. All this reflects the traditional picture of the continuous battle waged between the virtues and the vices described by Prudentius in the *Psychomachia*, by Cassian in the *Collationes* and the *Institutes* and then by Gregory the Great, *Moralia in Job*, XXXI.45. These authors are well known to Alcuin, and so was the description of this battle in Aldhelm's *De virginitate*, [15] a model for Alcuin's metrical verse.

The preceding analysis shows that Alcuin only repeats traditional commonplaces. His reference to the content of the treatise as *haec mea dicta* (in the dedicatory letter) is therefore not to

[13] Heinz Löwe in Wattenbach-Levison, *op. cit.*, p. 233.
[14] See above, Chapter I, n. 14.
[15] See the prose chs. 11 and 12, and metr., vv. 2454–2472, ed. R. Ehwald, *MGH*, *Auctores Antiquissimi* xv (1919).

be taken literally or seriously. The expression *mea dicta* also occurs in other epistles and belongs to the rhetorical style he employs in his letters.[16]

A critical investigation of the treatise will finally reveal how Alcuin excerpted his sources.

## THE SOURCES OF THE SECTION *DE VIRTUTIBUS*

Dom Rochais has recently published a study of the source said to underlie the first section of the treatise, which deals with the virtues.[17] He concludes that Alcuin used a *florilegium* of patristic authors and not their original writings. The intermediary is said to have been the *Liber scintillarum* of Defensor of Ligugé,[18] who during the last decades of the seventh century compiled a collection of *deflorationes* from the Old and New Testaments and from early and later patristic writings. Defensor always indicates in his *catenae* the authors of the quotations without expressly registering the fact that many of these quotations are not directly derived from their originals but from later *florilegia*, such as Isidore of Seville's *Synonyma* and *Sententiae*.

[16] Cf. *Epist.* 257, p. 415,24, addressed to Charlemagne, also *Epist.* 172, p. 284,22.

[17] H.-M. Rochais, "Le Liber de virtutibus et vitiis d'Alcuin: Note pour l'étude des sources," *Revue Mabillon* 41 (1951), 77–86. Dom Rochais has incorporated the results of our investigation (first published in 1955) in his edition of Defensor's *Liber scintillarum*, CCL 117 (Turnhout, 1957), XII; see further Rochais, "Defensoriana; Archéologie du *Liber scintillarum*," *Sacris Erudiri* 9 (1957), 264.

[18] PL 88, 597–718. See the studies of the *Liber scintillarum* by Dom Rochais in *Revue bénédictine* 58 (1948), 77–83; 59 (1949), 137–156; 61 (1951), 63–80; "Les manuscrits du L. Sc.," *Scriptorium* 4 (1950), 294–309. Furthermore A. Vaccari, "Il liber scintillarum del monaco Defensor," *Studi Medievali* 17 (1951), 86–92. Not listed by S. de Ricci and W. J. Wilson, *Census of Medieval and Renaissance Manuscripts in the United States*, are two MSS of Defensor, currently offered for sale by the New York firm of Bernard M. Rosenthal, Inc.; see nos. 2 and 32 of their *Catalogue I: Selections of Medieval Text Manuscripts* (New York, 1954), 2 and 21.

Dom Rochais believes that a similar method was adopted by authors who used Defensor's work: they never mention Defensor's name. "Une dépendance de ce genre apparaît dans le *Liber de virtutibus et vitiis* d'Alcuin: 130 passages de la Bible et des Pères sont communs aux deux florilèges, et la façon dont les cite Alcuin prouve qu'il les doit à Defensor." [19] But these and other conclusions of Rochais in his inquiry are untenable. That Alcuin was familiar with Defensor's compilation has not been proved by Dom Rochais, despite his lists of passages in both works which are in complete textual agreement. For many sections of Alcuin's treatise whose sources are not listed by Rochais, the underlying source is easy to see. Dom Rochais gives a synopsis of the parallel passages [20] in the first twenty-six chapters of Alcuin's treatise *and* in Defensor and also identifies the origin of Defensor's excerpts. Some parallels have escaped his attention. Besides those mentioned for various reasons in the course of our investigation, compare, for instance, the two following:

Alcuin, ch. 7, *De misericordia* (*PL* 101, 618B): in judice misericordia et disciplina debet esse, quia una sine altera bene esse non possit;

Defensor, ch. 43, *De misericordia* (*PL* 88, 674C): Gregorius. Disciplina sine misericordia multum destituitur, si una sine altera teneatur.

Alcuin, ch. 18, *De castitate* (627B): castitas hominem coelo conjungit;

Defensor, ch. 13, *De virginitate* (633A): Isidorus. Castitas hominem ad coelos conjungit: = Isidore of Seville, *Synonyma*, II.10 (*PL* 83, 847C): castitas hominem coelo jungit.

Dom Rochais misjudges the relation between the *Sententiae* of Isidore of Seville and the quotations from this work in Al-

---

[19] Rochais, "Contribution à l'histoire des florilèges ascétiques du Haut Moyen Age Latin: Le Liber Scintillarum," *Revue bénédictine* 63 (1953), 289.

[20] *Revue Mabillon* 41 (1951), 81–86. All subsequent references to Rochais are to this synopsis unless otherwise indicated.

cuin's treatise.[21] To be sure, the titles and some subject matter of Alcuin's first four chapters run parallel to the beginning of the second Book of the *Sententiae*.[22] The assertion, however, that Alcuin's text contains no part of the text of Isidore's *florilegium* which Alcuin could not have found among Defensor's many excerpts from the *Sententiae* is mistaken. Rochais does not furnish in his synopsis, for example, the source of Alc., ch. 11 (621A), "Quando ergo ista in corde hominis fiunt, sciendum est tunc esse Deum per gratiam suam cordi humano presentem," which is a literal quotation from *Sententiae* II.12.6 (*PL* 83, 614A). Alcuin's chapters 20 and 21, for which there is one lone parallel (overlooked by Dom Rochais) in Defensor (see below), correspond literally with the text of the *Sententiae*.

Alcuin, ch. 20, *De judicibus* (*PL* 101, 628C–629B), is made up of verbatim quotations from *Sententiae* III (*PL* 83, 724B–726B, *passim*) in the following sequence: III.52.4; 52.2; 52.6–7; 52.11–12; 52.16; 53.1–3. Of these passages only Alcuin 629B, "non est persona in iudicio consideranda, sed causa," occurs in Defensor, ch. 58 (*PL* 88, 692B).

Alcuin, ch. 21, *De falsis testibus* (629C–630A) runs parallel to *Sententiae* III.55.2.3.7; 54.7; 57.1.2.3.6 (*PL* 83, 727A–729A, *passim*).

There can be no doubt that Alcuin used the *Sententiae* directly.[23] Indeed it is a question whether Alcuin used Defensor at all when compiling his treatise. The mere list of parallel passages by Dom Rochais does not suffice as evidence for Alcuin's dependence on Defensor, especially when we see that Alcuin used one of the *florilegia* also used by Defensor.

Further, parallels to longer passages in Alcuin's treatise, for

---

[21] *Revue Mabillon* 41 (1951), 80.    [22] *PL* 83, 599–603.
[23] Alcuin repeatedly expressed special admiration for Isidore of Seville, especially in *Adv. Elipandum Libri Quattuor* II, 8 (*PL* 101, 266B): Isidori ...perplurima legebamus opuscula et in magna habemus veneratione. Alcuin's use of the *Sententiae* and *Synonyma* may be added to A. E. Anspach, "Das Fortleben Isidors im vii. bis ix. Jahrhundert," *Miscellanea Isidoriana* (Rome, 1936), 350 f.

which not many parallel texts occur in Defensor, are found in certain pseudo-Augustinian sermons (Ps.-Aug., *App.*) embedded in a fuller context.[24] A synoptic survey of the chapters in Alcuin's treatise and these apocryphal homilies will serve to illustrate the point.

| Alcuin, *PL* 101, 614 ff. chapter: | Ps.-Aug., *App.*, *PL* 39, 1932 ff. sermo: |
|---|---|
| 1. De sapientia | 302,1 |
| 2. De fide | |
| 3. De charitate | 108,1,4–5,2 |
| 4. De spe | |
| 5. De lect. studio | 302,2 |
| 6. De pace | 98,2 |
| 7. De misericordia | 304,1 |
| 8. De indulgentia | 304,2 |
| 10. De humilitate | 297,1 |
| 12. De confessione | 254,1–2 |
| 13. De poenitentia | 254,2–3 |
| 15. De timore Dei | 297,2 |
| 18. De castitate | 291,1,2,3. |

While the editors of the pseudo-Augustinian *Appendix* assume that the substance of Alcuin's treatise was incorporated into the context of the apocryphal homilies,[25] the editor of Alcuin's treatise refers to its individual chapters as portions evidently derived from Augustinian sermons.[26] We can find the relation between Alcuin and some of the homilies if we weigh internal evidence in the texts.

We read in Alcuin's ch. 8, *De indulgentia* (*PL* 101, 618D):

[24] *PL* 39, in appendice, subsequently always referred to as Ps.-Aug., *Appendix*. The editor of Alcuin in *PL* 101, 614 ff., refers to these sermons in the notes; but read 614B "*Serm.* 302," instead of 303; for ch. 6, *De pace*, the reference to *serm.* 98 (*PL* 39, 1933) is missing; 625 n. a, read '*serm.* 291,' instead of 91.

[25] See the b notes in *PL* 39, 1932, 2215, 2296, 2313, 2323, 2328.

[26] Cf. *PL* 101, 614b, 616c, 617a, 618b, 619a, 621a, 623a, 625a.

"Sciendum est certissime quod unusquisque talem indulgentiam accepturus est a Deo, qualem et ipse dederit proximo suo." Rochais adduces as the alleged source Defensor, ch. 5, *De indulgentia (PL* 88, 611B): "Augustinus. Unusquisque talem indulgentiam accepturus est a Deo, qualem et ipse dederit proximo suo." Augustinus, the source of Defensor's citation, is not identified by Rochais. The citation is from Ps.-Aug., *App., sermo* 304,2 *(PL* 39, 2329): "Sciendum est certissime quod unusquisque talem indulgentiam accepturus est a Deo, qualem et ipse dederit proximo suo." Since Alcuin's wording is closer to the text of the sermon than to the incomplete quotation of Defensor, Alcuin clearly used the sermon; and since Defensor obviously took the citation from the sermon, this apocryphal homily is older than both Defensor and Alcuin and is the source of both.

Another example of the same kind is found in Alcuin's ch. 15, *De timore Dei (PL* 101, 624B): "Qui timore sancto Deum metuunt, inquirunt quae bona placita sunt illi"; and "Homo sapiens in omnibus operibus suis metuit Dominum." Rochais refers to Defensor, ch. 12, *De timore (PL* 88, 630D): "Augustinus. Qui timent Dominum, inquirunt quae beneplacita sunt illi"; and "Homo sapiens in omnibus metuit." The two citations from "Augustinus" are not identified by Rochais. They occur, however, in Ps.-Aug., *App., sermo* 297,2 *(PL* 39, 2314): "Qui timore sancto Deum metuunt inquirunt quae beneplacita sunt illi"; and "Homo sapiens in omnibus operibus suis Deum timet." So, clearly, this homily also antedates Defensor and Alcuin.

For two sentences in Alcuin's ch. 11, *De compunctione cordis (PL* 101, 621A), Rochais refers to Defensor, ch. 6, where both are cited from "Augustinus." I have not identified the homily which may have served as the source of Defensor and Alcuin. Alcuin's chapters 11, 12, and 13 are also found in Ps.-Aug., *App., sermo* 254, and since Defensor quotes from an unidentified work of "Augustinus" which was also used by Alcuin in ch. 11, we must assume that Defensor and Alcuin used the same source, which was quite probably one of the apocryphal homilies ascribed to Augustinus.

Slight verbal parallels seem to join Alcuin, ch. 19 (*PL* 101, 627D–628A) to Defensor, ch. 77 (*PL* 88, 711A): "Augustinus. Ubi lucrum, et ibi damnum. Lucrum in arca, damnum in conscientia. Acquirit pecuniam, et perdit iustitiam." This quotation is from Ps.-Aug., *App.*, *sermo* 220,2 (*PL* 39, 2152), i.e., from Caesarius of Arles, *sermo* 222,3 (ed. G. Morin, in *Corpus Christianorum*, series Latina, 104 [Turnhout, 1953], 878 f.). Defensor and Alcuin used this homily. We note that the same "Augustinus" quotation is found in the report—written in 786—on an Old English synod which Alcuin attended (*Epist.* 3 D.26.4).

The "Augustinus" quotations of Defensor [27] and Alcuin prove that the apocryphal homilies 297 and 304 antedate both authors, and that Alcuin's chapters 11 and 19 contain similar pseudo-Augustinian materials. Eight "Augustinus" quotations of Defensor are traced by Dom Rochais [28] to certain sermons of Caesarius of Arles.[29]

One example will reveal the complications we encounter in dealing with a pseudo-Augustinian homily. The editor of *sermo* 98 (*PL* 39, 1932b) states that this sermon contains ch. 6, *De pace*, of Alcuin's treatise. He thus assumes that *sermo* 98 is a post-Alcuinian homily. Dekkers and Gaar [30] also hold No. 98 to be later than Alcuin, and find it in homily 52 of the homiliary of Hrabanus. There can be no doubt that the text of ch. 6 corresponds with homily 98. The question is whether Alcuin copied 98 or the author of 98 copied Alcuin. The first alternative is confirmed by the fact that the content of ch. 6 is traceable to

[27] Our conclusions presuppose that Defensor's Augustinus quotations are genuine parts of the *florilegium*.

[28] *Revue bénédictine*, 63 (1953), 284.

[29] Ed. Germain Morin, *S. Caesarii Arelatensis Sermones*, CCL 103–104.

[30] *Clavis patrum latinorum* (*Sacris Erudiri* 3, 1951), no. 368, p. 67.

homily 53 of Petrus Chrysologus (*PL* 52, 347). *Sermo* 98 itself
appears to be an expanded version of Ps.-Aug., *App.*, *sermo* 61,[31]
which in its turn is but another version of Chrysologus, *sermo*
53. The relation between 98, Alcuin, and Hrabanus seems to be as
follows: Hrabanus could have used homily 98 directly, since
the two variants (see below) *fratres* and *societatem habet* do not
occur in the present text of Alcuin. On the other hand, we find
(see below) that a considerable portion (five-sevenths) of
Alcuin's text is paralleled by certain sections in the text of fourteen homilies by Hrabanus. So it might well be that Hrabanus'
readings are traceable to the MS of Alcuin's treatise used by
him. That *sermo* 98 does antedate Alcuin may be inferred because the homily was used, more extensively than in ch. 6, in his
*Epistle* 219 (p. 363, 19, 23, 24), addressed to the monks of
Lérins, lauding their good reputation, and exhorting them to
mutual charity and peace. The *unanimitas pacis*, repeatedly
stressed in this letter, but not mentioned by Alcuin in ch. 6, is
a special point at issue discussed together with *caritas* in *sermo*
98, 4–5 (*PL* 39, 1933 f.).

The following excerpts of an identical passage in its five
different transmissions illustrate the possible interdependences
just discussed.

Petrus Chrysologus, *sermo* 53 (*PL* 52, 347C–348A):
    Pax plebis charissimi est gloria sacerdotis, et pacis plena laetitia est
    perfecta charitas filiorum. Sacerdotis est, admonere quod decet;
    plebis est, audire quod monet, quidquid non licet, pastoris est pro-
    hibere, gregis audire ac velle ne fiat.... Custodienda *prae omnibus
    virtutibus* pax est, quoniam Deus semper in pace est;
Ps.-Augustinus, *Appendix, sermo* 61,3 (*PL* 39, 1859):
    Pax plebis, gloria est sacerdotis: et parentum laetitia, perfecta chari-
    tas filiorum. Sacerdotis...[like Chrysologus, above] pastoris est pro-
    hibere ne fiat; gregis est audire, ut faciat... Custodienda *omnibus
    viribus* pax est; quoniam Deus semper in pace est;

[31] Add to *Clavis*, s.v., *sermo* 98: recensio amplificata sermonis 61.

Ps.-Augustinus, *Appendix, sermo* 98,2 (PL 39, 1933):

Pax plebis sanitas, gloria sacerdotis, et patriae laetitia, et terror hostium sive visibilium sive invisibilium. *Omnibus viribus* pax est custodienda, fratres, quia semper in Deo manet, qui in pace sancta manet, et cum sanctis Dei societatem habet. Sacerdotis est, in pace populum admonere quod debeat agere; populi est, in humilitate audire quae monet sacerdos. Quidquid non licet, pastoris est prohibere ne fiat; plebis, audire ne faciat;

Alcuin, ch. 6, *De pace* (PL 101, 617C):

Pax plebis est sanitas...[the remainder is identical with *sermo* 98]; there are some variants: Alcuin omits *fratres*, reads *manet* instead of *societatem habet*, and at the end *est* audire; cf. Alcuin, *Epist.* 18, p. 51, 29 "sanitas plebis";

Hrabanus Maurus, *Hom.* 52 (PL 110, 96A–B):

This text is identical with *sermo* 98; Hrabanus reads *fratres*, and *societatem habet*, and *est audire*.

The reading "custodienda *omnibus viribus* pax est" [32] as against Chrysologus' *prae omnibus virtutibus* is noteworthy. According to Chrysologus *pax* belongs to the *virtutes*, while the authors of the expanded version of his sermon evidently no longer shared this notion, which was known to the early Middle Ages, especially, also from Prudentius, *Psychomachia*, vv. 769 f.:

> Pax plenum virtutis opus, pax summa laborum,
> Pax belli exacti pretium est pretiumque pericli.

A summary of the preceding inquiry and comparison with the conclusions of Dom Rochais shows that Defensor's *florilegium* cannot have been Alcuin's source, for Alcuin excerpted some of the writings also excerpted by Defensor, such as Isidore of Seville's *florilegia* and pseudo-Augustinian homilies. One of these homilies was identified (above) with a homily of

---

[32] The reading appears in the so-called OE Alcuin: Seo sibb is mid ealle maeignen to healdene; see R. D-N. Warner, *Early English Homilies from the Twelfth Century MS. Vesp. D. XIV* (EETS, Original Series, 152; London, 1917), 95.

Caesarius of Arles, whose *sermo* 18, 2–6 (*CCL* 103, pp. 83–86), for example, supplied Alcuin with two-thirds of the text of ch. 14 (623B–D). It seems that Alcuin was also familiar with Pomerius, *De vita contemplativa*, since excerpts from Pomerius are found in Alcuin's ch. 23, *De superbia*.[33] The homiletic nature of at least the first part of Alcuin's treatise was obvious to Alcuin's unknown biographer, who wrote: "Scripsit et ad Widonem comitem *omelias* de principalibus vitiis et virtutibus."[34]

## THE SOURCES OF THE SECTION *DE VITIIS*

The second part of Alcuin's treatise, which is not investigated by Dom Rochais, is in eight chapters, each dealing with one of the chief vices (*principales*), namely, pride, gluttony, lust, avarice, anger, sloth, sorrow, and vainglory (chs. 26–34). The chapters on the vices are followed by a brief discussion of the four cardinal virtues (ch. 35) and a letter peroration, addressed to the recipient of the handbook. The last paragraph attached to the peroration (in Migne's edition) is a cento of Scriptural passages "On Friendship" (*PL* 101, 638CD) which is not an original part of the work. Its origin is not unknown, as Dom Rochais assumes.[35] The passages are taken from Defensor, ch. 63, *De amicitia* (*PL* 88, 696CD).

The fundamental sources of Alcuin's catalogue of vices are

[33] Compare this chapter and Pomerius, *PL* 59, 478A–B; also Alcuin, ch. 3 (*PL* 101, 615C) and Pomerius III, 13, 14, 15 (*PL* 59, 493C, 494A ff., 496B–C); A. M. Landgraf, *Dogmengeschichte der Frühscholastik* I, 1 (Regensburg a.D., 1952), 162 compares Pomerius III, 16 (*PL* 59, 498) and Alcuin, ch. 35. The first Pomerius item is listed by Dom Rochais, *Revue Mabillon* 41 (1951), 85. M. L. W. Laistner, *Studi e Testi* 122 (1946), 356, assumes that Alcuin was unfamiliar with Pomerius when writing his treatise.

[34] *Vita Alcuini* ch. 21, *MGH, Scriptores* XV.195.—There is no apparent connection between the homiletic materials of our treatise and the extant second volume of Alcuin's homiliarium; on the latter see the note in *Speculum* 29 (1954), 823. Cf. generally M. W. Bloomfield, *The Seven Deadly Sins* (East Lansing, Mich., 1952).

[35] *Revue Mabillon* 41 (1951), 73.

Gregory, *Moralia in Job* XXXI.45,[36] and Cassian, *Collatio* V.1 and V.16.5.[37] The themes at the end of each chapter—the specific virtue overcoming its opposing vice—are supplied by Isidore, *Sententiae* II.37.[38]

The sequence of chapters 27–34 follows with two exceptions the order of Cassian's classification of vices, though Gregory furnishes the description of the individual *vitia*. Since *acedia* is missing in Gregory's list, Alcuin in this instance follows (635A) Cassian. And although *superbia* is the last vice in Cassian's list, it becomes the first for Alcuin as being the worst vice. Occasionally, both basic sources conflate in Alcuin's description. *Haereses*, for example, derived from Cassian's treatment of *cenodoxia*, is inserted into the description of *superbia*, copied from Gregory. As a rule, the source actually used by Alcuin can be determined without great difficulty. *Malitia* in Alcuin's treatment of *tristitia*, a vice not found in Cassian, *Collatio* V.16.5, is taken from Gregory's list of vices (*PL* 76, 621B).

The occurrence of direct literal citations from Cassian has been wrongly denied by Albert Hauck;[39] for not only the *Collationes*, but also the *De institutis coenobiorum*[40] is excerpted by Alcuin. So when Alcuin says in ch. 32, *De acedia*, "Quae cum miserabilem obsidet mentem," he obviously follows Cassian, *De inst.* X.2: "Quae cum miserabilem obsederit mentem." Rather incongruously the "mala otiositas" (*De inst.* X.20) of the monk is mentioned and rejected in this chapter of our treatise written for a layman! The first bracketed section in *De superbia* (633B)

[36] *PL* 76, 620–622.

[37] Ed. M. Petschenig, *CSEL* 13 (Wien, 1886), 142 f.

[38] *De pugna virtutum adversus vitia* (*PL* 83, 638); cf. also Isidore's *Differentiae* II, chs. 39–40 (*PL* 83, 95 f.); *Quaestiones Testamentorum: In Deuteronomium* ch. 16 (*PL* 83, 366), following Cassian.

[39] Albert Hauck, *Kirchengeschichte Deutschlands* II (3rd and 4th eds.; Leipzig, 1912), 147 f.: Direkt aus Cassian entnommene Sätze habe ich nicht bemerkt.

[40] *De institutis coenobiorum et de octo principalium vitiorum remediis libri* XII, ed. M. Petschenig, *CSEL* 17 (Wien, 1888).—See Alcuin, *Epist.* 203, D.337.10, addressed to Charlemagne:...Cassiani exempla posui.

is drawn verbatim from *De inst.* XII.29. The chapter "On Vain-glory" (635A–D) contains longer excerpts derived word for word from *De inst.* XI.3.4.6, and 19.[41]

Thus, our study reveals the nature of the treatise on virtues and vices and its author's method of excerpting. The same method of borrowing may be observed in Alcuin's *Rhetoric* and in his grammatical treatise *De orthographia*.[42]

The system of eight vices is used in the treatise dedicated to Wido. In *De animae ratione*, however, written for Gundrada, sister of Charlemagne's trusted advisor Adalhard of Corbie, Alcuin enumerates only seven vices: "gastrimargia, fornicatio, phylargiria, tristitia, acedia, superbia, and cenodoxia." [43] *Ira* is missing.[44] Alcuin does not consider *ira* an individual vice, since it is assignable to the irascible part of the soul from which *tristitia* and *acedia* also spring. From the two other parts of the soul in this ancient division stem the remaining five vices, pride and vainglory from the rational part, gluttony, lust, and avarice from the concupiscent. *De animae ratione*, we note, was one of the sources [45] of *De spiritu et anima* by the Cistercian Alcher of Clairvaux.

Though the treatise *De virtutibus et vitiis*, as Schmitz [46] puts it, "s'inspire beaucoup de Saint Augustin," it is hard to identify

---

[41] *Ibid.*, pp. 195,18–26; 196,13–22; 197,6–10; 203,22–204,6.

[42] Ed. Aldo Marsili, *Alcuini Orthographia* (Pisa, 1952).

[43] *PL* 101, 640C–D; the treatise is partly edited by E. Dümmler in *MGH*, *Epist.* IV, no. 309, pp. 473–478.

[44] For the reason subsequently stated; cf. Karl Werner, "Der Entwicklungsgang der mittelalterlichen Psychologie von Alcuin bis Albertus Magnus," in *Denkschriften der K. Akademie der Wissenschaften Wien*, phil.-hist. Classe XXV (1876), 70–77.

[45] Alcuin, ch. 11 (*PL* 101, 644B–C) is verbatim copied in Alcher of Clairvaux's *De spiritu et anima* (*PL* 40, 788). On Alcher's authorship of this pseudo-Augustinian writing see H. S. Denifle, *Die deutschen Mystiker des 14. Jahrhunderts*, ed. Otwin Spiess (Freiburg, Switzerland, 1951), 81.

[46] Philibert Schmitz, *Histoire de l'Ordre de Saint-Benoît* II (Maredsous, 1949), 379.

in the tractate literal excerpts from genuine Augustinian writings, although the trace of a genuine Augustinian homily can occasionally be seen.[47] But in general there is no ground for thinking with Kleinclausz [48] "that most of the chapters on the virtues are literally indebted to sermons of the great African doctor," or that "Alcuin reasoned and thought independently in the chapters on the vices, especially where he dramatically confronts the virtues and the vices." Nor is there a basis for Kleinclausz' assumption that Cicero's *De officiis* supplied Alcuin with the definitions of the cardinal virtues (in ch. 35).

## THE INFLUENCE OF THE TREATISE

The treatise *De virtutibus et vitiis* was read and copied during the ninth and subsequent centuries. About 22 MSS, saec. IX–X, are still extant,[49] and more from the following centuries are found in the libraries of all Western and Central European countries. A lone MS copy of the work has just now reached this country.[50]

Carolingian writers used the treatise. The chapter on the cardinal virtues (ch. 35) was copied by Alcuin himself in his *Rhetoric*.[51] Some excerpts are inserted in an epistle of unknown

[47] Compare, for example, Alcuin, ch. 30 (*PL* 101, 634B) and Augustine, *sermo* 177, ed. D. C. Lambot, *S. Aurel. August. Sermones Selecti* (Stromata Patristica et Mediaevalia I; Utrecht-Bruxelles, 1950), 68; for Alcuin, ch. 14 see Appendix 2, and *Revue Mabillon* 41 (1951), 83.

[48] Arthur Kleinclausz, *Alcuin* (Paris, 1948), 221. There are slight verbal parallels between Alcuin's definition of *prudentia* (in ch. 35) and Cicero, *De officiis* I.153, but not enough to assume certain dependence. See the fine treatment of the four virtues by Harald Hagendahl, *Latin Fathers and the Classics* (Studia Graeca et Latina Gothoburgensia; Göteborg, 1958).

[49] Listed by Rochais, *Revue bénédictine* 63 (1953), 251 n. 4. On the oldest MS see E. A. Lowe, "A Manuscript of Alcuin in the Script of Tours," *Classical and Mediaeval Studies in Honor of E. K. Rand*, ed. L. W. Jones (New York, 1938), 191–193.

[50] This MS is listed in the sales *Catalogue I*, p. 2, no. 2, quoted in n. 18, above.

[51] Wallach, *Medievalia et Humanistica* 6 (1950), 41.

Frankish origin that was sent to Italy during the early ninth century.[52] Jonas of Orléans in *De institutione laicali*[53] acknowledges his indebtedness to the section on the vices. A contemporary of Louis the Pious dedicated to his sovereign distichs on the virtues and the vices for which he adopted thirty-two chapter titles in the sequence of Alcuin's treatise.[54] To these Carolingian witnesses we may add Halitgar of Cambrai and Alcuin's pupil Hrabanus Maurus.

Halitgar of Cambrai appropriated Alcuin's definitions of the four cardinal virtues (ch. 35) in five chapters of his *Penitential*, Bk. II.[55] Alcuin's influence is further noticeable in Bk. I, chs. 6, 10–12, and 14.

We have referred above to some homilies of Hrabanus Maurus. It can be shown that the text of twenty-five of the thirty-five chapters of Alcuin's treatise is paralleled by certain sections in the context of fourteen homilies by Hrabanus,[56] namely, nos. 45, 47–49, 51–56, 58–60, and 62. Hrabanus' sermons are always more extensive than the chapters of Alcuin. Some of Hrabanus' homilies could be combinations of individual chapters of Alcuin's treatise, as may be deduced from the following summary.

Chapters 1 and 5 of Alcuin correspond with *Homilia* 48 of Hrabanus; chs. 2, 3, 4 with hom. 45; ch. 6:hom. 52; chs. 7–8:hom. 51; chs. 10 and 15 with hom. 54; chs. 11, 12, 13:hom. 55; 14:56; 16:49; 17:53; 18:47; chs. 19 and 30:hom. 62; chs. 20 and 21:hom. 58; chs. 23 and 25:hom. 59; chs. 24 and 31:hom. 60. For eleven of Alcuin's chap-

---

[52] *MGH, Epistolae* IV, no. 2, pp. 484–491.

[53] In Lib. III, 6; cf. *PL* 106, 244–247A; compare also Alcuin, ch. 23 (630D), and the sentence from this chapter quoted by Jonas in III, 4 (*PL* 106, 239A).

[54] Omitting those of Alcuin's chs. 1, 20, 26; see Strecker, *MGH, Poetae* IV, pp. 924–927.

[55] In chs. 6–10 (*PL* 105, 673D–674A; 674D–675A; 675C; 676A); see Alcuin's chs. 22, 28, 30, and 33 in *PL* 105, 662B, 667B, 664D, and 665A.

[56] *Homiliae de virtutibus*, *PL* 110, 82 ff.

ters (9, 22, 26–29, 32–36) parallels seem to be absent in Hrabanus' homilies.

Some of Hrabanus' sermons are identified by Dekkers and Gaar [57] with pseudo-Augustinian homilies that are also used, as we saw, by Alcuin. These identifications can now be supplemented and corrected in accordance with our findings. Hrabanus indeed utilized some of these apocryphal sermons that were not excerpted by Alcuin, for instance, *serm.* 194, 280, and 290. But the statement in Dekkers and Gaar, *Clavis*, No. 368, s.v., *sermo* 98, "est in homiliario Hrabani Mauri homilia 52," can only refer to the identity of the texts and not to Hrabanus' authorship of the sermon, because its origin has been ascertained (see above). Since Alcuin used *sermo* 98 in his treatise, Hrabanus' authorship of no. 98 is impossible. The same conclusion holds for Ps.-Aug., *App.*, *serm.* 297 and 304, which are paralleled in the Clavis with hom. 54 and 51 of Hrabanus; the use made by Alcuin of nos. 297 and 304 forbids us to assume that Hrabanus was the author of these two pseudo-Augustinian homilies.

Hrabanus also copied for Book III of *De ecclesiastica disciplina* [58] from Alcuin's chapters 2, 4, 3, 6, 9, 23, 24, 28, and 30–32.

The definitions of virtue and the four cardinal virtues in Hrabanus' *De vitiis et virtutibus*, Bk. III,[59] whose first two Books are identical with Halitgar's *Penitential*, Bks. I–II, are not from Alcuin's ch. 35, but from Alcuin's *Rhetoric*, chs. 44–45.[60] Hrabanus here cites a sentence from Alcuin's *Rhetoric* [61] which does not occur in Alcuin's ch. 35.

---

[57] *Clavis*, pp. 67–70.

[58] *PL* 112, in the following sequence corresponding to the Alcuin chs. listed above: 1234A–C, 1236A–C, 1236D–1237B, 1257B, 1240D–1241A, 1242C, 1246B–C, 1245A, 1241D–1242A, and 1252A.

[59] *PL* 112, 1253D, 1254B, 1254D, 1255A.

[60] Ed. Carl Halm, *op. cit.*, p. 548 f.; Karl Werner, *Alkuin und sein Jahrhundert* (Paderborn, 1876), 257, wrongly assumes that Hrabanus followed *De virtutibus et vitiis*, ch. 35.

[61] Ed. Halm, p. 549, 27 f., from "Honor eximius...apud Deum;" compare the Hrabanus citation in *PL* 112, 1255A.

Onulf of Speyer, writing his *Colores rhetorici* in the seventies of the eleventh century, quotes [62] from Alcuin's ch. 35.

The definition of the three kinds of alms in the *Corpus iuris canonici,* decr. I, dist. 45, q. xii, seems to be derived from Alcuin's ch. 12, *De eleemosynis.*

A manuscript of the treatise which probably contained only the section on the vices was known to Wolfger of Prüfening,[63] who in his literary history, formerly ascribed to the so-called *Anonymus Mellicensis,* lists the writings of Alcuin and says: "Scribit de octo viciis ad Gwidonem comitem." [64]

Considerable use was made of Alcuin's treatise in Old and Middle English literatures. Aelfric inserted excerpts in his *Homiliae catholicae,*[65] and an Old English translation of the first sixteen chapters, preserved in a MS of the twelfth century,[66] probably was made in his period. About 1300, or perhaps a little later, Alcuin's work became the immediate source of the early English metrical poem, *Speculum Gy de Warewyke,*[67] and largely determined the trend of the argument. Finally, an Old Norse translation of the treatise is found in a MS of the twelfth or thirteenth century.[68]

[62] Wallach, "Onulf of Speyer: A Humanist of the Eleventh Century," *Medievalia et Humanistica* 6 (1950), 40.

[63] Now ascribed to him by H. von Fichtenau, "Wolfger von Prüfening," *Mitteilungen des Inst. für Oesterreich. Geschichtsforschung* 51 (1937), 341–351.

[64] *De scriptoribus ecclesiasticis,* ed. Emil Ettlinger (Karlsruhe, 1896), ch. 41, p. 70.

[65] Max Förster, *Anglia* 16 (1893–1894), 46 f.

[66] Referred to in n. 32, above.

[67] Ed. G. L. Morrill, *Speculum Gy de Warewyke* (EETS, Extra Series, 75; London, 1898), pp. xciii–cxiv and cxvii f., on Alcuin's influence on Gy.

[68] See G. T. Flom, *Codex AM 619 Quarto: Old Norwegian Book of Homilies...and Alcuin's De virtutibus et vitiis* (Univ. of Illinois Studies in Language and Literature 14, 4; 1929); Gustav Indrebø, *Gamal Norsk Homiliebok Cod. AM 619.4°* (Oslo, 1931); and the facsimile edition by Trygve Knudsen, *Gammelnorsk Homiliebok Etter AM 619 QV* (Corpus

The popularity of the treatise *De virtutibus et vitiis* during the Middle Ages, as evinced by the number of MSS and by its influence on authors from the ninth until the fourteenth centuries who wrote in Latin and in vernacular languages, calls for a new edition of the treatise. Migne's edition of 1851 is reprinted from the second volume of Alcuin's *Opera* published by Froben at Regensburg on-the-Danube in 1777. It is not based on the oldest and best MSS and is now inadequate in the light of modern standards of textual editing.

## APPENDIX

### 1. *Alcuin and the Commonitiuncula ad Sororem?*

An anonymous treatise, presumably from the second half of the seventh century, in the MSS ascribed variously to Augustine, Ambrose, Jerome,[69] or Caesarius of Arles, and by A. E. Anspach,[70] its most recent editor, assigned to Isidore of Seville, is said to have left traces in Alcuin's *De virtutibus et vitiis*. But the assumption of such an influence on Alcuin cannot stand the test of a critical examination. Careful comparison of both treatises does not disclose evidence to support the contentions made by Anspach and Vaccari.

The introductory letter of the *Comm(onitiuncula ad Sororem)* is not the source of Alcuin's dedicatory epistle to Wido. The purely Alcuinian origin of the epistle has been demonstrated in the first part of this chapter. Alcuin certainly needed no recourse to the exordium of the *Comm.*, "Tuae non immemor petitionis, o charissima mater, tibi

---

Codicum Norvegicorum Medii Aevi, ed. D. A. Seip, Quarto Serie I; Oslo, 1952).

[69] Cf. Alberto Vaccari, "Un trattato ascetico attribuito a S. Girolamo," *Mélanges offerts au R. P. Ferdinand Cavallera* (Toulouse, 1948), 147–162. Cf. Giorgio Brunoli, "Un opusculo pseudo-Geronimiano in un codice Farfense," *Benedictina* 9 (1955), 169–173.

[70] A. E. Anspach, *S. Isidori Hispalensis Episcopi Commonitiuncula ad Sororem* (Script. eccl. hispano-latini veteris et medii aevi, IV; Escorial, 1935); Dom Rochais, *Revue bénédictine* 63 (1953), 251 n. 1, offers a list of extant MSS.

ut rogasti, scribere studui," in order to say in his exordium (*Epist.*
305, D.464.11): "*Memor petitionis tuae et promissionis meae*, qua me
obnixe flagitasti aliquod tuae occupationi, quam te in bellicis rebus
habere novimus." This is merely a commonplace, repeated elsewhere.
For example, the same exordium is used in Alcuin's dedicatory letter
that accompanies parts of the *Commentary on John*, which he presented to Gisla, sister of Charlemagne (*Epist.* 214, D. 357.29): "*Memor petitionis vestrae et promissionis meae*, quamvis tardius implerem
propter occupationes perplurimas...." An often stereotyped exordial
technique is a feature of Alcuin's epistles. The formulalike phrase,
"*Memor condictae amicitiae inter nos*," for instance, occurs as the
exordium in seven of his letters.[71]

The testimonia of the *Comm.* allegedly preserved in Alcuin's chapters 3, 10, and 11, are hardly to the point. The slight similarities between the two texts can be explained; the authors of both writings
excerpted the same source. The medieval scribe of an expanded MS
tradition of the *Comm.* must have been aware of this source, since he
inserted into ch. XIII a passage from Isidore of Seville's *Sententiae*
III.8.2 (*PL* 83, 679B), which occurs also in Alcuin's ch. 5 (*PL* 101,
616D). Alcuin drew directly on Isidore's *florilegium*, which was—
as we have seen—one of the main sources of his treatise. The passage
in question assumed topical significance in Alcuin's epistolary style
and appears as such in at least three of his letters.[72] An interpolated
passage in MS E of the *Comm.* (ed. Anspach, p. 34), which is identical with the opening sentences of Alcuin, ch. 5 (*PL* 101, 614C), might
be traceable to a direct borrowing from Alcuin by the scribe of MS
E, or else be directly derived from the pseudo-Augustinian *sermo*
302,2 (*PL* 39), which contains the same sentences.

## 2. Alcuin and Caesarius of Arles

The relation between Alcuin and Hrabanus Maurus can be more
closely determined by an investigation of the use made by Alcuin of
Caesarius of Arles's *serm.* 18, 2–6 (ed. G. Morin, CCL 103, 83–86,

[71] *Epistles* nos. 11, 24, 108, 122, 128, 263, 298.
[72] *Epistle* 296, p. 455,26; 270, p. 429,6; 228, p. 372,7.

*passim*) in ch. 14 (*PL* 101, 623 f.).[73] The literal borrowings from this homily in ch. 14 are here printed in italics. Compare:

Legitur in litteris divinitus inspiratis dictum: "Fili, ne tardes converti ad Deum, quia nescis, quid futura pariat dies" (Eccli. 5:8). Qui tardat converti, periculum facit animae suae, quia "mors non tardat" (Eccli. 14:12). Quae si tardantem converti inveniet, ad tormenta deducit eum. *Dissoluta* et *paralytica cogitatio* est, de crastina cogitare conversione, et hodiernam negligere. Quid tu, peccator, *converti dissimulas, et non metuis, ne tibi mors repentina subripiat* diem conversionis? *Nonne homines subito moriuntur? Si bonum est* peccata dimittere, et ad Deum converti, *cito fiat. Deus* tibi *promittit* remissionem convertenti a peccatis, *securitatem* tibi non promisit diu vivendi. (Lege prophetas, lege Apostolum, et vide si tibi promissa sit hora aut dies). *Ideo convertat se* citius *unusquisque ad Deum*, et cum invenerit eum, derelinquat impius viam suam. Si *subito intrat dies extremus, perit dilatio, et restat damnatio*. Perire non vis, redi ad Deum, et vives. Noli desperare (MS: peccando sperare) de venia peccatorum, *nec de vita longiori confidere. Convertere ergo*, et poenitentiam age. *Cras, inquies*, convertam. *Quare non hodie? Quid mali*, dicis, *si cras* dicam? *Quid mali, si hodie?* Forte dicis: *Longa erit vita* mea. Dicam, *si longa erit, bona sit; si brevis, et ipsa bona sit. Quis ferat malum longum prandium? Longum non vis habere malum, et vitam longam vis habere malam? Villam emis; bonam* desideras. *Uxorem vis ducere; bonam* quaeris. *Filios tibi nasci vis; bonos optas. Et ut etiam de rebus vilissimis loquar, caligas emis, et non vis malas. Et vitam amas malam? Quid te offendit vita tua, quam solam vis malam, ut inter omnia bona tua solus sis malus?* "Neque tardes converti ad Dominum, et ne differas de die in diem" (Eccli. 5:8). *Verba Dei sunt, non mea. Non a me haec audisti, sed ego tecum audio* a Domino. Forte *respondes: Cras, cras. O vox corvina! Corvus non redi(i)t ad arcam, columba redi(i)t. Si enim tunc vis poenitentiam agere quando peccare non potes, peccata te dimiserunt, non tu illa.* Satis alienus a fide est, qui ad agendum poenitentiam tempus senectutis exspectat....

Alcuin's dependence on Caesarius' homily is obvious. Since the complete text of Alcuin's ch. 14 appears in Hrabanus Maurus' *sermo* 56 (*PL* 110, 104 f.), where it constitutes about one-half of the entire sermon, Hrabanus clearly inserted the text of Alcuin's chapter into

[73] Alcuin's familiarity with Caesarius' *Sermones* answers the question asked by M. L. W. Laistner, *The Intellectual Heritage of the Early Middle Ages* (Ithaca, 1957), 176.

his homily. The same relationship exists between all the other chapters of Alcuin's treatise and those homilies of Hrabanus' collection *De virtutibus* that borrowed from Alcuin's *De virtutibus et vitiis.* We finally note one of the rarely found literal borrowings from a genuine Augustinian sermon; the passage "Si enim tunc...non tu illa" is taken from Augustine's *sermo 393 (PL 39, 1715).*

The results of Ch. XII concerning *serm.* 98, 108, 254, 291, 297, 302, 304, are listed in the *Clavis Patrum Latinorum,* ed. Dekkers-Gaar (2nd ed., 1961), no. 368, s.v. Ps.-Augustinus, *Sermones spurii.* Alejandro Olivar, *Los sermones de san Pedro Crisologo* (Scripta et Documenta 13; Montserrat, 1962), 170 n. 89, states that Alcuin (above, p. 242 f.) reproduces phrases of Chrysologus, *serm.* 53. On Alcuin's authorship of the two official documents dealt with in Sect. I and II (above, pp. 147-65) see Bernhard Bischoff, "Aus Alkuins Erdentagen," *Medievalia et Humanistica* XIV (1962), 31-37, especially p. 34. Heinz Loewe, *Göttingische gelehrte Anzeigne* 214 (1962), 150, and *Deutsches Archiv* 18 (1962), 282 f., wrongly assumes that I used only the *Stilvergleich* for the establishment of Alcuin's authorship of certain Carolingian documents. Nor does he recognize that all these documents are also seen within the sphere and atmosphere of the administrative and diplomatic practice of established Carolingian traditions of government. See now the reasonable discussion and the conclusions by Herwig Wolfram, *Intitulatio I (MIOEG,* Erg.-Bd. 21; Wien, 1967), 241; also Wolfgang Edelstein, *eruditio und sapientia: Weldbild und Erziehung in der Karolingerzeit* (Freiburg i.Br., 1965), 50 and oftener; and Wilhelm Heil, "Der Adoptianismus, Alkuin und Spanien," in *Karl der Grosse* II: *Das Geistige Leben* (2nd ed.; Düsseldorf, 1966), 104 f.

# CHAPTER XIII

# The Epitaph of Alcuin: A Model of Carolingian Epigraphy

SINCE we have reason to believe that Alcuin was the author [1] of the epitaph of Hadrian I, there are grounds for supposing that Alcuin's epitaph, written by him shortly before his death on May 19, 804, resembled it in epigraphic workmanship.[2] The elegiacs of this inscription are extant in manuscripts alone; originally they were engraved on a bronze tablet.[3] Although it would be an easy task to reconstruct the original epigraphic appearance of the epitaph—undoubtedly in Roman square capitals with the proper ligatures, *nomina sacra*, and special letters as known to us from the preserved epitaph of

[1] Cf. Chapter X.

[2] See the facsimile of the Hadrian inscription provided by Stanley Morison, "The Art of Printing," *Proceedings of the British Academy*, XXIII (1937), Table I, and N. Grey, "The Palaeography of Latin Inscriptions in the Eighth, Ninth, and Tenth Centuries in Italy," *Papers of the British School at Rome*, XVI (1948), no. 76.

[3] *Vita Alcuini*, ch. 28, *MGH, Scriptores*, XV, 197: titulus quem ipse vivens dictaverat lamina scriptus in aerea parietique insertus.

Hadrian—nothing would be gained from such an exercise. Like Hadrian's, the epitaph of Alcuin was in all likelihood another product of the epigraphic school of Tours.[4] Since Alcuin's inscription became a formula and the model for other epitaphs of the Carolingian age, it is printed here with an epigraphic and literary commentary.[5] Alcuin's authorship, reported by his anonymous biographer, will be substantiated by the parallels between the epitaph and Alcuin's other poetry listed in the notes to the following text.[6]

### The Epitaph of Alcuin

1   Hic, rogo, pauxillum veniens subsiste viator,
     Et mea scrutare pectore dicta tuo,
     Ut tua deque meis agnoscas fata figuris:
      Vertitur o species, ut mea, sicque tua.
5   Quod nunc es fueram, famosus in orbe, viator,
     Et quod nunc ego sum, tuque futuris eris.
     Delicias mundi casso sectabar amore,
      Nunc cinis et pulvis, vermibus atque cibus.
     Quapropter potius animam curare memento
10    Quam carnem, quoniam haec manet, illa perit.
     Cur tibi rura paras? Quam parvo cernis in antro
      Me tenet hic requies: sic tua parva fiet.
     Cur Tyrio corpus inhias vestirier ostro,
      Quod mox esuriens pulvere vermis edet?
15   Ut flores pereunt vento veniente minaci,
     Sic tua namque caro, gloria tota perit.
     Tu mihi redde vicem, lector, rogo, carminis huius
      Et dic: "Da veniam, Christe, tuo famulo."
     Obsecro, nulla manus violet pia iura sepulcri,

---

[4] Cf. C. Chevalier, *Les Fouilles de Saint Martin* (Tours, 1888).

[5] See Ernst Dümmler, *MGH, Poetae,* I, 350–351; *Scriptores,* xv, 197.

[6] The following abbreviations are used in the commentary: *CIL— Corpus Inscriptionum Latinarum; CLE—Carmina Latina Epigraphica,* ed. Buecheler and Lommatzsch; Diehl—E. Diehl, *Inscriptiones Latinae Christianae Veteres,* I–III (Berlin, 1926–1931).

20      Personet angelica donec ab arce tuba;
        "Qui iaces in tumulo, terrae de pulvere surge,
        Magnus adest Iudex milibus innumeris."
        Alchuine nomen erat sophiam mihi semper amanti,
24      Pro quo funde preces mente legens titulum.
25      [Hic requiescit beatae memoriae domnus Alchuinus, abba,
        qui obiit in pace XIV Kal[endas] Iun[ias]. Quando
        legeritis, o vos omnes, orate pro eo et dicite: "Requiem
        aeternam donet ei Dominus." Amen].

## COMMENTARY

1      Cf. Alcuin, *Carmina*, ed. Ernst Dümmler, *MGH, Poetae*, I, no. cx, 18, 1 (p. 343); *Hic* fessus veniens primo *subsiste viator*; CXI.I (p. 343): *Hic* tu per stratam pergens *subsiste viator*; *CIL*, II, 4315 (Tarraco): Quisquis homo es, quaeres talem. *Subsiste viator,*/ Perlege, si memor es. On the *viator* formula in Roman epigraphy see Ludwig Friedländer, *Sittengeschichte Roms* III, 9th ed. (Leipzig, 1920), 299–300.

3–4      Alcuin, in the Poem of York, vv. 229–230 (p. 174 f.):
        Quod praeceps fortuna rotat, *fati*sque malignis
        *Vertitur*, et variis semper mutatur in horis;
        Alcuin, *De cella sua*, XXIII.23 (p. 244):
        *Vertitur* omne decus secli sic namque repente,
        Omnia mutantur ordinibus variis.
        Alcuin, IX.12 (p. 229): omnia vertuntur temporibus variis; Propertius, II.8.7: omnia vertuntur; Virgil, *Georg.* 1.420: verum vertuntur species animarum. For *vertitur* at the beginning of the verse cf. also *Aen.* II.250, and Ovid, *Met.* V.568. On *fata* cf. Ewald Lissberger, *Das Fortleben der römischen Elegiker in den Carmina Epigraphica* (diss. Tübingen, 1934), 19–21 and 24.

4      Dracontius, *Satisfactio*, 30: Vertuntur sensus vertitur et species.

5–6      This distich, an old Roman *memento mori*, occurs frequently, e.g., *CIL*, XI, 6243 (*Fanum Fortunae*): VIATOR VIATOR QVOD TV/ES EGO FVI QVOD NVNC SVM/ET TV ERIS; *CIL*, VIII, 9913 (*Mauretania Caesar.*): VIATOR QVOD TV ET/EGO QVOD EGO ET/OMNES; Diehl, 3865 (Rome), *saec.* VII, and *CLE*, 799 (Tabernae) from the twelfth century:
        Vos qui transitis, nostri memores rogo sitis.
        Quod sumus, hoc eritis, fuimus quandoque quod estis.
        Epit. Milonis et Hucbaldi, *MGH, Poetae*, III, no. x, 4: Fratres, quod estis, fuimus; quod sumus, eritis: mementote nostri.

A Spanish inscription of 1380, ed. Jaime Villanueva, *Viage literario a las Iglesias de España*, IX (Valencia, 1821), 16, reads:

Tú hom, quem guardes á mi,
Hom era axi com tú, é mori;
E tú morás, é seras axi com mi.

Cf. also Ovid. *Trist.* 3.11.15: non sum ego quod fueram, and 3.8.38; *Met.* 2.551; John 17:24.

7    Alcuin, XXIV.7 (p. 340): propter amorem/*delicias mundi;* XLI.3 (p. 253):. Delicias saecli; XI.15 (p. 236): Deliciasque poli; the same verse ending IX.93 (p. 231): complectit amore.

8    Gen. 18:27: cum sim pulvis et cinis; Job 21:26: in pulvere dormient, et vermes operient eos, and Gen. 3:19. *CLE,* 1158, 5: nunc cinis est, and often.

9    Alcuin, IX.119 (p. 232): *Quapropter potius* caelestia semper amemus.

9–10    Bede, *Hist. Eccl.* I.19: hi animas curare cupientes, hi corpora; *Disticha Catonis* IV.5: corpus curare memento; Isidore of Seville, *Etym.* IV.13.5. Alcuin, *De animae ratione,* PL CI, 643 B: Dum anima deserit corpus, moritur corpus; 639 A: Quid sum ego nisi anima et caro.

11    The same verse ending Virgil, *Ecl.* I.75: in antro; *Ecl.* I.46: ergo tua *rura* manebunt, may be compared with the sentiment expressed in verse 11.

12    Alcuin in Hadrian's Epitaph, v. 27 (p. 113): Haec tua nunc teneat requies.

13    Prudentius, *Psychomachia* 39: Floribus ardentique iubet *vestirier ostro;* the *Tyrio—ostro* formula also in Alcuin's Poem on York, v. 1272 (p. 197); in Bede, *Hist. Eccl.,* V.19, and *Vita Cuthberti,* XXI.552 (ed. Werner Jaager, *Palaestra,* 128; Leipzig, 1935, p. 99); Boethius, *Cons. phil.,* ch. 3, metr. 4.1; Virgil, *Georg.* III.17; Ovid, *Ep.* XII.179; *Met.* X.211.

15    *minaci* as verse ending also Alcuin, Poem on York, v. 178 (p. 173), and Fortunatus, *Vita Martini,* III.332 (p. 341).

16    *Sic namque,* Alcuin, *De cella sua,* XXIII.23 (p. 244); IX.48 (p. 230): laus tua *tota perit;* XI.12 (p. 236): nil est perpetuum, cuncta perire; IX.55 (230):

Sic fugit omne decus hominis quod dextera fecit,
Gloria seclorum sic velut umbra volat.

17    Alcuin, XXXIII.6 (p. 250): Sis memor Alchuine, *lector, rogo, carminis huius:* LXXXVIII.4.15–16 (p. 306):

Qui legit hos versus dicat, rogo, pectore puro:
Alchuino *veniam* scelerum *da,* Christe, precamur.

Cf. Ovid, *Amor.*, I.6.23: Redde vicem meritis; *Ex Ponto*, IV.2.23: da veniam.

19 Cf. Diehl, 808–851: *Iura Sepulchrorum*, e.g., no. 66, 21: istud nulla manus temptet violare sepulchrum, also Ovid, *Met.* XIII.472, and Gen. 23:4; see Lissberger, *op. cit.*, p. 69.

20 Alcuin, *Epitaph of Hadrian* I, vv. 29–30 (p. 113):
> Ultima quippe tuas *donec tuba* clamet in aures,
> Principe cum Petro *surge* videre deum;

In *Cimiterio S. Amandi*, XV.9–13 (p. 338):
> *Donec ab* aetheria clamet pius angelus *arce:*
> Surgite nunc prumptim *terrae de pulvere*, fratres,
> Vos vocat adveniens *iudex* e culmine caeli;

cf. I Cor. 15:52; I Thess. 4:16; Matt. 24:31.

22 Eccli. 10:27: Magnus, et iudex; Alcuin, Poem on York, v. 240 (p. 175): millibus innumeris.

23 Alcuin, *Praecepta vivendi*, LII.182 (p. 281): Diligit omnipotens *sophiam sibi semper amantem*. The parallel in Alcuin's epitaph has been overlooked by Marcus Boas, *Alcuin und Cato* (Leiden, 1937), p. 56; see also Alcuin, *De cella sua*, XXIII.33 (p. 244): Tu fugiens fugias, Christum nos semper amemus; *CV*.4.10 (p. 332): Pacificos mores, fratres, vos semper amate; Epitaph of Alcuin's teacher Aelbert, v. 4 (p. 206): qui semper sophiae magnus amator erat.— The verse ending *semper amanti* also Fortunatus, III.6.49.

24 Alcuin, LI.2.5 (p. 264): *Pro quo funde preces* solita pietate tonanti; LXXXVII.4 (p. 305): *Pro quo*, quisque legas, *funde preces* domino. The *funde preces* formula is found in Roman and Christian inscriptions; cf. e.g., *CLE*, 546, 9 (Rome); Virgil, *Aen.* VI.55; 2 Par. 6.19; Bar. 2:19.—For *mente* in the sense of *quietly* see Alcuin, CXI.2 (p. 343): Versiculos paucos studiosa *perlege mente*.—As a rule, people used to read aloud.

25 Dümmler fails to see that the prayer is from the introit of the *Missa pro defunctis* (4 Esdras 2:34 f.): Requiem aeternam dona eis, Domine. The writers of two MSS (see p. 351, *app. crit.*, note *e*) recognized this origin of the prayer, and therefore offer the continuation of the introitus: et lux perpetua luceat eis. The prayer is included in other Carolingian epitaphs of the ninth century directly in the context of inscriptions. Cf. Epit. of Meginoz, *MGH, Poetae*, IV, p. 1038, no. IV: Dic: "Requiem aeternam donet ei dominus," and *ibid.*, p. 1206, no. I, vv. 10 f., Epit. of Armannus of Lausanne:
> Donet ei Dominus requiem sine fine perhennem
> Et lux perpetui splendoris fulgeat ipsi.

The epitaph is an appeal of the departed to the traveler, who is asked to stop for a moment and read the inscription. The wayfarer is told of the inevitability of death; his future will be identical with that of him who lies buried in the tomb. The person addressed is advised that personal glory and the physical body perish; the soul alone survives, while the body returns to the dust of the earth whence it will rise again on Judgment Day.

The main topic of Alcuin's epitaph, the address of the departed to the living, is partly developed in earlier homilies. Caesarius of Arles, *Sermo* XXXI (ed. G. Morin; [Maredsous, 1937], 129), develops such a colloquy: "Clamat ad te mortuus de sepulchro...*Quod tu es, ego fui; quod ego sum, tu eris.*" The dead speaking from the grave to the living also appears in a homily of Ambrosius Autpertus: "...homo mortuus loqui de sepulcro: *Quod tu es, ego fui; et quod ego sum, tu* quoque post modicum *futurus es,*" (PL 89, 1287B).

Compared with Hadrian's epitaph, Alcuin's is of a simple nature. It is not an encomium like the former, and its contents are less rhetorical. The general tenor of the ideas on life and death expressed by Alcuin does not take Alcuin's personal salvation as the point of departure for the main concepts mentioned in the inscription, which are as a whole identical with those known from earlier Roman and Christian epitaphs.[7] Alcuin's views are closer to Roman than to basic Christian ideas, notwithstanding the occasional use made by him of Biblical phraseology. There was actually this double tradition of Roman and Christian ideas on life, death, and resurrection [8] in Alcuin's mind when he wrote the inscription. This fact should explain to a certain degree why, in contrast to Hadrian's epitaph with about twelve *nomina sacra*, Alcuin's has but one.

[7] For the contents of epitaphs see Richmond Lattimore, Chapter X, note 18.

[8] See above, Chapter X, p. 192.

Roman epigraphic *formulae* in the inscription are: the *viator* pattern of the epitaph that determines its literary form, and the reiterated comparative formula *ut mea sicque tua* (vv. 4, 12, 16);[9] the *memento mori* saying based on the present, past, and future tenses of *esse* with the interchanged personal pronoun (vv. 5–6); the ancient warning against the desecration of the tomb (v. 19). The literary influences in the epitaph, which is written without any special display of rhetorical ornaments, are rather cursory. Naturally, the prose legend attached at the end of the inscription is not by Alcuin; it was added after his death.

Alcuin's acquaintance with the species of the metrical epitaph is based not only on his familiarity with literary sources cultivating the species. One of his main models was the poetry of his favorite author Venantius Fortunatus, on whose poems he draws heavily for Hadrian's epitaph and for his other poetical products. Also, the sepulchral inscriptions inserted by Bede in the *Ecclesiastical History*[10] were naturally known to Alcuin, since Bede is the main source of the poem on his native York. In addition, we can hardly go amiss in assuming that Alcuin's antiquarian interests made it impossible for him to pass up the many Roman and Christian dedicatory and sepulchral inscriptions still preserved in his time. His own York stood on the walls and other remains of the Roman legionary fortress of *Eboracum*,[11] a fact he is well aware of when he says in his Poem on York, v. 19 f. (p. 170): "Hanc Romana manus muris et turribus altam/Fundavit primo." Alcuin must have read many inscriptions on his frequent travels in England, France, and Italy,

[9] Cf. Hans Walther, "Zur Geschichte eines mittellateinischen Topos: me tibi teque mihi," *Liber Floridus*, ed. B. Bischoff and S. Brechter (St. Ottilien, Bavaria, 1950), 153–164.

[10] Bk. II.3; v.7.8, and 19.

[11] See R. G. Collingwood and J. N. L. Myers, *Roman Britain and the English Settlements* (Oxford, 1936), *passim*, s. v. *Eboracum*; H. Leclercq, "Tours," in *Dictionnaire d'archéologie chrétienne et de liturgie*, xv (1952), 2570–2677.

and especially when visiting Rome. Like other pilgrims to the Eternal City, he too might have copied some of the numerous inscriptions to be found there. A collection of papal inscriptions by an English pilgrim in the time of Bede, the so-called *Sylloge of Canterbury*,[12] was obviously used by Alcuin—as we shall see —when he wrote some of his own inscriptions. The *Sylloge of Tours* (Diehl, 1195, 9 f.),

> Iustitiae cultor, vitae servator honestae,
> Pauperibus dives, sed sibi pauper erat,

is used by Alcuin in the Poem on York, v. 134 (p. 172):

> Cui datur antistes *vitae servator honestae,*
> Nomine Paulinus,.../ Qui fuit.../
> *Iustitiae cultor,* verus pietatis amator,

and not (as one might be inclined to believe at first glance) Lucan, *Pharsalia* 2.389: Iustitiae cultor, rigidi servator honesti.

Alcuin's name indeed survived, as he had hoped, in the memory and in the literary tradition of the ninth century. Like some of his *Letters*,[13] certain inscriptions he wrote became *formulae* and were used as models for other inscriptions. Thus Angilbert,[14] the son-in-law of Charlemagne, imitates some of his metrical inscriptions. Compare, for instance, the following inscription of Angilbert (b) with two *tituli* by Alcuin: [15]

a. Alcuin, *MGH, Poetae*, I, no. 88, 14, 3 (p. 308), *Inscriptiones Elnonensis Monasterii:*

> Non parcens opibus; miseris nam quidquid habebat
> Sparserat et Christi compsit sacra templa sacerdos.

---

[12] Ed. Angelo Silvagni, "La Silloge Epigrafica di Cambridge," *Rivista di archeologia cristiana* 20 (1943).

[13] Included as *formulae* in the *Formulae Salzburgenses,* ed. Zeumer, *MGH, Formulae Merowingici et Karolini Aevi,* pp. 438 ff.

[14] Ludwig Traube, *Karolingische Dichtungen* (Berlin, 1888), 55; Otto Schumann, "Bernowini Episcopi Carmina," *Historische Vierteljahrschrift,* XXVI (1931), 253.

[15] Cf. Wilhelm Levison, *England and the Continent in the Eighth Century* (Oxford, 1946), 162 n. 2.

b. Angilbert, *ibid.*, no. 4, 5–6 (p. 364):
> Non parcens opibus *propriis*. Nam quidquid habebat
> Ecclesiae *larga* iam pietate dedit.

c. Alcuin, *ibid.*, no. 66, 2, 8 f. (p. 286):
> Non parcens *propriis* opibus. Nam quidquid habebat,
> Distribuit *larga* mente in donaria Christi.

d. Alcuin, *ibid.*, Poem on York, v. 284 (p. 176):
> O pietas, o celsa fides! Nam quicquid habebat,
> Prodigus in domini gazarum sparsit honorem.

Alcuin's own model for the two *tituli* (a, c) is the epitaph of Pope John VII (d. 707), which was known to him probably from the inscription's unique transmission in the *Sylloge of Canterbury:* [16]

> Non parcens opibus, pretiosum quicquid habebat
> In tua distribuit munera, sancta parens.

It is evident that Angilbert (b) does not imitate these verses directly, but in the parallel versions of Alcuin (a, c), while the author of the papal epitaph copies from Ennodius, *Carmina* II, 39 (*MGH, Auctores Antiquissimi*, VII, 147, no. CLXIIb):

> Horrea parva licet, sed mens est largior illis.
> *Non parcens opibus* divitias merui.

Like some of his *tituli*, Alcuin's own epitaph became a literary model for other inscriptions. As such it is included—without his name—in two Carolingian syllogae of inscriptions from the ninth century in the Paris MSS 4841 and 4629.[17] Indeed, the epitaph of Angilbert, which was reconstructed by Ludwig Traube,[18] copies a number of elegiacs from Alcuin's metrical epitaph. That of a certain Ardo of Aniane [19] imitates three verses.

---

[16] Ed. Silvagni (see n. 12), p. 112, no. 41, vv. 9–10.

[17] J. B. de Rossi, *Inscriptiones Christianae vrbis Romae*, II, 1 (Rome, 1888), p. 277, no. XXXI, C.

[18] See n. 14 above.

[19] Ed. Karl Strecker, *MGH, Poetae*, VI, 1 (1951), p. 141; see my review of this volume in *Speculum* 28 (1953), 212–217.

The epitaph by Walafrid Strabo for Abbot Wolfhart,[20] and an epitaph written by an unknown versifier for Strabo himself,[21] also used the verses of Alcuin. An astonishing lack of originality is revealed in one of the two sepulchral inscriptions for the famous Archdeacon Pacificus (d. 846) in the cathedral of Verona.[22] No less than nineteen of its twenty-two verses are taken word for word from the twenty-four lines of Alcuin's epitaph. Two verses of the metrical epitaph of one Crescentius (d. 1010) at Rome [23] may partly have been copied from vv. 5, 6, and 8, of Alcuin's inscription.

The systematic investigation of Carolingian epitaphs will perhaps bring to light additional traces of the popularity of Alcuin's epitaph, a translation [24] of which follows:

1  Here, I beg thee, pause for a while, traveler,
    And ponder my words in thy heart,
  That thou mayest understand thy fate in my shadow:
    The form of thy body will be changed as was mine.
5  What thou art now, famous in the world, I have been, traveler,
    And what I now am, thou wilt be in the future.
  I was wont to seek the joys of the world in vain desire:
    Now I am ashes and dust, and food for worms.
  Remember therefore to take better care of thy soul
10   Than of thy body, because that survives, and this perishes.
  Why dost thou look for possessions? Thou see'st in what a little cavern
    This tomb holds me: Thine will be equally small.

---

[20] *MGH, Poetae*, II, p. 410, no. LXX.

[21] *Ibid.*, p. 424, no. 11; cf. also p. 640, no. IV, 1.

[22] *Ibid.*, p. 656, no. IX; cf. L. Billio, "Le Iscrizioni Veronesi dell'Alto Medioevo," *Archivio Veneto*, 16 (1934), 49–61, and Table 8; Augusto Campana, "Veronensia," *Studi e Testi*, 122 (1946), 67–77.

[23] F. Schneider and Walther Holtzmann, *Die Epitaphien der Päpste und andere stadtrömische Inschriften* (Rome, 1933), no. 53.

[24] A free translation in blank verse is offered by Helen Waddell, *Mediaeval Lyrics* (4th ed.; New York, 1933).

Why art thou eager to deck in Tyrian purple thy body
  Which soon in the dust the hungry worm will devour?
15 As flowers perish when comes the menacing wind,
  So also thy flesh and all thy glory perish.
Give me, I beg thee, O reader, a return for this poem,
  And pray: "Grant, O Christ, forgiveness to thy servant."
I implore thee, let no hand profane the holy rights of this tomb,
20   Until the angelic trumpet announces from Heaven high:
"Thou who liest in the tomb, rise from the dust of the earth,
  The Mighty Judge appears to countless thousands."
My name was Alchuine, and wisdom was always dear to me.
24   Pour out prayers for me when thou quietly readest this inscription.
25 [Here doth rest the Lord Alchuine of blessed memory, the Abbot, who died in peace on the 19th of May (804). When you read, all of you, pray for him and say: "The Lord grant unto him eternal rest." Amen].

# CHAPTER XIV

# The Origin of the Manuscript Collections of Alcuin's Letters

PUPILS and admirers of Alcuin are customarily named as the probable originators of the manuscript collections of Alcuin's voluminous correspondence. Wattenbach [1] assumes that most of the letters are not derived from a "copy-book" as are other collections of epistles.[2] But contrary to these assumptions, Alcuin kept, if not an actual book of minutes (*Konzeptbuch*), then at least *copies* of his letters, which he frequently used later as sources of epistolary *formulae*. These facts will be substantiated here in connection with the investigation of an unknown Anglo-Saxon translation of one of Alcuin's letters.

The Old English version (OE) of the enlarged Rule of Chrodegang of Metz,[3] the Latin original of which was compiled

[1] Wilhelm Wattenbach, *Deutschlands Geschichtsquellen im Mittelalter* I (7th ed., 1904), 189; the same view is repeated by Heinz Löwe in Wattenbach-Levison, II. Heft (Weimar, 1953), 235.

[2] Bernhard Schmeidler in *Historisches Jahrbuch der Görresgesellschaft* 62–69 (1949), 320–338.

[3] A. S. Napier, *The Old English Version with the Latin Original of the Enlarged Rule of Chrodegang* (EETS 150; London, 1916), 90–94; *PL* 89.1092–1094.

after the Synod of Aix-la-Chapelle of 816,[4] offers as ch. 80 an anonymous letter addressed to an unnamed bishop. Its hitherto unknown source is a letter by Alcuin [5] sent to his friend Rado of St. Vaast at Arras, who at one time also belonged to the staff of the royal chancery as Charlemagne's chancellor. The OE version of Alcuin's *Epistle* 74 (pp. 92.25–94.11 in the edition of Napier) corresponds to pp. 116.8–117.25 of Dümmler's edition. The OE follows closely its Latin original. Not infrequently the translation helps in determining the variant in the Latin MS of the translator. Alcuin's *fratres*, for instance, which is changed in Chrodegang's version to *cleri* or *cleros*, is translated with *preostas*, and *fili*, similarly changed to *pastor*, is rendered *hyrde*. A slight trace of paraphrase [6] is found in the following passage:

> Nyd eac þine preostas þæt hi geornlice leornion 7 raedan halige gewrytu;
> Cleros quoque coortare ut sanctas scripturas diligentissime legant.

There is no Latin equivalent for OE *leornion*, which is, however, justifiable on the basis of the context. The two Biblical quotations in the OE text are almost identical with extant Anglo-Saxon translations of the Gospels.[7]

The OE version of Alcuin's epistle is not written in the vernacular of Northumbria, the native country of Alcuin, but in a Saxon dialect, and probably belongs to the age of Aelfric. This date is based on the following observations. The OE *Preface* of the enlarged Rule of Chrodegang is not sufficiently like its Latin source to be called a literal translation. The reference to a Coun-

---

[4] Cf. Otto Hannemann, *Die Kanonikerregeln Chrodegangs von Metz und der Aachener Synode von 816* (Greifswald, 1914), overlooked by Napier; E. Morhain, in *Miscellanea Pio Paschini* I (Rome, 1948), 173–185.

[5] Ed. Dümmler, *MGH, Epistolae* 4, no. 74, pp. 116–117; cf. n. 16, below, on another edition of the same letter.

[6] Ed. Napier 93.34.

[7] See W. W. Skeat, *The Gospel According to Saint John in Anglo-Saxon, Northumbrian, and Old Mercian Versions* (Cambridge, 1887), 138; the same, *Matthew* (1887), 208.

cil of Nicaea, not to be found in the Latin *Preface* of the Rule, seems traceable to a similar one in Aelfric's letter addressed to Wulfsige.[8] On the basis of this probable connection we can assign to the age of Aelfric the OE version of the enlarged Rule of Chrodegang, and therefore also that of Alcuin's letter.

Aelfric and his age have provided us also with OE translations of two of Alcuin's treatises.[9] The *Interrogationes Sigewulfi presbyteri in Genesin* were translated by Aelfric himself,[10] who used them furthermore in the *Homiliae Catholicae*.[11] An OE version of the first sixteen chapters of Alcuin's *De virtutibus et vitiis* is preserved in a MS of the twelfth century.[12] This moralizing manual is quoted by Aelfric in the same collection of homilies,[13] and about 1300 in the *Speculum Gy de Warewyke*.[14] There is also an Old Norse translation [15] of the manual in a MS

---

[8] See Bernhard Fehr, *Die Hirtenbriefe Aelfrics* (Bibliothek der Angelsächsischen Prosa 9; Hamburg, 1914), 1 ff. "þe Preoste Synode," especially pp. 2.12–3.2 and the reference to the Council of Nicaea in the OE, ed. Napier, 1.25–2.2.

[9] The account given of Alcuin by G. K. Anderson, *The Literature of the Anglo-Saxons* (Princeton, 1949), 233–237, 251–254 nn. 57–68, is unsatisfactory. Anderson is not familiar with the modern editions of Alcuin's treatises and epistles and speaks of Alcuin's "few poems" (p. 234) although the *Carmina* comprise 182 pages in large quarto in Dümmler's edition.

[10] Edited by G. E. MacLean, "Aelfric's Version of Alcuin's Interrogationes in Genesin," *Anglia* 7 (1884), 1–59; F. H. Mitchell, *Aelfric's Sigewulfi Interrogationes in Genesin* (diss. Zürich, 1888); A. Tessmann, *Aelfrics altenglische. Bearbeitung der Interrogationes* (diss. Berlin, 1891); M. M. Dubois, *Aelfric: Sermonnaire, docteur et grammairien* (Paris, 1943), 92, 248–251.

[11] M. Förster, "Ueber die Quellen von Aelfrics exegetischen *Homiliae Catholicae*," *Anglia* 16 (1893–1894), 46.

[12] See R. D-N. Warner, *Early English Homilies from the Twelfth Century* (EETS 152; London, 1917), 91–105; an older edition by B. Assman appeared in *Anglia* 11 (1889), 371–391.

[13] Förster in *Anglia* 16 (1893–1894), 46–47.

[14] J. E. Wells, *A Manual of the Writings in Middle English* (New Haven, 1916), 275.

[15] See Chapter XII n. 68.

of the twelfth or the thirteenth century. Additional testimonies of Alcuin will be found in all probability in other collections of OE homilies.

Alcuin's letter no. 74, inserted in the enlarged version of Chrodegang's Rule, provides a hint as to the origin of the manual. The letter might have been used as a formulary by the compiler of the version, because it is the dedicatory epistle which accompanies Alcuin's revision of the older *Vita Vedastis*,[16] which he sent to Rado, the restorer of the buildings of St. Vaast. The most complete manuscript of inscriptions written by Alcuin for this occasion has come to light recently.[17]

The letter to Rado is not the only epistle that became a formulary. Other letters of Alcuin are included as *formulae* in a collection of model letters from the ninth century, the so-called *Formulae Salzburgenses*.[18] Even Alcuin's epitaph,[19] written by himself shortly before his death in 804, was used, like some of his other metrical inscriptions, as a model for inscriptions.

*Epistle* 74 offers a good example of the use made by Alcuin of his own letters as formularies, as can be shown by parallels to this letter which are found in his correspondence.

A = Alcuin, *Epist.* 74 (Dümmler 116–117):

A 116.21: *nullis horis canonicis se* divinis *subtrahat* laudibus, *ne...;*

    269 (D.428.19): Quapropter *nullus se subtrahere* debet *horis canonicis* ecclesiasticis officiis, *ne* forte...;

    43 (D.88.14): nec aliquis *se canonicis horis* a communione... separet.

---

[16] Ed. Bruno Krusch, *MGH, Script. Rer. Merov.* 3 (1896), 414–416.

[17] Cf. J. Lestocquoy, "Notes sur l'épigraphie de l'abbaye de S. Vaast: Les inscriptions d'Alcuin," *Bulletin de la Commission départementale des monuments historiques du Pas-de-Calais* NS. 7 (1941), 54–59; E. A. van Moé, *Bibliothèque de l'École des Chartes* 102 (1941), 292.

[18] Ed. Karl Zeumer, *MGH, Formulae Merowingici et Karolini Aevi* pp. 438 ff.

[19] See Chapter XIII, p. 262.

A 116.27: *Seniores bonis exemplis* et sedula ammonitione *erudiant iuniores* illosque diligant ut filios, *et illi quasi* patres eos honorificent, illorum omni alacritate obediant praeceptis;

    269 (D.428.23): *Seniores bonis exemplis iuniores* aedificent *et illi* devota humilitate *quasi* filii Deo digni patrum sequantur exempla;

    280 (D.437.36): non solum *seniores* verbis ammoneant *iuniores* suos, verum etiam *bonis exemplis erudiant* illos;

    278 (D.434.37): *Seniores* inter vos *iuniores erudiant,...iuniores* debitum honorem senioribus inpendant; cf. 250 (D.405.24).

A 117.2: *sobrietate* ornati, *non ebrietate* adsueti;

    30 (D.71.29): sobrietatis non ebrietatis; 20 (D.58.2): sunt tibi epule non in ebrietate, sed in sobrietate; 114 (D.168.29) non sint ebrietatis sectatores, sed sobrietatis amatores; cf. Hans Lewy, *Sobria Ebrietas* (Giessen, 1929), 138 ff.

A 117.8: magister virtutum, *moribus honestus;*

    20 (D.58.1): sit tuus comitatus *honestus moribus.*

A 117.10: non confidant in linguae notitia, sed in veritatis intelligentia, *ut possint contradicentibus veritati resistere;*

    280 (D.437.20): ut habeant orthodoxae fidei praedicatores, quo *possint contradicentibus veritati resistere;*

    168 (D.276.35): *ut resistere valeatis contradicentibus veritati;*

    Alcuin, *De fide s. trinitatis* (PL 101.143C): *ut possint veritati contradicentibus resistere.*

A 117.12: *Sunt tempora periculosa,* often in the letters: 280 (D.437. 16); 116 (D.171.17); 193 (D.320.10); 206 (D.342.29); cf. II Tim. 3:1.

    Alcuin, *Carmina* 48.21 (ed. Dümmler, *MGH, Poetae* I.261): Tempora sunt nimium variis nunc plena periclis.

A 117.13: *novas introducentes sectas;*

    also *Epistles* 280 (D.437.22); 291 (D.449.17); 137 (D.211.12); 138 (D.220.1); 200 (D.332.28); cf. II Pet. 2:1.

A 117.17: has vero...litterulas *non quasi nescienti* direxi, *sed* ut;

    145 (D.232.25): *non* vobis *quasi nescienti, sed* quasi probanti.

These textual parallels to Alcuin's *Epistle* 74 come from seventeen of his others letters. There are five distinct parallels between

*Epistles* 74 and 280. All these parallels can best be explained if we assume that Alcuin used some of his own letters as epistolary models. Of the many similar instances that occur in his correspondence we may quote the following:

*Epist.* 296 (D.455.26–30):
   Quid dulcius debet esse, quam Deum audire loquentem?
*Epist.* 270 (D.429.6–9):
   Quid dulcius est, quam hac vicissitudine frui cum Deo?
*Epist.* 228 (D.372.7–9):
   Quid dulcius est, quam Dei omnipotentis frui confabulatione?

These passages show in addition a unique adaptation of the Augustinian concept of *fruitio Dei* [20] to the reading of the Bible, elsewhere very succinctly described by Alcuin: [21] "When we pray we are speaking with God, and when we read the Bible God converses with us" (nam cum oramus ipsi cum Deo loquimur; cum vero legimus, Deus nobiscum loquitur).

The interrelation that exists between the letters of Alcuin cannot be based solely on his memory but must reflect the repeated use of his own letters as epistolary models. This conclusion presupposes that copies of his earlier letters were always available to him. He himself confesses that he does not blush when rewriting what he has said before and when repeating his own words: "ideo non erubesco prius dicta rescribere et iterare quae ante dixi" (*Epist.* 161, D.260.10). He could accordingly write to Arno of Salzburg: "I have sent you the letter which I directed to the King on the same subject a few days ago" (misi tibi epistolam quam ante paucos dies domno regi de hac eadem re direxi).[22] Thus Alcuin could provide his friend Arno with the

[20] Cf. Rudolf Lorenz, "*Fruitio Dei* bei Augustin," *Zeitschrift für Kirchengeschichte* 63 (1950), 75–132.
[21] Alcuin, *De virtutibus et vitiis* 5 (*PL* 101.616D), following Isidore of Seville, *Sententiae* III.8.2 (*PL* 83.679B) or Ps.-Augustinus, *Serm.* 302.2 (*PL* 39.2324).
[22] *Epist.* 112 (D.162.28); cf. Dümmler, "Alcuinstudien," *SB. Akademie*

text of an earlier letter addressed to Charlemagne because he kept copies of his correspondence.[23]

The evidence, then, points clearly to the fact that Alcuin [24] retained copies of his letters. Some of the extant MSS of his Epistles,[25] or their archetypes, must actually be derived from such a collection of copies, which was either edited by the author himself or by his disciples. Such an edition, however, does not exclude the possibility of smaller, separate editions of certain groups of the letters by some of the recipients. The transmission of letters by Charlemagne in MSS of Alcuin's correspondence might be traceable to still another MS collection, and also to Alcuin's very probable authorship of royal epistles. Of these, Halphen [26] indeed designates Charlemagne's famous letter to Pope Leo III as the product of Alcuin's pen. Charlemagne's letter to Elipand (C), which belongs to the stray tradition of Alcuin's epistles, is the first document of the Frankish king for which Alcuin's authorship can be positively established. In this connection we should further point out that Alcuin's share in the writing of the great educational capitularies of Charlemagne

---

*Berlin* (1891), 501 n. 3. Cf. Luc. 9:26; Cicero, *Ad Fam.* 5.12.1; Terence, *Eunuch* 41: "nullum est iam dictum quod non sit dictum prius."

[23] This fact cancels out the assumption of T. Sickel, *Historische Zeitschrift* 32 (1874), 365, that the repetition of "certain ideas, formulae, and quotations" in the letters of Alcuin is indicative of their respective dates.

[24] Or his notaries; see Alcuin, *Vita Richarii*, ed. Krusch, *MGH, Script. Rer. Merov.* 4 (1902) 389; *Epist.* 242 (D.387.30): "vocato notario" and "accito notario." On the functions of the *notarius* see Wilhelm Wattenbach, *Das Schriftwesen im Mittelalter* (3rd ed.; Leipzig, 1896), 421.

[25] See J. Ramackers, "Eine unbekannte Handschrift der Alchuinbriefe," *Neues Archiv* 50 (1935), 425–428.—A revised dating is suggested by Hermann Nestler, "Ein Beitrag zur Datierung der Briefe Alkuins," *Verhandlungen des historischen Vereins der Oberpfalz* 77 (1921), 48–52, for *Epist.* 264 (autumn, 799) and 265 (Easter, 804).

[26] L. Halphen, *Charlemagne et l'empire carolingien* (Paris, 1947), 121; see the evidence for Alcuin's authorship above in Chapter I and n. 42; and *ibid.*, n. 66, on Alcuin's authorship of Charlemagne's letter to King Offa of Mercia, 796.

has never been investigated. Future diplomatic inquiry will probably solve this problem [27] as well as that of the unknown authorship of other letters by Charlemagne which are included in MSS of Alcuin's epistles.

The stray tradition of letters by Alcuin suggests an early ninth-century edition, based on the copies of finished letters or "preliminary notes" (*Konzepte*). Such an edition must have represented a selection from Alcuin's voluminous correspondence, as is evinced by the dates of some of the single letters discovered during recent decades. The selective character of its archetype is obvious because at least two of the stray letters (below, nos. 3, 6) originated during a period of Alcuin's life that is otherwise well represented in the manuscripts of the collected letters. Since the edition of Alcuin's *Epistolae* by Ernst Dümmler, nine items have been added to the *Corpus Epistolarum Alcuini:*

1. The *Preface* of Alcuin's supplement to his edition of the *Sacramentarium Gregorianum,*[28]

2. A letter addressed to King Offa of Mercia, discovered by Paul Lehmann;

3. A letter to Beatus of Liébana, found by Dom De Bruyne and Agustin Millares Carlo; [29]

[27] Friedrich-Carl Scheibe, "Alcuin und die Admonitio generalis," *Deutsches Archiv für Erforschung des Mittelalters* 14 (1958), 221–229, following my suggestion first made in *Traditio* 9 (1953), 153, shows Alcuin's co-authorship of the named capitulary.

[28] Edited in *MGH, Epistolae,* 5.579 as a letter by Grimald of St. Gall; but see Suitbert Bäumer, *Historisches Jahrbuch der Görresgesellschaft* 14 (1893), 259; Hans Lietzmann, *Petrus und Paulus* (2nd ed.; Berlin-Leipzig, 1927), 50–51. See the critical edition by R. Amiet, "Le prologue *Hucusque* et la table des Capitula du Supplément d'Alcuin au Sacramentaire Grégorien," *Scriptorium* VII (1953), 177–209.

[29] Nos. 2 and 3 were re-edited by W. Levison, *England and the Continent,* 244–246, 314–323. On no. 3 see J. F. Rivera, "A propósito de una carta de Alcuino recientemente encontrada," *Revista española de teologia* 1 (1940–41), 418–433, who assumes that the letter was written at the begin-

4. A letter to an unknown woman, on the canonical hours, published by Leone Mattei-Cerasoli; [30]

5. The Frankish *Synodica* of the Council of Frankfurt.[31]

6. Charlemagne's letter to Elipand of Toledo.[32]

7.–9. Charlemagne's Epistles 85, 93, 100, the co-authorship of which Scheibe convincingly ascribes to Alcuin.[33]

---

ning of the year 800. C. Erdmann in *Deutsches Archiv für die Erforschung des Mittelalters* 6 (1943), 565, suggests the second half of 798, Levison 797–798.

[30] "Una lettera inedita di Alcuino," *Benedictina* 2 (Rome, 1948), 227–230, from MS 3 of La Cava, saec. XI, f. 318–319. Considerations of style and direction, however, militate against accepting Alcuin's authorship of this letter without a note of doubt.

[31] See Chapter IX, Pt. II.

[32] *Ibid.*, Pt. I.

[33] Friedrich-Carl Scheibe, "Alcuin und die Briefe Karls des Grossen," *Deutsches Archiv für Erforschung des Mittelalters* 15 (1959), 181–193.

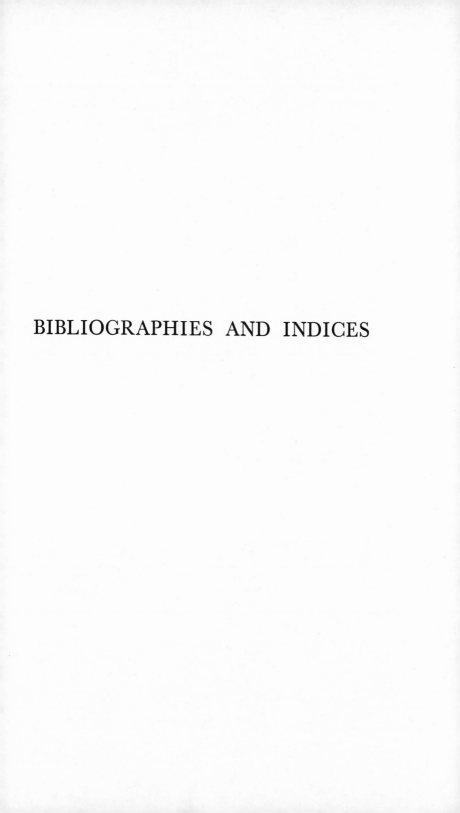

BIBLIOGRAPHIES AND INDICES

# A. Select Bibliography

AMANN, E. *L'époque carolingienne.* (Histoire de l'église, ed. A. Fliche and V. Martin, 6.) Paris, 1936.

AMIET, R. "Le prologue *Hucusque* et la table des Capitula du supplément d'Alcuin au sacramentaire grégorien," *Scriptorium* 7 (1953), 177–209.

———. "Les sacramentaires 88 et 137 du Chapitre de Cologne," *Scriptorium* 8 (1955), 76–84.

ATKINS, J. W. H. *English Literary Criticism: The Medieval Phase.* Cambridge, Eng., 1943.

BENNER, C. "Les rélations de Charlemagne et d'Alcuin avec l'Alsace," *Revue d'Alsace* 81 (1934), 42–51.

BLASCHKA, A. "Der Topos scribendo solari—Briefschreiben als Trost," *Wissenschaftliche Zeitschrift der Martin Luther Universität Halle-Wittenberg* 5 (1956), 637–638.

BOAS, M. *Alcuin und Cato.* Leiden, 1937.

BROWNE, G. F. *Alcuin of York.* London, 1908.

BUCHNER, R. *Die Rechtsquellen.* (Beiheft to WATTENBACH, LEVISON, and LOEWE, see below.) Weimar, 1953.

BULST, W. "Alchuuines *Ecloga de Cuculo*," *Zeitschrift für deutsches Altertum und deutsche Literatur* 86 (1955), 193–196.

CAPELLE, B. "Alcuin et l'histoire du symbole de la messe," *Recherches de théologie ancienne et médiévale* 6 (1934), 249–260.

———. "L'introduction au symbole à la messe," *Mélanges Joseph de Ghellinck* 2 (Gembloux, 1951), 1003–1027.

CARENA, C. *Flaccus Albinus Alcuinus: Canti.* Florence, 1956. (A reprint of some poems.)

CASPAR, E. *Das Papsttum unter fränkischer Herrschaft.* Darmstadt, 1956.

CAVALLERA, F. "Un problème de paternité littéraire: Alcuin ou Léon III," *Bulletin de littérature ecclésiastique* (1934), 229–230.

CHARLIER, C. "Alcuin, Florus et l'apogryphe hiéronymien *Cogitis me* sur l'Assomption," *Studia Patristica* I (Berlin, 1957), 70–81.

CURTIUS, E. R. *European Literature and the Latin Middle Ages.* (Bollingen Series, 36.) New York, 1953.

DE BRUYNE, Edgar. *Etudes d'Esthétique Médiévale.* Brugge, Belgium, 1946.

DELARUELLE, E. "Charlemagne et l'église," *Revue d'histoire de l'église de France* 39 (1953), 165–199.

DELIUS, E. "War Alcuin Mönch?" *Theologische Studien und Kritiken* 103 (1931), 464–473.

DROEGEREIT, R."Kaiseridee und Kaisertitel bei den Angelsachsen," *Zeitschrift der Savigny-Stiftung für Rechtsgeschichte* 69 (Germ. Abt., 1952), 24–73.

DUCKETT, E. S. *Alcuin, Friend of Charlemagne.* New York, 1951.

DÜMMLER, E. "Alcuinstudien," *Sitzungsberichte, Preussische Akademie* (Berlin, 1891), 495–523.

——. "Zur Lebensgeschichte Alcuins," *Neues Archiv der Gesellschaft für ältere deutsche Geschichtskunde* 18 (1893), 51–70.

ELLARD, G. *Master Alcuin, Liturgist.* Chicago, 1956.

ERDMANN, C. *Forschungen zur politischen Ideenwelt des Frühmittelalters.* Ed. Friedrich Baethgen. Berlin, 1951.

FICHTENAU, H. *Das Karolingische Imperium: Soziale und geistige Problematik eines Grossreiches.* Zürich, 1949.

——. "Karl der Grosse und das Kaisertum," *Mitteilungen des Instituts für Oesterreichische Geschichtsforschung* 61 (1953), 257–334.

——. "Il concetto imperiale di Carlo Magno," *Settimane di Studio del Centro Italiano di Studi sull'alto medioevo* 1. Spoleto, 1954.

——. *The Carolingian Empire.* Oxford, 1957.

FISCHER, B. *Die Alkvin Bibel.* (Aus der Geschichte der lateinischen Bibel, I.) Freiburg i. Br., 1957.

FLOM, G. T. *Codex AM 619 Quarto: Old Norwegian Book of*

*Homilies containing the Miracles of Saint Olaf and Alcuin's* De virtutibus et vitiis. (Univ. of Illinois Studies in Language and Literature, 14.4.) Urbana, 1929.

FORTGENS, H. W. "De paedagoog Alcuin en zijn *Ars grammatica*," *Tijdschrift voor Geschiedenis* 60 (1947), 57–65.

FUENTES ARROYO, E. "La institución de la Iglesia segun Alcuino," *Revista española de teologia* 8 (1948), 231–274.

GANSHOF, F. L. "La révision de la Bible par Alcuin," *Bibliothèque d'humanisme et renaissance* 9 (1947), 7–20.

——. *The Imperial Coronation of Charlemagne: Theories and Facts.* Glasgow University Publications, 1949.

——. *Wat waren de Capitularia?* Brussel, 1955.

——. "Recherches sur les Capitulaires," *Revue historique de droit français et étranger*, sér. 4e, 35 (1957), 33–87, 196–246.

GEISELMANN, J. "Ps.-Alcuins *Confessio Fidei*...eine antiberengarianische Ueberarbeitung der *Expositio missae* des Florus von Lyon," *Theologische Quartalschrift* 105 (1924), 272–295.

——. *Studien zu frühmittelalterlichen Abendmahlschriften.* Paderborn, 1926. (Contains an expanded version of preceding item.)

GERHARDT, D. "Ueber Bruchstücke von Alkuins Grammatik in der Bibliothek des Meneburger Domstiftes," *Thüringisch-Sächsische Zeitschrift für Geschichte und Kunst* 27 (1940), 27–48.

GROSJEAN, P. "Le *De excidio* chez Bede et chez Alcuin," *Analecta Bollandiana* 75 (1957), 222–226.

HADOT, P. "Marius Victorinus et Alcuin," *Archives d'histoire doctrinale et littéraire du moyen âge* 29 (1954), 5–19.

HALPHEN, L. *Charlemagne et l'empire carolingien.* Paris, 1949.

HEIMING, O. "Aus der Werkstatt Alkuins," *Archiv für Liturgiewissenschaft* 4 (1956), 341–357.

HOCQUARD, G. "Quelques réflexions sur les idées politico-religieuses d'Alcuin," *Bulletin des facultés catholiques de Lyon* 74 (1952), 13–30.

HOHLER, C. Review of G. Ellard (see above), in: *Journal of Ecclesiastical History* 8 (1957), 222–226.

HOWELL, W. S. *The Rhetoric of Alcuin & Charlemagne.* (Princeton Studies in English, 23.) Princeton, 1941.

INDREBØ, G. *Gamal Norsk Homiliebok Cod. AM 619.4°.* Oslo, 1931.

Jones, L. W. "The Text of the Bible and the Script and the Art of Tours," *Harvard Theological Review* 28 (1935), 139–197.

Klauser, T. "Die liturgischen Austauschbeziehungen zwischen der römischen und der fränkisch-deutschen Kirche," *Historisches Jahrbuch der Görresgesellschaft* 53 (1933), 169–189.

Kleinclausz, A. *Alcuin*. (Annales de l'Université de Lyon, III.15.) Paris, 1948.

Knudsen, T. *Gammelnorsk Homiliebok Etter AM 619 QV*. (Corpus Codicum Norvegicorum Medii Aevi, ed. D. A. Seip; Quarto Serie, I.) Oslo, 1952.

Koehler, W. "Turonische Handschriften aus der Zeit Alkuins," *Mittelalterliche Handschriften: Festgabe H. Degering* (Leipzig, 1926), 172–180.

——. *Die karolingischen Miniaturen*. Vol. I, 1. Berlin, 1930.

Kowalski-Fahrun, H. "Alkuin und der ahd. Isidor," Braune's *Beiträge zur Geschichte der deutschen Sprache und Literatur* 47 (1923), 312–322.

Laistner, M. L. W. *Thought and Letters in Western Europe*. London and Ithaca, 1957.

Lehmann, P. "Cassiodor-Isidor-Beda-Alchvine," *Philologus* 74 (1917), 357–383.

——. *Fuldaer Studien: Neue Folge*. (Sitzungsberichte, Bayerische Akademie, No. 2.) Munich, 1927.

Lestocquoy, J. "Notes sur l'épigraphie de l'abbaye de Saint-Vaast: Les inscriptions d'Alcuin," *Bulletin de la Commission dép. des monuments histor. du Pas-de-Calais* 7 (1941), 54–59.

——. "Les saints et les églises de l'abbaye de Saint-Vaast d'Arras au VIIIe siècle," *Revue du Nord* 26 (1943), 197–208.

Levison, W. "An Eighth-Century Poem on St. Ninian," *Antiquity* 14 (1940), 280–291. (On Bamberg Ms B II.10, a sylloge ascribed to Alcuin.)

——. *England and the Continent in the Eighth Century*. Oxford, 1946.

Lienard, E. "Alcuin et les *Epistolae Senecae et Pauli*," *Revue belge de phil. et d'histoire* 20 (1941), 589–598.

Lietzmann, H. *Das Sacramentarium Gregorianum nach dem Aachener Urexemplar*. Münster, 1921.

——. "Handschriftliches zu Alkuins Ausgabe und Sakramentarium," *Jahrbuch der Liturgiewissenschaft* 5 (1925), 68–79.

LOEWE, H. "Zur Geschichte Wizos," *Deutsches Archiv für Geschichte des Mittelalters* 6 (1943), 363–373.

——. "Von Theoderich dem Grossen zu Karl dem Grossen," *Deutsches Archiv für die Erforschung des Mittelalters* 9 (1952), 353–401.

——. see WATTENBACH-LEVISON, and LÖWE, below.

LONG, O. F. "The Attitude of Alcuin toward Virgil," *Studies in Honor of Basil L. Gildersleeve* (Baltimore, 1902), 377–386.

LOWE, E. A. "A Manuscript of Alcuin in the Script of Tours," *Classical and Mediaeval Studies in Honor of Edward Kenneth Rand* (New York City, 1938), 191–193.

MANITIUS, M. *Geschichte der lateinischen Literatur des Mittelalters.* Vol. I. Munich, 1911.

MANZ, G. *Ausdrucksformen der lateinischen Liturgiesprache bis ins elfte Jahrhundert.* (Texte und Arbeiten, ed. Erzabtei Beuron, I Abt., 1. Beiheft.) Beuron, 1941. (Deals with Alcuin, pp. 29–42.)

MARSILI, A. *Alcuini Orthographia.* Pisa, 1952.

MARTIN, J. "Zu den Rhetores Latini Minores," *Würzburger Jahrbücher für die Altertumswissenschaft* 3 (1948), 319.

MATTEI-CERASOLI, L. "Una lettera inedita di Alcuino," *Benedictina* 2 (1948), 227–230.

NESTLER, H. "Ein Beitrag zur Datierung der Briefe Alkuins," *Verhandlungen des histor. Vereins der Oberpfalz* 77 (1927), 48–52.

OTTAVIANO, C. "Un opusculo inedito di Alcuino," *Aevum* 2 (1928), 3–16. (Edition of a ps.-Alcuinian text.)

PALLASSE, M. "Brève histoire d'un schème cicéronien au moyen âge," *Revue du moyen âge latin* 1 (1945), 35–42.

PAPETTI, M. "Intorno ai viaggi di Alcuino in Italia," *Sophia* 3 (1935), 216–218.

PSEUDO-ALCUINIANA. See GEISELMANN, OTTAVIANO, RYAN, WILMART.

RABY, F. J. E. *A History of Christian Secular Poetry.* 2nd ed. Oxford, 1953.

RAIS, A. "Une mise au point: La Bible de Grandval, dite d'Alcuin," *Revue d'histoire ecclésiastique suisse* 26 (1932), 145–153.

RAMACKERS, J. "Eine unbekannte Handschrift der Alcuinbriefe,"

*Neues Archiv der Gesellschaft für ältere deutsche Geschichtskunde* 50 (1933), 425–428.

RAND, E. K. "A Preliminary Study of Alcuin's Bible," *Harvard Theological Review* 24 (1931), 323–396.

REUSCHEL, H. "Kenningar bei Alkuin," Braune's *Beiträge zur Geschichte der deutschen Sprache und Literatur* 62 (1938), 143–155.

RIVERA, J. F. "A propósito de una carta de Alcuino recientemente encontrada," *Revista española de teologia* 1 (1941), 418–433.

ROCHAIS, H.-M. "Le *Liber de virtutibus et vitiis* d'Alcuin," *Revue Mabillon* 41 (1951), 77–86.

RYAN, J. J. "Pseudo-Alcuin's *Liber de divinis officiis* and the *Liber Dominus vobiscum* of St. Peter Damiani," *Mediaeval Studies* 14 (1952), 159–168.

SANFORD, E. M. "Alcuin and the Classics," *Classical Journal* 20 (1925), 526–533.

SCHEIBE, F. C. "Alcuin und die *Admonitio Generalis*," *Deutsches Archiv für Erforschung des Mittelalters* 14 (1958), 221–229.

SCHROEBLER, I. "Zu den *Carmina rhythmica*...oder über den Stabreim in der lateinischen Poesie der Angelsachsen," Braune's *Beiträge zur Geschichte der deutschen Sprache und Literatur* 79 (1957), 1–42.

SECKEL, E. "Studien zu Benedictus Levita, VIII," *Neues Archiv der Gesellschaft für ältere deutsche Geschichtskunde* 40 (1916), 101–103.

SOLANO, J. "El concilio de Calcedonia y la controversia adopcionista del siglo VIII en España," *Das Konzil von Chalkedon* 2 (Würzburg, 1953), 841–871.

STANGL, T. "Zur Kritik der lateinischen Rhetoren und Grammatiker," *Xenien: Der 41. Versammlung deutscher Philologen dargeboten* (Munich, 1891), 27–38.

STENGEL, E. E. *Urkundenbuch des Klosters Fulda* I.2. (Die Zeit des Abtes Baugulf.) Marburg, 1956.

SUCHIER, W., and DALY, L. W. *Disputatio regalis et nobilissimi iuvenis Pippini cum Albino scholastico*, in: *Altercatio Hadriani Augusti et Epicteti philosophi*. (Illinois Studies in Language and Literature, 24 nos. 1–2.) Urbana, 1939.

TAYLOR, P. "The Construction *Habere-with-Infinitive* in Alcuin as an Expression of the Future," *Romanic Review* 15 (1924), 123–152.

TRAUBE, L. *Karolingische Dichtungen*. Berlin, 1888.

ULLMANN, W. *The Growth of Papal Government in the Middle Ages*. London-New York, 1956.

WALLACH, L. "Amicus amicis, inimicus inimicis," *Zeitschrift für Kirchengeschichte* 52 (1933), 614–615.

——. "Onulf of Speyer, a Humanist of the Eleventh Century," *Medievalia et Humanistica* 6 (1950), 35–56.

——. "Alcuin's Epitaph of Hadrian I: A Study in Carolingian Epigraphy," *American Journal of Philology* 72 (1951), 128–144.

——. "Charlemagne's *De litteris colendis* and Alcuin: A diplomatic-historical study," *Speculum* 26 (1951), 288–305.

——. "Charlemagne and Alcuin: Studies in Carolingian Epistolography," *Traditio* 9 (1953), 127–154.

——. "Education and Culture in the Tenth Century," *Medievalia et Humanistica* 9 (1955), 18–22.

——. "The Genuine and the Forged Oath of Pope Leo III," *Traditio* 11 (1955), 37–63.

——. "Alcuin on Virtues and Vices," *Harvard Theological Review* 48 (1955), 175–195.

——. "Alcuin on Sophistry," *Classical Philology* 50 (1955), 259–261.

——. "The Epitaph of Alcuin: A Model of Carolingian Epigraphy," *Speculum* 30 (1955), 367–373.

——. "The Roman Synod of December 800 and the Alleged Trial of Leo III," *Harvard Theological Review* 49 (1956), 123–142.

——. "Berthold of Zwiefalten's Chronicle," *Traditio* 13 (1957), 153–248.

——. "A Manuscript of Tours with an Alcuinian Incipit," *Harvard Theological Review* 51 (1958), 255–261.

——. Review of L. Arbusow, *Colores Rhetorici* (Göttingen, 1948), in: *Speculum* 24 (1949), 416–418. (See my reference to Geoffrey of Vinsauf's anonymous quotation from Alcuin's *Rhetoric*.)

——. Review of A. Kleinclausz (see above), in: *Speculum* 24 (1949), 587–590.

——. Review of B. Bischoff and S. Brechter (eds.), *Liber Floridus:*

*Mittellateinische Studien* (St. Ottilien, 1950), in: *Speculum* 26 (1951), 705–707. (See p. 706, the unacknowledged quotation by Lupus of Ferrières from Alcuin's poem 35.20.)

——. Review of E. S. Duckett (see above) in: *Speculum* 27 (1952), 102–106.

——. Review of Karl Strecker and Otto Schumann, *Nachträge zu den Poetae Aevi Carolini* (*MGH, Poetae* VI.1; Weimar, 1951), in: *Speculum* 28 (1953), 212–217. (See the remarks about Walther of Speyer and the Waltarius.)

——. Review of Wattenbach-Levison (see below), Fasc. I–III, in: *Speculum* 29 (1954), 131–137, 820–825; 34 (1959), 343-44.

——. Review of A. P. McKinlay, *Aratoris Subdiaconi de Actibus Apostolorum* (*CSEL* 72; Vienna, 1951), in: *Speculum* 29 (1954), 145–150. (See p. 147; six of the seven verses of Alcuin's poem 114.3 are from Arator's poem I.1070–1076.)

——. Review of R. Buchner (see above), in: *Speculum* 30 (1955), 92–96.

——. Review of G. Ellard (see above), in: *Thought* 32 (1957), 468–469.

WATTENBACH, W., LEVISON, W., and LOEWE, H. *Deutschlands Geschichtsquellen im Mittelalter*. Fasc. I–III. Weimar 1952–57. Beiheft, see BUCHNER (above).

WERNER, K. *Alkuin und sein Jahrhundert*. Paderborn, 1865.

WILMART, A. *Auteurs spirituels et textes dévots du moyen âge: Etudes d'histoire littéraire*. Paris, 1932. (Deals with pseudo-Alcuinian writings.)

——. "Le lectionnaire d'Alcuin," *Ephemerides Liturgicae* 51 (1937), 93–135.

WILMART, A., and BISHOP, E. "La réforme liturgique de Charlemagne," *Ephemerides Liturgicae* 45 (1931), 186–207.

*See also* pp. 4, 28, 33, 82, 101, 177, 197, 226, 254.

# B. Text Editions Used

Abbreviations:

*BSGRT—Bibliotheca scriptorum graecorum et romanorum Teubneriana*
*CCL—Corpus Christianorum, series latina*
*CSEL—Corpus scriptorum ecclesiasticorum latinorum*
*EETS—Early English Text Society*
*MGH—Monumenta Germaniae historica*
*PL—Patrologia latina*, ed. J. P. Migne
*SCBO—Scriptorum classicorum bibliotheca Oxoniensis*

ACTA CONCILIORUM:
*Acta conciliorum oecumenicorum* II.ii.1, rec. Eduard Schwartz. Berlin-Leipzig, 1932.
*MGH, Concilia aevi Merovingici*, rec. Friedrich Maassen. Hannover, 1893.
*MGH, Concilia aevi Karolini*, I., rec. Albert Werminghoff. Hannover-Leipzig, 1906.
ACTA SANCTORUM:
*Acta Sanctorum Junii* VII.2. Brussels, 1867.
*Acta Sanctorum Novembris* III. Brussels, 1910.
ACTUS SILVESTRI:
ed. Bononius Mombritius, *Sanctuarium seu Vitae Sanctorum* II. 2nd ed; Paris, 1910.

AELFRIC:
"Aelfric's version of Alcuin's *Interrogationes in Genesin*," ed.
G. E. MacLean, *Anglia* 7 (1884), 1–59.
*Die Hirtenbriefe Aelfrics*, ed. Bernhard Fehr, *Bibliothek der angel-
sächsischen Prosa* 9; Hamburg, 1914.

ALCHER OF CLAIRVAUX:
*De spiritu et anima*, PL 40.779–832.

ALCUIN:
*Adv. Elipandum Libri* IV, PL 101.231–300.
*Adv. Felicem libri* VII, PL 101.119–230.
*Adv. Felicis haeresin*, PL 101.87–120.
*Ars grammatica*, PL 101.849–902.
*Carmina*, ed. Ernst Dümmler, *MGH, Poetae latini aevi carolini*
I (Berlin, 1881), 160–351, no. 1–124; additions *ibid.* II (Berlin,
1884), 690–693; VI (Weimar, 1951), 159 f.
*Carmina rhythmica*, ed. Karl Strecker, *MGH, Poetae latini aevi
carolini* IV (Berlin, 1923), 903–910.
*Comm. in Ecclesiasten*, PL 100.665–722.
*Comm. in Joannem*, PL 100.743–1008.
*De animae ratione*, PL 101.639–649; excerpts published as Alcuin's
*Epistle* 309 by Ernst Dümmler, *Epistolae* IV (Karolini aevi II;
Berlin, 1895), 473–478.
*De dialectica*, PL 101.951–976.
*De fide sanctae et individuae trinitatis*, PL 101.9–58.
*De orthographia*, ed. Aldo Marsili. Pisa, 1952.
*De rhetorica et de virtutibus*, ed. Carl Halm, *Rhetores latini mi-
nores* (Leipzig, 1863), 525–550.
*De virtutibus et vitiis*, PL 101.613–638.
*Epistolae*, ed. Ernst Dümmler, *MGH, Epistolae* IV (Karolini
aevi II; Berlin, 1895), 1–481, nos. 1–311; additions *ibid.* V
(Karolini aevi III; Berlin, 1899), 643–645.
*Expositio in Psalmum* 118, PL 100.597–620.
*Interrogationes et responsiones in Genesin*, PL 100.516–566.
*Vita Richarii confessoris Centulensis*, ed. Bruno Krusch, *MGH,
Scriptores rerum Merovingicarum* IV (Hannover-Leipzig,
1902), 381–401; see Alcuin's source, the *Vita Richarii sacerdotis*

*Centulensis,* ed. Bruno Krusch, *ibid.* VII (Hannover-Leipzig, 1920), 438–453.

*Vita Vedastis episcopi Atrebatensis,* ed. Bruno Krusch, *MGH, Scriptores rerum Merovingicarum* III (Hannover, 1896), 414–427; see additions *ibid.* IV (Hannover-Leipzig, 1902), 770, and *ibid.* VII (Hannover-Leipzig, 1920), 819–820.

*Vita Willibrordi archiepiscopi Traiectensis* [Liber primus], ed. Wilhelm Levison, *MGH, Scriptores rerum Merovingicarum* VII (Hannover-Leipzig, 1920), 81–141; additions *ibid.,* pp. 856–858.

*De vita Sancti Willibrordi episcopi libri secundi,* ed. Ernst Dümmler, *MGH, Poetae latini aevi Carolini* I (Berlin, 1881), 207–220.

*Vita Willibrordi,* prose and metrical versions, ed. Albert Poncelet, *Acta Sanctorum Novembris* III (Brussels, 1910), 435–457.

*Vita Alcuini,* ed. Wilhelm Arndt, *MGH, Scriptores* XV.1 (Hannover, 1887), 182–197.

Old-English Alcuin: R. D.-N. Warner, *Early English homilies from the twelfth century Ms. Vesp. D. XIV. EETS,* Original Series 152; London, 1917.

ALDHELM:

*Aldhelmi Opera,* ed. Rudolf Ehwald, *MGH, Auctores Antiquissimi* XV; Berlin, 1919.

AMBROSE:

*De officiis ministrorum, PL* 16.23–184.

AMBROSIUS AUTPERTUS:

*Sermo de cupiditate, PL* 89.1277–1292.

ANGILBERT:

*Carmina,* ed. Ernst Dümmler, *MGH, Poetae latini aevi carolini* I (Berlin, 1881), 355–366.

ANNALES LAURESHAMENSES:

ed. G. H. Pertz, *MGH, Scriptores* I (Hannover, 1826), 22–39.

ANNALISTA SAXO:

*Chronicon,* ed. Georg Waitz, *MGH, Scriptores* VI (Hannover, 1849), 542–777.

ANTHOLOGIA LATINA:

Pars prior: *Carmina in codicibus scripta,* rec. Alexander Riese. Leipzig, 1894; vols. II and III see *Carmina Latina Epigraphica.*

ARATOR:
*Aratoris subdiaconi De actibus apostolorum,* ed. A. P. McKinlay, *CSEL* 72; Wien, 1951.

AUGUSTINUS:
*De beata vita libri duo,* ed. Pius Knöll, *CSEL* 63; Wien-Leipzig, 1922.

*De civitate dei libri* XXII, rec. Emanuel Hoffmann, *CSEL* 40; Wien, 1899–1900.

*De diversis questionibus* 83, *PL* 40.11–100.

*De doctrina christiana, PL* 34.15–122; ed. H. Vogels, *Florilegium patristicum,* 24; Bonn, 1930.

*Enchiridion,* ed. Otto Scheel. 2nd ed.; Tübingen, 1930.

*Sermones, PL* 39; *Sermones* selecti, ed. D. C. Lambot, *Stromata patristica et mediaevalia,* I; Utrecht-Bruxelles, 1950.

AULUS GELLIUS:
*Noctium Atticarum libri xx,* rec. M. Hertz, ed. Carl Hosius, *BSGRT;* Leipzig, 1903.

BEDA VENERABILIS:
*Venerabilis Baedae opera historica* I-II, ed. Charles Plummer. Oxford, 1896.

*Bedas metrische Vita Sancti Cuthberti,* ed. Werner Jaager, *Palaestra,* ·128; Leipzig, 1935.

*Bibliotheca scriptorum graecorum et romanorum Teubneriana;* Leipzig, 1849–

BILLIO, L. "Le iscrizioni Veronesi dell'alto medioevo," *Archivio Veneto* 16 (1934), 49–61.

BOETHIUS:
*Commentarii in librum Aristotelis...*ΠΕΡΙ ΕΡΜΗΝΕΙΑΣ, I–II, rec. Carl Meiser, *BSGRT;* Leipzig, 1877–1880.

*Philosophiae consolationis libri quinque,* rec. Wilhelm Weinberger, *CSEL* 67; Wien, 1934.

*Philosophiae consolatio,* ed. Ludovicus Biehler, *CCL* 94; Turnholti, 1957.

*Henry Bradshaw Society for editing rare liturgical texts;* London, 1891–

BREVIARIUM ALARICIANUM:
*Lex Romana Visigothorum,* ed. Gustav Haenel. Leipzig, 1849.

*Codex Theodosianus* I.2, ed. T. Mommsen and Paul M. Meyer. Berlin, 1905.

CAESARIUS:

*Sancti Caesarii Arelatensis Sermones* I–II, rec. Germain Morin, ed. altera, *CCL* 103–104; Turnholti, 1953.

CARMINA LATINA EPIGRAPHICA:

*Carmina Epigraphica (Anthologia Latina* II.1), conlegit Franz Buecheler. Reprinted Leipzig, 1930;

*Carmina Latina Epigraphica (Anthologia Latina* II.2), conlegit Franz Buecheler. Leipzig, 1897;

*Carmina Latina Epigraphica (Anthologia Latina* III, Supplement.), cur. Ernst Lommatzsch. Leipzig, 1926.

CASSIAN:

*Conlationes XXIII*, ed. Michael Petschenig, *CSEL* 13; Wien, 1886.

*De institutis coenobiorum et de octo principalium vitiorum remediis libri XII*, rec. Michael Petschenig, *CSEL* 17; Prague-Wien-Leipzig, 1888.

CASSIODORUS:

*Historia ecclesiastica tripartita*, rec. Waltarius Jacob, ed. Rudolfus Hanslik, *CSEL* 71; Wien, 1952.

*Institutiones*, ed. R. A. B. Mynors. Oxford, 1937.

*Variae*, rec. T. Mommsen, *MGH, Auctores Antiquissimi* XII; Berlin, 1894.

CHARLEMAGNE:

*Capitularia: MGH, Capitularia regum Francorum* I, ed. Alfred Boretius. *Legum Sectio* II, t. I; Hannover, 1883.

*Diplomata: MGH, Diplomata Karolinorum* I, ed. Engelbert Mühlbacher. Hannover, 1906.

*Epistolae:* see in: *MGH, Epistolae Karolini aevi* II (*Epistolae* IV; Berlin, 1895); *MGH, Concilia aevi Karolini* I (Hannover-Leipzig, 1906); *MGH, Epistolae Karolini aevi* III (*Epistolae* V; Berlin, 1899). See also *Libri Carolini*.

CHRODEGANG:

*The Old-English Version with the Latin Original of the Enlarged Rule of Chrodegang*, ed. A. S. Napier, *EETS* 150; London, 1916.

CICERO:

*De officiis*, rec. C. Atzert, 3rd ed.; Leipzig, 1949.

*Epistularum ad familiares*, rec. H. Sjögren. Leipzig, 1925.
*Rhetorici libri duo qui vocantur De inventione*, rec. Eduard Stroebel, *BSGRT;* Leipzig, 1915.
*Clavis Patrum Latinorum*, ed. Eligius Dekkers and Aemilius Gaar, *Sacris Erudiri* III, 1951.

CODEX CAROLINUS:
ed. Wilhelm Gundlach, *MGH, Epistolae Merovingici et Karolini aevi* I (*Epistolae* III; Berlin, 1892), 469–657.

COLLECTIO HIBERNENSIS:
ed. Herrmann Wasserschleben, *Die Irische Kanonensammlung*, 2nd ed.; Leipzig, 1885.

COMMONITIUNCULA AD SOROREM:
ed. A. S. Anspach in: *Scriptores ecclesiastici hispano-latini veteris et medii aevi* IV; Escorial, 1935.

*Corpus Christianorum*, series latina; Turnholti, 1953–

CORPUS INSCRIPTIONUM LATINARUM:
Vol. II—*Inscriptiones Hispaniae Latinae*, ed. Aemilius Hübner. Berlin, 1869.
Vol. VIII.2—*Inscriptiones Africae Latinae*, ed. Gustavus Wilmanns. Berlin, 1881.
Vol. XI.2,1—*Inscriptiones Aemiliae Etruriae Umbriae Latinae*, ed. Eugenius Borman. Berlin, 1901.

*Corpus iuris canonici*, ed. E. A. Friedberg. Leipzig, 1879–1881.
*Corpus scriptorum ecclesiasticorum latinorum;* Wien, 1864–

CREEDS:
*Bibliothek der Symbole und Glaubensregeln der alten Kirche*, ed. August Hahn, 3rd ed.; Breslau, 1897.
*Enchiridion symbolorum*, ed. H. Denzinger and I. B. Umberg. Freiburg i. Br., 1932.
I. Ortiz de Urbina, *El Simbolo Niceno*. Madrid, 1947.
J. Madoz, *Le symbole du XIe concile de Toledo*, Spicilegium Sacrum Lovaniense 19; Louvain, 1938.

DEFENSOR:
*Liber scintillarum, PL* 88.597–718.
Ed. H. M. Rochais, *CCL* 117 (Turnholti, 1957), 1–308.

DEGRASSI, Attilio. "Epigrafia Romana," *Doxa* 2 (1949), 111–119.

DHUODA:

*Le Manuel de Dhuoda,* ed. E. Bondurand. Paris, 1887.

DIEHL:

*Inscriptiones latinae christianae veteres* I–III, ed. Ernestus Diehl. Berlin, 1925–1931.

DIPLOMATA MEROWINGICA:

Ed. K. A. F. Pertz, *Diplomata regum Francorum e stirpe Merowingica (Diplomatum imperii* I, in folio). Hannover, 1872.

DISTICHA CATONIS:

*Disticha Catonis,* rec. Marcus Boas, cur. H. J. Botschuyver. Amsterdam, 1952.

DRACONTIUS:

*Blossii Aemilii Dracontii Carmina,* ed. Friedrich Vollmer, *MGH, Auctores Antiquissimi* XIV; Berlin, 1905.

*Early English Text Society;* London, 1864–

EDICTUM THEODERICI REGIS:

*Fontes iuris romani antejustiniani* II, ed. Johannes Baviera (Florence, 1940), 682–710.

EILBERT:

*Ordo judiciarius,* ed. Ludwig Wahrmund, *Quellen zur Geschichte des römisch-kanonischen Processes* I, Heft 5. Innsbruck, 1906.

EINHARD:

*Vie de Charlemagne,* ed. et trad. Louis Halphen, *Les classiques de l'histoire de France au moyen âge* I; Paris, 1923.

ELIPAND OF TOLEDO:

*Epistles* 182, 183, see: *MGH, Epistolae* IV (*Karolini Aevi* II; Berlin, 1895.)

*Epistle* 19 A, see: *MGH, Concilia* II (*Aevi Karolini* I.1; Hannover-Leipzig, 1906.)

ENNODIUS:

*Opera,* rec. Friedrich Vogel, *MGH, Auctores Antiquissimi* VII; Berlin, 1885.

EPISTOLAE SYNODICAE:

See: *MGH, Concilia aevi Karolini* I.1, ed. Albert Werminghoff (Hannover-Leipzig, 1906), nos. 19 D-E.

ERMENRICH OF ELLWANGEN:

*Epistola ad Grimaldum abbatem,* ed. Ernst Dümmler, *MGH, Epistolae Karolini aevi* III (Berlin, 1899), 534–579.

EUTROPIUS:

*Breviarium ab·urbe condita,* ed. H. Droysen, *MGH, Auctores Antiquissimi* II; Berlin, 1879.

FELIX OF URGEL:

*Epistle* 199, ed. Ernst Dümmler, *MGH, Epistolae* IV ( *Karolini aevi* II; Berlin, 1895), 329–330.

*Fontes iuris romani antejustiniani* II, ed. Johannes Baviera. Florence, 1940.

FORMULAE:

*Formulae Merowingici et Karolini Aevi* I.1–2, ed. Karl Zeumer, *Legum Sectio* V; Hannover, 1886.

FORTUNATIANUS:

*Ars rhetorica,* ed. Carl Halm, *Rhetores latini minores* (Leipzig, 1863), 81–134.

FORTUNATUS:

*Opera...poetica,* ed. Friedrich Leo, *MGH, Auctores Antiquissimi* IV.1; Berlin, 1881.

GELASIUS I:

*Epist. ad Anastasium imperatorem,* excerpt in: Carl Mirbt, *Quellen zur Geschichte des Papsttums* (4th ed.; Tübingen, 1924), no. 187; ed. Eduard Schwartz, *Publizistische Sammlungen zum Acacianischen Schisma* (Abhandlungen Bayerische Akademie der Wiss., phil.-histor. Abt., Heft 10; Munich, 1934), no. 8, pp. 19–24.

GESTA ABBATUM FONTANELLENSIUM:

ed. F. Lohier and J. Laporte. Rouen, 1936;

excerpts ed. G. H. Pertz, *MGH, Scriptores* II (Hannover, 1829), 270–300.

GILDAS:

*De excidio et conquestu Britanniae,* ed. T. Mommsen, *MGH, Auctores Antiquissimi* XIII (Berlin, 1898), 25–85.

*Grammatici latini* I–VII, ed. Heinrich Keil. Leipzig, 1857–1880; Supplementum: *Anecdota Helvetica,* ed. Hermann Hagen. Leipzig, 1870.

GREGORIAN SACRAMENTARY:
  ed. H. A. Wilson, *The Gregorian Sacramentary under Charles the Great, Henry Bradshaw Society;* London, 1915.
GREGOROVIUS, Ferdinand. *Le tombe dei papi*, 2nd ed. by C. Hülsen; Rome, 1931.
GREGORY I:
  *Dialogi libri* IV, ed. U. Moricca, *Fonti per la storia d'Italia* 57; Rome, 1924.
  *Lib. regulae pastoralis*, PL 77.13–128.
  *Moralia in Iob*, PL 75.515–576. 782.
HALITGAR OF CAMBRAI:
  *Penitential*, PL 105.651–710.
HINCMAR:
  *De ordine palatii* in *MGH, Capitularia regum Francorum* II, ed. Alfred Boretius and Victor Krause (Hannover, 1897), 517–530.
  *De regis persona et de regis ministerio, PL* 125.833–856.
HRABANUS MAURUS:
  *Carmina*, ed. *MGH, Poetae latini aevi Carolini* II (Berlin, 1884), 159–244, additions *ibid*. p. 700.
  *De eccl. disciplina*, PL 112.1191–1262.
  *De institutione clericorum*, ed. Alois Knoepfler. Munich, 1900.
  *De vitiis et virtutibus*, PL 112.1335–1398.
  *Homiliae*, PL 110.9–468.
*Inscriptiones christianae urbis Romae septimo saeculo antiquiores* I–II.1, ed. J. B. de Rossi. Rome, 1888.
*Inscriptions chrétiennes de la Gaule antérieures au VIIIe siècle* I, ed. Edmond Le Blant. Paris, 1856.
INSCRIPTIONS:
  see Billio, L.; *Carmina Latina Epigraphica;* DeGrassi, A.; *Corpus Inscript. Lat.;* Diehl, E.; Gregorovius, F.; *Monumenta Epigraphica;* Schneider, F.; *Sylloge of Canterbury.*
ISIDORE OF SEVILLE:
  *Differentiae*, PL 83.69–98.
  *Etymologiae sive Origines Libri XX*, rec. W. M. Lindsay, *SCBO;* Oxford, 1911.
  *Questiones in Vetus Test.*, PL 83.207–424.

*Sententiae, PL* 83.537–738.

*Synonima, PL* 83.825–868.

IUVENCUS:

    *Iuvenci Evangeliorum Libri Quattuor,* rec. Iohannes Huemer, *CSEL* 24; Prag-Wien-Leipzig, 1891.

JEROME:

    *Dialogi contra Pelagianos, PL* 23.495–590.

    *Epistulae,* rec. Isidor Hilberg, *CSEL* 54; Wien-Leipzig, 1910.

    *Praefationes Bibliae vulgat. editionis,* see: VULGATE, Vatican edition.

    *Pre-Vulgate translation of Job, PL* 29.61–114.

JONAS OF ORLÉANS:

    *De institutione laicali, PL* 106.121–278.

    *De institutione regia,* ed. J. Réviron, *Les idées politico-religieuses d'un évêque...Jonas d'Orléans et son* De institutione regia. Paris, 1930.

JULIUS VICTOR:

    *Ars rhetorica,* ed. Carl Halm, *Rhetores latini minores* (Leipzig, 1863), 371–448.

KAROLUS MAGNUS ET LEO PAPA:

    Epic poem, ed. Ernst Dümmler, *MGH, Poetae latini aevi Carolini* I (Berlin, 1881), 366–379.

LEO I:

    *Tomus Leonis,* ed. August Hahn, *Bibliothek der Symbole und Glaubensregeln der alten Kirche* (3rd ed.; Breslau, 1897) no. 36; ed. Eduard Schwartz, *Acta conciliorum oecumenicorum* II.ii.1 (Berlin-Leipzig, 1932), no. 5.

LIBER PONTIFICALIS:

    I–III, ed. Louis M. Duchesne, *Bibliothèques des écoles françaises d'Athènes et de Rome,* 2nd ed.; 1955–57.

*Libri Confraternitatum,* ed. Paul Piper, *Monumenta Germaniae Historica;* Berlin, 1884.

LIBRI CAROLINI:

    *Libri Carolini sive Caroli Magni Capitulare De Imaginibus,* rec. Hubert Bastgen, *MGH, Legum Sectio* III, *Concilia* II, *Supplementum.* Hannover-Leipzig, 1923. See *Charlemagne.*

LITURGICAL TEXTS:
 Gerd Tellenbach, *Römischer und christlicher Reichsgedanke in der Liturgie des frühen Mittelalters.* Sitzungsbericht, Heidelberg Akademie; 1934. See *Creeds, Stowe Missal, Gregorian Sacramentary.*

LUCAN:
 *M. Annaei Lucani Belli Civilis libri decem,* ed. A. E. Housman. Oxford, 1926 (1950).

LUCRETIUS:
 *T. Lucreti Cari De rerum natura,* rec. Josef Martin, *BSGRT;* Leipzig, 1934.

LUPUS OF FERRIÈRES:
 *Epistolae,* ed. Ernst Dümmler, *MGH, Epistolae Karolini Aevi* IV (Berlin, 1925), 1–126.

MARBOD OF RENNES:
 *De ornamentis verborum, PL* 171.1687–1692.

MARIUS VICTORINUS:
 *Explanationum in rhetoricam M. Tulli Ciceronis libri duo,* ed. Carl Halm, *Rhetores latini minores* (Leipzig, 1863), 153–304.

MARTIAL:
 *M. Valerii Martialis Epigrammaton libri,* rec. Wilhelm Heräus, *BSGRT;* Leipzig, 1925.

MIRACULA NYNIE EPISCOPI:
 ed. Karl Strecker, *MGH, Poetae latini medii aevi* IV (Berlin, 1923), 943–962.

*Monumenta epigraphica Christiana saeculo XIII antiquiora quae in Italiae finibus adhuc exstant* I, ed. Angelo Silvagni. Rome, 1938.

MONUMENTA GERMANIAE HISTORICA:

| | |
|---|---|
| *Auctores antiquissimi;* | *Leges* (series *in folio*); |
| *Concilia;* | *Legum sectiones* I–V; |
| *Diplomata;* | *Libri confraternitatum;* |
| *Epistolae;* | *Poetae latini medii aevi;* |
| *Formulae;* | *Scriptores* (series *in folio*); |

 *Scriptores rerum Merovingicarum.*

ONULF OF SPEYER:
 Wilhelm Wattenbach, "Magister Onulf von Speyer," *Sitzungsberichte, Berlin Akademie* (1894), 361–386.

OROSIUS:
  *Pauli Orosii historiarum adversum paganos libri* VII, rec. Carl
  Zangemeister, *CSEL* 5; Wien, 1882.
OVID:
  *Fasti*, ed. F. W. Lenz. Leipzig, 1932.
  *P. Ovidius Naso* ex R. Merkelii recognitione edidit Rudolf Ehwald,
  *BSGRT;* Leipzig, 1888–1897 (in part reissued 1905, 1907, etc.).
PASCHASIUS RADBERTUS:
  *Vita Adalhardi, PL* 120.1507–56; excerpts, ed. G. H. Pertz, *MGH*,
  *Scriptores* II (Hannover, 1829), 524–532.
*Patrologia latina*, ed. J. P. Migne; Paris, editio prior, 1844–1864.
PAULI SENTENTIAE:
  *Fontes iuris romani antejustiniani* II, ed. Johannes Baviera (Flor-
  ence, 1940), 317–417.
PAULINUS OF AQUILEIA:
  *Libellus sacrosyllabus episcoporum Italiae*, ed. A. Werminghoff,
  *MGH, Concilia* II (*Aevi Karolini* I; Hannover-Leipzig, 1906),
  130–142.
  *Liber exhortationis ad Heiricum, PL* 99.197–282.
PAULUS DIACONUS:
  *Carmina*, ed. Ernst Dümmler, *MGH, Poetae latini aevi Carolini* I
  (Berlin, 1881), 27–77.
  Paul Neff, *Die Gedichte des Paulus Diaconus.* Munich, 1908.
PELAGIUS:
  *Libellus fidei*, ed. August Hahn, *Bibliothek der Symbole* (3rd ed.;
  Breslau, 1897), 288–292.
PETRUS CHRYSOLOGUS:
  *Sermones, PL* 52.183–666.
POMERIUS:
  *De vita contemplativa, PL* 59.415–520.
PORFYRIUS:
  *Carmina*, ed. Elsa Kluge, *BSGRT;* Leipzig, 1926.
PROPERTIUS:
  *Sexti Properti Carmina*, rec. E. A. Barber, *SCBO;* Oxford, 1953.
PRUDENTIUS:
  *Aurelii Prudentii Clementis Carmina*, rec. Ioannes Bergman, *CSEL*
  61; Wien-Leipzig, 1926.

Pseudo-Augustinus:
*Sermones, PL* 39.1735–2354.

Pseudo-Benedictus Levita:
*Benedicti Capitularia,* ed. F. H. Knust. *MGH, Legum* (in folio) II, pars altera. (Hannover, 1837), 17–158.

Pseudo-Cyprian:
*De XII abusivis saeculi,* ed. Siegmund Hellmann, in *Texte und Untersuchungen,* ed. Adolf Harnack and C. Schmidt 34.1; Leipzig, 1909.

Pseudo-Isidorian Decretals:
*Decretales Pseudo-Isidorianae,* ed. Paul Hinschius. Leipzig, 1863.

Regesta Imperii:
J. F. Böhmer, *Regesta Imperii I: Die Regesten des Kaiserreichs unter den Karolingern.* 715–918, ed. Engelbert Mühlbacher and Johann Lechner, 2nd ed.; Innsbruck, 1908.

Regesta Pontificum:
*Regesta pontificum romanorum* I–II, ed. Ph. Jaffé, editio altera, supervised by Wilhelm Wattenbach, ed. by S. Löwenfeld, F. Kaltenbrunner, and P. Ewald. Leipzig, 1885–1888.

Regula S. Benedicti:
*S. Benedicti Regula Monachorum,* ed. Benno Linderbauer. Metten, 1922.
*Sancti Benedicti Regula Monasteriorum,* ed. C. Butler. Freiburg i. Br., 1927.

*Rhetores latini minores,* ed. Carl Halm. Leipzig, 1863.

Rhetorica ad Herennium:
*Incerti auctoris De ratione dicendi Ad C. Herennium libri IV,* rec. Friedrich Marx. Leipzig, 1894; editio minor, *BSGRT;* Leipzig, 1923.
*Rhetorica ad Herennium,* trans. and ed. Harry Caplan. *Loeb Classical Library;* Cambridge, Mass.-London, 1954.

Rhetorica Ecclesiastica:
ed. Ludwig Wahrmund, *Quellen zur Geschichte des römisch-kanonischen Processes* I, Heft 4. Innsbruck, 1906.

Richer:
*Historiae,* ed. Robert Latouche. *Les classiques de l'histoire de France au moyen âge,* 12 and 17; Paris, 1930–1937.

SACRA SCRIPTURA, see VULGATE.

SCHNEIDER, Fedor, and HOLTZMANN, Walther, *Die Epitaphien der Päpste und andere stadtrömische Inschriften.* Rom, 1933.

*Scriptorum classicorum bibliotheca Oxoniensis;* Oxford.

SEDULIUS:

> *Sedulii opera omnia,* rec. Iohannes Huemer, *CSEL* 10; Wien, 1885.

SEDULIUS SCOTTUS:

> *De rectoribus christianis,* ed. Siegmund Hellman, *Sedulius Scottus* in *Quellen und Untersuchungen zur lateinischen Philologie des Mittelalters* I.1; Munich, 1906.

SILVAGNI, Angelo, see *Monumenta epigraphica, Sylloge of Canterbury.*

SMARAGDUS OF ST. MIHIEL:

> *Via regia, PL* 102.933–970.

SPECULUM GY DE WAREWYKE:

> ed. G. L. Morrill, *EETS,* Extra Series 75; London, 1898.

STOWE MISSAL:

> ed. G. F. Warner, *Henry Bradshaw Society;* London, 1906, 1915

SULPICIUS SEVERUS:

> *Sulpicii Severi Libri qui supersunt,* ed. Carl Halm, *CSEL* I; Wien. 1864.

SYLLOGE OF CANTERBURY:

> Angelo Silvagni, "La Silloge di Cambridge," *Rivista di archeologia christiana* 20 (1943), 49–112.

TERENCE:

> *P. Terenti Afri Comoediae,* rec. Robert Kauer and W. M. Lindsay, *SCBO;* Oxford, 1926.

TERENTIANUS MAURUS:

> *De litteris syllabis et metris Horatii,* ed. Heinrich Keil, *Grammatici latini* VI (Leipzig, 1874), 325–413.

THEODULPH OF ORLÉANS:

> *Carmina,* ed. Ernst Dümmler, *MGH, Poetae Latini aevi Carolini* I (Berlin, 1881), 437–581; *ibid.* II (Berlin, 1884), 694–697.
>
> *De spiritu sancto, PL* 105.239–276.

VEGETIUS:

> *De re militari: Epitoma rei militaris,* rec. C. Lang. ed. altera, *BSGRT;* Leipzig, 1885.

VIRGIL:

*P. Vergili Maronis Opera*, rec. Remigius Sabbadini. Rome, 1930.

VULGATE:

*Biblia Sacra iuxta latinam vulgatam versionem*...praeside Aidano Gasquet...edita. Romae, 1926–

*Novum Testamentum Latine*, rec. I. Wordsworth and H. I. White. Editio minor; Oxford, 1911.

*Concordantiarum Universae Scripturae Sacrae Thesaurus* auctoribus Peultier, Etienne, Gantois. Paris, 1897.

WALAFRID STRABO:

*Libellus de exordiis et incrementis rerum ecclesiasticarum*, in: *MGH, Capitularia regum Francorum* II, ed. Alfred Boretius and Victor Krause (Hannover, 1897), 473–516.

WALTHER OF SPEYER:

*Vita S. Christopheri*, ed. Karl Strecker, *MGH, Poetae latini medii aevi* 5 (Leipzig, 1937), 1–79.

WOLFGER OF PRUEFENING:

*De scriptoribus ecclesiasticis*, ed. Emil Ettlinger. Karlsruhe, 1896.

# C. Index of Sources

# D. General Index